Great ~~~
Abroad

Arthur H. Bell, Ph.D.

McGraw-Hill

New York San Francisco Washington, D.C. Auckland Bogotá
Caracas Lisbon London Madrid Mexico City Milan
Montreal New Delhi San Juan Singapore
Sydney Tokyo Toronto

Library of Congress Cataloging-in-Publication Data

Bell, Arthur H. (Arthur Henry), [date]
    Great jobs abroad / Arthur H. Bell.
        p.   cm.
    Includes index.
    ISBN 0-07-005839-3 (pbk)
    1. Employment in foreign countries.   2. Americans—Employment—
Foreign countries.   3. Job hunting—United States.
    4. International business enterprises—Personnel management.
    I. Title.
    HF5549.5.E45B449   1997
    650.14—dc21   96-49935
                                                                                CIP

Copyright © 1997 by The McGraw-Hill Companies, Inc. All rights
reserved. Printed in the United States of America. Except as permitted
under the United States Copyright Act of 1976, no part of this publication
may be reproduced or distributed in any form or by any means, or stored
in a data base or retrieval system, without the prior written permission of
the publisher.

3 4 5 6 7 8 9 10   FGRFGR   9 9 8 7

ISBN 0-07-005839-3

*The sponsoring editor for this book was Betsy Brown, the editing
supervisor was Fred Dahl, and the production supervisor was Suzanne
W. B. Rapcavage. It was set in Palatino by Inkwell Publishing Services.*

This publication is designed to provide accurate and authoritative
information in regard to the subject matter covered. It is sold with the
understanding that the publisher is not engaged in rendering legal,
accounting, or other professional service. If legal advice or other expert
assistance is required, the services of a competent professional person
should be sought.

 This book is printed on recycled, acid-free paper containing a minimum of 50 percent recycled de-inked fiber.

McGraw-Hill books are available at special quantity discounts to use as
premiums and sales promotions, or for use in corporate training programs.
For more information, please write to the Director of Special Sales,
McGraw-Hill, 11 West 19th Street, New York, NY 10011. Or contact your
local bookstore.

Contents

Turn the Dream into a Reality!	v
1. How to Get a Job Abroad	1
2. Focusing on Who You Are and What You Want	9
3. Assembling Your Application Package	19
4. Meet Sixteen People Who Did It	39
5. Preparing for an International Job Interview	45
6. What You Need to Know about Passports, Visas, and Work Permits	57
7. Using the Internet to Find Jobs Abroad	71
8. 150 Jobs Available Almost *Everywhere*	81
9. 192 Major Companies in 49 Countries	109
10. 100 Non-U.S. Employers in 25 Job Areas	135
11. Eight Areas for Temporary International Employment	151

Appendix A. State-by-state U.S. Employers with Foreign Offices ... 157

Appendix B. Selected Foreign-based Companies with U.S. Offices ... 215

Appendix C. Using a World Trade Center in the Job Search ... 219

Appendix D. Obtaining Information and Applications from Embassies ... 229

Appendix E. Finding International Jobs with Councils, Associations, and Government Agencies ... 237

Appendix F. Using Federal Information Centers in Your Job Search ... 241

Appendix G. Obtaining Country and Business Information from the U.S. Department of Commerce ... 245

Appendix H. An Entrepreneur's Directory to Foreign Service Officers ... 255

Appendix I. Personality Profile Evaluation for Career Choices ... 353

Appendix J. Helpful Reference Guides for the International Job Search ... 365

Index ... 368

Turn the Dream into a Reality!

Have you harbored the dream of working in a foreign country, of adding something special to your career by gaining exposure to new cultures, new ideas, and new people? If so, the time for dreaming is past—it's time to start your international career.

Great Jobs Abroad gives you tested, practical ways of finding international employment. The techniques presented here work for seasoned employees considering a job change, those between jobs, and recent graduates looking for a first position. There are also helpful contacts for jobseekers seeking summer and temporary work.

The hundreds of pages of reference materials in *Great Jobs Abroad* give detailed information on:

- U.S. companies in your own state or region that send employees abroad—at U.S. wages!
- Foreign corporations that hire U.S. workers.
- Internet listings of current international job openings—more than 100,000 of them!
- Company and employer profiles.
- Contacts for information and assistance from embassies, consulates, U.S. foreign service officers, and federal job centers.
- Dozens of recommended reference works for finding out more about companies, countries, and job descriptions.

Your international career may be just a postage stamp, telephone call, e-mail message, or fax away. *Great Jobs Abroad* has one primary purpose: to put you in touch with the international employer who will say, "You're hired."

Acknowledgments

More than one hundred international personnel directors, human resource specialists, and corporate executives have contributed to the concept and entries in this book. To each of them, I extend my sincere thanks. Special appreciation goes to the following individuals, whose friendship, counsel, and expertise have been invaluable to me during this project: Mr. Chen and Mr. Liu, China Resources, Ltd.; Mr. He and Mr. Zhao, Guangdong Enterprises, Ltd.; Koichiro Hirouchi, Nippon Telephone and Telegraph; Jackie McCoy, Northern Ireland Small Business Institute; John Elterton, British Telephone; Montse Serra, Hewlett-Packard/Spain; Helmut Schmidt, Deutsche Telekom; Joan Fujii and Allison Ross, Cost Plus World Markets; Thomas Housel, Telecom Italia; and Gary Rothschild, Israel Customs. Many of my academic colleagues at the McLaren School of Business, University of San Francisco, have also enriched my knowledge of the international employment picture. I thank them all for their interest in my work, their guidance, and most of all their wonderful anecdotes of work experiences abroad. Research assistants Joe Parente, Clem Moore, and David Harband contributed significantly to the scope and depth of the book. I thank Betsy Brown at McGraw-Hill and Fred Dahl at Inkwell Publishing Services for their expertise, hard work, and good humor. Finally, I want to remember the patience and love of my family during "writing weekends."

Great Jobs Abroad is dedicated to my students—past, present, and future—at the McLaren School of Business, University of San Francisco.

ARTHUR H. BELL

About the Author

Arthur H. Bell is Professor of Management Communication at the McLaren School of Business, University of San Francisco. He holds a Ph.D. from Harvard University and is the author of more than 30 books on business careers, interviewing, intercultural communication, resume preparation, and management skills. He has taught, worked, and traveled in dozens of countries and, through his San Francisco-based firm, consults regularly for such companies as Lockheed, PaineWebber, American Stores, Hewlett Packard, Sun Microsystems, Star-Kist, Southern Pacific, Global Technologies, the U.S. State Department, Bain and Company, Cost Plus World Markets, ANA, and TRW.

1
How to Get a Job Abroad

You know where you'd like to be: managing that chic restaurant in Italy ... learning the London version of investment banking ... serving as an import/export representative in Tokyo ... or in Paris, if only for the summer, if only selling baguettes.

How to Make It Happen

This book offers the advice, examples, recruiter names, and addresses you will need for finding international employment. Hundreds of opportunities are described here for people seeking careers in the $25,000 to $100,000+ range, for entrepreneurs who want to start a business abroad, for those interested in international volunteer work, and for people looking for summer work and short-term positions.

As you thumb through the book, you'll immediately notice that most of the pages are devoted to company, government, association, and embassy names, addresses, and telephone/fax numbers. These are actual sources you can begin contacting today about international employment possibilities. Also listed are commonly available library resources that describe companies and their products in detail and provide more information about the cultures and people of foreign countries.

Cutting to the Chase

To secure a job abroad, you need to do four things:

1. *Investigate* companies, organizations, and job descriptions that interest you (Chapters 7–11)

2. *Prepare* a persuasive application letter and compelling resume (Chapter 3)
3. *Interview* for the position with skill and confidence (Chapter 5)
4. *Obtain* the necessary visas and work permits you will need to begin work abroad. (Chapter 6)

A word of caution: The exciting prospect of working abroad, surrounded by new sights, sounds, and foods, can spill over into false expectations. It's tempting to view the international job search as an endless line of benevolent employers all bidding for your services. Think again. You will find wonderful opportunities abroad, but also many closed doors. Some of the companies you contact will not respond with a warm, encouraging call or letter and on-the-spot job offer. Just as in domestic job applications, you will have to convince international employers that your talents fit their needs. In short, finding international employment requires courage and persistence.

But remember: Hundreds of thousands of U.S. citizens are working abroad at this moment. You *can* be one of them.

Your Best Shot May Be an American Company or Organization

Statistically, most Americans working in other countries have been sent there by their American employers. Therefore, this book emphasizes U.S. companies and organizations prepared to hire you stateside, train you for international service, and pay for your relocation.

Working abroad as an American employee has several benefits:

- You can apply and interview for a position in your own city, state, or region.
- Your U.S. company will go to bat for you in obtaining visas and work permits.
- You may be paid at American salary rates while living in low cost-of-living foreign locations.
- You probably will have "retreat rights" to return to a stateside position with the company if things don't work out abroad.
- You will participate in your U.S. employer's health, retirement, and other benefit programs that probably exceed those available from a foreign employer.

To help you take this well-traveled route to a job abroad, Appendix A presents a state-by-state listing of companies near you that have international branches. Appendixes B–H list U.S. government organizations, associations, and other groups that regularly send employees abroad. Chapter 9 lists more than two hundred U.S. companies categorized by the foreign countries in which they maintain offices and manufacturing facilities.

Making Direct Contact with International Employers

At the same time you are applying to U.S. companies and organizations, you can also be sending application letters directly to foreign employers. Many jobseekers have found that the same resume turned down in Peoria was dynamite in the Paris job market. In other words, skills and knowledge that may be relatively available to U.S. employers may be rare and highly sought after by foreign companies. Basic skills in word processing and spreadsheets, for example, may get you the job in Italy that you couldn't land in the U.S.

Applying directly to foreign firms gives you the additional advantage of having an indigenous firm helping you with work permits, living arrangements, language proficiency, and social connections. To help you connect directly with many of the world's most prominent non-U.S. companies, Chapter 10 lists names and addresses for applying directly to more than one hundred corporate giants in twenty-five countries.

Why Think International?

Let's begin at the beginning. What gave you the notion to seek employment in Singapore instead of Cincinnati? I asked that question of four U.S. citizens now working abroad—one in Japan, two in Europe, and one in Brazil. I promised them anonymity on the condition that they "tell it like it is." Here are the reasons—some of them quite personal—why they chose international careers:

Phyllis
> "I'm designing microcomputers for a major Japanese company in Kyoto. I left a job in Silicon Valley when a major contract was canceled and, frankly, after a painful divorce. The career possibilities over here intrigued me. In my industry, the Japanese tend to plan in a more thorough and long-term way. After three years here, I feel that I'm on a true career path instead of a roller coaster."

It's a theme you'll hear often when talking to international businesspeople: stability. Many of these men and women have left behind the ups and downs of positions in U.S. "go-go" companies to associate themselves with international corporate giants. Phyllis, our Japanese transplant, says she feels like she really belongs—that she won't be squeezed out or overlooked in corporate restructuring. (I'm not asserting that all international positions are more stable and secure than all U.S. positions. It is true, however, that many employees have found the kind of long-term career environment they were seeking in international employment.)

David
> "I'm working in England because of all the nonwork advantages. My family and I walk to famous museums, art galleries, and theatres. We can take the train on a Saturday morning to the countryside or seashore. On even a short vacation—say, a three- or four-day weekend—we pop across the Channel to France, Germany, or the Netherlands. My children are receiving superb public educations. I wouldn't trade this stage in my career for a huge raise and promotion stateside. Besides, I'm making quite decent money here."

This is a second common theme for international workers: the sheer fun and personal enrichment of intercultural experience. But again, the response is deeply personal and individual. For every employee thrilled with the excitement of a new culture there's at least one who misses McDonald's and can't wait to return stateside.

Paul
> "I manage an airline office for a major air carrier in France. I'm here instead of my former home, Denver, because of career advancement. Given the seniority system within my company, several very healthy senior managers in the Denver area would have had to die or quit before I would get my turn as manager. I just didn't want to commit several years of my life to the waiting game. Here I'm doing the job I do best, as top manager. It puts me in a good position for administrative promotions in the U.S. when openings occur."

An employee in an American company with foreign branches often finds that an international position can offer career advancement. Instead of being just one more face in the Chicago office, he or she is "our Paris representative." In many industries, there's less competition for advancement in international offices and agencies. And often there's considerable freedom. Many international managers find it easier to run the kind of operation that gets one noticed by top management.

Lillith
> "I'm employed as a sales/marketing agent for a food producer here in Brazil. While I don't want to talk exact numbers, I'll admit that I'm here strictly for the money. In the U.S., commissioned salespeople are often held back by an elaborate quota system—the idea is to keep them from making more than their office-bound, salaried bosses. But in South America, the sky is still the limit for someone who can put deals together. We call it the 'wild, wild West.' I probably made fifty percent more last year here in Brazil than in my previous year as a food broker in the U.S. Many of my major accounts are in the U.S., so I get home to California several times each year."

As U.S. manufacturers reach out to international sources for materials, fabrication, and affordable labor, the potential for English-speaking entrepreneurs (whether inside or outside the company) is unlimited.

But Phyllis, Dave, Paul, and Lillith suggest only a few of the reasons for seeking international employment. What are your reasons? Perhaps you haven't spelled them out, or even thought them through in a conscious way. There's no time like the present. On a separate sheet of paper, list your top three reasons for wanting an international work experience. (Fight the impulse to skip on with your reading. Actually writing down your reasons for seeking international employment will set you on your way to determining what you want to do and where you want to do it.)

The Right Idea at the Right Time

We can't peek over your shoulder, of course, to kibbitz on whether an international career is the right move for you. But we can tell you that many U.S. organizations, companies, and business-related academic and professional programs are now looking to Europe, Asia, Africa, Latin America, and elsewhere for business relations. In 1995, more than one-fifth of all agricultural products and manufactured goods produced in the U.S. were exported abroad. And we imported even more than we exported, for an import-export total of $800 billion. That number is a headline—Jobs Here!—for someone seeking international employment.

Business schools in the U.S. were among those to read the headline. Harvard, Georgetown, Stanford, Wharton, Virginia, and others are now gearing up for what *Fortune* called a global vision: "Students will have to master a foreign language and culture as well as the usual tough material on marketing and finance." Schools offering bona fide degrees in international management, such as Arizona's American Graduate School of International Management, have rocketed in prestige, with dozens of major corporations coming each year to court their graduates.

Congressional and corporate leaders have found the scent as well. In 1989, a broad-based group of top politicians and CEOs published "An Action Agenda for American Competitiveness," which called for a strengthening of "international studies courses—language, cultural, political, and economic." These government and business leaders have glimpsed the "Sold War" that will replace the "Cold War"—the European Economic Community closing its ranks, the Pacific Rim looming larger (if that's possible) as a trading force, and Russia and China getting down to fighting weight. Certainly the twenty-first century will be the era of the international worker.

But you didn't need a college bulletin or a Congressional mailing to remind you that international careers were opening up. You've probably seen the new international emphasis in your newspaper's classified section.

Take the time this week to buy several major-city newspapers at your newsstand or bookstore. If possible, also purchase a few papers from foreign capitals (many of these newspapers are available in English). Read the classified "Help Wanted" sections with care. In the U.S. papers, notice the many ads for positions abroad; you may want to clip them out for later consideration. In the foreign papers, notice how many ads invite application from English-speaking noncitizens and promise help with the work permit process. You may also want to peruse the *National Employment Weekly*, a compilation of some of the best job possibilities published in major newspapers. These ads frequently refer to "possible foreign placement," "preference to candidates willing to relocate abroad," and "frequent foreign travel" as part of the job descriptions.

Burying a Few Myths

Wrong assumptions about international employment often lead to career mistakes. We can avoid some of the traditional potholes on the road to application success by discussing and discrediting several myths about international employment:

- **Myth:** *To be considered for employment, you must speak a foreign language as well as the natives in the country of your intended career.*

Some foreign language ability is advantageous for most international employment applications and interviews. But employers rarely expect native speaking ability. At Japan's Fujitsu Corporation, the company's current efforts to attract non-Japanese engineers, programmers, technical writers, and others would be stifled if the company considered only those who spoke flawless Japanese.

- **Myth:** *There's a single book that contains, country by country, the job openings that are currently available to Americans.*

No book, including the dozens listed for your reference in this book, can claim to list actual job openings available for your application. Most international openings are not advertised in the traditional American way. Many are known only to the company itself and to employment agencies.

- **Myth:** *To get an international position, you have to know someone.*

There's no denying that many people get jobs through friends, relatives, acquaintances, and friends of friends. Some books assert (without empirical data) that 85 percent of international hiring happens through such personal contacts. This figure is grossly exaggerated, especially for the hundreds of American firms hiring for their foreign branches. Most companies are constrained by federal and state guidelines in their hiring practices, and can't afford to hire simply on the basis of personal contacts.

If your friends and relatives can't deliver names and addresses of potential international employers, don't despair. With a polished and well-written application letter and resume, you'll definitely be in the running for consideration.

- **Myth:** *International employers don't care about your education; they just want to know about your work experience.*

Nothing could be further from the truth for the great majority of career positions in international companies. Respect for education is greater in most countries than it is in the U.S. Your training certificates, college degree(s), and other marks of educational accomplishment will definitely be key assets in your application.

International employers, like U.S. employers, do want to see a pattern of experience and practical responsibility in addition to education. Your resume and application letter should portray a balance.

- **Myth:** *You should take any job, even menial work, to get your foot in the door of a foreign company. You'll quickly be moved up to where you belong.*

Turning janitors to generals isn't common in any corporation, domestic or foreign. As a rule, international corporations don't want a cadre of Ph.D.'s sweeping the floors. (The result might be dirty floors!) Don't seek out a position substantially beneath your training and expertise. This is not to say that you can't get by in London by washing dishes—just don't expect to climb from dishwasher to business manager within the same company. It's an unusual career path at best.

- *Myth: Once you've taken an international position, you've burned your bridges for comparable positions within the U.S. You're "out of the loop."*

As demonstrated by the movement of managers within such international corporations as Heinz, IBM, and Nestlé, a stint as an international manager or employee usually adds to a worker's attractiveness for the company. Thanks to fax machines, electronic mail, teleconferencing, and other communication technologies, the loop connecting employees is electronic, not physical. You can't have coffee with the gang in Chicago as you sit in your office in Bombay, but you can still communicate with them (daily, if necessary), attend their meetings by teleconference, and fly on short notice to their conventions. The company need not forget you while you're abroad. And you'll be the resident expert when the company prepares to meet the global trading challenges of the twenty-first century.

- *Myth: For the employee, most foreign employment situations are cultural successes but financial disasters.*

Those who believe this myth haven't checked on the latest monetary rates for Germany, Switzerland, France, Great Britain, Japan, and other trading nations. Your international salary often compares quite favorably to your U.S. numbers. Employees from the U.S. are often pleasantly surprised when they add up their housing allowance, travel funds, salary, tax advantages, and other aspects of compensation. But for your own sake, don't trust anyone's estimate or general arithmetic. Find out what your living expenses and other costs will be before accepting a particular salary.

2
Focusing on Who You Are and What You Want

In Chapter 1, you jotted down your reasons for seeking an international career. Let's assume that you're satisfied with those reasons and they make sense to you, although your mother still thinks you should be a dentist in St. Paul. Your reasons seem to be compelling enough to carry you through the interesting, but difficult, work of locating appropriate positions and applying for them.

The hard work begins not by investigating companies or countries but by investigating yourself. Only by knowing yourself well can you plan effectively for successful job applications.

If you were to seek the help of trained career counselors in considering jobs for which you are best suited, they would probably administer the Myers-Briggs Type Inventory, an extensive and often expensive measurement of your strong and weak suits in eight basic dimensions of personality. A similar but shorter version of a personality profile evaluation is included in Appendix I. It will take you less than 30 minutes to work through this evaluation. The results will help you make informed decisions about what kinds of jobs you want to pursue. After all, the wrong job in even the best foreign location can often be disastrous to your personal happiness and professional progress.

Viewed as concentric circles, your search comprises three areas. The largest, What You Can Do, includes all those skills, abilities, and competencies that you've learned. On a separate sheet of paper, make a list of what you can do. Put down not only tasks you've performed at work ("handled payroll") but also those skills and abilities you've demonstrat-

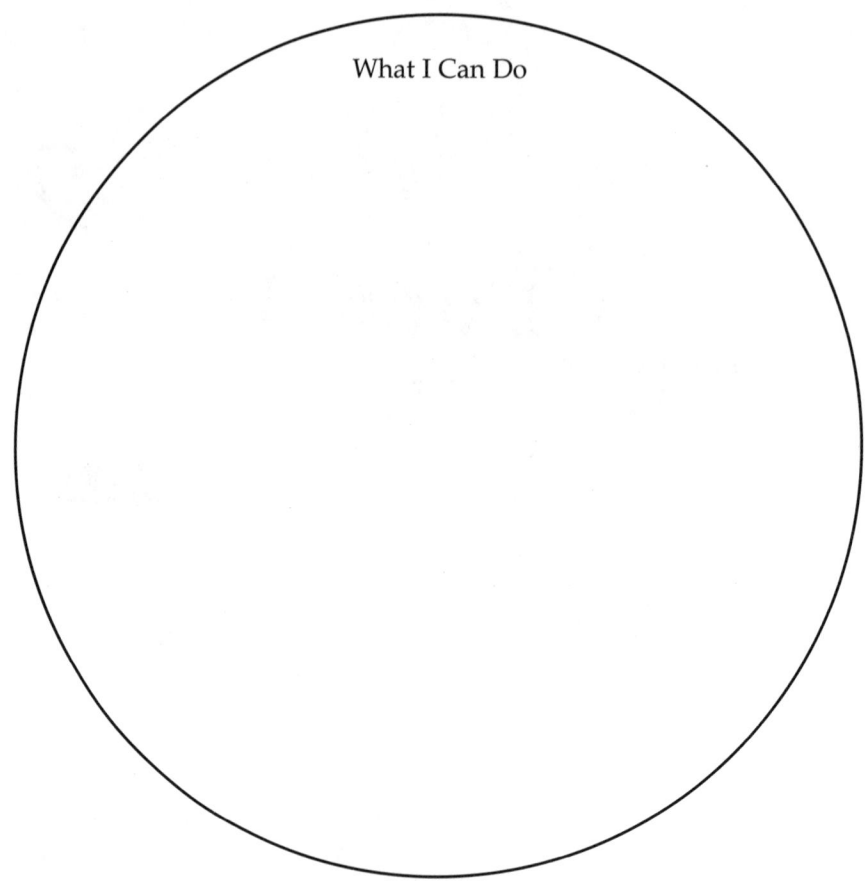

ed in organizations and civic life ("very organized," "a good public speaker"). Orient your list toward items a potential employer will value.

Unhappy employees are often those people who are doing what they know they can do, but dislike doing it. In the inner circle on the next page, therefore, consider what you like to do. These items will be drawn from your previous list. Set down those career-related skills, activities, and competencies that give you pleasure, satisfaction, or a feeling of accomplishment. Let's say, for example, that you're good at public speaking, but hate, hate, hate to do it. Leave it in the outer circle.

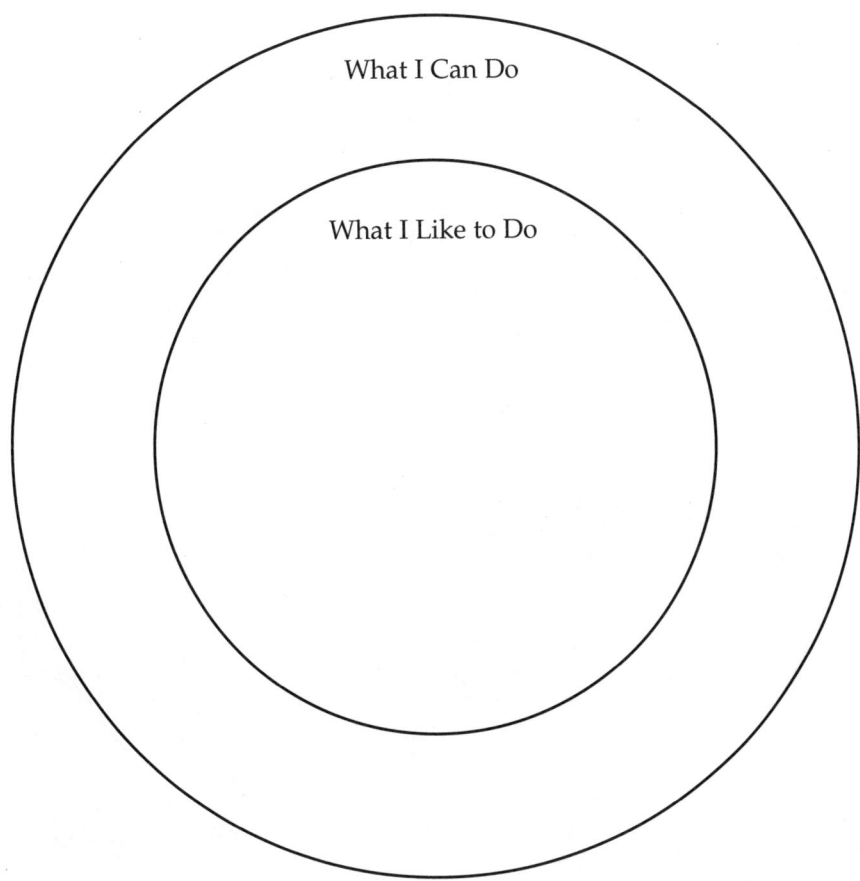

In this inner circle, you've defined the "heart" of what you have to offer to an employer—those things that you'll do with energy, enthusiasm, and caring. These are the items that make work seem like a form of "serious play." At the end of a day you've had more pleasure than pain, and at the end of a career more satisfaction than disappointment. Perhaps, as Thoreau said, "the mass of men lead lives of quiet desperation." But not you.

Now for the difficult—and humbling—part. Review your second list to locate those items that you not only like to do, but also have proven your skill in. For example, if you mentioned in your second list that you "like to work with people," you should now put down an actual example (e.g., "sales clerk of the month") of your skill. As much as possible, these examples should come from real-world work situations.

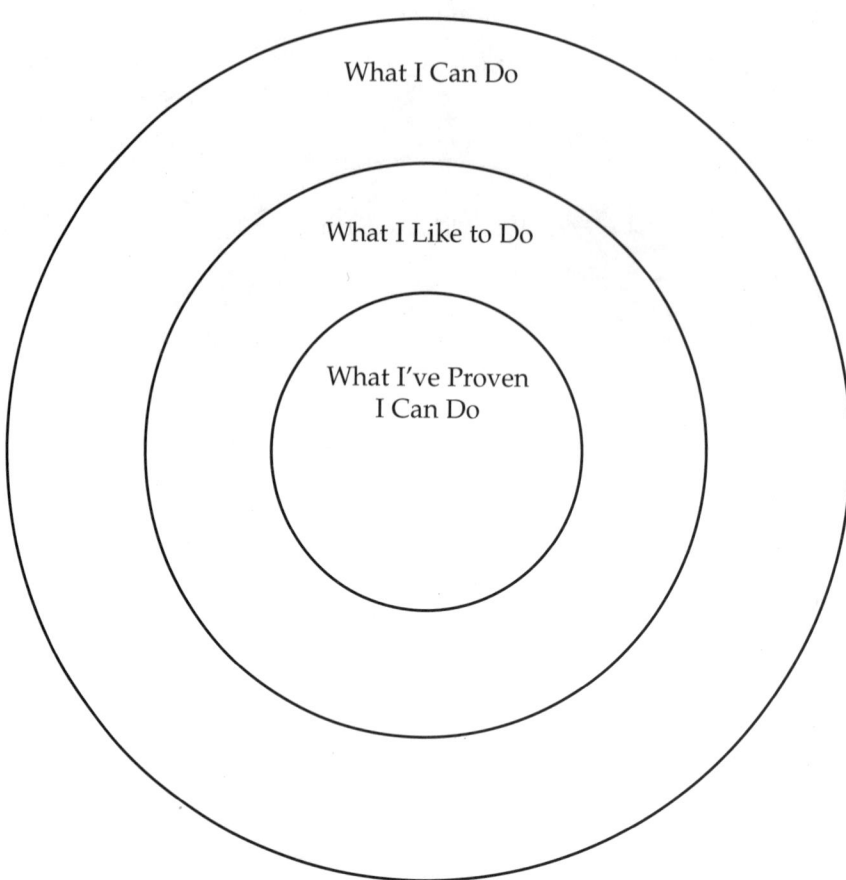

In preparation for a winning resume and for great interview responses, we shall now expand a bit on each of your proven skills listed above. Use your own paper as necessary to fill in these blanks for each of your proven abilities:

Proven Ability: _____
Past Proof: _____
Present Proof: _____
Future Proof: _____

Here are some quick definitions that may make your job easier: Past Proof (something from the past that demonstrates the ability), Present Proof (something you're doing now that demonstrates the ability), and Future Proof (something you plan to do that will require the ability).

In making your list, consider both paid and unpaid experiences. At this stage in your analysis, don't ignore seemingly marginal or insignificant activities, positions, or associations. Consider not only your present occupation, but also avocations, memberships, volunteer work, church and charity associations, civic involvement, and academic interests.

In completing your Future Proof, send yourself back to the future for a moment. Consider those short-term and long-term plans that will prove your abilities in the future. It may be a somewhat strange thought at first to contemplate how future events will prove your abilities. Perhaps the analogy of a fruit tree can help: How will the seeds you're planting in the present bear fruit? What will you be doing six months from now, a year from now, two years from now that will prove particular abilities? For example, how will your participation in an upcoming convention or trade show demonstrate your professionalism? How will your promotion to a supervisory position demonstrate your leadership skills? How will your attainment of a certificate, license, or degree demonstrate your competence? In drawing up this list, let your imagination go. Your future employer, after all, is hiring you for what lies ahead, not behind, in your productive life. The act of drawing up this list gives you a chance to face that future—and shape it to your advantage.

The Hand You Hold for International Employment

In assembling your past, present, and future proven abilities, you're looking at the hand that you bring to the table of employment application. On the basis of this hand, you can make quite accurate estimates of what kind of jobs to apply for, how to approach employers, and what to expect in your international career path.

Choosing a Career Field

There's no better time to contemplate exactly what you want to do than now, with your past, present, and future proven abilities laid out before you. You may have already made up your mind—an accountant, an engineer, a salesperson, and so forth. But, for the international employment arena, you may want to throw a wider net in considering related occupations you would also qualify for. Many jobseekers within the U.S. and abroad have come up empty in their search only because they confined their search too narrowly.

To help you throw open the gates of imagination, read through the job titles in Chapter 8. The list, of course, isn't complete by any means. But it does include many emerging careers named by the *New York Times* as "the best opportunities of tomorrow." You may want to investigate several of these careers to determine if they make use of your abilities. For detailed descriptions of each, see the *American Almanac of Jobs and Salaries* and *The New York Times Career Planner*.

Spend an afternoon or evening at your public library browsing through the career section in search of possible career areas that fit your skills and interests.

Strengthening the Hand You Hold for International Employment

Before we begin to play your hand for high stakes in the international job market, let's see if we can strengthen it in key areas.

Languages

Put yourself in your employer's position. If you were doing the hiring for a sales position, let's say, within the United States, would you require fluency in English? Of course. Your new hire would be paralyzed without such ability.

Which leads to the question that discourages many people interested in international careers: How's your foreign language ability? Put another way, can you read and speak with ease in the language of the country where you want to work?

That question can't be answered by school transcripts: "Well, I had French in high school and for two semesters in college." Many of us (your author included) had good grades in school language classes, but heaven help us if we had to speak and write in all those languages on the job tomorrow. And "tomorrow" is just the point: When you mail off a job application to Germany, let's say, you may well receive a phone interview the next week—*auf Deutsch*! Your language skills should be at their peak when you mail off your application.

But let's be practical. Most of us probably aren't going to speak or write superb German, French, Spanish, or another foreign language as a prerequisite for seeking international employment. We're going to learn what we can, then hope our prospective employer gives us time to play catch-up in the first few months on the job. Many jobs in Europe, Asia, and Latin America require only social language skills at the beginning—the ability to lunch with a client, keep up with small group conversation, and answer the telephone.

Unfortunately, those are precisely the skills that American language instruction often fails to address during high school and college. A Washington, DC, executive complained to me recently that "I have a minor in Spanish. I can translate Borges. But take me to a Chicano neighborhood and I'm tongue-tied. I can't even ask directions without getting flustered."

Begin to strengthen your hand for international employment, therefore, by enrolling in the kind of language instruction that will give you quick, solid results in terms of practical, day-to-day language ability. You may be lucky enough to have such a program at a local university or community college. Check particularly with extended or continuing education programs, many of which meet in evening hours.

If you can't find a suitable college class, bite the bullet and pay for an intensive language course through a commercial school. The organizations listed below are famous for their ability to turn a sheepish grin—"Uh, I don't speak any French"—to confident fluency.

But brace yourself: The instruction is far from cheap. You may want to attend a class or two on a trial basis before signing on as a contracted student. And don't waste your money, by the way, on those omnipresent cassette tapes promising to "teach Italian in six easy lessons." For meaningful competence, you need face-to-face instruction with a trained teacher.

Here are U.S. offices and phone numbers for some of the most prominent and reputable language schools. All have programs and schedules geared to fit your business or academic day. When you call, be sure to describe in detail the kinds of positions you'll be seeking abroad. You don't want to get stuck in a tourist language class ("Would the beautiful lady care to dance?") when you need a battery of business phrases.

Berlitz Language Centers
1050 Connecticut Ave.
Washington, DC 20008
(202) 331-1160

Inlingua Schools of Language
1030 15th St. NW
Suite 828
Washington, DC 20005
(202) 289-8666

Linguex
1255 23rd St. NW
Suite 285
Washington, DC 20005
(202) 296-1112

International Center for Language Studies
727 15th St. NW
Suite 400
Washington, DC 20005
(202) 639-8800

As your language instructor will probably recommend, surround yourself with foreign language materials—magazines on your coffee table, a novel by your bed, a foreign language videotape in your VCR. Try as much as possible to "live" in the foreign language of your choice when you're home. Talk yourself through the names of household items when you cook or clean. Talk out loud in the car if you drive to work: to yourself, give directions and point out sights in the foreign language. Most of all, try to find someone among your acquaintances who speaks the language well. Talk his or her ear off several times a week.

By using this type of language immersion, you'll be amazed how quickly you can become comfortable and confident in speaking (and, later, writing) your newly acquired language. As the old joke goes, foreign languages must be easy—even two-year olds learn them overseas.

You'll have to be the judge of when and how to use your foreign language ability in applying for an international position. As a general rule, do not write your application letter in a foreign language unless 1) you can be absolutely sure that your letter is correct in grammar, style, form, and mechanics, and 2) you can reflect the same level of language competence in speaking. Many international employers have received flawless, native-language letters from job applicants only to discover later (usually in the first telephone interview) that the letters were written by hired language instructors.

If your first contact with your prospective employer is in person or by phone, it is courteous to greet the person in his or her native language, then to move as graciously as possible to a mutually comfortable language. (Many French employers, for example, prefer to conduct interviews somewhat haltingly in English rather than in the applicant's bad French.)

It may help to remind yourself that employers abroad are probably not expecting you to speak like a native your first day on the job. They will expect, however, that you are taking steps to master the language and are willing to use it, albeit tentatively, in social and business situations.

Your Growing Work Experience

Another way to build your international employment profile is to create some kind of business or quasi-business experience, however slight, in your intended career area. For example, an Iowa elementary school teacher wanted to teach for a year in England. While on summer vacation there, she took time to visit two schools and was invited to participate in classes. On her eventual application, she was able to state truthfully that she had "enjoyed helping to teach classes during visits to public schools at Manchester and Leeds." That sentence stood out like a beacon on her successful application.

Focusing on Who You Are and What You Want

Here are four other quick examples to give you the idea:

1. An Accounting major volunteers time for a semester to help keep association books for the Mexican American Business League (thus strengthening his resume for Latin American positions).
2. A computer programmer puts together a short program on social customs a German manager needs to know when visiting America. For $80 he markets it, with moderate success, through a couple of classified ads in German newspapers. But his real "score" comes when he includes this entrepreneurial activity on his application for a systems analyst position in Germany—and gets the job.
3. An advertising major makes a hobby for several months of clipping interesting print advertisements out of French magazines. In an interview for an advertising job in Paris, the candidate can talk about actual French ads and so appears head and shoulders above her competition.
4. An assistant manager in a grocery store sets up a "Foods of Italy" display in the deli section of his store. This item becomes one small but telling bit of evidence on his application to be an import broker for a major Italian food distributor.

The point is that you too can take steps now to position yourself well for international employment. A sound guide to your efforts is simply to put yourself in the place of your potential employer: What kinds of experiences and interests would you be pleased to find in an application? These activities and involvements shouldn't be phony, of course, or merely drummed up for the sake of the resume. But there is every reason to shape your choice of activities toward your goal of international employment.

You've now strengthened your international employment profile by brushing up (or acquiring) language skills and creating business-related experiences that will attract the eye of an international employer. We're ready to commit those strengths to writing, in your resume and application letter.

3
Assembling Your Application Package

In this chapter, we'll walk through the application process step by step, giving examples of all forms of communication—resumes, letters, interviews, and phone calls—used in that process. Applications differ somewhat, however, depending on whether your response involves a blind advertisement, a "full disclosure" ad, a cold call, or a personal recommendation. We'll term these various approaches Paths A, B, C, and D.

The Application Package

No matter what path of application you are pursuing, you will be sending your "application package" to potential employers. This package is made up of the following items:

1. A cover letter expressing your interest in a position, highlighting your education and experience, and setting the stage for an interview, even if only by telephone.
2. A resume setting forth your career goals, education, experience, special skills, personal background, and references.
3. Optional letters of recommendation and samples of your work.

We'll see examples of this package customized to each of the application paths.

Path A: Responding to a Blind Ad

You open the classified pages of the *New York Times* and spot this "blind" ad ("blind" because it doesn't let you see the name of the company or its representative):

> Opportunities in Europe for creative individuals with business experience and/or business degrees. Top salaries, benefits, travel allowances. Send resume, Box 293, New York Times.

Your imagination works overtime as you contemplate your ideal position—blind ads encourage such flights of fancy. But you gradually come down to earth as you begin to wonder why a reputable company would hide its name, the nature of its business, and even its address and country from you.

Blind ads make up about one-fifth of all classified job advertising. Sometimes a company chooses the "blind" approach for sound reasons. Perhaps it doesn't want to expose specific personnel needs, as in the case of a hospital desperately seeking qualified nurses. (An ad specifying that need would be bad advertising for the hospital.) Or a company may want to find "fresh blood" without letting its present employees know that it is trying to fill vacancies. A company may want to limit the number of inquiries it receives to a single box or telephone number instead of clogging company mail and telephone channels.

Just as often, however, blind ads are written in an effort to deceive the job applicant. You respond in good faith with your resume only to discover that the company behind the ad has little to offer you.

Let's pursue the blind ad above, although it includes no name, company, or specific position information. We'll then see if it turns out to be our ticket abroad or just another con job.

Here is the type of letter you might write in response to a blind advertisement. Note that we haven't lowered the tone or reduced the amount of detail in the letter or accompanying resume. Just because you're responding to a blind ad doesn't mean that decision makers in major corporations may not be reading your application package.

Assembling Your Application Package 21

7432 W. 45th St.
Washington, DC 29953

Nov. 29, 1996

Personnel Director
Box 293
New York Times

Dear Director:

    I'm interested in the career opportunities you advertised in the *New York Times,* Nov. 28, 1996, and would appreciate receiving more information.

    I graduated from the University of Maryland in 1995 as a Marketing major. Since that time I have been employed as an assistant manager in charge of wholesale accounts at Revex, a large Maryland pharmaceutical chain. In that capacity, I supervise eight employees and manage an administrative budget of $540,000. I enjoy working closely with clients on a day-to-day basis and encourage good communication skills among my employees.

    It has long been my goal to apply my business training to an international position involving retail or wholesale marketing. I'm willing to undertake intensive language training if required by the positions you offer.

    I look forward to hearing more from you regarding these opportunities. Thank you for considering my qualifications and strong interest.

Sincerely,

Rebecca R. Johnson

    Rebecca mails this letter along with her resume. (She could have included general letters of reference, but decides to hold these back until she finds out what kind of positions are available.) She has gone to the trouble of sending a full letter and resume rather than just a note (e.g., "Yes, I'm interested. Please send details.") She reasons that the employer will respond first to expressions of serious interest—and her time and effort in writing a detailed letter will demonstrate that level of interest.

    Four days pass and then the phone rings. Here's what Rebecca hears: "This is Ted Conway, vice president at Trans-Atlantic Associates. We represent several large European corporations who are about to open up new managerial positions in Paris, Amsterdam, Rome, and London. I'm calling to thank you, Rebecca, for your response to our *New York Times* advertisement. Your credentials certainly are impressive, and we'd like to pursue the possibilities of employment with you." (Pause.)

    Rebecca can't quite "read" the conflicting messages she's receiving. What companies are hiring? For what positions? When? She decides to find out: "I'd like that too, Mr. Conway."

He continues: "As you probably realize, Rebecca, it takes many skills to participate effectively in the international business community." And as his voice drones on, Rebecca's hopes fade. It turns out that "Trans-Atlantic Associates" is nothing more than a school trying to sell language tapes and correspondence courses in intercultural relations. Following successful completion of their courses, Rebecca would be given access to the company's "private data base" of current openings throughout Europe and Asia. She would be "virtually assured" of receiving a position abroad.

Rebecca indicates that she's not interested and hangs up. She feels she has wasted considerable effort in responding to this blind ad.

Up to half of all blind ads turn out to be smokescreens for people who are selling something, not hiring you. But don't let that fact discourage you from exploring very real career opportunities that may be available through such ads. Just listen carefully for the first hints of monetary "investment" on your part as a requisite to the hiring process. That's usually your key that you're not dealing with a bona fide company wanting to hire you.

Some employment agencies routinely run blind ads, but honestly set forth the terms under which they do business. In some cases, the company will require an advance fee for the services it renders in finding you an international position.

Path B: Responding to a "Full Disclosure" Advertisement

In this case, you know the name of the company, the person to whom you're writing, and many of the details of the position offered. This information will allow you to adapt and personalize somewhat the model letter reproduced in Path A. Obviously, the more convincingly you can target your skills and accomplishments to the needs identified in the ad, the greater your chances for success.

Path C: Making a Cold Call

The great majority of job openings at all levels never get advertised, or perhaps are advertised in newspapers and magazines you don't see. The key to finding such positions is the cold call—the unsolicited call or letter expressing your interest in exploring career possibilities with a particular company.

Assembling Your Application Package   23

It's not a matter of asking "Are you hiring?" Few companies are willing to send lists of open positions to anyone. Instead, use your letter of inquiry (as in the example below) to sell yourself. Positions have a way of becoming available when the right person comes along—and you want to be that right person.

In the following letter, Andrea Wu pays a "cold call" on NVK Microcomputer Systems of Taiwan. She has found the name of the company's personnel director and the address of company headquarters in *Asia's Top 7500 Companies,* one of the directories available at her library. Andrea begins her letter by showing that she's interested in recent company developments, then goes on to show how she can be useful to the firm. A growing company in need of skilled employees will find it hard to resist Andrea's logic and enthusiasm:

Dec. 2, 1996
300 Levett St.
Alexandria, VA 22304

Mr. Zhou Chang
Director of Personnel
NVK Microcomputer Systems
687-A South Extension
Taipei, Taiwan NW8923

Dear Mr. Chang:

In the Nov. 27, 1996, *Wall Street Journal,* I read with great interest of your success in developing a prototype Pentium laptop computer in the U.S.$1000 price range. As the first manufacturer in this market, surely you will enjoy strong sales, no doubt with the need for an expanded staff.

I would like to join NVK as a systems architect and United States marketing specialist. My resume (enclosed) sums up my academic training in Electrical Engineering and Business as well as my experience as a systems designer for NCR Corporation. You may be particularly interested in my design for a CAD software package at NCR—the kind of development software that you may be contemplating for production of your new laptop.

Thank you for reviewing my qualifications and for considering my interest in a career at NVK. I would welcome a telephone call or letter from you. I'm eager to learn more about NVK and to answer your questions about my background and skills.

Sincerely,

Andrea Wu

In her resume, Andrea identifies the location of her colleges and workplaces. International employers may not be as familiar as domestic employers with, say, Rice University. But they may well know of Houston, and associate the college favorably with that business center.

Nor does Andrea presume that an international employer will know intuitively what a computer programmer/analyst at NCR Corporation does. She breaks out a thorough description of her tasks and accomplishments there in hopes that one or more of these items will strike the interest of the employer. She uses both spelled-out and abbreviated forms of some key terms—e.g., "printed circuit board" (PCB)—to make sure the reader understands. She wisely chooses not to spell out well-known computer terms (CAD, etc.) so as not to seem naive or inexperienced to those evaluating her resume.

Under "Volunteer Work" Andrea includes material that also could have been grouped under "Personal Background" or a similar category. Knowing that NVK will need skilled English speakers and writers to sell its laptop to the United States market, she makes a point of mentioning her work as an English tutor for Asian refugees.

ANDREA K. WU
1509 N. Jackson Avenue, #24
Alexandria, VA 22304
(703) 555-9293

EDUCATION

Capital University, Washington, DC
M.B.A., expected May 1997.
- Member, Graduate Marketing Association and American Marketing Association.
- Member, Production and Operations Management Club.

Rice University, Houston, TX.
B.S. Electrical Engineering, May 1994.
Area of Concentration: Computer Engineering.

WORK EXPERIENCE

NCR CORP., Wichita, Kansas.
Computer Programmer/Analyst, VLSI CAD/CAE group.   June 1994–July 1996.
- Developed a new release of a CAD software package used extensively company-wide for both in-house and customer chip design analysis.
- Provided ongoing maintenance and support for existing in-house CAD software.
- Transported software written for VAX hardware to the Mentor workstation environment.
- Wrote and updated software documentation.
- Participated in planning printed circuit board (PCB) simulation strategy and prepared current databases and tools for simulation.

Assembling Your Application Package   25

- Studied process flow of engineering bill of materials creation to target areas for automation.
- Implemented an automated backup system for PCB symbol libraries and menus on the Mentor workstation platform.

RICE UNIVERSITY, Houston, Texas.
Lab/Teaching Assistant, Electrical Engineering Dept.   August 1993–May 1994.
- Conducted a digital logic design lab class.
- Graded lab reports and exams.
- Maintained lab equipment.

NCR CORP., Wichita, Kansas.
Summer Intern, VLSI CAD/CAE group.   May–August 1993.
- Developed a menu-based interface for a CAD software tool.

VOLUNTEER WORK

Rape Crisis Hotline Counselor. Houston Women's Center, Houston, Texas.
English as a Second Language Tutor (Specifically, for Southeast Asian Refugees). Houston Community College, Houston, Texas.

COMPUTER SKILLS

Excellent command of Lotus 1-2-3, WordPerfect, Microsoft Word, Flowcharting II+, MS-DOS and UNIX operating systems. Functional knowledge of C, Pascal, Modula-2, and Basic programming languages.

LANGUAGES

Fluent in Mandarin, Cantonese, and French.

REFERENCES   Available upon request.

To highlight the skills that will matter most to NVK, she creates a special category, "Computer Skills." Here she recaps many of the skills that were implicit from her list of job tasks and experiences. She knows that such skills should not be suggested only implicitly, and so spotlights them explicitly to end her resume with power.

For a different employment opportunity—one, perhaps, utilizing her business skills more than her computer skills—Andrea would have drawn up an entirely different resume highlighting her M.B.A. studies and supervisory experience at NCR.

So: What happened as a result of all this? Within two weeks, Andrea received a thick packet of employment information from NVK, along with a warm letter of interest from Mr. Chang. He referred to the inevitable obstacles of interviewing Andrea at such a great distance, but went on to ask if she would be willing to travel to New York to meet with the company's senior United States trade representative. Andrea's cold call had worked like a charm.

How many such inquiries can you make at once? Thanks to the resources of word processing, you can make as many contacts by letter as you wish. Be careful, however, not to blanket the world with a standard, catch-all resume that speaks to no one because it tries to speak to everyone. Employers have a right to expect that you have tailored your application materials to their needs and type of business.

In general, you will have much more success targeting a dozen or so businesses or organizations for a customized, personalized application than in mailing a standard letter and resume to a hundred or more companies. It's still a "people" world where real individuals read your letters and decide whether to respond. Employment directors around the world get reams of "junk mail" from applicants each year. Make your application the one that distinguishes itself by a personal touch, a sincere interest in the company, and a customized description of your background and skills.

Mail Merge to the Rescue

The task of creating such tailored communications need not be arduous. Virtually all popular word processing systems now allow you to create a relatively standard letter text with interspersed "field markers" where you can put customized material (including company information, names, and so forth).

Your resume, similarly, can be customized to include the name of your prospective employer in your statement of your career objective (e.g., "To begin as a systems architect with NVK; with experience, to assume responsibility for technical product adjustments to the United States market.") Personnel directors, like the rest of us, love to see their names and/or the company name mentioned in your letter. Whenever possible, find out the name of the personnel director before writing your letter. (Often this involves just a quick phone call to the company's receptionist—at most a $3 to $4 expense.)

Making the Cold Call by Telephone

Using the directories listed in the appendix, you can find the main telephone number for virtually any major company in the world. And given the recent lowering of international telephone rates, you can talk to just about any location on earth for less than $10 for 3 minutes. But here's the question: How are your nerves? Making an international cold call for employment brings a cold sweat to many applicants, especially those whose foreign language skills aren't up to par. Probably the best advice in the matter of telephone cold calls is to follow your intuition. If you feel that you have the personal charisma, gung-ho spirit, and financial resources to win a personnel director's attention by an initial call, dial away.

If your "nerves show," however, on such occasions and you forget every bit of your foreign language under pressure, send a letter. For many countries, letters will be the expected means of communication. In France, Germany, Latin America, and large parts of Asia, a personnel director will be surprised (sometimes unpleasantly so) to receive an out-of-the-blue phone call from a United States job applicant. The effect for these cultures is not unlike the feeling you may have when a salesperson comes uninvited to knock at the door of your residence. In England, Australia, New Zealand, and above all in the United States itself, personnel directors are more used to applicants who come on strong in an initial contact over the phone.

Path D: Using a Personal Contact in Your Application

Often your route to a job application has been greased for you by the supportive words of a mutual acquaintance—perhaps a friend of an executive in the company, an employee in the company, or an academic or professional bigwig known to you and the company. Every survey of how people actually get jobs underlines the importance of these personal contacts. People get jobs through people more often than through paper.

The trick is to use personal contacts without abusing them. Notice in the following job application letter how Blair Fallows gets maximum mileage out of his personal contact without appearing to "ride on the coattails" of his reference.

389 Western St.
Toronto, Canada SW893

Dec. 4, 1996

Ms. Virginia Walsch
Director, Optical Scanning Laboratory
Forbst Optical Systems
Berlin, West Germany

Dear Ms. Walsch:

Professor Samuel Owens, who directed my senior thesis at the University of Waterloo, suggested that I write to you regarding possible career opportunities at Forbst in laser optics or allied fields. Professor Owens mentioned how much he enjoyed meeting you at the recent Laser Optics convention in Paris, and hearing of your exciting research in microlaser applications.

As my enclosed resume suggests, I have been active in the development of new laser optical systems since 1991 for PRA International and Waterloo Scientific, Inc. You may have stopped by the Waterloo Scientific booth at the Laser Optics convention; our representatives were unveiling there the company's new laser microscope (written up in the September, 1996, issue of *Optics*). You may be particularly interested in my computer training, a background more and more necessary in developing sophisticated laser applications.

To work effectively in Germany, I recognize that I'll require an intensive course in written and spoken German. Such a course is available through Waterloo University, in partnership with Berlitz, and I am certainly ready to enroll in it if an employment opportunity arises with Forbst.

I'm eager to learn more about current lines of research at Forbst and your staffing needs. Thank you for reviewing my resume and considering my desire to join your optics team.

Sincerely,

Blair Fallows

Here's what actually took place between Professor Owens and Virginia Walsch at the Laser Optics convention in Paris. Professor Owens delivered a paper, after which Virginia Walsch introduced herself and expressed interest in Owens' topics. They chatted briefly and exchanged business cards. The whole social transaction took no more than five minutes.

But that five minutes proves crucial to Blair Fallows' job search. When Professor Owens gives Blair permission to use his name in a letter to Virginia Walsch, he gives Blair access to the German firm on a higher level than off-the-street candidates have. In receiving Blair's letter of inquiry, Virginia Walsch associates this applicant with the brilliant paper she has just heard in Paris. She's interested in hiring Blair partly for his own merits but also partly because it helps to create a ongoing link between Forbst and Professor Owens.

Blair would have ruined the usefulness of mentioning Professor Owens by stating it too baldly: "Professor Owens said you were hiring ..." or "I studied under the world-famous Professor Samuel Owens, whom you approached at ...." Be careful not to undo the power of personal contacts through overkill.

Blair received a letter from Virginia Walsch indicating that Forbst was in the midst of a temporary hiring freeze. He was invited, however, to participate in a company-sponsored symposium on optics, to be held in Switzerland the following summer. At that time, Ms. Walsch suggested, there would be time to explore career possibilities more seriously. Blair wrote a gracious letter of acceptance in which he again expressed his interest in joining the company. This time he included a letter of recommendation written for him by Professor Owens. At the Switzerland symposium Virginia Walsch offered Blair an attractive position with the company.

BLAIR FALLOWS

P.O. Box 4621, Capital University
Washington, DC
(202) 555-1117

EDUCATION

University of Waterloo, Waterloo, Canada
BSc (Co-op) Honors Applied Physics, Management Studies minor, April 1996.
- Received Mike Moser Award for Academics, Athletics, and Activities, 1996.
- Received Alexander Rutherford Scholarship, 1995.

WORK EXPERIENCE

University of Waterloo, Waterloo, Canada
Department of Science
Teaching Assistant
Sept 1995–April 1996
- Assisted a technical writing and speaking course.
- Tutored students in the use of microcomputer networks and word processors.
- Experienced in technical report writing.

Waterloo Scientific Inc., Waterloo, Canada
Scanning Laser Microscopes
Project Assistant
May 1995–August 1995
- Led project involving the development of a Scanning Photoluminescence Microscope.
- Coordinated software and hardware design modifications.

Research Assistant
Sept 1994–Dec 1994
- Performed outside contract research with prototype Laser Microscope.
- Author, Contract Research study, 1994.

PRA International, Inc., London, Canada
Optical Scientific Equipment
Technician/Demonstrator
Sept 1993–April 1994
- Explained uses and applications for spectrometers and lasers at International and Canadian conferences.
- Conducted application experience on a new type of spectrometer.
- Contributing Author, *Pittsburgh Conference (Spec) paper 621, 1994.*

Esso Resources, Calgary, Canada
Quirk Creek Sour Gas Plant
Operator
Jan 1992–May 1993

- Controlled all process functions and detected Hydrogen Sulphide leaks.
- Assumed Fire Control officer and Safety Officer duties.

Physical Metallurgy Labs, Ottawa, Canada
Metals/Mining Research Group
Software Developer
April 1991–Aug 1991

- Wrote software in "C" and Assembler to control x-ray diffractometer.
- Executed various research experiments.

INTERESTS/ACTIVITIES

- Reporter, University of Waterloo "Imprint," 1995–1996.
- Athletic Dept. Mascot, "The Warrior," 1995–1996.
- President, University Residents' Council, 1994.
- Varsity Rugby, Waterloo, 1992–1995; elected Captain, 1994, Vice Captain, Treasurer, 1995.
- Organized West Coast Tour, April 1996; toured United Kingdom, 1995; Eastern U.S., 1993.

LANGUAGES

- Conversational ability in French and German.
- Basic reading skills in Italian.

Those Pesky Application Forms

Because job applicants often fail to include necessary information in their resumes and cover letters, more and more companies are using lengthy job application forms. These forms frustrate applicants by requiring large answers in small spaces, or asking obtuse and ambiguous questions. As a result, the forms are often dispatched quickly and carelessly by many applicants—especially those who don't get the jobs.

Take the preparation of an application form as seriously as you take the preparation of your resume. Attach an extra page where space doesn't allow for a complete answer. Type whenever possible. Above all, write well in response to questions asking for your written opinion. Spelling, grammar, and mechanics should be flawless—and no less so if you are writing in a foreign language.

Neat, complete, typed answers convey an impression of the applicant as professional, skilled, and interested in the company.

What to Do When a Response Comes

Make it a practice always to have the last word in any application process. For example, let's say that you have sent your application package to the TWA office in Cannes. You receive a short letter from the director of the office there, M. Oberge, informing you that no positions are open. He thanks you for your interest and wishes you well in your job search.

Ninety-five percent of job applicants would leave the matter there. But you're part of that distinctive five percent who always try to turn "no" into "maybe." You respond with a brief personal note:

Dec. 10, 1996

M. Pierre Oberge
Director, TWA District Office
Cannes, France OA7898

Dear Mssr. Oberge:

 Thank you for taking time to consider my application for employment and for responding so promptly.

 I'd like to check with you again this summer to see if openings are available. In the meantime, I'm participating in TWA's domestic internship program for management trainees through my university and polishing my French.

 Thanks for keeping me in mind as career opportunities arise in your office.

With best regards,

Michele Covington

 Though Michele didn't find the opening she wanted, she has put herself in a good position for further correspondence and contact with this international employer. In short, she hasn't just let things drop. She's left a final, positive impression that may help her with the company at a later date.

Having the last word to a positive reply to your application is easy: Say thank you, repeat the gist of the letter or call you've received, and indicate what action you are taking.

Dec. 10, 1996

M. Pierre Oberge
Director, TWA District Office
Cannes, France OA7898

Dear M. Oberge:

I am delighted to accept your offer for a summer, 1997, position in your office. I understand that I will be assisting you in implementation of a computer scheduling system for area travel agents. You also mentioned that TWA would provide transportation to and from Cannes.

I look forward to making final arrangements for what I hope will be an ongoing association with TWA. Feel free to call me at home (389) 987-7987 or send messages via fax (389) 389-3892.

With best wishes,

Michele Covington

What about Fax?

International letters still can take ten days or more to reach their destination in Europe or Asia, and often longer for parts of Africa. Can't you speed the job application process by faxing your cover letter and resume?

It depends. In many company cultures, the use of the fax machine is reserved for high-priority matters—the kind of thing that used to require courier or express mail. When an applicant's cover letter and resume arrive on this sacrosanct machine, the company may react adversely. "The medium is the message," as McLuhan claimed, and the medium (fax) can undo the message (your application) in such companies.

Other firms have embraced the future and use fax for all kinds of communications, including employment matters. But how do you know when to fax and when not to?

Probably the safest course is to send your initial inquiry via traditional mail, but then to invite the employer's response to you by fax. You say you don't own a fax machine and don't plan to buy one? Not to worry. In virtually every city, town, and hamlet in the United States are "mail stop" shops offering public fax availability. For a dollar or so per page, these shops will receive your fax message for you and telephone you to report that the message has arrived. Simply call a mailstop or other fax merchant in your town and make arrangements to refer to the shop's fax number in your letters to employers (as in Michele's letter).

Keys to an Effective International Resume

As suggested by the resumes that appear earlier in this chapter, international resumes differ from domestic resumes in at least five ways:

1. Names of companies, colleges, and organizations should not be referred to in abbreviated form alone (USC, YMCA, etc.). International decision makers may not recognize the abbreviated form. After spelling out the term at least once in your letter or resume, you may refer to it by abbreviations thereafter, so long as the reference is clear.

2. Places of study and employment should be specified (George Mason University, Fairfax, Virginia). International employers are used to reviewing resumes from applicants who have worked and studied in a half dozen countries or more. Only American resumes seem to presume that everyone knows where Colgate is located, and so forth. By specifying location, you gain the additional advantage of "gilt by association"—that is, favorable associations based on location. An international employer who has never heard of Macy's may nonetheless be impressed that you worked in its Washington, DC, or New York City locations.

3. College studies and job responsibilities should be spelled out in more detail on international resumes. Typical American college majors such as economics or management may leave international employers wondering precisely what you studied and what you can do. You may want to list five or six of your major courses, by title, to suggest the nature of your academic training. Job responsibilities, similarly, should be defined thoroughly: What projects you supervised, why the results were important for the company, how many people you oversaw, where your products were distributed, and so forth. To avoid heavy paragraphs of prose, use bullets to break out these responsibilities beneath the name and location of the company and your job title.

4. While references may be available upon request, many international employers prefer that recommendation letters simply be sent along with the application package. Then all materials necessary for decision making are at hand, without waiting (sometimes for weeks) for recommendation letters to arrive. To assemble your recommendation letters, simply inform your reference sources that you will be photocopying their letters and sending them to several companies. Your resume can then offer "Additional References Available Upon Request" for those companies that desire confidential or personalized reference letters.

5. Consider providing personal background about yourself and a professionally appropriate photograph. Employers within the United States prefer not to see your picture along with your resume simply because they are constrained by law not to consider race, age, or sex in hiring decisions. International employers, as a rule, are not so constrained, and often welcome the chance to get an impression of you as a person. For personal data, you might consider describing your outside interests, sports involvement, volunteer work, hobbies, civic involvement, and family life. (You must be the judge of when such information will be an appropriate and advantageous addition to your resume. For some positions—international finance, for example—a more austere and impersonal resume may be desirable.)

An Example of a Personal Background Statement at the End of a Resume

PERSONAL BACKGROUND. I'm a 24-year-old entrepreneur who enjoys working closely with people to actualize new ideas. As a member of Rotary International since 1991, I've led seminars on intercultural management and now serve as chapter president for the Toledo, Ohio, club. I maintain an active physical life through jogging, swimming, and skiing. My avocations include computers, HAM radio, and volunteer work at a local hospital.

What about Desktop Publishing?

Desktop published resumes, like those included at the end of this chapter, have become the standard for international resumes. Others done in ordinary ribbon-type look amateurish by comparison.

If you don't have desktop publishing equipment, check with a university computer center or commercial photocopy center for the use of software such as Page Maker (Apple) or Ventura (IBM) to use in connection

Assembling Your Application Package

with a laser printer. Photocopy centers usually rent time on their computers (perhaps Macintosh) for desktop publishing. You'll want to have your resume and cover letter composed before renting such time—at $8 to $10 per hour, "writer's block" can be expensive!

Many resume and secretarial services offer desktop published resumes from either your paper draft or word processing disk. There are advantages, however, to undertaking the somewhat painful process of learning to use desktop publishing yourself. You will find it possible to make customized changes in your resume according to the company you're sending it to. Those kinds of changes are usually not possible or practical when you're relying on (and paying for) a resume service for alterations.

Sample International Resumes

The following resumes are presented not as perfect models but as various approaches to the crisp, clear communication of business and personal information.

Maureen Connell
435-F South Lark Road
Arlington, Virginia 22206
(703) 555-2233

EDUCATION

Georgetown University, Washington, DC 1994–1996. Master of Business Administration candidate Emphasis: International Business

St. Joseph's University, Philadelphia, PA 1989–1993. Bachelor of Arts in Political Science

University of Paris, La Sorbonne, Paris, France 1992. Foreign Exchange program, spring semester

EXPERIENCE

U.S. House of Representatives, Washington, DC Office of the Republican Leader — Fall, 1996
Intern.
Worked with Leadership staff of Representative Robert H. Michel on budget reconciliation and Congressional redistricting.

Republican Research Committee — 1994–1996
Senior Research Analyst for House Leadership Committee.
Worked with Republican Members and Committee staff. Directed nine task forces for the development, introduction and implementation of specific legislation and general policy initiatives. Participated in strategy sessions and briefings between Members, White House personnel, and Administration officials. Worked with national political party organization and special interest groups.

Budget Committee, Minority Staff — 1992–1994
Policy Analyst.
Tracked legislation, wrote staff reports and legislative summaries. Analyzed budget proposals, worked with other Congressional staff, House and Senate committees, and federal agencies. Coordinated Congressional activities with the Office of Management and Budget.

Children, Youth, & Families Committee, Minority Staff — 1990–1992
Staff Assistant.
Assisted with committee projects, Congressional and constituent inquiries, drafted correspondence. Organized local and national hearings. Acted as committee liaison to Republican Congressional Offices and to outside organizations.

Fund for a Conservative Majority, Washington DC — 1989–1990
Receptionist for Political Action Committee.
Assisted staff in preparation of direct mail campaigns, preparation of Federal Committee Reports.

ACTIVITIES

Georgetown International Business Forum, Georgetown M.B.A. Yearbook, Georgetown M.B.A. "Annual Report" student review.

OTHER

Proficient in WordPerfect, Lotus 123. Conversational French. Reading ability in Russian and Japanese.

William Gorka
1724 Downey Lane, NW, Washington, DC 20007
(202) 555-9125

EDUCATION

LAW: Georgetown University Law Center J.D., Washington, DC, May 1996

BUSINESS: Georgetown University School of Business Administration M.B.A., May 1996

ENGINEERING: University of California, Los Angeles Ph.D. Mechanical Engineering, June 1994; M.S. Mechanical Engineering, June 1990; B.S. Mechanical Engineering, June 1988, cum laude

PROFESSIONAL EXPERIENCE

Lyon & Lyon, Los Angeles, California May 1996 to August 1996
Summer Associate
Researched and drafted legal memoranda; conducted patent disclosures; drafted patent application; composed patent amendment and restriction requirement.

CADAM INC, Burbank, California June 1993 to August 1995
Product Analyst
Supported intellectual property copyright litigation; managed specialized marketing and development projects; conducted legal, marketing, and technical research; provided marketing competitive analyses; developed research-oriented software in LISP; conducted dealer training and trade show demonstrations (both domestically and in South America).

Jet Propulsion Laboratory, Pasadena, California June 1991 to June 1993
Technical Aide B
Designed and built various scientific and technical apparatuses; operated machine shop equipment; conducted laboratory experiments.

ORGANIZATIONS

Georgetown University Law Center, American Criminal Law Review, Georgetown Law & Business Society (Chairman—High Tech Committee), The James Brown Scott Society of International Law.

University of California, Los Angeles, Tau Beta Pi (Engineering Honor Society), Phi Eta Sigma (Freshman Honor Society), Engineering Society of the University of California, Bruin Christian Fellowship, Golden Key National Honor Society Order of the Engineer.

Professional: American Bar Association (ABA), Society of Manufacturing Engineers (SME), Computer Automated Systems Association (CASA), National Society of Professional Engineers (NSPE), California Society of Professional Engineers (CSPE), American Society of Mechanical Engineers (ASME), Christian Legal Society (CLS).

HONORS AND SCHOLARSHIPS

University of California, Los Angeles, UCLA Alumni Scholarship, UCLA Chancellor's Scholarship, Department Scholar American Society of Cost Engineers Scholarship, National Dean's List (1987–1988), Fourragere Bearer (Top 15% of graduating class).

LANGUAGES

Proficient in written and conversational French, Italian, and Spanish.

4
Meet Sixteen People Who Did It

Often the best information about the methods used in an international job search comes from Americans who have already worked abroad. In the following interview segments, sixteen such people respond to two questions: How did you get your international job? How do you recommend that others go about getting a job abroad? Then, at the conclusion of the chapter, six foreign businesspeople in a variety of fields offer their advice to U.S. citizens seeking international work in their countries.

Brad Eberhart, a broker for Pacific Sun Financial:
   "I worked in London as a researcher for an investment banking firm. I got the job simply by responding to an ad in the *New York Times*. A friend of mine also obtained a position as an exporter for Izod in Paris by applying directly to the company. My advice to others? Get your application package in top shape and stick it out there."

Matthew Meyer, a bond broker for Gintelco, Inc.:
   "It may sound like a typical story, but I got my job as a corporate bond broker in London through my Uncle Vincent. He knew the managing director of the London office and put in a good word for me. I would advise jobseekers to scan their relatives and acquaintances carefully to look for people who have international contacts. The inside track really helps."

Bob Foster, a systems analyst for TRW:
   "I was hired by the Mitsubishi Corporation in the United States, and was then sent to Japan for a year of training. It was an incredible year, filled with wave after wave of new learning experiences. I would recommend that anyone seeking work in Japan try to make connections first through a United States branch of the company."

Andrea Liu, a computer programmer/analyst for NCR Corporation:
> "I'm now seeking an international position in the Far East, so I can't speak from actual experience yet. But I have a good friend who got a job in Switzerland under an internship program for programmers. The process of finding that international job wasn't hard at all: He simply watched for foreign companies who were recruiting at his school, the University of Colorado. I think your college recruitment office is one of your best tickets abroad."

Brenton R. Babcock, a product analyst for CADAM, Inc.:
> "Our parent company, Lockheed, has offices throughout the world. I accepted foreign assignment to Santiago, Chile, as a product analyst and trainer. One of the highlights of my stay was participation in an international trade show there. Talk about contacts! You meet people in your industry from all over the world. I was passing out and collecting business cards like mad. I guess my advice to others would be to link up with a company that offers the possibility of international assignment."

Maureen Mingey, a policy analyst for the State Department:
> "It doesn't always appear on my resume, but I worked as a nanny for a year while attending school in Germany. In my case, the job was arranged through the college placement office. But it provided me with an opportunity to get to know a prominent family and their friends. I learned about a lot of career opportunities that never appeared in the want ads. My roommate, however, didn't need personal contacts at all to get her first international position. She saw an ad in *The Wall Street Journal,* sent in her resume and cover letter, and three weeks later was on her way to Europe for a career in sales and marketing. So I would advise others to try several channels of application—at the same time, if possible."

Michael J. Farrand, Senior Associate, ICF Corporation International:
> "I worked as an English instructor in Rome, and got my job the old-fashioned way: by knocking on doors of private language schools there. Needless to say, my moderate competency in Italian was absolutely necessary to getting an interview. The instructors all spoke English, of course, but they only wanted to hire people who could communicate with clients. My advice to international jobseekers is to go to the country you're interested in, then try to make social and business connections. Often you can get your foot in the door by sending letters of inquiry in advance of your visit. Even though they may not offer you a job on the basis of your letter, they may invite you to stop by their place of business. That can lead to contacts, information, and eventually a job. Be aware of work permit regulations in the country you're visiting. Sometimes your employer can get you the necessary permits or can invent creative ways around them."

Richard Larson, a history professor in California:
"Four of my college friends and I saw an ad in the *Los Angeles Times* from an employment agency looking for teachers of English to send to a company school in Japan. On a lark, we all sent our resumes in, not expecting much. To our surprise, all five of us were interviewed by a company manager within a week and had offers of employment in Japan within two weeks. Only two of us accepted, but I was amazed at how streamlined the hiring process can be for jobs 10,000 miles away. Based on our experience, I would recommend that jobseekers watch the classified ads in major city newspapers and contact employment agencies that specialize in foreign positions."

Jennifer McCullough, a registered representative for Drexel Burnham Lambert, Inc.:
"Through relatives, I heard that positions were often open at United States Embassies abroad. I applied to our Belgian embassy, and landed a job as Assistant Immigrant Visa Counselor. My advice to others would be to send your resume along with a dynamite cover letter to as many embassies as possible. But be prepared to move quickly if a job offer comes. The embassy jobs tend to be here today, gone tomorrow."

Cynthia North, a tax accountant with Price Waterhouse:
"Just out of college I accepted an entry-level accounting position with a 'Big 6' firm with branch offices in Canada. I flew up on assignment for a week, and eventually ended up there for several years. I suppose I trace my international employment experience back to one question I asked in my initial job interview: 'Does your company do work outside the United States?' I made my selection of employers on that basis."

Craig Walker, a sales representative for Lanier:
"I had the time of my life as a claims broker for Lloyd's of London (in London) for six months. It may sound like boring work, but my cases brought me in contact with all kinds of people and situations. I think I learned more about international business in those six months than in any other period of my life. I got the job through a friend of my family. He knew of the opening, and made a phone call for me. But, once, there, I worked with a lot of non-British employees who had simply applied for their positions without personal contacts. Those seeking international jobs shouldn't despair if they don't have influential family members or friends to help them out."

Joan Stein, a software consultant for American Management Systems:
"It wasn't the most lucrative job of my career, of course, but I wouldn't have traded the experience for anything: my months working on a communal farm—a *kibbutz*—in Israel. I made a few calls in Tel Aviv and located the Central Office where assignments were made to such jobs. It was one of those situations, however, where I had to 'be there.' The process couldn't have taken place very well by

mail. On the other end of the financial spectrum, I might mention a friend who got a marketing position for Avon in Japan. He had taken a series of intensive Japanese courses and applied through Avon's home office in the United States. Knowing a language well really sets you apart from the competition."

Sprague Simonds, a research analyst for Citibank:
"In one of the wildest years of my life, I was a whitewater river leader in a job that took me to several continents. I had always wanted to turn my avocation into an occupation. So I watched travel ads in the newspaper and magazines for agencies that were putting trips together. I went in person to see if they needed a trained leader, and got the job. Even though the resume is important, I would recommend that jobseekers set up the nerve to simply show up and shake some hands in the application process."

Bob Karig, operations officer, United States Army:
"I took the ads seriously about 'Join the Army and see the world.' I accepted an assignment as executive officer for a United States Army Aviation battalion in Germany. Without sounding like a recruiter, I want to tell those looking for international positions not to ignore the many, many opportunities in the armed services. It's hard to think of a business or technical field that isn't represented in some form within the military."

Becky Bleich, a corporate assistant with Alex Brown & Sons, Inc.:
"My sister has all the luck. She worked as a marketing researcher at Interior Selections, a fabric-making and interior design firm in London. The job came about when the general manager of the firm mentioned to my parents that he needed help with a marketing project. I would advise those seeking international jobs to tell parents, aunts, uncles, grandparents, and extended family to keep their eyes and ears open for job possibilities. Many times these people have built up terrific contacts over the years."

Deborah Rich, new products supervisor, Cornnuts, Inc.:
"I literally walked into my international position. I was visiting the University of Madrid, and wondered what kind of positions were posted on the 'Employment Available' board for students there. One posting advertised a position for an English teacher—which turned out to be me. I would advise jobseekers to turn a vacation into a job search. Find an area you really like, then spend time around the university or town center finding job leads and making personal contacts. If you're in college in the United States now, consider asking some of your professors for contacts abroad. Often they have colleagues who need research assistants or teaching aides."

Finally, we asked several nationals in major trading regions to offer their advice to United States citizens seeking international employment.

Meet Sixteen People Who Did It

Yazuto Wakatsuki, Staff Member, International Planning Department, The Saitama Bank, Ltd., Japan:

"Americans are generally unaware how aggressively Japanese banks, insurance companies, security firms, and others are recruiting foreign employees. In most cases, Japanese firms are more interested in your academic preparation than in your work experience. They are especially interested in finance and economics majors. You can locate such firms by watching for their advertisements in *The Wall Street Journal, New York Times, Washington Post,* and other papers. Or you can make direct contact with Japanese companies by consulting the directories in your college careers office.

"Don't be discouraged if you don't speak or write flawless Japanese. Few Americans do. Japanese companies will appreciate it if you have taken an intensive course to give you the basics of the language, but all job interviews and initial job assignments will be in English, not Japanese.

"One word of advice, however: Do study Japanese management techniques and Japanese culture. Foreign employees are hired in part on their likelihood of 'fitting in' to the company and country. You can help your application by knowing how the Japanese relate at work and in their social lives."

Jean-Michel Beghin, software engineer, Hewlett-Packard, France:

"It is very difficult for a non-citizen to get a work permit for a career position in France without the assistance of a company or trade association. It makes best sense, therefore, to contact French companies that have branch offices here in the United States. For instance, 'Societe Generale' is a large French bank that has offices in New York City. These branch offices will know of hiring opportunities in France, and will be able to provide the kind of introduction and assistance for you that will avoid permit problems.

"Especially when seeking employment in France, know the language well. Your usefulness to a French company will be very limited if you cannot speak French with a high level of competency."

Barbara Thwaites, Consultant, Rehabilitation Services:

"In the Caribbean, newspapers are filled with job ads but hiring usually takes place through personal references and contacts. If you have a friend in Jamaica, for example, ask him or her to find out about potential jobs for you. Once you have entrée to the company, send a complete resume and follow up, if possible, by a visit to the company. Latin cultures pay much more heed to your personal presence (an expression of sincere interest) than to the fanciest of resumes or application letters."

Amit Pande, Chartered Accountant, Mohinder Puri & Co., Chartered Accountants:

"The private sector in India is exploding with business opportunities, and the need for American liaisons and joint ventures has never been greater. Indian business leaders will take your paperwork very seriously, and often hire on the basis of it. Spend time putting together a flawless, complete application package. You may not get a second chance to add material later. Language competence is helpful, but most Indian firms will be looking primarily for your business or technical skills. Emphasize what you can do in your resume. At some point in the job application process, you will have to meet with your prospective employee or his representative in the United States. You may want to read about Indian culture prior to this meeting to understand customs, religion, diet, and so forth."

Mohammed Shanshal, Construction Manager:

"In Canada, the first step in your job search should be to apply through the Immigration Service for a work permit. Few career opportunities will be open to you without this necessary legal step. Thereafter, the application process is very similar to that in the United States. In French-speaking portions of Canada, you will want to demonstrate not only your language ability but also your respect for things French. Canadians dislike American applicants who 'have all the answers'—United States answers—from the beginning; better to show sincere interest in the Canadian approach to things."

Luis Edvardo Bravo, Financial Analyst, Central Bank of Chile:

"Latin American companies put great stock in formal introductions. It would be best if one of their trusted branch managers or trade representatives in this country wrote a letter (or made a call) of introduction to the home office prior to the arrival of your job application. Once you've been introduced, the company will probably follow up with a brief letter of interest inviting you to apply. You'll then have the name and direct address of one or more decision makers in the company.

"Business documents, including applications, run somewhat longer in Chile and other Latin American countries than in the United States. A short, snappy resume, therefore, may do you more harm than good. Take time—and several pages, if necessary—to explain your education, your experience, your special skills, and your career goals. Your Latin American reader will take this volume of language as a sign of sincere interest and respect. Your cover letter should be similarly courteous and fulsome. If you do not speak Spanish, take the kind of course that will give you basic business and social phrases. Latin American companies resist interviewing or hiring applicants who have made no effort to learn Spanish."

5
Preparing for an International Job Interview

You're on the phone with an employer based in London. Jill Tervorson, personnel manager for an investment banking firm, has just called to express her interest in interviewing you for a summer internship, with long-term career possibilities.

What should you expect? No, she probably won't offer to send you a ticket for the Concorde, or any other airliner for that matter. In most cases, foreign employers will arrange an in-the-States interview, at least for the first screening. Jill's company, for example, is associated with Lloyd's Bank in New York. You're invited there for the interview. But wait a minute. You live in Cincinnati. Does she expect you to get to New York at your own expense, simply in hopes of getting the internship?

The painful answer to that question is yes. In many cases, international employers, particularly in Europe, think of major cities as closely linked by rail and air. A London student, for example, would think nothing of popping up to Manchester on the train for an interview. International employers often aren't aware that distances and transportation costs within the United States can pose a significant hurdle for the jobseeker on a budget.

Be sure to clarify, therefore, who's picking up the tab for your interview travel and lodging. For example, you may ask, "Does your company usually pay for travel and lodging expenses, or would these by my responsibility?" Jobseekers often discover that foreign employers think Oklahoma City is just down the road from Minneapolis. Once they understand the distances involved, most companies are willing to assist with transportation and lodging costs. By clarifying where you are in relation to where they plan the interview, you may save yourself needless expense.

I'm not suggesting, by the way, that all international employers will arrange a first interview for you within the United States. Some, particularly in Asia and South America, will assume that you plan a trip to their region in the near future and can be interviewed on-site at that time. Use vacation travel wisely, therefore, in coordination with your international job search.

But back to the future: You're invited to an interview at Lloyd's Bank in New York City. Jill Trevorson tells you that the company's London-based recruiting director will be in New York to interview you and other candidates. Here are ten things you can expect in an international employment interview. Forewarned is forearmed!

1. *You will be judged in part by how you look.* Like it or not, your clothing and grooming play a significant (though not decisive) role in your hiring. And "Dress for Success" books notwithstanding, there is no one formula for how to dress. (For instance, personnel managers scoff at one popular book's advice on "power suits" for women. "I'm sick of seeing a gray suit, white blouse, and red accessories," one personnel manager told me. "We're not going to hire someone who thinks professionalism means a certain uniform.")

    Better advice, he says, is to "dress to express, not impress." Wear business attire that suits you and the situation. If you have to choose between more conservative or liberal clothing, lean toward the conservative side.

2. *You may overlook some of the key decision makers.* Many job candidates have sat silently, even sullenly, waiting in a reception room for their interview. They make no effort to get to know the secretary, and may even be curt with him or her. What a mistake! The impressions of the office staff are often invited by the interviewing manager or volunteered by staff members. The intuitions of a seasoned secretary mean much to his or her superior.

    Take time, therefore, to make appropriate small talk with people you meet before the interview. Often they can give you valuable information ("Mr. Sajaki loves to talk about golf") and tips ("The company seems especially interested in your proposal-writing skills"). For that matter, look around the reception room. If annual reports, company literature, or company-related business articles are set out on the tables, they're probably there for a reason. Be the one candidate who can say in the interview, "Yes, I noticed in your annual report that..."

3. *First impressions matter.* The first five minutes of an interview are crucial. Interview research suggests that many interviewers make up their minds about a candidate in those first few minutes, and then spend the remainder of the interview confirming their impressions. But what sort of questions make up the first five minutes, and how can a job candidate prepare?

   In most international employment interviews, the "tough" questions for which you have rehearsed answers don't occur at the outset of the interview. Instead, this time is devoted to ice-breakers—small talk about the weather, parking, traffic, your hometown, your hotel, and so forth. Too many candidates make the mistake of giving minimal "yes/no" responses to these efforts of the interviewer to become acquainted. Don't make this mistake. It is as much your responsibility to put the interviewer at ease as it is his or her responsibility to make you feel comfortable. You have everything to gain by presenting yourself at the beginning of the interview as a sociable, friendly conversationalist.

   You may, for example, want to notice what's on your interviewer's walls or desk. Are those soccer (i.e., "football") trophies on top of the cabinet? Is that a picture of a large family or new baby on the desk? Many of the most productive topics for opening "small talk" are staring at you from the interviewer's office.

4. *Your interview answers shouldn't sound like lectures.* Watch the hands and eyes of your interviewer to know when enough is enough. Nonverbal signals such as averted eyes, hand movements, shifting posture, and other signs tell you that the interviewer has heard enough in response to one question and is ready to move on.

5. *Give headlines before launching into a long story.* It is not uncommon in international employment interviews to face unwieldy, complex questions such as "Tell me about your preparation," or "What challenges do you foresee in this position?" If you know in advance that you'll be talking for two minutes or more in response to such questions, establish the structure of your answer at the outset. For example, your answer to the question regarding your preparation might begin with this kind of headline: "I'll try to answer that question by telling you about my education, my primary work experiences, and my work habits." There—you've established an agenda, a shopping list, for both you and the interviewer. Your answer seems organized and satisfying precisely because you have set out the ground rules for what you will and won't discuss. The much less attractive alternative to such headlining is the kind of rambling answer we've all heard in interviews: "Well, let's see. I graduated from high school in 1982 and then..."

6. *Give eye contact to all participants in the interview.* When being interviewed by more than one person in a room, it's common to give eye contact almost exclusively to the person asking the questions. Let's take the case of an interview I observed recently in San Juan, Puerto Rico. The candidate faced an interview panel of three executives—a bank vice president, the personnel manager, and the marketing manager. You can guess who did virtually all of the questioning: the two subordinates in the room. The vice president sat back as a silent observer, only nodding occasionally. In this hour-long interview, the candidate made the mistake of looking only at the personnel manager and marketing manager. He never once met and held the eyes of the vice president.

   When the interview ended, the interviewers' impressions of the candidate fell strictly in line with the amount of eye contact they received during the interview (a phenomenon borne out by interview research). The personnel manager and marketing manager liked the candidate, and used words such as "direct," "honest," and "personable" to describe her characteristics. But the most important decision maker in the room—the vice president who had received virtually no eye contact—had different impressions: "a bit stand-offish," "not a good fit," and "nervous or somewhat hostile."

   Obviously, the candidate should have looked directly at her questioner at the beginning of her answer, and then distributed her direct eye contact to each person in the room for the remainder of the answer. Remember, the most important people in the room usually ask the fewest questions.

7. *Expect interruptions and deal with them graciously.* In many, if not most, international employment interviews, the phone will ring, the secretary will pop in for an urgent question, or the intercom will blare. Don't show even the hint of annoyance at such interruptions, even if your interviewer shows his or her irritation. If you've lost your train of thought due to such intrusions, politely ask the interviewer's help in getting back on track: "May I ask you to repeat your question?" "We were discussing my educational background. Did you want to hear more about my graduate degrees?"

8. *Your responses should sound natural, not memorized.* You score no points with an interviewer by rattling off a rehearsed answer. When the international interviewer's English skills are less than yours, you may actually sabotage the interview by a slick answer delivered at machine-gun pace. Instead, try to give the interviewer the answers. In most interviews, you will be asked, "Do you have any questions about the company?" The only wrong answer to this question is, "No,

I think we've covered everything." Consider: You're asking for the company's interest in you as an employee but, in return, you aren't able to come up with a single expression of interest in the company? It doesn't compute.

Some good standby questions are the following:

(Asked of the interviewer) "What has been your experience with the company? Have you been happy here?"

"Where do you see the company going in the next three (five, etc.) years?"

"How would you describe employee relations at the company?"

It's tempting, but usually unwise, to ask self-serving questions regarding raises, vacations, and so forth. (There will be an appropriate time for such questions after you've established the company's interest in hiring you.) You may want or need to ask rather blunt questions about salary. This line of questioning can be pursued without putting interviewers off: "What is the usual salary range for this position?" Notice that you haven't asked "What will I be paid?" Interviewers may not be willing or able to name an exact number in the interview. And by asking for the usual pay range you have put yourself in position to ask for more, because you are by no means a usual employee, right?

What Will They Ask?

Bearing in mind that your answers should never sound memorized, you may nevertheless want to think through and practice answering aloud the most common interview questions:

Questions about Your Education

- What do you consider your successes in school?
- What kinds of subjects did you dislike or avoid in school?
- What kind of jobs did you hold while in school?

Questions about Your Skills and Work Experience

- What can you offer this company at the beginning of your job here?
- What specific strengths made you effective in previous positions?
- How would you go about managing a budget for your work unit?

- What do you consider some of the most important ideas you contributed in previous positions?
- Describe a typical day in a previous position.
- Evaluate a previous boss. What did you like or dislike about his or her managerial style?
- Tell me about some of the people you worked with in previous positions. How did you relate to them?
- What do you think it takes to be successful in the position you seek?

Questions about Your Attitudes and Intelligence

- What would you like to be doing two years from now?
- What risks did you take in a previous position, and what were the results of those risks?
- Tell me about a failure of some sort in your professional life, and how you handled that failure.
- Describe the best boss you ever had.
- What kinds of things do you think this company might do to make you more successful in your position?
- What do you know about this company?

Such challenging interview questions, of course, are open-ended, requiring more than a "yes/no" response. You may want to talk out answers to these questions into a tape recorder. Simply listening to the quantity, quality, stops, and starts of your answers can be the best way to improve your interviewing manner. As you listen (sometimes a painful experience), jot down notes on specific ways in which you can improve. For example, you might want to note "avoid umms, get right to the point, keep examples and anecdotes brief," and so forth. With these goals in mind, practice your answers again on tape. With even a few practice sessions, you'll hear definite improvement and feel your confidence rising.

Here are 65 more questions that I've collected over the years from observing and participating in employment interviews:

1. Please tell me about your previous job.
2. What do you believe were your major responsibilities in that job?
3. What kind of job experiences have you had that relate to this position?

4. What aspects of your previous job did you like?
5. What aspects of your previous job did you dislike?
6. What are some of the things you spent the most time on in your previous job?
7. What are some of the assignments in your previous job that you did particularly well? Why?
8. What are some of the assignments in your previous position that you found difficult to do? Why?
9. Tell me about a problem you solved on your previous job.
10. What did you do when you couldn't solve a problem in your job?
11. Describe your boss's method of management.
12. For what things did your boss compliment you?
13. In your previous job, how much work was done on your own? As part of a team?
14. What was the most innovative idea you introduced in your previous job?
15. Describe your techniques for getting the job done.
16. What schooling have you had that can be helpful in performing the job for which you are applying?
17. What are your own objectives with regard to this position?
18. What are your long-term career objectives?
19. In your own career, where do you want to be one (three, five) year(s) from now?
20. What do you plan to do to reach your career objectives?
21. How do you feel about the progress you've made so far in your present or previous job?
22. Do you believe your talents and abilities are well matched to this job? How and why?
23. What are your greatest assets?
24. How did you choose the school you attended?
25. Did you change your course of study? Why?
26. Did you change schools? Why?
27. Why did you major in your particular field?
28. In what extracurricular activities were you involved in school?

29. What made you choose those particular activities?
30. What accomplishments did you feel proud of at school?
31. What experiences at school do you wish you had a chance to do over? Why?
32. How did you pay for your education?
33. Did you hold any leadership positions in school?
34. What things interest you outside of work?
35. What do you like to do best?
36. What things give you the greatest satisfaction?
37. Have your interests changed in recent years?
38. How well did you do in school?
39. What grades did you receive?
40. In what courses did you do best? Why?
41. With what courses did you have the most trouble?
42. From what courses did you get the most benefit? Why?
43. From what courses did you get the least benefit? Why?
44. Do you feel that your grades fairly reflect your ability? Why or why not?
45. If you had it to do over again, would you take the same course of study?
46. How do you view the job for which you are applying?
47. If you were to get this job, in what areas could you contribute immediately? Where would you need training?
48. What barriers do you see that might prevent you from performing your job as effectively as you would like?
49. Do you have the tools and support that you need to do your job?
50. What do you understand to be the purpose or mission of the company?
51. How do you feel about the day-to-day work tasks involved with this position?
52. How well do you work under pressure? Give me some examples.
53. How well do you get along with your peers?
54. What kind of people rub you the wrong way?
55. How do you go about motivating people?

Preparing for an International Job Interview

56. What kinds of problems do you enjoy solving?
57. What can you tell me about your level of ambition?
58. How do you spend your free time?
59. What newspapers and magazines do you read regularly?
60. What is your definition of success?
61. What did you learn from a previous position?
62. What can you tell me about your level of creativity?
63. Do you work better alone or as part of a team? Explain.
64. What motivates you?
65. Why should this company hire you?

After the Interview

Few job offers are made on the spot. Within a matter of days (sometimes weeks), you may receive a verbal or written job offer, or you may be invited for further interviews. Given the distances involved, some of these later interviews may be by phone.

But the period immediately following your initial interview shouldn't be considered merely a waiting game. You should write a thank-you letter to your company host and/or interviewer. This message need not be long, but should express your appreciation for their interest in you and your impression of the company. Here's a sample:

Dear Sr. Ortiz:

    I enjoyed our discussion yesterday and want to thank you for your hospitality during my visit to Zapata Industries. I was particularly impressed by my tour of the new Juarez production facility and by the cooperative spirit among your employees.

    Please don't hesitate to contact me if you need further information helpful to your decision making. I look forward to hearing from you.

If you spent time with several employees during your visit, name them in your thank-you letter: "I enjoyed meeting Frank Rodriguez, Rosa Sanchez, and you during my visit, and thank you all for ..." In the rush and possible anxiety of an interview visit, you may tend to forget the names of people you meet. Get business cards or jot down names in preparation for writing a thank-you letter.

The days immediately following a job interview are an excellent time to check out the claims made by the company during your visit. You may soon be asked to commit a significant portion of your life to the company—you certainly want to make sure that you haven't been hyped during your interview. Relocating to Calcutta for a company that will go into receivership within six months isn't what you had in mind by an international work experience.

If you receive no word for ten days after an interview, it's appropriate to write a brief, polite letter of inquiry or make a phone call to your contact at the company. Here's a sample "what's-going-on" letter:

Dear M. Villan:

I'm writing to reemphasize my interest in the position we discussed during my visit to your corporate headquarters on May 9. If I can be helpful in supplying further information or materials, please don't hesitate to call or write.

I look forward to our next conversation.

With best regards,

Accepting, Postponing, or Refusing an International Job Offer

Just as you had hoped, you receive the job offer by phone. If you like what you hear, you may want to give your tentative acceptance on the phone—subject to your review of the written job offer (which you have every right to request). In that written offer you should ask that the following matters be specified:

- The job for which you are being hired, including any provisions or terms you have negotiated with the company.
- The amount you will be paid, and any currency or tax understanding you've reached with the company. Is the stated salary in American dollars? In highly inflationary economies, have you protected yourself from drastic losses in the real value of your salary? Do you know how that salary will be taxed?
- The kind of benefits package, severance agreement, and other matters that have been agreed upon.
- Who will pay for relocation expenses.
- The date you are expected to report for work.

It's crucial to get these matters in writing prior to formal acceptance of an international job offer. Too often, some presumed understandings get "lost in translation," leaving both employer and new employee unsure of who said what. If a company representative is unwilling to put the job commitment in writing, you've located a definite red flag to your future association.

Your formal acceptance should similarly be in writing, as in this sample letter:

Dear Mr. Peters:

I am pleased to accept the position as described in your letter of May 18. I understand that the company wishes to approve my relocation expenses in advance of my move. After receiving bids this week from trans-Atlantic shippers, I'll forward them to you by express mail.

Thank you for your kind offer to meet me at Heathrow Airport at 9 a.m., June 1, gate 37. I'll look forward to seeing you then.

With best regards,

If you're fortunate enough to have more than one international employment offer on your desk at the same time, you will want to send a postponement letter. Sending this communication is much better than simply letting time pass without any message to prospective employers.

Dear Mr. Peters:

I deeply appreciate the position offered in your letter of May 18. May I request a period of ten days to consider it? You'll have my answer by express mail no later than May 28.

Thank you for considering this request and, again, for the position offered.

Sincerely,

Or you may have changed your mind about the position altogether. In this case, take the time to thank the company that has probably invested a thousand dollars or more in the hiring process for you. It's not only the right thing to do, but makes good business sense. You may be knocking on this employer's door at some point in the future.

Dear Mr. Peters:

Thank you for offering the position described in your letter of May 18. Unfortunately, I have made other professional commitments that will not make it possible for me to accept your offer.

Please accept my very best wishes for the future.

Sincerely,

If you're new to the international interview process entirely, or need to brush up your skills, three helpful videotapes may be available through your local university or public library:

Face to Face Payoff: Dynamics of Interviewing. Available through Video Software and Production, Yonkers, New York.
The Colonel Comes to Japan. Available through LCA Video Films, New York.
Going International: Bridging the Culture Gap. Available through Copeland Griggs Productions, San Francisco, CA.

6

What You Need to Know about Passports, Visas, and Work Permits

Probably the most important advice for anyone seeking a job abroad is this: Do *not* travel to your target country without making work arrangements, with all the paperwork required, in advance. Too many Americans have the idea that they can get off the plane with a tourist visa in Frankfurt, Tokyo, or London and find work in the classified ads as easily as they would in Chicago or New York.

No so. This chapter presents the harsh realities of finding work abroad as a non-EU (European Union) citizen. EU citizens, including residents of Belgium, Great Britain, Denmark, France, Germany, Greece, the Netherlands, Ireland, Italy, Luxembourg, Portugal, and Spain, and EEA (European Economic Area) residents (Austria, Finland, Iceland, Norway, and Sweden) are not required to obtain work permits in one another's countries, and can use the substantial network of government employment services available to EU and EEA jobseekers.

As a U.S. citizen, however, you have no intrinsic right to work in other countries. If you do accept work without appropriate permits, you are subject to fines and deportation; your employer can also be penalized. Have American citizens found nonpermit work for short stints abroad as au pair caregivers, fruit harvesters, and the like? Of course. But don't count on it for yourself. Foreign countries, under pressure from unemployed citizens of their own, are becoming much more strict about even letting you inside their borders unless you can demonstrate sufficient means of support for your stay and return airfare. If you're depending on a decent paying job to pay for your stay abroad, *get your work permit before you leave,* even though the process may take time and persistence.

Obtaining Your Passport

Except for short-term tourist travel to Canada and Mexico, U.S. citizens will require a valid passport to live and work abroad. U.S. passports are now issued for a ten-year period—but don't try to obtain visas and work permits if your passport is within one year of expiring. Many countries will issue these documents only to those with more than one year remaining before passport expiration. All family members traveling with you are now required to hold their own passports.

Begin your application process for a passport by obtaining a U.S. Department of State form DSP-11 or form DSP-82. These are available at the passport agencies listed in this chapter, at many main branches of the post office, and at your county clerk's office. When you have completed the form, you must appear in person along with any family members also applying for passports at a passport office or post office. You will have to show proof of U.S. citizenship, in the form of a certified copy of your birth certificate (available from the clerk of records or state bureau of vital statistics in the city or state of your birth). If your formal birth record has been lost or destroyed, ask for a letter from the clerk or bureau of vital statistics stating that fact. Present instead a hospital birth record, baptismal certificate, family Bible record, or affidavit from someone who can attest to the facts of your birth. For citizens not born in the U.S., present a Certificate of Citizenship, a Certificate of Naturalization, or forms FS-240, 545, or 1350 available from the passport agency or U.S. Department of State, Passport Services, 1425 K St. NW, Washington, DC 20524, (202) 646-0518.

You will also have to demonstrate that "you are you," by showing a photo ID bearing your signature and a clear picture of your face. A valid driver's license or government employee ID is acceptable, but your social security card or credit card is not. You will be asked to attach to your application two identical photographs of yourself in head-and-shoulders view, 2" × 2" format, taken within the last six months. Most photography stores offer instant passport photo service for $10 to $15. The application fee for a U.S. passport is currently $40 for those under 18 and $65 for those over 18.

If you prefer, you can handle the entire application process by mail if you have held a valid passport issued within the last twelve years (it must be turned in with your application) on or after your sixteenth birthday. Your name must not have changed, except for marriage or court order. If your name has changed since you got your old passport, fill out form DSP-19, available through a passport agency or the U.S. Department of State at the address above, and submit it with the divorce decree, court order, marriage certificate, or other document verifying your name change.

Regional Passport Agencies

Boston Passport Agency
Federal Bldg., Rm. 247
Ten Causeway St.
Boston, MA 02222
(614) 565-6990

Chicago Passport Agency
Federal Bldg., Ste. 380
230 S. Dearborn St.
Chicago, IL 60604
(312) 353-7155

Honolulu Passport Agency
Federal Bldg., Rm. C-106
300 Ala Moana Blvd.
Honololy, HI 96850
(808) 541-1918

Houston Passport Agency
Concord Towers
1919 Smith St., Ste. 1100
(713) 653-3153

Los Angeles Passport Agency
11000 Wilshire Blvd., Rm. 13100
Los Angeles, CA 90024
(213) 209-7075

Miami Passport Agency
Federal Bldg., 16th Fl.
51 Southwest First Ave.
Miami, FL 33130
(305) 536-4681

New Orleans Passport Agency
Postal Services Bldg., Rm. T-12005
701 Loyola Ave.
New Orleans, LA 70113
(504) 589-6161

New York Passport Agency
Rockefeller Center, Rm. 270
630 Fifth Ave.
New York, NY 10111
(212) 541-7710

Philadelphia Passport Agency
Federal Bldg., Rm. 4426
600 Arch St.
Philadelphia, PA 19106
(215) 597-7480

San Francisco Passport Agency
525 Market St., Ste. 200
San Francisco, CA 94105
(415) 974-9941

Seattle Passport Agency
Federal Bldg., Rm. 992
915 Second Ave.
Seattle, WA 98174
(206) 442-7945

Stamford Passport Agency
One Landmark Square
Broad and Atlantic Streets
Stamford, CT 06901
(203) 325-3538

Washington, DC, Passport Agency
1425 K St. NW
Washington, DC 20524
(202) 647-0518

Obtaining Necessary Visas

In addition to your country's passport, you will have to obtain permission in the form of a visa stamp in your passport booklet from the country you intend to enter. If you have traveled as a tourist recently from the U.S. to Great Britain, Japan, or major European countries, you may think of the visa application process as "no sweat"—at most, a few hours standing in line, showing your passport, and filling out brief forms at the embassy or consulate of the country you want to visit. That's because most "tourist nations" are signatories to the Visa Waiver Program, which minimizes the bureaucratic approval process for granting visas to tourist travelers.

To work abroad, however, you will require a business visa, work visa, permanent resident visa, or other form of entry permission. Unfortunately, the application process for these documents ranges from taxing to downright discouraging. Embassy or consulate officials will require that you describe your work plans in writing, complete an often lengthy application form, submit additional photographs of yourself and family members traveling with you, and then wait—six weeks is not unusual—for the bureaucracy to approve or disapprove your application.

Listed in the next section are visa requirements related to work applications for twenty-five major countries. More detailed descriptions of visa types and application procedures for all countries can be found in Government Publication M-264, "Foreign Entry Requirements," available from the Department of State at the address above or from the U.S. Consumer Information Center, Pueblo, CO 81009.

Obtaining Your Work Permit

Holding a U.S. passport and an entry visa to your destination country do not by themselves give you the right to apply for work in that country. The foreign company for which you intend to work must apply to its local Ministry of Labor, or equivalent office, for permission to hire you. The application process for work permits differs substantially from country to country. As a general rule, countries with high unemployment and faltering economies are stricter about granting employment permission to noncitizens than are countries with booming economies.

If you have been hired by a U.S. company for employment at one of its foreign branches (see a list of such companies in Chapter 9), that company will probably handle the work permit application process for you. Similarly, large foreign companies (see Chapter 10) usually have staff assigned to assist you in obtaining a work permit. But in all cases, the key guideline is "don't leave home without it." You probably will not be granted a business or work visa by the embassy or consulate of your destination country without your work permit in hand.

And, as a general rule, don't risk obtaining a work permit *after* you've entered a country in the guise of a tourist. Most countries have strict regulations requiring you to physically leave the country for what can often be a period of months while you complete the work permit application process at one of the country's embassies or consulates. In other words, if you attempt to get a work permit after entering the country, you probably will find yourself back at square one filling out the application you should have completed prior to your travel. As discussed in Chapter 5, it's wise to have a written understanding with your prospective foreign employer regarding whose responsibility it is to obtain required work permits. As part of the process, you will probably be asked to provide evidence from police agencies that you do not have a criminal record, certification of good health from a physician, and (increasingly) X-rays and AIDS test results. Some countries will also require proof of academic degrees and verification of your professional qualifications.

There's good news, however, for U.S. citizens who are full-time students aged 18 or over. The Work Exchange Program administered by the Council on International Exchange (CIEE) will provide permission to work in nine countries for specified times:

Australia: Six months work permission

Canada: From May 1 to October 1

Costa Rica: From June 1 to October 1

France: Up to three months any time of the year

Germany: Up to three months between May 15 and October 15

Ireland: Up to four months any time of the year

Jamaica: From June 1 to October 21

New Zealand: From April 1 to October 21

United Kingdom: Up to six months any time of the year

Application for this program must be completed within the U.S. before your departure. Full details and application forms can be obtained from CIEE, 205 E. 42nd St., New York, NY 10017, (212) 972-1414, fax (212) 661-3231.

Visa and Work Permit Requirements for Twenty-five Countries

The following information is up to date as of the time of publication. It's prudent, however, to check with the embassy or consulate of your destination country for their latest visa and work permit requirements. One note of caution: U.S. citizens are used to looking upon bureaucratic requirements as hurdles that must simply be surmounted, sometimes with considerable persistence, for a happy result. This is *not* the case with the following work permit and visa requirements. There is no guarantee that even the tidiest application will receive approval. Many countries, in fact, have mandated to their immigration and labor offices that work can be permitted for a noncitizen only when no citizen is available to take the job. Time delays are often used as part of the process to discourage noncitizen jobseekers; work permit approvals from embassies and consulates can often take six months or more.

For better or worse, the fact is that big companies have far better luck getting work permits for noncitizen employees than do small firms or individual employers. The paperwork alone is daunting in many cases. In addition, big companies have often worked out public or private agreements with government agencies for a quota of desired foreign workers. None of this is said to dampen your enthusiasm for a job abroad. Just don't imagine that the work permit approval process is automatic.

Australia

Work permit and visa: These documents are issued together by the Australian High Commission or Australian Embassy. A work permit is typically good for 13 months. Australia imposes tight restrictions on age, family status (number of children), resources, and health verifications (particularly AIDS testing) in determining nontourist visas and work permits.

Austria

Work permit: Your intended employer must obtain this permit *(Arbeitsbewillingung)* from the local labor office and send it to you *before* you enter the country. Work permits are seldom granted after a jobseeker has entered Austria.

Visa: A business or permanent resident visa is required of anyone staying in the country for more than 90 days.

Canada

Work permit: The Canadian Immigration Office decides whether to issue Work Authorizations to noncitizens intending to work for any amount of time. Contact the Canadian Embassy, 501 Pennsylvania Ave. NW, Washington, DC 20001, (202) 682-1740 for application procedures.

Visa: A permanent resident or business visa is required for anyone staying longer than three months.

Denmark

Work permit: Required for all noncitizen employees and obtained prior to entry into the country by the Danish employer from the local labor authority.

Visa: A business visa or permanent resident visa is required for anyone staying longer than three months.

Finland

Work permit: Application should be made to the Finnish Embassy accompanied by a letter from your Finnish employer verifying your employment contract and term.

Visa: A business visa or permanent resident visa is required for anyone staying longer than three months.

France

Work permit: The intended French employer applies to Office des Migrations Internationales in Paris and then provides it to the noncitizen employee prior to entry into France.

Visa: A business visa or permanent residence visa is required for anyone staying longer than three months.

Germany

Work permit: The German Embassy issues this permit upon written confirmation of the employment contract and terms by the intended German employer.

Visa: A business visa or permanent residence visa is required for anyone staying longer than three months.

Greece

Work permit: The prospective Greek employer must obtain this permit from the local labor authority before the noncitizen employee enters the country. Entry may be denied without this work permit.

Visa: A business visa or permanent visa is required for anyone staying longer than three months.

India

Work permit: Application should be made by the noncitizen employee to an Indian Embassy or Consulate prior to entering the country. A copy of the employment contract must be provided.

Visa: Required for any length or purpose of stay. AIDS testing may be required.

Ireland

Work permit: The prospective employer obtains this permit from the Irish Ministry of Labor before the noncitizen employee enters the country.

Visa: A business visa or permanent residence visa is required for anyone staying longer than 90 days.

Israel

Work permit: The prospective employer obtains this permit from the Israeli Ministry of the Interior. The noncitizen employee must present this document upon entering the country.

Visa: A business visa or permanent residence visa is required for anyone staying more than three months.

Italy

Work permit: The prospective employer must obtain this permit from the local labor authority and send it to the noncitizen employee before entry into the country.

Visa: A business visa or permanent residence visa is required for anyone staying more than three months.

Japan

Work permit: Application for a work permit, including verification from the prospective employer of the contracted position and term, must be presented in person at the Japanese Embassy or Consulate before a visa is issued.

Visa: A business visa or permanent residence visa is required for anyone staying more than 90 days.

Luxemborg

Work permit: The prospective employer must obtain a work permit from the Administration de l'Emploi in Luxemborg and send it to the noncitizen employee prior to entry into the country.

Visa: A business visa or permanent residence visa is required for anyone staying more than three months.

Mexico

Work permit: The prospective employer must obtain a work permit from Mexican Immigration Authority before the noncitizen employee enters the country.

Visa: A business visa or permanent residence visa is required for anyone staying more than 90 days.

Morocco

Work permit: The prospective employer obtains this permit from the Ministry of Labor. The noncitizen employee can obtain this permit after entry into the country and finding work.

Visa: A business visa or permanent residence visa is required for anyone entering the country to work rather than as a tourist.

The Netherlands

Work permit: The prospective employer must obtain the work permit from the local labor authority and send it to the noncitizen employee before entry into the country.

Visa: A business visa or permanent residence visa is required for anyone staying more than 90 days.

New Zealand

Work permit: Can be obtained while in the country from Immigration Service Office by the noncitizen employee with proof of contracted employment, or before entry into the country from the New Zealand Embassy or Consulate.

Visa: A business visa or permanent residence visa is required for anyone staying more than three months.

Norway

Work permit: Prior to entry into the country, a noncitizen must submit applications forms to the Norwegian Embassy or Consulate which, in turn, sends them to the Directorate of Immigration in Oslo. Proof of contracted employment is required in this application.

Visa: A business visa or permanent residence visa is required for anyone staying more than three months.

Portugal

Work permit: For jobs lasting more than 30 days, a prospective employer must obtain a work permit from the Ministry of Labor and send it to the noncitizen worker before entry into the country. For jobs lasting fewer than 30 days, written permission from the Ministry of Labor (obtained by the prospective employer) is sufficient.

Visa: A business visa or permanent residence visa is required for anyone staying more than 60 days.

Russia

Work permit: A letter of invitation specifying contracted work and term must be provided to the prospective noncitizen employee in order to obtain a business visa.

Visa: Required for any visit for any length or purpose.

Spain

Work permit: The prospective employer must obtain this document from the Delegacion Provincial de Trabajo y Seguridad Social and send it to the noncitizen employee before entry into the country.

Visa: Business visa or permanent residence visa is required for anyone staying more than six months.

Sweden

Work permit: A written offer of employment must be presented as part of the noncitizen employee's application for the work permit from the Swedish Embassy or Consulate before entry into the country.

Visa: A business visa or permanent residence visa is required for anyone staying more than three months.

Switzerland

Work permit: The prospective employer makes application on behalf of the noncitizen employee before entry into the country. A valid work permit must be presented by the employee to the Immigration Officer upon entering the country to work.

Visa: A business visa or permanent residence visa is required for anyone staying more than three months.

Turkey

Work permit: The noncitizen employee must submit a contract of employment in applying for this permit from the Turkish Consulate General before entry into the country.

Visa: A business visa or permanent residence visa is required for anyone staying more than three months.

For Non-U.S. Nationals: How to Work Legally in the United States

As is true in most countries, United States laws related to immigration and work permits change frequently. The following information is based on legislation in effect at the time of publication.

Since the passage of the 1986 Immigration Reform and Control Act, United States employers face legal and financial penalties if they do not verify the citizenship and work status of their employees. As a non-U.S. national, therefore, you should not expect to talk your way into long-term or career-oriented work experiences in the United States. Employers have too much at stake to accept you. Even traditionally loose areas of black market labor such as agriculture, kitchen help, and hotel services are now heavily scrutinized by the Immigration and Naturalization Service (INS).

The easiest legal route to a United States job, therefore, is to enter the country under a student visa. These are relatively simple to obtain once you have been accepted for study by an American college or university. You will be classified as an F-1 or J-1 student, depending upon your country of origin, proposed college program, and other factors. In either case, you are granted substantial access to American jobs.

For example, during the period of your student visa you can work on campus up to twenty hours per week during the school session and up to forty hours per week during vacations without authorization from the INS. It is more difficult, but not impossible, to work off-campus as a foreign student. You must demonstrate to the INS that you have experienced an unforeseen financial need; this need must be documented thoroughly on form I-538. Typical circumstances justifying such INS authorization are the death of a supporting parent, a parent's bankruptcy, or a natural disaster affecting your level of support from your home country. If granted, the permit for off-campus employment allows you work up to twenty hours per week off-campus.

The INS also has a program for practical training authorization for qualifying foreign students. Practical training is work experience related to the student's course of study and not available in the home country. A computer science student, for example, could apply for practical training with IBM on the grounds that state-of-the-art computing facilities were unavailable in his or her home country.

Students holding F-1 visas are allowed a total of twelve months' practical training eligibility before graduation and twelve months' after graduation. The pregraduation period of practical training is often used in co-op work/study programs. The postgraduation portion of the practical training allowance is granted by the INS in two 6-month segments. The first segment can be authorized by the foreign student advisor on campus. The second segment is granted by the INS only if you can demonstrate that you have a job. (Certain forms and binding deadlines pertain to this application; get the latest information from your student advisor.)

Students holding J-1 visas cannot obtain practical training before graduation, but are eligible for eighteen months of such work experience following graduation. Like F-1 students, they must prove that the work experience is related to their course of study and is not available in their home country. If you do not have a job at the time of application, you may be granted only six months of practical training authorization which then may be extended if you find a job within that period.

To work in the United States beyond the time limits granted under practical training, students must undergo the lengthy and often difficult process of switching their visa status. You will want to investigate H-1 and J-2 visas (usually applied for through your employer) or permanent residency status.

To achieve permanent residency status, you will have to obtain one of the very limited numbers of green card visas given by the INS through a complex system of quotas and categories. Having a spouse or relative in the United States is usually helpful, but by no means decisive, in this long application process. Nonnationals can also obtain a coveted green card through Labor Certification—that is, by demonstrating with the help of their employer that no United States citizen with comparable skills is available for employment. Non-United States nationals frequently find it advantageous to pursue specialized fields in which they do not compete directly with large numbers of native United States job applicants.

But be forewarned: The road to long-term legal employment in the United States is by no means easy. The patient cooperation of your employer and often the services of an immigration attorney may be required.

7
Using the Internet to Find Jobs Abroad

Wouldn't it be splendid if international employers simply entered their job openings on a computer bulletin board that you could access anytime, anywhere in your job search? Even more, wouldn't it be terrific if you could enter your resume and career wish-list so that international employers could look you over electronically? Finally, it would be the icing on the cake if the computer would simply match up your career desires with available jobs, and send you a list each week or so of international jobs that seem particularly right for you.

That day, happily, has arrived. As this chapter will make clear, the Internet is the repository of literally hundreds of thousands of current job openings around the world. An earnest plea: If you're not now an Internet user, don't skip over this chapter. Getting on the "Net" is easy through one of the many user services such as America Online, CompuServe, Prodigy, Microsoft Network, and others. Your local computer store can help you get online with the Internet, or you can access the Net using computers increasingly available at work, college computer facilities, libraries, and, of course, friends' homes.

The Internet is changing the way companies do business and the way they hire. Online commerce and e-mail connections offer companies, clients, and jobseekers instant access to global products, information, and opportunities. In 1996, there were over thirty million users on the Internet, with 100,000 more joining each month.

From 1989 to 1993 the "Net" was used primarily by scientists, engineers, and hobbyists. With the advent of the World Wide Web and powerful search software, the doors to global communication from your PC keyboard have been thrown open.

Proprietary services (listed above) are the primary means by which most PC users (now 30 percent of all U.S. households) connect to the Internet. This chapter will assume that you now have access to the Internet, or are motivated enough by what you read here to get access as soon as possible.

Searching for Company Job Listings

Thousands of companies now make use of the Internet, by means of "home pages," to provide basic company information, advertise products and services, and post current job listings. To find our target company on the Internet, simply enter its name using one or more of the "Web crawlers" or search mechanisms. The best of these are:

Architect, Mountain View, CA
http://www.atext.com

Open Text, Waterloo, Ontario
http://www.opentext.com

InfoSeek, Santa Clara, CA
http://www.infoseek.com

WebCrawler, San Francisco, CA
http://www.webcrawler.com

Lycos, Pittsburgh, PA
http://www.lycos.com

MetaCrawler, Seattle, WA
http://www.metacrawler.com

McKinley Group, Inc., Sausalito, CA
http://www.mckinley.com

Yahoo!, Mountain View, CA
http://www.yahoo.com

Others that you may want to investigate are Excite, The Electric Library, Alta Vista, A2Z, HotBot, Magellan, AccuFind, Point, IBM InfoMarket, and DejaNews. For those new to the Internet, there's good reason to use more than one search service: Each will turn up somewhat different lists of job sites. Yahoo!, for example, yields 39 responses to the search term, "international jobs." The same search term on Excite yields more than 500 responses.

A "response" is simply a place you can look, described by its computer address on the World Wide Web (www), for listings of international jobs. To access these job sites, you type in the computer address and, voilà, you're sitting with sometimes thousands of current job possibilities before you from employers around the world.

Getting Where You Want to Go Quickly

This chapter lists the brightest and best of the international job sites now available on the Internet. Some of these sites are specialized for particular occupations; others are massive collections of job listings of all types.

Using the addresses provided here, you'll have to "surf the Net" a bit to discover which international job sites are most pertinent to your needs.

All search programs will ask you to enter search words or descriptor terms. By entering the name of your target company—Nippon Telephone and Telegraph, for example—you will quickly find dozens of "hits," that is, places to look on the Internet for information about the company, including its employment needs. Charles Schwab, Inc. is among the companies that make a practice of listing all their job openings on the Internet. Schwab feels it has nothing to lose and everything to gain by letting the whole world know about its employment opportunities. Or you can enter more generic search words in combination, such as "international employment" and "investment banking." This entry may bring back literally hundreds of hits, some of which will be just what you're looking for: current job ads for careers.

Certainly one of the quickest ways to sort through the dozens of job sites to find the most current, complete, and reliable is to use (for free) the services of professionals at career centers at colleges and universities. These job counselors review available job sites on an ongoing basis and list the best as part of their university's home page.

Here's a concrete example. If you type in the address http://www.usfca.edu, you will be connected with the home page of the University of San Francisco. That page offers you several menu choices. By clicking on the "Career Center" item, you will be routed to an astounding collection of domestic and international job listings. From this list, click on "International Jobs" to see these categories:

Asia

- AsiaNet
- Asia Pacific Management Forum
- Malaysia
- Project Aspire
- TKO Personnel, Inc.

Australia

- Australian University Jobs
- Employment in Australia

Canada

- Canadian Association of Career Educators and Employers (CACEE)
- The Career Centre

Europe
- Employment in Ireland
- The Employment Network
- EuroJobs
- More European Jobs
- Russian and Eastern European Internships
- Swiss Jobs
- Work in France

Global Resources
- Contact: International Nonprofit Information
- Council on International Educational Exchange (CIEE)
- The Directory: Global Academic Recruiters
- The Employment Network
- Internet Job Surfer
- Job Hunt
- Overseas Job Express
- The Riley Guide Masterlist
- Working and Living Overseas

By clicking on any of the bulleted items, you can quickly be connected to literally thousands of current job openings, arranged for each searching according to the country and type of job you're interested in. If you want to go directly to the University of San Francisco's international job listings without visiting its home page, use this address:

http://www.usfca.edu/career/International.html.

Many other universities and colleges have similar job services available for free through the Internet. Visit the home page of the university or college to be directed to these career services.

Using the Monster Board

By far the largest collection of current job ads can be found at the address http://www.monster.com. More than 55,000 job ads, both domestic and international, are gathered here by job category, region, and company. You can spend many hours harvesting outstanding job possibilities from this source. In many cases, you can apply electronically by registering your resume at this job site (directions provided on the Monster Board) and having the service match up your abilities and background with likely jobs.

Be aware, however, that companies are more diligent about getting ads *on* the Monster Board than taking them *off*, once they have been filled or are no longer active. You will no doubt encounter a few deadends on the Monster Board in your search for the right international position.

Other Valuable Jobs Sites on the Internet

Here is an address collection of other worthwhile sites you can visit to speed your search for the right job in the right place.

www.cyberss.com/software-source

This service specializes in placing data processing professionals in U.S. and international positions. The hiring companies pay all fees.

www.oai.com/jobs

Optical Access International lists its current jobs openings here.

www.indirect.com/spectra/legal.html

At this address you will find international jobs associated with the legal profession.

www.194.151.8.68/job hunt/reader22.htm

This is a particularly valuable site for European jobs and contacts with headhunters.

www.camrev.com.au/share/jobs.html

Here are listed international academic jobs of all types.

www.snowmass.zdv.gov:8080/jobs.html

This site lists international job openings and also provides an extensive list of international job search resources.

www.expat.gulliver.frl

Here you'll find a wonderful resource—the International Jobs Magazine online. It contains not only current job listings but also helpful articles and testimonials by those who have found international careers.

www.netline.com

This is the justly famous Career Center, with click-on connections to the following categories:

- Career Connections—Direct connection between the candidate and the international job recruiter. The service is available 24 hours a day.
- California Career and Employment Center—International jobs, not just California listings.
- Career Magazine
- Career Mosaic—14,000 current job listings and profiles of employers.
- Career Path—Classified "help wanted" ads from major city newspapers.
- Jobs—Hundreds of international positions and contact information for recruiters.
- Intellimatch Online Career Services—Register your resume here and specify companies and individuals (such as your current employer!) that can't have access to it.
- Job Trak—A superb site for college students and recent graduates. Three hundred colleges participate in this site in partnership with 150,000 employers.
- Recruiters Online Network—The largest site list of recruiters, employment agencies, and search firms.
- Virtual Job Fair—A site specializing in domestic and international job placement for high technology careers.

www.nationjob.com/rob half

This is the international job site for Robert Half International, one of the largest employment and search firms in the world.

www.kishbaugh.com

This site specializes in international jobs for executives and senior management.

www.renard-international/com/

Here you will find hundreds of listings for jobs in the hospitality industry (restaurants, hotels, tours, etc.) worldwide.

www.scopeinc./com/

A wide range of international jobs and employer lists is posted at this site.

www.icpa.com/

This site focuses on international jobs in technology, marketing, and finance throughout Asia and the Pacific Rim.

www.summerjobs.com/

At this site you will find thousands of listings for domestic and international short-term and summer jobs.

www.jobsource.com

This collection of job listings and employer profiles also features a resume generator so you can enter your information efficiently for review by international employers.

www.espan.com

This site is rich in international job listings.

www.occ.com

Here at the Online Career Center is another collection of thousands of current job listings.

www.jobtrack.com/jobguide

This address takes you to Margaret Riley's Job Guide. You'll be amazed at the range and number of job listings and other career services available here.

www.kaplan.com

The Kaplan Online Career Center offers many international career possibilities.

www.peoplebank.com/

This is an international database of jobs and jobseekers.

www.oconnell.co.ok

This engaging site goes by the name "Searching the Universe" and focuses particularly on recruitment for international finance positions.

http://BizServe.com//greenlake/ERI/getjob.html

This site is called "Executive International Employment" and lives up to its name.

www.universal.nl/jobhunt/

At this address you will find the International Headhunters Guides, providing hundreds of headhunter addresses on the Internet, employment contacts, and current international job listings.

www.dmcl.com/it/

This site is the International IT Recruitment Exchange specializing in information technology recruitment and job listings.

www.cegos.fr/

This site, called Jobs Online, is limited to specific job offers from French and other European employers along with company profiles.

www.jobcontacts.com/ijc/

The InfoHighway Job Contacts site located at this address is Canada's largest database of international jobs.

www.itjobs.co.uk/

This site, ARC International, specializes in technical job openings in the United Kingdom.

www.hway.net/kcswis

This is the Directory of American Employers for International Professions. Look here for U.S. employers that will send you abroad.

Using the Internet to Find Jobs Abroad   **79**

http://hosea.atc.ll.mit.educ.8000/jobs.html

This site, called International Job Search Resources, is an excellent gathering of listings, employers, and recruiters.

http://asiafacts.kingston.net

This is probably the best site for information about jobs, particularly teaching careers, in Japan, Korea, Taiwan, and other Asian countries.

www.tvp.com/jintl.html

The name of this site, TVP's Job Information Center: International Job Opportunities, describes what you'll find here.

www.streamjobs.com/

The Stream International Jobs site is yet another extensive collection of short- and long-term international job openings.

www.hway.net/jandl/jobs/jobs.htm

This site is titled J & L's Job Classified, with thousands of current listings.

interbiznet.com/hunt/newsint.html

Here you will find International Newsgroups, a site focusing on information exchange and shared job listings among those holding international jobs and those seeking these careers.

www.zynet.co.uk/bpark/bpchem.html
www.zynet.co.uk/bpark/bpoppo.html

These addresses are but two of the several sites making up the UK Business Park. The first address above specializes in careers in chemistry and pharmaceuticals throughout the United Kingdom. The second address is a more general listing of international job opportunities.

www.purdue.edu/homes/swlodin/jobs.html

Called Employment Resources on the Internet, this site (like the University of San Francisco example provided earlier in this chapter) provides a wealth of international career listings, resume advice, and other resources.

http://phoenix.placement.oakland.edu/career/internet.htm

This site is titled The Definitive Internet Career Guide and measures up to its name.

http://quintus.universal.nl/jobhunt

This is the Avotek International Home Page providing access to international jobs in dozens of categories and countries.

www.webcom.com/scope/correct.html

This is one of many maintained by 1-Stop Careers. By visiting this site you can gain access to several related sites, all of which provide international job listings.

Happy job hunting on the Internet!

8

150 Jobs Available Almost *Everywhere*

A teacher posed this question to a youngster in her third-grade class: "How would you go about finding a needle in a haystack?" She expected an answer having something to do with a magnet, magnifying glass, or metal detector. To her surprise, the youngster responded, "Add a bunch of needles to the haystack. Then one will be easier to find."

Finding a job abroad gets much easier when you have many needles in your haystack of possibilities. This chapter asks you to consider one hundred fifty jobs that are available, in one form or another, throughout most of the world. The commentary on each position isn't intended to belabor what you already know about these well-known jobs, but instead to give you insight into international aspects of the positions and tips for application.

As you skim through this list of jobs, the chances are excellent that you'll spot several that you could pursue with pleasure and profit, even if they haven't been your main occupation lately. In many cases, your first job with an international employer, though not your first choice, may be your "foot in the door," putting you in position for other, more suitable jobs as they open up in the company.

Broadening your range of possible jobs can often lead to unexpected success and career satisfaction. Probably the classic story of someone willing to stretch for new career opportunities is that of a senior vice president at Boeing. In his early twenties, he graduated with a degree in English from an East Coast college and sought work the following summer in Europe. Failing at first to find any position in line with his English degree, he filled out job applications wherever he could, including one at a Boeing installation in Germany. That particular application asked him to specify the field in which he earned his degree. Without intending to deceive anyone, he wrote the abbreviation "ENG" for "English." He was hired as an Engineer Apprentice and, over the years, proved to be one of Boeing's most outstanding employees and, eventually, a corporate leader. He still takes ribbing from Boeing colleagues, however, on his leap from English to Engineering.

So, whether you now call yourself a banker, baker, or candlestick maker, read through the following list with an imaginative spirit willing to consider second- and third-choice jobs in case your first-choice positions don't pan out right away.

Accounting/Bookkeeping/Tax Preparation

These positions are available wherever money changes hands. Be prepared in many countries, however, to comply with lengthy and often complicated licensing and certification requirements. Often American enclaves within a country can form a sufficient clientele for a profitable accounting or tax practice.

Advertising

Advertising Sales

Can you call on businesses to secure advertising orders for phone books, newspapers, magazines, billboards, and media spots? If so, consider the highly lucrative field of advertising sales. Your U.S. contacts can give you an edge in placing foreign advertisements in American publications and electronic media. Wouldn't you like to have the BMW account?

Copy Writer

This position requires a flair for imaginative, motivating language. Be aware, of course, the U.S. advertising lingo may fall flat in other cultures. Chevrolet, for example, advertised its Nova automobile in Spanish-speaking countries without foreseeing a devastating language pitfall: "no va" in Spanish means "won't go."

Design/Layout Specialist

If you have experience in this field, you will want to brush up not only your computer skills in cutting-edge layout software, but also some of the pre-1980 methods of cut-and-paste layout. In many developing countries, advertising layout is still done the old-fashioned way—with galleys, scissors, and paste-up.

Applied Sciences
Chemist
If you've had U.S. training and experience in chemistry, you're highly attractive to foreign industrial firms. Your resume should emphasize accomplishments and areas of expertise more than academic degrees.

Engineer
Similarly, a U.S.-trained mechanical, structural, or electronic engineer is "gold" to many companies abroad. Make sure your application materials communicate your ability to understand and use foreign measurement terms and standards.

Laboratory Technician
This position is readily available in developed countries and pays relatively well. If you bring considerable experience to the position, you may quickly find yourself in a training role for indigenous employees.

Marine Biologist
Every country with a coastline has employment opportunities for marine biologists. Often, these countries are less interested in pure science than in how their marine resources can be harvested profitably and protected from others.

Art Opportunities
Art Liaison
The international art market is "back," with galleries and auction houses showing record sales and profits. You can be the liaison or broker connecting sales outlets with artists. Your U.S. connections can be extremely useful in placing foreign artists in American galleries and American artists in galleries or publications abroad.

Gallery Sales/Management

Have you noticed how many gallery managers and assistants in the U.S. speak with a British, French, or other accent? Your accent, whatever it may be, may be a useful and charming asset in meeting a foreign clientele.

International Representative

Picasso, for all his talent, owed his prominence and price in worldwide galleries and museums to shrewd representation. Consider a career as a representative of a group of artists or galleries to the U.S. marketplace.

Automotive Services

Auto Rental

Fees for auto rentals in most of the world are at least twice what we are used to paying in the U.S. You can participate in this profitable sector as an owner, an investor, a rental agent, or a maintenance worker in one capacity or another.

Auto Repair

Auto technologies have become virtually universal, with auto mechanics in the U.S. knowing as much about Toyotas, Mercedes, and Fiats as their Japanese and European equivalents. This job choice is highly portable. You will find positions widely available in urban centers throughout the world.

Retail Sales

Auto sales staff—even "used car salesmen"—enjoy more prestige throughout the world than they do in the U.S. You don't necessarily have to know only foreign cars to work in retail sales abroad; the best-selling make of automobile in Europe, after all, is Ford.

Charitable/Religious Organizations

Field Worker

There is probably no better way to get to know the people of another country than to circulate among them as a field worker. This position is the final point of distribution of aid, information, and training provided by charities and churches. Contact your religious organization or foreign-oriented charity for placement in this immensely important job.

Fundraiser

Foreign charities, churches, and even governments have strong interest in hiring individuals who can raise funds in more affluent countries. This job often entails considerable travel—to the U.S., for example, to raise funds and then back to a foreign country for a period of needs assessment and project planning. Fundraisers are often paid a combination of salary and a percentage of the money they raise.

Grant Manager

Charities and churches hate to see funds misspent by inefficient or less than honest administrators in foreign countries. There are frequent openings, at reasonable pay, for individuals willing to oversee and account for the distribution of charitable funds and other grants abroad.

Computing

Assembly

Your personal computer is probably a virtual United Nations of parts—chips from Indonesia, boards from Japan, cables from Ireland, and so forth. If you know and enjoy computer assembly, you can probably find a job in the dozens of countries where PCs are hatched.

Programmer

The responsibilities associated with this position range from highly complex—for example, developing programs for currency conversion—to simple and straightforward—an inventory program, for example, for a retail shop. Few foreign businesses can fill their computing needs by buying off-the-shelf software packages. A skilled programmer is required to custom fit these packages to the particular requirements of the business at hand. One point of entrance to foreign careers in programming is through U.S.-based firms such as Oracle that specialize in custom-designed software applications.

Sales

The curve of PC sales throughout the world is still steeply upward. This job involves contact with a wide variety of people, comfortable working conditions, and (often) bonus or commission arrangements that reward exceptional sales skill.

Service

"The damn thing doesn't work!" That approximate complaint echoes wherever computers are sold. If you know PC repair, you're "occupationally attractive" in most countries.

Systems Analyst

This position requires extensive training in computer science. Major computer manufacturers such as IBM and Sun Microsystems often place systems analysts in foreign posts, at advantageous U.S. salaries.

Training

A computer-literate workforce is emerging as a baseline requirement for countries seeking to participate in the Information Revolution. You can find a good-paying niche position as a company-employed or independent trainer in relatively elementary computer skills such as word processing, business graphics, spreadsheets, and accounting software.

Construction

Architect/Drafting

Construction skills of all types are sought after by countries with aging infrastructures as well as by countries beginning new residential and commercial projects. An individual adept in architecture and drafting will have many government and commercial opportunities available.

Cabinet Maker

This is one of the best-paying construction trades, with the advantages of inside work and relatively controllable safety factors. In many countries, cabinet makers have the chance to work with exotic woods and cabinetry styles not common in the U.S.

Carpenter

This catch-all category includes all levels of woodcraft from framing to finish work. Investment in tools is usually minimal and pay is based on hourly rates. Be aware that construction jobs in many countries, as in the U.S., are restricted to union or guild members. As a handyman, however, you may be able to make a good living abroad working in private residences and commercial building on a more casual, nonunion basis.

Contractor/Contractor's Representative

This individual gets to wear the white collar (as well as a hard hat on the job site). He or she negotiates term with clients, sees plans through review and regulatory agencies, and oversees construction. Contractors and their representatives are often paid on a percentage basis—typically 10 to 20 percent—of the total project cost. Contracting licenses are required in most countries.

Electrician

This trade, although governed by strict licensing standards in the U.S., is treated more casually abroad. In England, for example, an electrician requires no special certification, even though household voltages are double the U.S. 110-volt standard. Pay is most commonly based on an initial project bid rather than hourly rates.

Floorcovering Specialist

This occupation includes tile and carpet layers as well as hardwood floor installers. Pay rates are usually determined on a square-foot basis rather than by the hour.

Glass Specialist

Glaziers work with prefabricated and traditional windows, mirrors, glass doors, shower and bath enclosures, and skylights. Pay is based on bid.

Painter

Commercial painters in the U.S. do most interior and exterior work with high-pressure spray equipment. This cost-effective system is not common in many countries, where paint is traditionally applied by brush or roller. The opportunity exists, therefore, for highly profitable start-up ventures abroad using the latest spray equipment.

Plumber

As in the U.S., this trade earns high hourly rates in most developed countries. It also entails work that can be downright miserable, in dank, odiferous conditions and at all hours of the day or night. Plumbers working abroad have to get used to marrying new plumbing to old, and often ancient, systems.

Project Foreman

This individual has on-site responsibility for work standards, schedules, and safety factors. The job pays well and is usually less physically strenuous than any of the construction trades.

Roofer

Keeping the rain outside is a challenge that faces both great cathedrals and humble dwellings. Composite asphalt products typically used for roofing in the U.S. are less well known abroad, where roofs may be made of slate, earthen tile, or even thatch.

Structural Engineer

This position requires a thorough working knowledge of stress factors for various bearing structures. A structural engineer usually reviews building plans before construction begins and certifies compliance as construction proceeds. Building collapses (particularly due to earthquakes) in countries such as Mexico and China have underlined the dangers of poorly engineered structures and the need to hire structural engineers.

Consultant

Cultural Coach

As a consultant to foreign businesses, you can equip company representatives with the cultural knowledge they will need to do business effectively in the U.S. or elsewhere. Many foreign business people hoping to do business in the U.S. are understandably unsure about how to behave at business meetings and business-related dinners, how to write proposals and business correspondence for a U.S. audience, and how to make effective business presentations.

Industrial Troubleshooting

If you have considerable experience in a particular industry or business, you probably are well equipped to help foreign firms in those areas locate the glitches in their operations. Your best calling card for this form of consulting is your claim that you can save companies many times your fee or salary.

International Liaison

Many firms abroad want a man or woman ready to represent their interests in other countries. Pay often involves a retainer as well as an hourly rate (much like compensation for lawyers in the U.S.).

Management Processes

Many international consultants specialize in helping foreign companies design, monitor, and change their management processes. This form of consulting will involve you in focus groups, executive training, and reengineering efforts.

Market Analyst

It is not uncommon for companies abroad to put the cart before the horse—that is, to line up raw materials, a trained workforce, and suitable technologies before a secure market has been defined for the goods or services produced. That's where you come in. As a market analyst, you help companies determine where to target their marketing efforts. Your pay can be fee-based or, in many companies, calculated on "gain-sharing" (a compensation system in which you receive a percentage of gains achieved by the company as a result of your work).

Domestic Services
Chauffeur

In the U.S. this position is associated most frequently with wealthy individuals who can afford a private driver. In many countries, however, groups of chauffeurs are employed by companies as drivers for executives and visiting VIPs. China Resources, Ltd., in Hong Kong, for example, employs more than a dozen chauffeurs.

Child-/Eldercare

Virtually every developed industrial country makes better provision for child- and eldercare than does the U.S. In France, for example, some 79,000 infants are cared for in 1,497 childcare centers *(creches)*, only 167 of which are private. Half of all Danish children under three and two-thirds of those between the ages of three and five are enrolled in public childcare. Although positions in these centers do not pay particularly well, the work is steady and, if you like kids, very fulfilling.

Cook/Chef

Affluent families in many foreign countries employ kitchen staff. Room and board in virtual palaces is often part of the deal.

Personal Secretary

This position has a long and honorable history. Samuel Taylor Coleridge, for example, served as personal secretary to the governor of Malta. The personal secretary typically handles appointments, travel arrangements, correspondence, and telephone business. Salaries are often quite good, especially when room and board provisions are included in the deal.

Residence Manager

Large estates often require the services of a residence manager. If you have experience managing apartment buildings or motels in the U.S., you probably have many of the skills necessary for managing large private residences.

Security

Protective services inevitably involve a degree of personal danger, especially in countries prone to kidnapping of prominent citizens, Mafia crimes, or civil unrest. Before taking a security position for a company or individual, assess the risk in relation to the rewards.

Tutor

Institutional instructors are discussed under "Education/Training." Domestic tutors are those hired by affluent families to handle the children's education—in short, the Julie Andrews role in *Mary Poppins* and *The Sound of Music*. Room and board are often included, although you may not end up marrying the lord or lady of the manor.

Education/Training

Business Skills Trainer

As organizations of all kinds get used to the idea that they must constantly *learn* to survive, the need for qualified trainers increases exponentially. This is one of the easier entry positions, since no special degrees are mandatory. Prior experience in some form of training and development can often get you in the door.

Educational/Training Sales

Americans may tend to forget that the vast majority of educational institutions abroad are for-profit businesses. As such, they sell educational services—and require salespeople to represent them in the marketplace. Santa Clara Schools International in Barcelona, for example, contracts for executive training for Hewlett-Packard managers throughout Europe. A sales position in the educational/training field can be particularly lucrative, since most sales are to groups and repeat business from client companies is common.

Language Coach

English is still the stepladder to success for businesspeople in an increasingly global economy. Your abilities as a native speaker of English plus some teaching experience, however minimal, can qualify you for a position in the hundreds of English language schools through Europe, Asia, and South America. Don't expect to get rich as a language coach. The real payoff is in the friendships that evolve from close contact with people of other cultures.

Teacher

It's well known that teachers in the U.S. are often paid less than streetsweepers. Although your pay as a teacher will not be substantially more abroad, the level of respect you receive from your students and your community will soar. A credential and good references from a U.S. teaching experience will qualify you for application to a wide range of challenging and rewarding teaching positions abroad. Look into foreign exchange programs sponsored by your professional association.

Testing Specialist

Far more than in the U.S., a student's progress in foreign education is determined by uniform resting. The English poet Gerard Manley Hopkins earned his living for many years as an examination grader. If you have expertise in academic testing, you may find interesting employment in countries where tests are used almost exclusively to separate the sheep from the goats.

Entertainment

Musician, Actor, Comedian, etc.

A Biblical quotation can be altered as follows: "An entertainer is not without honor, save in his own country." Many jazz musicians, for example, find themselves famous in Frankfurt after years of being broke in Boston. If you have the capacity to entertain, urban centers throughout the world have venues waiting for you. Your best point of entry is a U.S. talent agency that places entertainers abroad.

Talent Agent

If you're not the one with talent, perhaps you're the representative for entertainers. Talent agents make the rounds of clubs, theatres, college venues, and concert series throughout the world to place their people, usually at a nice profit for all concerned.

Entrepreneurial Ventures

Business Broker

Your tax dollars pay for a bevy of well-trained, well-connected commercial officers and aides throughout the world. Their mission is primarily to aid U.S. businesspeople seeking to establish trade relations. They are *not* employment counselors and should not be contacted for specific job opportunities abroad. But if you want to establish a company abroad or broker the sale of an existing company, these men and women can be extremely helpful.

Franchiser

One way to see the world and make a mint at the same time is to travel as part of a franchise team for a well-established food or service company. McDonald's, Kentucky Fried Chicken, Taco Bell, and many other U.S. companies have vastly expanded their customer and revenue base by opening franchises abroad. If you have a track record or strong interest in franchising, target several companies that want to go international.

Small Business Owner

Contemplating that small marina in Costa Rica? The hamburger restaurant in Manchester? Your entrepreneurial ideas and money will be welcomed, especially if you can offer jobs to local workers. Use your trade representative (see Appendix H) to help you find your way through the often dense woods of licenses, certificates, and permissions necessary to do business in your target country.

Venture Capitalist

As American stock markets, particularly the NASDAQ, have listed more and more international stocks, venture capitalists have been increasingly attracted to foreign businesses as investment vehicles. Again, your trade representative attached to the U.S. embassy in your target country or region can be of help in identifying local business and brokerage contacts for venture capital investment. Be aware, of course, that legally binding agreements differ widely from country to country. In Japan and China, for example, personal relationships and eye-to-eye understandings carry as much weight as signed contracts.

Financial Services/Banking

Administrative Assistant

Because most international banks serve a culturally diverse clientele, an employee with native English writing and speaking skills is usually a welcome addition. The position of administrative assistant is often a good stepping-stone to better, higher paying positions in the institution.

Appraiser

Any financial institution that makes residential or commercial loans relies upon a staff of appraisers to estimate the value of real estate and other tangibles securing those loans. One of the key benefits of this position is the opportunity to get to know a wide variety of people and places within your territory.

Bank Teller

Comfortable working conditions, constant contact with the public, and good networking possibilities are among the key benefits of this position. International banks with branches in the U.S. can be a good point of entry and information for those interested in working in banking careers abroad.

Document Processor

This backroom position requires good math and written communication skills. Other than telephone work, there is usually little direct contact with the public. This can be an excellent way to get to know the business and legal practices of another country.

Investment/Portfolio Manager

Many foreign financial institutions have significant holdings in U.S. companies and U.S.-backed bonds. If you are knowledgeable about this investment sector, you may find a satisfying and high-paying career as an investment/portfolio manager. You can use this position to broaden your investment knowledge of companies abroad.

Loan Agent

This is the bank employee who meets with the loan applicant, often off-site, to ascertain needs, fill out applications, and facilitate loan processing. Loan agents are often paid both a salary and a commission based on the number and dollar amount of the loans they bring in.

Garment Industry

Fabricator

The garment industry has the ill-founded reputation of only producing clothes in sweatshop conditions. In fact, many tailors, seamstresses (male and female), and other experts in garment alteration and fabrication enjoy good working conditions and pay, especially in clothes-conscious urban centers throughout the world.

Modeling

It's a truism in modeling that European and Scandinavian models work in New York, and that American models are most likely to find their fame abroad. To break into modeling abroad, you may want to work through a modeling agency that specializes in foreign placement.

Promotions

Garment manufacturers rely upon engaging, powerful marketing campaigns to sell their wares. If you have skills and background in marketing, you could do well in targeting the garment industry for your career abroad. Your knowledge of and connections with major U.S. department stores can serve you well in designing promotional efforts for foreign garment lines.

Sales Representative

In this position, you are the person who carries dress samples to Barcelona boutiques or supervises a booth at a Paris garment show. You'll travel widely and make good use of your language skills in this potentially lucrative job.

Government

Customs

Your language skills may qualify you for customs work. Work conditions are usually comfortable, if a bit intense, and work-related travel is common.

Document Processor

Governments everywhere are awash in documents of all kinds. If you have excellent writing, translating, and organizational skills, you may well qualify for a government position in some form of document processing. Be aware that governments are under strong pressure to give any available jobs to citizens, no matter how qualified a noncitizen may be.

Embassy Attaché

Your country's embassy in a foreign nation may have a variety of positions open, ranging from secretarial assistance to information gathering to translation services. You can open doors to more advanced positions in diplomatic service—and you may get a diplomatic license plate for your car.

Public Services

All of the governmental services provided to the public in a given country are labor-intense. Check with the government personnel office in your target country for positions available to noncitizens.

Healthcare

Counselor

"Triage" counseling interviews are performed in many countries by paramedical personnel before the patient sees a physician. A background in social work, paramedic services, or mental health work may qualify you for work in these positions.

Health Plan Sales/Administration

The health maintenance organization (HMO) movement is now worldwide, even in countries such as England and Scandinavia where basic health care is provided by the government. Your background in health-related sales or administration may help you land a high-paying job in selling and managing private health care plans abroad.

Hospital Maintenance Worker

In many European countries, these positions are held primarily by work-permitted noncitizens. Italians keep hospitals clean in Switzerland, for example, and Alergians workers form a significant percentage of French hospital maintenance employees.

Laboratory/Diagnostic Technician

Your training and background as a lab tech in the U.S. will probably put you at the head of the employment line for this position in government-run and private laboratories abroad. In your resume, indicate the specific lab technologies and procedures you're familiar with.

Massage

Once you build a steady clientele, this position can be highly profitable and replete with networking possibilities for other positions. But getting started—there's the rub (so to speak). Advertisements for massage in urban newspapers abroad are often disguised ads for prostitution. Work through a health organization, exercise facility, or social club to make sure your professional intentions are clear to your clients.

Nurse

If you have spent time in a U.S. hospital in recent years, you know that a significant portion of nurses there are work-permitted non-natives (particularly Filipino). The "nurse crunch" is as severe abroad as it is in the U.S. As a trained, degreed nurse, your chances of obtaining a position in a foreign hospital are excellent. You will probably find that your range of responsibilities and sphere of influence are much greater abroad than in the American health care system. Some U.S. nurses report feeling more like physicians in their foreign positions.

Office Administrator/Assistant

Running a medical office or serving as an administrative assistant, receptionist, or secretary in a hospital or doctor's office requires good organizational, language, and people skills. You'll find excellent opportunities to get to know other cultures in these positions.

Personal Health Assistant

Social service organizations abroad as well as affluent individuals hire assistants to serve as something less than a nurse and more than a fitness coach. In social service jobs, these workers check in on elderly and homebound patients. In private placement, personal health assistants are responsible for diet and exercise regimens for their employers.

Physician

The American Medical Association can provide a wide-ranging listing of foreign opportunities for licensed physicians, including teaching opportunities in hospitals and medical schools abroad.

Hospitality Industry

Bartender

If this is your thing, it pays reasonably well abroad if tips and free food are calculated in.

Caterer

Affluent people abroad, and common folk too on special occasions, are much more likely to cater a social event at home or at a rented hall than to go to a restaurant. In most urban centers abroad, there are many openings, often without too many questions about work eligibility, in the catering field.

Food Preparation

Airlines, hotels, and, of course, restaurants have frequent jobs available in all phases of food preparation. These usually are not "move-up" positions, but they do provide steady work almost everywhere.

Hotel/Restaurant Management

If you've served in these capacities successfully, there's a good chance you can qualify for such jobs abroad. Many U.S. hotels such as Sofitel have more properties outside the U.S. than inside it. Check with the personnel offices of large hotel and restaurant chains to see if they can place you in an international position, perhaps after a probation period at a U.S. site.

Promotions/Group Sales

Hotels and restaurants (as well as the convention offices of major cities) hire sales representatives to attract tours, conventioneers, and other groups to their establishments. These positions are usually paid a combination of salary and commission, and involve a great deal of travel.

Wait Staff

Being a waiter abroad, especially in a high-class restaurant, is an occupation with approximately the same prestige as, say, a travel agent or policeperson. Your skills will be greatly appreciated by restaurant guests, who will also have high expectations about your knowledge of foods, wines, and gracious service.

Import/Export

Merchandiser

This occupation is literally shopping for a living. U.S. companies such as Pier One Imports and Cost Plus World Markets employ dozens of buyers who travel throughout the world to stock store shelves with attractive items of all types. Check with these companies and others as a good place to begin your search for a job as an international merchandiser.

Sales Representative

Every foreign manufacturer with an eye toward global markets needs sales representatives. Your facility with languages and your prior knowledge of product lines will give you an edge in application for these potentially lucrative positions.

Shipping Specialist

Whatever gets imported or exported goes through the hands of shippers. Your background in air, rail, or ship freight may qualify you for a position abroad in this field. Begin your job inquiries with major shippers that have U.S. offices, such as Maersk and Continental Cargo. They can tell you about openings abroad.

Insurance

Claims Processor

This position is filled everywhere by people who never intended to be claims processors. (No college, after all, offers courses in this specialty.) As an up-by-your-own-bootstraps job, this position offers the chance for travel within your territory, daily contact with the public, and decent pay. Some experience in auto or property claims can be as important as academic degrees in applying for this position.

Office Manager/Administrative Assistant

Managing or assisting in an insurance office (or "assurance office," as it is called in much of the world) requires a passion for detail, excellent time management, and patience with phones and paperwork. This is relatively prestigious work abroad and offers good pay.

Sales Agent

As a general rule, citizens of other developed countries are relatively underinsured by U.S. standards. The persuasive appeals you may have used with limited success on U.S. customers may be far more potent in countries where the idea of life or property insurance is relatively new.

Interior Design/Decorating

In the U.S., these careers are often stand-alone operations, with a sole decorator or small group trying to staff an office, call on clients, and provide contracted services. In most other countries, interior designers and decorators are employees of furniture, antique, or paint/wallpaper companies. To apply for such positions, make sure you have assembled an impressive portfolio of your prior work.

Legal/Paralegal Services

Lawyers, barristers, solicitors, and their ilk are established players in the business and government life of all countries. One particularly useful niche for finding international work in this area is maritime law, where international treaties and agreements hold sway. Another fruitful area for work abroad is patent and copyright law, especially as large corporations try to protect their intellectual property rights from infringement in foreign countries.

Manufacturing

Line Worker

That's you, riveting away or attaching strut "D" to part "A." Wages are excellent in many developed countries; German factory workers average more than $50,000 U.S. per year. To qualify for employment, you may have to wade through the process of joining a worker's association or union.

Manufacturer's Representative

"Repping" for a manufacturer can be highly profitable, especially if you have a guaranteed territory or exclusive product line as part of your employment contract. If you know a region of the world or market sector that could use a particular manufacturer's wares, contact the manufacturer with a proposal for your representation services. It's a "something for nothing" proposition for the manufacturer.

Mechanical Specialist

Things that go buzz and whirr in a factory also go clunk occasionally. If you have a background in mechanical systems, you have an excellent chance of finding work in heavily industrialized countries.

Personnel Specialist

Hiring, evaluating, promoting, firing, providing benefits, and maintaining employee records are some of the key duties of personnel officers in international organizations. A background in human resources and appropriate academic degrees (especially an MBA) will put you in line for serious consideration in this area.

Process Engineer

Just as Japanese management practices were "hot" in the 1980s, so American management practices are considered cutting edge in the 1990s, even in Japan. If you have substantial experience in managing organizations and some theoretical background in management science, you may be ideal for a position as a process administrator or engineer with a company abroad.

Quality Inspector

Most manufacturing operations have inspectors of some kind, and heaven knows more quality control is needed. If you've done this job before or know manufacturing operations well, you will probably qualify for work in this position.

Training Specialist

Much of what you're now doing in the U.S. or elsewhere may be highly marketable abroad as a trainer. Everything from bar code scanning to customer-savvy shelf arrangements to advanced management techniques is sought after by foreign companies hoping to compete in the global marketplace.

Media: Radio, Television

Announcer/Host

In the days when only a handful of radio and TV channels were on the air, the idea of finding work as a program host, reporter, or interviewer was quixotic at best. But the telecommunications revolution is already increasing the number of media outlets exponentially in developed countries, with accompanying increases in openings for talented on-air employees. A video or audio portfolio of your previous work will definitely increase your chances of finding work in this area.

Program Specialist

U.S. television programs remain the most popular in syndication throughout the world. The number one television show internationally at present is *Baywatch,* and reruns of *Charlie's Angels, Bonanza,* and *Star Trek* are global favorites. If you know U.S. radio and television programs well and have worked in a programming capacity, you may qualify for employment as a program specialist with a media company abroad.

Sales

Television and radio survives financially through it advertising. Although experience in this field may help get you an interview, you may also be able to talk your way into an entry-level sales position through persistence, charm, and energy. The job can pay well if commissions are included in the compensation plan.

Technician

Technologies used in radio and television broadcasting do not differ substantially from country to country. A trained U.S. radio or TV technician can quickly make a transition to systems used abroad.

Writer

News anchors and program hosts, for all their sophistication, are usually dependent upon scripts written by someone else. If you have training and experience in such writing and can handle the language demands of a position abroad, there are many openings for skilled writers in radio and television.

Pet Services

Pet Grooming/Care

These sorts of jobs are obviously found primarily in affluent areas. The concept of pet grooming services is not uniquely American. The French, for example, have pampered their dogs for generations, even to the point of taking them along to the fanciest restaurants. Before committing your own money to a start-up venture, you may want to work as an employee in a pet services business to get a feel for the local market.

Pet Sales

If you have contacts with pet breeders and can adapt to the jungle of regulations related to the importing of animals, you may find a profitable career in pet sales. Pet shops are as common in urban centers throughout most of the world as they are in the United States.

Veterinarian

In the United States, veterinary practice is usually separated into "large animal" (horses, cows) and "small animal" (dogs, cats, etc.) divisions. That separation is less common abroad, where veterinarians can be expected to minister to parakeets one minute and to stallions the next. Fees tend to be somewhat lower than U.S. averages, but the potential market for services is often larger.

Publishing: Books, Magazines, Newspapers

Acquisitions Editor

This individual contacts potential authors, works with established authors, attends conferences and conventions in search of authors, negotiates contract terms, and often oversees schedules for production of books (or articles, in the case of magazines and newspapers). Publishing is among the most global of industries; McGraw-Hill, for example, has international offices in Auckland, Bogotá, Caracas, Lisbon, London, Madrid, Mexico City, Milan, Montreal, New Delhi, Paris, San Juan, Sydney, Tokyo, and Toronto. A good entry point for information about and perhaps placement in a foreign publishing position is any major U.S. publisher with branch offices abroad.

Copyreader

Are you good—no, great—as a prose stylist and expert on matters grammatical? Copyreading can be interesting and steady work. Contacts are the same as those described for editors above.

Developmental Editor

T.S. Eliot wrote that "between the conception and the reality falls the shadow." Authors often have bold designs that they can't or won't carry through in actual words. Developmental editors are midwives (and sometimes surrogate parents) to the creative process. They do what it takes to pull manuscripts together into publishable works.

Graphics Specialist

Books and articles accompanied by pictures and graphics of one kind or another require the expertise of graphics specialists. This field has been revolutionized by computer graphics systems. If you know your craft, you can probably market it to international publishers. A portfolio of your previous work is a must in the application process.

House Writer

Believe it or not, the words you find in books and articles (this book excepted, of course) are not all written by the author named on the cover. Virtually all publishers have writers on staff or on call who can be pressed into service to generate or revise manuscript copy. Writing samples (preferably published ones) will add credibility to your application.

Journalist

American newspapers and magazines place journalists and other press professionals in foreign locations. Whether you are already an experienced journalist or a beginner in the profession, check with these U.S. sources first for positions abroad.

Layout/Design Specialist

This specialty trade, like publication graphics, has been revolutionized by new computer software packages. If you know these new systems well, you may be highly attractive to international publishers who are a bit behind on the technology learning curve.

Photographer

This career is often listed by successful professionals in other fields as the most desirable "road not taken." It offers a chance to exercise creativity, meet a wide range of people, visit exotic locations, and experience adventures. Needless to say, a portfolio of your published work counts a great deal in the job search process.

Printer

This trade has gone international for even the smallest U.S. publishers. It is not uncommon for a book "published" in New York to have been printed in Hong Kong with color covers from Indonesia. As suggested for editors above, your best point of initial contact for job information abroad is the major U.S. publishing houses or printers with foreign offices.

Sales/Marketing Representative

Books and magazines don't sell themselves. As a sales representative for an international company, you will call on book and magazine distributors, major retailers of books, and schools and colleges. Pay is usually a combination of salary and commission.

Real Estate

Agent

Sales agents abroad differ little in their modus operandi from their American counterparts: advertising and showing property, facilitating negotiations, and steering the purchase through escrow. Interestingly, pay is often fee-based in much of the world rather than commission-based. The fee is sometimes paid by the seller and sometimes by the buyer, or may be shared by both.

Document Processor

Real estate transactions everywhere involve extensive paperwork: property descriptions, appraisals, loan papers, title certification, disclosures, and the like. If you've had experience in a U.S. escrow office, you can make a strong case for your ability to learn the ropes of documentation processing abroad.

Property Management

As a general rule, landlords like to receive rent but hate to deal with tenants, oversee maintenance, and keep detailed records. That's where property managers come in and earn their money. Particular if you have had experience managing apartments or other rental property, you can qualify for the many property management jobs available in urban and suburban areas abroad.

Retail/Wholesale

Buyer

Retailers and wholesalers abroad employ buyers (or merchandisers) to acquire goods to sell. The position entails extensive travel and "red carpet treatment" by manufacturers eager to market their wares.

Sales/Stocking Clerk

This is one of the most available positions, though not the best paying, in cities of all sizes abroad. Essential skills are good communication abilities, a pleasant manner, and dependability. A track record of successful clerking should be emphasized in your application or resume.

Store Management

If you're somewhat of a jack-of-all-trades prepared to do whatever it takes to keep the store open and attractive, you're a good prospect for store or shop management. Payment for this position is commonly a combination of salary and a percentage of total store sales. Good communication, team-building, and organizational skills are essential. Emphasize any prior experience you've had in store management in your application.

Sports

Coach

Especially in international sports, including soccer, baseball, tennis, ping-pong, and track, American coaches and athletes can find steady work abroad at levels ranging from school intramurals to professional levels. Because it's difficult to demonstrate one's coaching abilities in a resume or application, you may want to prepare a video portfolio of yourself in action as a coach.

Fitness Instructor

Spas, hotels, schools, athletic clubs, and affluent individuals all hire fitness instructors. Your prior experience as an aerobics instructor or personal fitness coach can help qualify you for this position.

Tourist Industry

Tour Guide

Hundreds of schools and colleges in the U.S. and scores of tour agencies advertising in travel magazines and newspapers offer guided tours of foreign lands. Your experience as a youth counselor, history or geography buff, or adult group leader can be excellent background for application as a tour guide. Once abroad, you can also investigate work for foreign tour companies.

Travel Agent

This highly competitive field requires specific training. Once you have it, door open everywhere for work. If you decide to remain stateside as your base, you can nevertheless travel on "comp" visits to foreign destinations. Or you can seek placement in an agency abroad through a travel business in the U.S. that has international branches.

Transportation: Air, Rail, Bus

Coach Driver

The luxury tourist coach is more familiar throughout the rest of the world than it is in the U.S. Drivers from U.S. bus and truck companies usually have the basic credentials to pursue good-paying and scenic work as coach drivers for tourist jaunts abroad.

Dispatcher

Cab companies, private coaches, and trucking firms employ dispatchers. If you have experience in this field, draw up a resume that lists your specific skills and responsibilities.

Mechanic

All forms of transportation require expert maintenance and repair. The best-paying of these positions abroad is airline maintenance, followed by rail and bus repair. International airlines often train mechanics in the U.S., then place them in foreign locations.

Ticket Clerk

Airlines, rail companies, bus lines and other modes of transportation employ counter clerks and ticket agents. These positions pay reasonably well and offer opportunities for a change of location from time to time with the same international employer.

9
192 Major Companies in 49 Countries

As discussed in Chapter 1, one of the most effective ways to find a job abroad is to hire on with an American company that sends many of its employees to international posts. What are your chances of working abroad? Consider the numbers: Raytheon has 2,500 U.S. employees in foreign positions; Litton has 10,000 of its U.S. workers abroad; W. R. Grace has 16,000 U.S. employees working outside the country; Exxon, Chevron, Citicorp, Lockheed, and dozens of other companies have 500 or more of their employees in international jobs.

This chapter obviously cannot list all American companies doing business in the countries listed here. But these companies will give you a representative sample and a good starting place for employment opportunities with firms that maintain a strong international presence. The company information is necessarily brief, but can nevertheless stimulate your interest in finding out more about countries and companies that may be good targets for your job applications. Please note that most of these firms are multinationals with branches in several countries. Write, call, or fax the company for further information about its placement of employees in jobs abroad.

Argentina

The Coca-Cola Company
One Coca-Cola Plaza
Atlanta, GA 30301 USA
Products: Beverages and food products
Recruiter: **Linda Bullard**
Human Resources Department
P.O. Drawer 1734
Atlanta, GA 30301
Tel: (404) 676-3478
Fax: (404) 515-2560

Eli Lilly and Company
Lilly Corporate Center
Indianapolis, IN 46285 USA
Products: Pharmaceuticals and medical instruments
Recruiter: **Ron Anglea**
Manager, Corporate Recruitment
Lilly Corporate Center
Indianapolis, IN 46285
Tel: (317) 276-1050

Premark International, Inc.
1717 Deerfield Rd.
Deerfield, IL 60015 USA
Products: Plastic storage and serving containers (Tupperware)
Recruiter: **George Shafer**
Human Resources
1717 Deerfield Rd.
Deerfield, IL 60015
Tel: (708) 405-6000
Fax: (708) 405-6311

Standard Commercial Corporation
2201 Miller Rd.
P.O. Box 450
Wilson, NC 27893 USA
Products: Tobacco and wool
Recruiter: **Keith H. Merrick**
Treasurer
2201 Miller Rd.
Wilson, NC 27893
Tel: (919) 291-5507
Fax: (919) 237-1109

Australia

Allen-Bradley Company, Inc.
P.O. Box 2086
Milwaukee, WI 53201 USA
Products: Industrial controls, motor starters, relays
Recruiter: **William Fletcher**
Senior VP International
P.O. Box 2086
Milwaukee, WI 53201
Tel: (414) 382-2000
Fax: (414) 382-4444

Ansell International
2500 Corporate Exchange Dr.,
Suite #200
Columbus, OH 43231 USA
Products: Plastic and rubber products
Recruiter: **Lynn Phillips**
Senior VP, HR/Administration
2500 Corporate Exchange Dr.,
Suite #200
Columbus, OH 43231
Tel: (614) 891-0033
Fax: (614) 891-2816

Black & Decker Corporation
701 E. Joppa Rd.
Towson, MD 21286 USA
Products: Tools and home maintenance/repair products
Recruiter: **Patricia Rogers**
Human Resources TW270
701 E. Joppa Rd.
Towson, MD 21286
Tel: (410) 716-3900
Fax: (410) 583-3967

Pittway Corporation
200 S. Wacker Dr.
Chicago, IL 60606 USA
Products: Publishing and security systems
Recruiter: **Peggy Odegaard**
Office Manager, Recruitment
200 S. Wacker Dr., Suite #700
Chicago, IL 60606
Tel: (312) 831-1070
Fax: (312) 831-0828

Austria

American Standard, Inc.
1114 Avenue of the Americas
New York, NY 10036 USA
Products: Plumbing, brake, heating, and air conditioning devices
Recruiter: **Steve Wilson**
Personnel Department
1114 Avenue of the Americas
New York, NY 10036
Tel: (212) 703-5100
Fax: (212) 703-5352

DDB Needham Worldwide, Inc.
437 Madison Ave.
New York, NY 10022 USA
Products: Advertising
Recruiter: **Ed Flathers**
Personnel Department
437 Madison Ave.
New York, NY 10022
Tel: (212) 415-2000
Fax: (212) 415-3562

Modine Manufacturing Company
1500 DeKoven Ave.
Racine, WI 53403 USA
Products: Heating, ventilating, and evaporative devices
Recruiter: **Abe Bixler**
Recruitment Coordinator
1500 Dekoven Ave.
Racine, WI 53403
Tel: (414) 636-1200
Fax: (414) 636-1424

Sensormatic Electronics
500 NW 12th Ave.
Deerfield Beach, FL 33442 USA
Products: Surveillance equipment
Recruiter: **Bill Beach**
Manager, Human Resources
500 NW 12th Ave.
Deerfield Beach, FL 33442
Tel: (305) 427-9700
Fax: (305) 428-9523

Belgium

Calgon Corporation
P.O. Box 1346
Pittsburgh, PA 15230 USA
Products: Industrial chemicals and personal hygiene items
Recruiter: **Michael Knoll**
Manager, Employment and Staffing
P.O. Box 1346
Pittsburgh, PA 15230
Tel: (412) 777-8000
Fax: (412) 777-8104

Ingersoll-Rand Company
200 Chestnut Ridge Rd.
Woodcliff Lake, NJ 07675 USA
Products: Industrial machinery
Recruiter: **Donna Vandermark**
Manager, Int'l Salaried Administration
200 Chestnut Ridge Rd.
Woodcliff Lake, NJ 07675
Tel: (201) 573-3138
Fax: (201) 573-3168

Russell Corporation
P.O. Box 272
Alexander City, AL 35010 USA
Products: Leisure and athletic apparel
Recruiter: **Bob Scire**
Manager, International Operations
P.O. Box 272
Alexander City, AL 35010
Tel: (205) 329-4000
Fax: (205) 329-5045

Wang Laboratories, Inc.
600 Technology Park Dr.
Billerica, MA 01821-4130 USA
Products: Information processing systems
Recruiter: **Edward J. Devin**
Senior VP, Human Resources
One Industrial Ave.
Lowell, MA 01851
Tel: (508) 967-5000
Fax: (508) 967-0436

Brazil

Borden, Inc.
277 Park Ave.
New York, NY 10172 USA
Products: Food products and industrial products
Recruiter: **Philip E. Perry**
Corp. Director,
Staffing/Development
180 E. Broad St.
Columbus, OH 43215
Tel: (614) 225-4505
Fax: (614) 225-7263

Holiday Inns Worldwide
Three Ravinia Dr.
Atlanta, GA 30346 USA
Products: Hotel services
Recruiter: **John Hager**
Staffing/Recruitment
Three Ravinia Dr.
Atlanta, GA 30346
Tel: (404) 604-5337
Fax: (404) 604-5548

Phillips-Van Heusen Corporation
1290 Avenue of the Americas
New York, NY 10104 USA
Products: Petroleum and natural gas
Recruiter: **Personnel Director**
1290 Avenue of the Americas
New York, NY 10104
Tel: (212) 541-5200
Fax: (212) 468-7064

Universal Foods Corporation
P.O. Box 25099
Richmond, VA 23260 USA
Products: Agricultural, tobacco, and lumber products
Recruiter: **Kathy Deubig**
Corporate Personnel
P.O. Box 25099
Richmond, VA 23260
Tel: (804) 359-9311
Fax: (804) 254-3584

Canada

Bristol-Meyers Squibb
345 Park Ave., 3rd Fl.
New York, NY 10154 USA
Products: Healthcare, pharmaceutical, and consumer products
Recruiter: **Michael McDonnell**
Director, Consumer Products
Group-International
345 Park Ave., 3rd Fl.
New York, NY 10154-0037
Tel: (212) 546-3751
Fax: (212) 546-9707

CUC International, Inc.
707 Summer St.
Stamford, CT 06901 USA
Products: Personnel and consumer services
Recruiter: **Felice Jaquim**
Benefits Manager
707 Summer St.
Stamford, CT 06901
Tel: (203) 324-9261
Fax: (203) 324-3468

Falk Corporation
P.O. Box 492
Milwaukee, WI 53201 USA
Products: Transmission equipment, drives, and gears
Recruiter: **Charles Kendall**
Human Resources
P.O. Box 492
Milwaukee, WI 53201
Tel: (414) 342-3131
Fax: (414) 937-4359

Motorola, Inc.
1301 Algonquin Rd.
Schaumburg, IL 60196 USA
Products: Consumer electronics, semiconductors
Recruiter: **James Donnelly**
Executive VP, Personnel Department
1301 Algonquin Rd.
Schaumburg, IL 60196
Tel: (708) 576-5000
Fax: (708) 576-8003

Chile

Bechtel Group, Inc.
P.O. Box 193965
San Francisco, CA 94119-3965 USA
Products: Engineering and construction
Recruiter: **Bryon Sanderson**
Staffing/Recruitment
MS-14-014
P.O. Box 193965
San Francisco, CA 94119-3965
Fax: (415) 768-3247

Eastman Kodak Company
343 State St.
Rochester, NY 14650 USA
Products: Photographic and chemical products
Recruiter: **Director, Recruitment/Staffing**
343 State St.
Rochester, NY 14650
Tel: (716) 724-4000
Fax: (716) 724-0633

Lubrizol Corporation
29400 Lakeland Blvd.
Wickliffe, OH 44092 USA
Products: Chemicals
Recruiter: **Elizabeth Martin**
Supervisor, Employee/College Relations
29400 Lakeland Blvd.
Wickliffe, OH 44092
Tel: (216) 943-4200
Fax: (216) 943-5337

McCann-Erickson Worldwide
750 3rd Ave.
New York, NY 10017 USA
Products: Advertising services
Recruiter: **Kathleen Yuill**
Human Resources
750 3rd Ave.
New York, NY 10017
Tel: (212) 697-6000

China

Corning Incorporated
Houghton Park
HP CBI-8
Corning, NY 14831 USA
Products: Kitchenware, laboratory services, optical equipment
Recruiter: **Michelle Cox**
Recruitment Department
Houghton Park, HP CBI-8
Corning, NY 14831
Tel: (607) 974-9000
Fax: (607) 974-8711

Goldman Sachs & Company
85 Broad St.
New York, NY 10004 USA
Products: Investment banking and brokerage
Recruiter: **Jim Morrison**
VP, Personnel
85 Broad St.
New York, NY 10004
Tel: (212) 902-7300
Fax: (212) 902-4079

Ralston Purina Company
Checkerboard Square
St. Louis, MO 63164-0001 USA
Products: Pet products, pet foods, batteries
Recruiter: **Ron Young**
Director, Human Resources
Checkerboard Square
St. Louis, MO 63164
Tel: (314) 982-1000
Fax: (314) 982-1211

3M Company
3M Center
St. Paul, MN 55144-1000 USA
Products: Chemicals, adhesives, abrasives, consumer products
Recruiter: **Bruce Hoeffel**
International Operations
3M Center
St. Paul, MN 55144-1000
Tel: (612) 733-1110
Fax: (612) 736-2041

Colombia

Core Laboratories
10205 Westheimer, 4th Fl.
P.O. Box 1407
Houston, TX 77251 USA
Products: Petroleum testing
Recruiter: **Jay G. Milner**
Human Resource Manager
10205 Westheimer, 4th Fl.
P.O. Box 1407
Houston, TX 77251
Tel: (713) 972-6318
Fax: (713) 972-6322

Goodyear Tire & Rubber Company
1144 E. Market St.
Akron, OH 44316 USA
Products: Vehicle tires
Recruiter: **D. C. Jones**
Manager, Corporate College Relations
1144 E. Market St., Dept. #806
Akron, OH 44316
Tel: (216) 796-7990
Fax: (216) 796-4099

Nalco Chemical Company
One Nalco Center
Naperville, IL 60563-1198 USA
Products: Water treatment chemicals, petroleum products
Recruiter: **Lou Habermas**
Human Resources Coordinator
One Nalco Center
Naperville, IL 60563-1198
Tel: (708) 305-1000
Fax: (708) 305-2920

Triton Energy Corporation
6688 N. Central Expressway
Dallas, TX 75206 USA
Products: Oil and gas exploration and production
Recruiter: **David Mormon**
Human Resources
6688 N. Central Expressway, Suite #1400
Dallas, TX 75206
Tel: (214) 691-5200
Fax: (214) 987-0571

Costa Rica

Clipper Cruise Lines
7711 Bonhomme Ave.
St. Louis, MO 63105-1908 USA
Products: Leisure cruise services
Recruiter: **Louann Ayer**
Director, Employment
7711 Bonhomme Ave.
St. Louis, MO 63105
Tel: (314) 727-2929
Fax: (314) 727-6576

Exxon Chemical Company
580 Westlake Blvd.
Houston, TX 77079-2638 USA
Products: Oil and gas exploration and production
Recruiter: **M. Asif Beg**
Manager, Human Resources
580 Westlake Blvd.
Houston, TX 77079-2638
Tel: (713) 584-7600
Fax: (713) 584-7926

Gerber Products Company
445 State St.
Fremont, MI 49413 USA
Products: Baby food products and child products
Recruiter: **Melissa Redinger**
International Operations
445 State St.
Fremont, MI 49413
Tel: (616) 928-2000
Fax: (616) 928-2819

VF Corporation
P.O. Box 1022
Reading, PA 19603 USA
Products: Sports and occupational clothing
Recruiter: **Frank Urban**
VP, Finance & Administration
P.O. Box 1022
Reading, PA 19603
Tel: (215) 378-5511
Fax: (215) 371-0749

Denmark

AMP, Inc.
441 Friendship Rd.
Harrisburg, PA 17111 USA
Products: Electronic components and connectors
Recruiter: **Donald Prowell**
Director, Employment/Employee Relations
441 Friendship Rd.
Harrisburg, PA 17111
Tel: (717) 564-0100
Fax: (717) 780-7019

General Motors Corporation (GM)
3044 W. Grand Blvd.
Detroit, MI 48202 USA
Products: Automotive vehicles and parts
Recruiter: **Richard J. Rachner**
Director, International Personnel
3044 W. Grand Blvd.
Detroit, MI 48202
Tel: (313) 556-7637
Fax: (313) 556-5108

Rosemount, Inc.
12001 Technology Dr.
Eden Prarie, MN 55344 USA
Products: Industrial and aerospace instruments
Recruiter: **Douglas Walters**
Manager, International Human Resources
12001 Technology Dr.
Eden Prairie, MN 55344
Tel: (612) 941-5560
Fax: (612) 828-7795

SPS Technologies, Inc.
900 Newtown-Yardley Rd.
P.O. Box 1000
Newtown, PA 18940 USA
Products: Engineering and industrial manufacturing
Recruiter: **John McGrath**
VP, Corporate Services
Highland Ave.
Jenkintown, PA 19046
Tel: (215) 860-3000
Fax: (215) 860-3034

Egypt

The Bank of New York Company, Inc.
One Wall St., 13th Fl.
New York, NY 10028 USA
Products: Banking and investment services
Recruiter: **Douglas Tantillo**
Vice President, Human Resources
One Wall St., 13th Fl.
New York, NY 10028
Tel: (212) 635-7735
Fax: (212) 635-7910

Ecology and Environment, Inc.
368 Pleasantview Dr.
Lancaster, NY 14086 USA
Products: Toxic and hazardous waste disposal
Recruiter: **Janet A. Steinbruckner**
Personnel Director
368 Pleasantview Dr.
Lancaster, NY 14086
Tel: (716) 684-8060
Fax: (716) 684-0844

General Electric Company (GE)
3135 Easton Turnpike
Fairfield, CT 06431 USA
Products: Consumer electronics, engines, industrial electronics, consumer products
Recruiter: **Thomas Dexter**
International Recruitment
3135 Easton Turnpike
Fairfield, CT 06431
Tel: (203) 373-2211
Fax: (203) 373-3131

Sonat Offshore
Four Greenway Plaza
Houston, TX 77046 USA
Products: Offshore well drilling services and equipment
Recruiter: **Bob Labbe**
Offshore Personnel
Four Greenway Plaza
Houston, TX 77046
Tel: (713) 871-7500
Fax: (713) 850-3817

Finland

Computer Associates International, Inc.
One Computer Associates Plaza
Islandia, NY 11788-7000 USA
Products: Development and distribution of computer software
Recruiter: **Lisa Mars**
Senior VP, Personnel
One Computer Associates Plaza
Islandia, NY 11788-7000
Tel: (516) DIAL-CAI
Fax: (516) DIAL-FAX

ITT Corporation
1330 Avenue of the Americas
New York, NY 10019 USA
Products: Telecommunications and defense contracting
Recruiter: **Lynda Sussman**
Director, International Personnel
1330 Avenue of the Americas
New York, NY 10019
Tel: (212) 258-1000

McKinsey & Company, Inc.
55 E. 52nd St.
New York, NY 10022 USA
Products: Business consulting
Recruiter: **Kathy Focht**
Manager, International Recruiting
485 Madison Ave.
New York, NY 10022

Tel: (212) 446-7000
Fax: (212) 832-0514
Free: (800) 221-1026

Tellabs Operations, Inc.
4951 Indiana Ave.
Lisle, IL 60532 USA
Products: Communication equipment
Recruiter: **Jim Coppens**
International Human Resources
4951 Indiana Ave.
Lisle, IL 60532
Tel: (208) 955-3153
Fax: (208) 955-0424

France

American Express Company—Travel Related Services
TRS Services
American Express Tower
World Financial Center
New York, NY 10285 USA
Products: Credit and travel services
Recruiter: **Barbara Kurz**
Director, Management Resources
American Express Tower
World Financial Center
New York, NY 10285
Tel: (212) 640-5548
Fax: (212) 619-9769

Armstrong World Industries, Inc.
P.O. Box 3001
Lancaster, PA 17604 USA
Products: Flooring, insulation, furniture
Recruiter: **B. G. Spitler**
Manager, College Relations
P.O. Box 3001
Lancaster, PA 17604
Tel: (717) 396-2541
Fax: (717) 396-2126

Cargill Incorporated
P.O. Box 9300
Minneapolis, MN 55440 USA
Products: Food products, seeds, agricultural consulting
Recruiter: **Christie L. Newman**
Human Resources Department
P.O. Box 9300
Minneapolis, MN 55440
Tel: (612) 475-7833
Fax: (612) 475-6208

Merck & Company, Inc.
P.O. Box 2000
Rahway, NJ 07065-0909 USA
Products: Pharmaceuticals, pesticides, chemicals
Recruiter: **Steven Darien**
Vice President, Worldwide Personnel
1 Merck Dr.
P.O. Box 100
Whitehouse Station, NJ 08889-0100
Tel: (908) 423-1000
Fax: (908) 423-2958

Germany

Block Drug Company, Inc.
257 Cornelison Ave.
Jersey City, NJ 07302-9988 USA
Products: Consumer, dental, and pharmaceutical items
Recruiter: **Thomas McNamara**
VP, Human Resources
257 Cornelison Ave.
Jersey City, NJ 07032-9988
Tel: (201) 434-3000
Fax: (201) 451-8424

Fritz Companies
735 Market St.
San Francisco, CA 94103 USA
Products: Import and export documentation and transportation services

Recruiter: **Robert Davidson**
Director, Human Resources
735 Market St.
San Francisco, CA 94103
Tel: (415) 904-8227
Fax: (415) 904-8326

Pfizer, Inc.
235 E. 42nd St.
New York, NY 10017 USA
Products: Over-the-counter medicines, pharmaceuticals, chemicals
Recruiter: **Marjory Bot**
Personnel, International Operations
235 E. 42nd St.
New York, NY 10017
Tel: (212) 573-2323
Fax: (212) 573-1240

Toys "R" Us, Inc.
461 From Rd.
Paramus, NJ 07652 USA
Products: Toys
Recruiter: **Jim Gorenc**
Manager, Recruitment/Placement
461 From Rd.
Paramus, NJ 07652
Tel: (201) 262-7800
Fax: (201) 262-8112

Greece

Bose Corporation
100 The Mountain Rd.
Framingham, MA 01701 USA
Products: Audio and video equipment
Recruiter: **Director**
Personnel Department
100 The Mountain Rd.
Framingham, MA 01701
Tel: (508) 879-7330

Kraft General Foods International
800 Westchester Ave.
Rye Brook, NY 10573 USA
Products: Food products, consumer items
Recruiter: **Susan Holsneck**
Manager, Expatriate Program
800 Westchester Ave.
Rye Brook, NY 10573
Tel: (914) 335-1626
Fax: (914) 335-1468

Penrod Drilling Corporation
2200 Thanksgiving Tower
Dallas, TX 75201 USA
Products: Oil drilling equipment and services
Recruiter: **Jay Hunt**
Personnel Manager
1405 Pinhook
Layfayette, LA 70503
Tel: (318) 232-7032
Fax: (318) 231-1745

Schlegel Corporation
P.O. Box 23197
Rochester, NY 14692 USA
Products: Sealing systems
Recruiter: **James Faulkner**
Director, Human Resources
P.O. Box 23197
Rochester, NY 14692
Tel: (716) 427-7200

Hong Kong

Clorox Company
1221 Broadway
Oakland, CA 94612 USA
Products: Household cleaning products, charcoal, salad dressing
Recruiter: **Ben Lawrence**
Director, Human Resources-International
1221 Broadway
Oakland, CA 94612
Tel: (510) 271-4900
Fax: (510) 271-7883

Johnson & Johnson
One Johnson & Johnson Plaza
New Brunswick, NJ 08901 USA
Products: Consumer health-related products and pharmaceuticals
Recruiter: **Michael Langua**
Director, International Recruitment
One Johnson & Johnson Plaza
New Brunswick, NJ 08901
Tel: (908) 524-3454
Fax: (908) 524-2587

Otis Elevator Company: World Headquarters
Ten Farm Springs Rd.
Farmington, CT 06032 USA
Products: Elevator design, installation, and maintenance
Recruiter: **Deborah Wilson**
Human Resources Representative
Ten Farm Springs Rd.
Farmington, CT 06032
Tel: (203) 674-4000

Tyson Foods, Inc.
P.O. Box 2020
Springdale, AR 72764 USA
Products: Food products
Recruiter: **Karen Percival**
Compensation/HRIS
P.O. Box 2020
Springdale, AK 72764
Tel: (501) 756-4000
Fax: (501) 290-7903
Free: (800) 643-3410

Hungary

Ernst & Young
787 7th Ave.
20th Fl.
New York, NY 10019 USA
Products: Business accounting and consulting
Recruiter: **David Nugent**
International Recruitment
787 7th Ave., 20th Fl.
New York, NY 10019
Tel: (212) 773-3000
Fax: (212) 977-8163

Guardian Industries Corporation
43043 W. Nine Mile Rd.
Northville, MI 48167 USA
Products: Glass products and insulation
Recruiter: **Robert Merrick**
Personnel Director
43043 W. Nine Mile Rd.
Northville, MI 48167
Tel: (313) 347-9102
Fax: (313) 347-9108

Macro Systems, Inc.
8630 Fenton St., Suite 300
Silver Spring, MD 20910 USA
Products: Marketing research, consultation
Recruiter: **Tracy Williams**
Director, Human Resources
8630 Fenton St., Suite 300
Silver Spring, MD 20910
Tel: (301) 588-5484
Fax: (301) 588-4731

Rubbermaid, Inc.
1147 Akron Rd.
Wooster, OH 44691-6000 USA
Products: Plastic and rubber products
Recruiter: **Larry Blackburn**
VP, International
1147 Akron Rd.
Wooster, OH 44691-6000
Tel: (216) 264-6464
Fax: (216) 287-2739

India

DH Technology, Inc.
15070 Ave. of Science
San Diego, CA 92128 USA
Products: High-speed printers
Recruiter: **David T. Ledwell**
VP, Operations
15070 Ave. of Science
San Diego, CA 92128
Tel: (619) 451-3485
Fax: (619) 451-3573

Dow Chemical Company
2030 Willard H. Dow Center
Midland, MI 48674 USA
Products: Chemicals, consumer storage items
Recruiter: **James E. Townsend**
Manager, University Relations
2030 Willard H. Dow Center
Midland, MI 48674
Tel: (517) 636-1463
Fax: (517) 636-0922
Free: (800) 258-9002

Lintas: Worldwide
One Dag Hammarskjöld Plaza
New York, NY 10017 USA
Products: Advertising
Recruiter: **Gary Billings**
International Recruitment
One Dag Hammarskjöld Plaza
New York, NY 10017
Tel: (212) 605-8000
Fax: (212) 486-8099

Whirlpool Corporation
2000 M-63
Benton Harbor, MI 49022-2962 USA
Products: Home appliances
Recruiter: **Linda Krager**
Recruitment/International
2000 M-63
Benton Harbor, MI 49022-2962
Tel: (616) 926-5000
Fax: (616) 926-3568

Indonesia

Freeport-McMoran, Inc.
1615 Poydras St.
New Orleans, LA 70151 USA
Products: Mining and natural resource development
Recruiter: **John Brouilette**
Manager, Expatriate Employment
P.O. Box 51777
New Orleans, LA 70151
Tel: (504) 582-4000
Fax: (504) 582-1639

Kimberly-Clark Corporation
P.O. Box 619100
Dallas, TX 75261-9100 USA
Products: Paper, disposable diapers
Recruiter: **Glenn Guthrie**
International Recruitment
P.O. Box 2001
Neenah, WI 54956
Tel: (414) 721-2000
Fax: (414) 721-4315

Rowan Companies, Inc.
2800 Post Oak Blvd., Suite #5450
Houston, TX 77056 USA
Products: Offshore drilling services
Recruiter: **Robert J. Tedrett**
Director, Human Resources
2800 Post Oak Blvd., Suite #5450
Tel: (713) 621-7800
Fax: (713) 960-7560

Union Carbide Corporation
39 Old Ridgebury Rd.
Danbury, CT 06817 USA
Products: Chemicals and solvents
Recruiter: **Malcolm A. Kessinger**
VP, Human Resources
39 Old Ridgebury Rd.
Danbury, CT 06817
Tel: (203) 794-2000
Fax: (203) 794-4336

Ireland

AT&T International
32 Avenue of the Americas
New York, NY 10013 USA
Products: Telecommunications equipment and services
Recruiter: **Kenneth Magnani**
Manager, Personnel Administration
P.O. Box 1955
Morristown, NJ 07960-1955
Tel: (201) 898-8000
Fax: (201) 898-8712

California Pellet Mill Company
150 Burke St.
Nashua, NJ 03061 USA
Products: Pellet machinery
Recruiter: **John Clancy**
VP, Employee Relations
150 Burke St.
Nashua, NJ 03061
Tel: (603) 882-2711
Fax: (603) 883-7328

Conoco, Inc.
600 N. Dairy Ashford Rd.
Houston, TX 77079 USA
Products: Oil exploration and production
Recruiter: **Tom Pauldine**
International Recruitment
600 N. Dairy Ashford Rd.
Houston, TX 77079
Tel: (713) 293-1000
Fax: (713) 293-4476

Lotus Development Corporation
55 Cambridge Pkwy.
Cambridge, MA 02142 USA
Products: Computer software
Recruiter: **Russell J. Campanello**
VP, Human Resources
55 Cambridge Pkwy.
Cambridge, MA 02142
Tel: (617) 577-8500
Fax: (617) 613-1213

Israel

AVX Corporation
750 Lexington Ave.
New York, NY 10022-1208 USA
Products: Ceramic capacitors
Recruiter: **Richard Aiosa**
VP, Human Resources Manager
P.O. Box 867
Myrtle Beach, SC 29578
Tel: (803) 448-9411
Fax: (803) 448-7139

Encyclopedia Britannica, Inc.
310 S. Michigan Ave.
Chicago, IL 60604 USA
Products: Home and school reference works
Recruiter: **Susan Marynowski**
Director, International Marketing
310 S. Michigan Ave.
Chicago, IL 60604
Tel: (312) 347-7000

LTV Steel Co.
P.O. Box 6778
Cleveland, OH 44115 USA
Products: Steel and steel processing equipment
Recruiter: **Chuck Butters**
Director, Human Resources
P.O. Box 6778
Cleveland, OH 44115
Tel: (216) 622-5000
Fax: (216) 622-1066

Vishay Intertechnology
63 Lincoln Hwy.
Malvern, PA 19355-2120 USA
Products: Electronic components
Recruiter: **William J. Spires**
VP, Human Resources
63 Lincoln Hwy.
Malvern, PA 19355-2120
Tel: (215) 644-1300
Fax: (215) 296-0657

Italy

Baxter Healthcare Corporation
One Baxter Pkwy.
Deerfield, IL 60015-4625 USA
Products: Health care products
Recruiter: **Anne Vexter**
International Recruitment
One Baxter Pkwy.
Deerfield, IL 60015-4625
Tel: (708) 948-4198
Fax: (708) 948-4353

Figgie International, Inc.
4420 Sherwin Rd.
Willoughby, OH 44094 USA
Products: Security and fire protection products and services
Recruiter: **William Sickman**
Manager, Manpower/Employment
4420 Sherwin Rd.
Willoughby, OH 44094
Tel: (216) 946-9000
Fax: (216) 951-1724

Primerica Corporation
65 E. 55th St.
New York, NY 10022 USA
Products: Financial and insurance services
Recruiter: **Barry L. Mannes**
Senior Vice President, Human Resources
1355 Avenue of the Americas
New York, NY 10022
Tel: (212) 891-8900
Fax: (212) 891-8910

Trinova Corporation
3000 Strayer
P.O. Box 50
Maumee, OH 43537-0050 USA
Products: Industrial components
Recruiter: **Cindy Gordon**
International Human Resources
3000 Strayer
P.O. Box 50
Maumee, OH 43537-0050
Tel: (419) 867-2200
Fax: (419) 867-2390

Jamaica

Cuna Mutual Insurance Group
5910 Mineral Point Rd.
Madison, WI 53705 USA
Products: Insurance
Recruiter: **Ann Roberts**
Staffing/Recruitment

5910 Mineral Point Rd.
P.O. Box 391
Madison, WI 53705
Tel: (608) 238-5851
Fax: (608) 238-0830

Northwest Airlines, Inc.
5101 Northwest Dr., A2060
St. Paul, MN 55111 USA
Products: Commercial airline services
Recruiter: **International Operations**
Director, International Operations
5101 Northwest Dr., A2060
St. Paul, MN 55111-3034
Tel: (612) 727-4864
Fax: (612) 726-6911

Reynolds Metals Company
P.O. Box 27003
Richmond, VA 23261-7003 USA
Products: Aluminum and plastic products
Recruiter: **John McGill**
VP, Human Resources
P.O. Box 27003
Richmond, VA 23261-7003
Tel: (804) 261-2000
Fax: (804) 261-4160

Union Camp Corporation
1600 Valley Rd.
Wayne, NJ 07470 USA
Products: Paper, chemicals, and wood products
Recruiter: **Gary Scott**
Personnel Supervisor
1600 Valley Rd.
Wayne, NJ 07470
Tel: (201) 628-2000
Fax: (201) 628-2592

Japan

Bausch & Lomb, Inc.
42 East Ave.
Rochester, NY 14673 USA
Products: Health care equipment, optical products, pharmaceuticals

Recruiter: **James Greenawalt**
Corporate Vice President, Human Resources
1 Lincoln 1st Square
Rochester, NY 14604
Tel: (716) 338-6873
Fax: (716) 338-6000

Colgate-Palmolive Company
300 Park Ave.
New York, NY 10022 USA
Products: Cosmetics, hygiene products
Recruiter: **Allison Good**
Benefits Administrator
300 Park Ave.
New York, NY 10022
Tel: (212) 310-2000
Fax: (212) 310-3284

Elizabeth Arden Company
1345 Avenue of the Americas
New York, NY 10105 USA
Products: Cosmetics
Recruiter: **Charlene Mullen**
Human Resources
1345 Avenue of the Americas
New York, NY 10105
Tel: (212) 261-1000
Fax: (212) 261-1303

Southland Corporation
2711 N. Haskell Ave.
Dallas, TX 75204-7011 USA
Products: Convenience store operations
Recruiter: **David M. Finley**
Human Resources
2711 N. Haskell Dr.
Dallas, TX 75204-7011
Tel: (214) 828-7011
Fax: (214) 828-7848

Kuwait

Dresser Industries, Inc.
1600 Pacific Building
Dallas, TX 75221 USA
Products: Industrial equipment

Recruiter: **Danny Sanchez**
Personnel Manager
1600 Pacific Building
Dallas, TX 75221
Tel: (214) 740-6000
Fax: (214) 740-6715

KFC Corporation
P.O. Box 32070
Louisville, KY 40232 USA
Products: Fried chicken restaurants
Recruiter: **Olden Lee**
Senior VP, Human Resources
P.O. Box 32070
Louisville, KY 40232
Tel: (502) 456-8393
Fax: (502) 454-2195

Parker Drilling Company
Parker Building
8 E. 3rd St.
Tulsa, OK 74103 USA
Products: Oil drilling
Recruiter: **Brent Thompson**
Director, Human Resources
Parker Building
8 E. 3rd St.
Tulsa, OK 74103
Tel: (918) 585-8221
Fax: (918) 631-1368

Raytheon Company
141 Spring St.
Lexington, MA 02173 USA
Products: Electronics, engineering services, appliances
Recruiter: **Frank Umanzio**
Vice President, Human Resources
141 Spring St.
Lexington, MA 02173
Tel: (617) 862-6600
Fax: (617) 860-2172

Luxembourg

Amerace Corporation (Elastimold)
Esna Park
Hackettstown, NJ 07840 USA
Products: Plastic and rubber products, chemicals
Recruiter: **Sid Ellis**
Human Resources Director
Esna Park
Hackettstown, NJ 07840
Tel: (908) 852-1122
Fax: (908) 852-6168

Commercial Intertech Corporation
1775 Logan Ave.
Youngstown, OH 44501 USA
Products: Fluid purification and hydraulic equipment
Recruiter: **Jack Savage**
Director, Employee Relations
1775 Logan Ave.
Youngstown, OH 44501
Tel: (216) 746-8011
Fax: (216) 746-1148

Malaysia

Cabot Corporation
75 State St.
Boston, MA 02116 USA
Products: Chemicals and natural gas importing
Recruiter: **Sarah Cuthill**
Manager, International Assignments
75 State St.
Boston, MA 02116
Tel: (617) 345-0100
Fax: (617) 342-6103

General Instrument Corporation
181 W. Madison Ave.
49th Fl.
Chicago, IL 60602 USA
Products: Electronic components and instruments
Recruiter: **Lee Keenan**
Director, Human Resources
181 W. Madison Ave., 49th Fl.
Chicago, IL 60602
Tel: (312) 541-5000
Fax: (312) 541-5049

Ogilvy & Mather
309 W. 49th St.
New York, NY 10019 USA
Products: Advertising
Recruiter: **Patty Enright**
Human Resources
309 W. 49th St.
New York, NY 10019
Tel: (212) 237-4000
Fax: (212) 779-7717

Texas Instruments, Inc.
13500 N. Central Expressway
Dallas, TX 75265 USA
Products: Electronic products, computers, and calculators
Recruiter: **Stephanie Vann**
Corporate College Relations
13500 N. Central Expressway,
Dallas, TX 75265
Tel: (214) 995-2011
Fax: (214) 995-3340

Mexico

American Greeting Corporation
10500 American Rd.
Cleveland, OH 44144 USA
Products: Greeting cards and related items
Recruiter: **Ron Novack**
Employment Manager
10500 American Rd.
Cleveland, OH 44144
Tel: (216) 252-7300
Fax: (216) 252-6519

Del Monte Corporation
One Market Plaza
P.O. Box 193575
San Francisco, CA 94119 USA
Products: Food products
Recruiter: **Richard Muto**
Vice President, Employee Relations
One Market Plaza
P.O. Box 193575
San Francisco, CA 94119
Tel: (415) 247-3000
Fax: (415) 247-3565

Playtex Apparel, Inc.
Ridgley St.
P.O. Box 631
Dover, DE 19903-0631 USA
Products: Leisure, sports, and intimate apparel
Recruiter: **Richard Smith**
VP, Human Resources
Ridgley St.
P.O. Box 631
Dover, DE 19903-0631
Tel: (302) 674-6666
Fax: (302) 674-6938

Rohm & Haas Company
Independence Mall West
Philadelphia, PA 19105 USA
Products: Chemicals and plastics
Recruiter: **Maurice Marietti**
Director, Human Resources
Independence Mall West
Philadelphia, PA 19105
Tel: (215) 592-3000

Sun Electric Corporation
One Sun Pkwy.
Crystal Lake, IL 60014 USA
Products: Automotive test equipment
Recruiter: **Betty Zambon**
Manager, Human Resources
One Sun Pkwy.
Crystal Lake, IL 60014
Tel: (815) 459-7700
Fax: (815) 459-7852

Netherlands

Emery Worldwide
3350 W. Bayshore
Palo Alto, CA 94303 USA
Products: Air freight transportation
Recruiter: **Thomas Rink**
Director, Employee Relations
3350 W. Bayshore
Palo Alto, CA 94303
Tel: (415) 855-9100
Fax: (415) 857-0745

H. J. Heinz Company
P.O. Box 57
Pittsburgh, PA 15230-0057 USA
Products: Food products, spices, sauces
Recruiter: **William Fera**
1060 Progress St.
Pittsburgh, PA 15212
Tel: (412) 456-5700
Fax: (412) 456-6128

Medtronic, Inc.
7000 Central Ave., NE
Minneapolis, MN 55432-3576 USA
Products: Medical devices
Recruiter: **Peggy Quirk**
International Human Resources
7000 Central Ave., NE
Minneapolis, MN 55432-3576
Tel: (612) 574-4000
Fax: (612) 574-4720
Free: (800) 328-2518

Sara Lee Corporation
Three First National Plaza
Chicago, IL 60602 USA
Products: Food products, consumer goods
Recruiter: **Lena C. Coldras**
Staffing/Recruitment
Three First National Plaza
Chicago, IL 60602
Tel: (312) 726-2600
Fax: (312) 726-3712

New Zealand

Cigna Corporation
One Liberty Pl.
1650 Market St.
Philadelphia, PA 19192-1550 USA
Products: Financial and insurance services
Recruiter: **Susan Wood**
Director, Human Resources
Two Liberty Pl.
1601 Chestnut St.
Philadelphia, PA 19192
Tel: (215) 761-4829
Fax: (215) 761-5482

Helene Curtis Industries, Inc.
325 N. Wells St.
Chicago, IL 60601 USA
Products: Cosmetics, beauty, and hygiene products
Recruiter: **Maile Mulligan**
Human Resources
325 N. Wells St.
Chicago, IL 60601
Tel: (312) 222-1589

Redken Laboratories, Inc.
6625 Variel Ave.
Canoga Park, CA 91303 USA
Products: Skin and hair products
Recruiter: **Treva Vohnig**
Manager, Human Resources
6625 Variel Ave.
Canoga Park, CA 91303
Tel: (818) 992-2700

Textron, Inc.
40 Westminster St.
Providence, RI 02903 USA
Products: Financial services, aerospace technology, commercial products
Recruiter: **Donna Blaney**
Vice President, Staffing
40 Westminster St.
Providence, RI 02903
Tel: (401) 421-2800
Fax: (401) 421-2878

Norway

Associated Press
50 Rockefeller Plaza
New York, NY 10020-1666 USA
Products: News gathering and distribution

Recruiter: **Jack Stokes**
Director, Human Resources
50 Rockefeller Plaza
New York, NY 10020-1666
Tel: (212) 621-1500
Fax: (212) 621-5447

Digital Equipment Corporation
146 Main St.
Maynard, MA 01754-2571 USA

Products: Computing systems

Recruiter: **R. Johnson**
Corporate Employment
146 Main St.
Maynard, MA 01754-2571
Tel: (508) 493-5111
Fax: (508) 493-9490

Monsanto Company
800 N. Lindbergh Blvd.
St. Louis, MO 63167 USA

Products: Chemicals, pesticides

Recruiter: **Robert J. Mason**
Director, University Relations
800 N. Lindbergh Blvd.
St. Louis, MO 63167
Tel: (314) 694-1000
Fax: (314) 394-7625

US West, Inc.
9785 Maroon Circle
Englewood, CO 80112 USA

Products: Telecommunication services and equipment

Recruiter: **Beth Moise**
Executive Director, Org. Development
9785 Maroon Circle, Suite #210
Englewood, CO 80112
Tel: (303) 649-4600
Fax: (303) 793-6654

Pakistan

Ebasco Overseas Corporation
Two World Trade Center
New York, NY 10048 USA

Products: Power generating plants

Recruiter: **William Bosakowski**
Recruitment Division
Two World Trade Center
New York, NY 10048
Tel: (212) 839-2658
Fax: (212) 849-4574

Phillips Petroleum Company
Plaza Building
Bartlesville, OK 74004 USA

Products: Petroleum and natural gas products and services

Recruiter: **E. L. Baughn**
Director, Employee Relations
Plaza Building
Bartlesville, OK 74004
Tel: (918) 661-6600
Fax: (918) 661-7636

Searle Company
5200 Old Orchard
Skokie, IL 60077 USA

Products: Pharmaceuticals

Recruiter: **Personnel Director**
5200 Old Orchard
Skokie, IL 60077
Tel: (708) 922-7000
Fax: (708) 470-6258

Skidmore, Owings & Merrill
220 E. 42nd St.
New York, NY 10017-5806 USA

Products: Engineering and architectural services

Recruiter: **Personnel Manager**
224 S. Michigan, Suite #1000
Chicago, IL 60604
Tel: (312) 554-9090
Fax: (312) 360-4545

Peru

Citicorp
575 Lexington Ave., 12th Fl., Zone 3
New York, NY 10043 USA

Products: Banking, financial services

Recruiter: **Hoyle Jones**
Director, Global MA Programs
575 Lexington Ave., 12th Fl., Zone 3
New York, NY 10043
Tel: (212) 559-1664
Fax: (212) 793-6434
Free: (800) 285-3000

E.I. Du Pont de Nemours and Company
1007 Market St.
Wilmington, DE 19898
Products: Fuels, pesticides, consumer products, pharmaceuticals
Recruiter: **Daniel W. Burger, Jr.**
Vice President, Human Resources
1007 Market St.
Wilmington, DE 19898
Tel: (302) 774-1000
Fax: (302) 774-7321

Liquid Carbonic Corporation
135 S. LaSalle St.
Chicago, IL 60603 USA
Products: Chemicals, compressed gases
Recruiter: **Jim Morgan**
Employee Relations
135 S. LaSalle St.
Chicago, IL 60603
Tel: (312) 855-2500
Fax: (312) 855-2797

Philippines

Columbian Rope Company
P.O. Box 270
Guntown, MS 38849 USA
Products: Rope, fiber, cable products
Recruiter: **Joseph Westmoreland**
Human Resources Representative
P.O. Box 270
Guntown, MS 38849
Tel: (601) 348-2241
Fax: (601) 348-5749

Intel Corporation
3065 Bowers Ave.
Santa Clara, CA 95052 USA

Products: Computer chips and components
Recruiter: **Carlene M. Ellis**
Director, Human Resources
3065 Bowers Ave.
Santa Clara, CA 95052
Tel: (408) 765-8080
Fax: (408) 765-3979

Levi Strauss Associates, Inc.
1115 Battery St.
San Francisco, CA 94111 USA
Products: Clothing
Recruiter: **Kathy Bornstein**
Personnel Manager
1115 Battery St.
San Francisco, CA 94111
Tel: (415) 544-6000
Fax: (415) 544-1468

William Wrigley Jr. Company
410 N. Michigan Ave.
Chicago, IL 60611 USA
Products: Chewing gum and gum products
Recruiter: **Warren Barshes**
Director, International Personnel
410 N. Michigan Ave.
Chicago, IL 60611
Tel: (312) 644-2121
Fax: (312) 644-0353

Poland

Newsweek International
444 Madison Ave.
New York, NY 10022 USA
Products: News reporting and publishing
Recruiter: **Jeanne Sakas and Cathy Fernandez**
Staffing/Recruitment
444 Madison Ave.
New York, NY 10022
Tel: (212) 350-4000

Teledyne, Inc.
1901 Ave. of the Stars
Los Angeles, CA 90067 USA
Products: Specialty metals, aerospace products, consumer services
Recruiter: **Lee Raspa**
Manager, Executive Placement
1901 Ave. of the Stars
Los Angeles, CA 90067
Tel: (301) 277-3311
Fax: (301) 551-4365

Portugal

ConAgra, Inc.
One ConAgra Dr.
Omaha, NE 68102 USA
Products: Foods and food materials
Recruiter: **Gerald B. Vernon**
VP, Human Resources
One Conagra Dr.
Omaha, NE 68102
Tel: (402) 595-4365
Fax: (402) 595-4707

General Tire, Inc.
One General St.
Akron, OH 44329 USA
Products: Tires, inner tubes
Recruiter: **David Mallory**
Director, Staffing & Development
One General St.
Akron, OH 44329
Tel: (216) 798-3000

ICF Kaiser Engineers
1800 Harrison St.
Oakland, CA 94612 USA
Products: Engineering and architectural services
Recruiter: **Dorothy Reihl**
Recruitment/International
1800 Harrison St.
Oakland, CA 94612
Tel: (510) 419-5235
Fax: (510) 419-5355

Seagate Technology, Inc.
920 Disc Dr.
Scotts Valley, CA 95066 USA
Products: Computer disk drives and related components
Recruiter: **Robert Morquecho**
Staffing/Recruitment
920 Disc Dr.
Scotts Valley, CA 95066
Tel: (408) 438-6550
Fax: (408) 438-6172

Russia

Dow Jones & Company, Inc.
200 Liberty St.
New York, NY 10281 USA
Products: Financial and business news reporting and publishing
Recruiter: **John Sax**
Employee Relations Manager
200 Liberty St.
New York, NY 10281
Tel: (212) 416-3530
Fax: (212) 416-4348

Pacific Architects & Engineers, Inc.
1601 N. Kent St., Suite #900
Arlington, VA 22209 USA
Products: Architectural and engineering consulting
Recruiter: **David Terrar**
Director, Recruitment
1601 N. Kent St., Suite #900
Arlington, VA 22209
Tel: (703) 243-6464
Fax: (703) 243-5607

Tambrands, Inc.
777 Westchester Ave.
White Plains, NY 10604 USA
Products: Feminine hygiene products
Recruiter: **Kevin Paradise**
VP, International Human Resources
777 Westchester Ave.
White Plains, NY 10604
Tel: (914) 696-6000
Fax: (914) 696-6757

Saudi Arabia

Boeing Company
7755 E. Marginal Way South
Seattle, WA 98108 USA
Products: Aircraft and aircraft parts
Recruiter: **William Cracker**
Human Resources Manager
P.O. Box 3707
Mail Stop 31-11
Seattle, WA 98124
Tel: (206) 655-2121
Fax: (206) 393-6370

Rust International, Inc.
P.O. Box 101
Birmingham, AL 35201 USA
Products: General contracting
Recruiter: **Donald Hayslett**
Manager, Recruitment
P.O. Box 101
Birmingham, AL 35201
Tel: (205) 995-7878
Fax: (205) 995-7684

SRI International
333 Ravenswood Ave.
Menlo Park, CA 94025 USA
Products: Research and consulting
Recruiter: **Allison Highlander**
Human Resources Representative
333 Ravenswood Ave.
Menlo Park, CA 94025
Tel: (415) 859-5211
Fax: (415) 859-2125

VTN Corporation
500 S. Main St., Suite #1123
Orange, CA 92668 USA
Products: Engineering and architectural services
Recruiter: **Howard Elliot**
Staffing/Recruitment
500 S. Main St., Suite #1123
Orange, CA 92668
Tel: (714) 547-4100

Singapore

Bell Helicopter Textron, Inc.
P.O. Box 482
Fort Worth, TX 76101 USA
Products: Aircraft and defense-related products
Recruiter: **Dick Davies**
Vice President, Human Resources
P.O. Box 482
Fort Worth, TX 76101
Tel: (817) 280-2011
Fax: (817) 280-2321

Compaq Computers Corporation
P.O. Box 692000
Houston, TX 77269-2000 USA
Products: Portable computers
Recruiter: **Mike Berman**
Senior VP, Human Resources
P.O. Box 692000
Houston, TX 77269-2000
Tel: (713) 370-0670
Fax: (713) 370-1740

Domino's Pizza, Inc.
30 Frank Lloyd Wright Dr.
P.O. Box 997
Ann Arbor, MI 48106-0997 USA
Products: Retail food
Recruiter: **Dan Foley**
VP, Human Resources
30 Frank Lloyd Wright Dr.
P.O. Box 997
Ann Arbor, MI 48106-0997
Tel: (313) 930-3030
Fax: (313) 668-4614

Reed Tool Company
6501 Navigation Blvd.
Houston, TX 77011 USA
Products: Industrial and commercial tools
Recruiter: **Tim Bruegger**
Manager, Compensation & Employment
6501 Navigation Blvd.
Houston, TX 77011
Tel: (713) 747-4000
Fax: (713) 747-5667

South Africa

Baker Hughes, Inc.
3900 Essex Ln.
P.O. Box 4740
Houston, TX 77210-4740 USA
Products: Consulting, products, and services for the petroleum and natural gas industries
Recruiter: **Shannon Nini**
International Recruitment
P.O. Box 4740
Houston, TX 77210-4740
Tel: (713) 439-8417
Fax: (713) 439-8782

Masonite Corporation
One S. Wacker Dr.
Chicago, IL 60606 USA
Products: Wood products and consumer items
Recruiter: **Mary Kurylo**
Human Resources Representative
One S. Wacker Dr.
Chicago, IL 60606
Tel: (312) 750-0900
Fax: (312) 750-9502

Quaker Chemical Corporation
Elm & Lee Sts.
Conshohocken, PA 19428 USA
Products: Chemicals
Recruiter: **Cliff Montgomery**
VP, Human Resources
Elm & Lee Sts.
Conshohocken, PA 19428
Tel: (215) 832-4000
Fax: (215) 832-4494

Simplicity Pattern Company, Inc.
200 Madison Ave.
New York, NY 10016 USA
Products: Clothing patterns
Recruiter: **Joanne Bowman**
Manager, Human Resources
200 Madison Ave.
New York, NY 19916
Tel: (212) 576-0500
Fax: (212) 576-0628

South Korea

L. A. Gear, Inc.
4221 Redwood Ave.
Los Angeles, CA 90066 USA
Products: Clothing and footwear
Recruiter: **Carolyn Harper**
Human Resources
4221 Redwood Ave.
Los Angeles, CA 90066
Tel: (213) 822-1995
Fax: (213) 822-0843

Litton Industries, Inc.
360 N. Crescent Dr.
Beverly Hills, CA 90210 USA
Products: Electronics, resource exploration equipment, industrial automation products
Recruiter: **Karen R. Smith**
Personnel Director
360 N. Crescent Dr.
Beverly Hills, CA 90210
Tel: (310) 859-5940

Rockwell International Corporation
2201 Seal Beach Blvd.
Seal Beach, CA 90740-8250 USA
Products: Automotive parts, electronics, and aerospace technologies
Recruiter: **Robert H. Murphy**
Senior VP, Human Resources
2201 Seal Beach Blvd.
Seal Beach, CA 90740-8250
Tel: (310) 797-5066
Fax: (310) 797-5690

Sotheby's Holdings, Inc.
1334 Avenue of the Americas
New York, NY 10021 USA
Products: Auctions and real estate sales
Recruiter: **Susan Garbrecht**
Senior VP, Human Resources
1334 Avenue of the Americas
New York, NY 10021
Tel: (212) 606-7000
Fax: (212) 606-7028

Spain

Borland International, Inc.
1800 Green Hills Rd.
Scotts Valley, CA 95066 USA
Products: Software
Recruiter: **Jull Stanger**
Staffing/Recruitment
1800 Green Hills Rd.
Scotts Valley, CA 95067-0001
Tel: (408) 8400
Fax: (408) 439-9327

Fuller Company
2040 Ave. C
Bethlehem, PA 18017-2188 USA
Products: Industrial processing equipment
Recruiter: **Joseph Mangan**
Manager, Employee Development
2040 Ave. C
Bethlehem, PA 18017-2188
Tel: (215) 264-6011
Fax: (215) 264-6170

Hertz Corporation
225 Brae Blvd.
Park Ridge, NJ 07656-0713 USA
Products: Vehicle rental services
Recruiter: **Joanne Petraglia**
Employee Relations Manager
225 Brae Blvd.
Park Ridge, NJ 07656-0713
Tel: (201) 307-2000
Fax: (201) 307-2644

Perkin-Elmer Corporation
761 Main St.
Norwalk, CT 06859 USA
Products: Computers and analytical electronic equipment
Recruiter: **Michael J. McPartland**
VP, Human Resources
761 Main St.
Norwalk, CT 06859
Tel: (203) 761-2590
Fax: (203) 274-1268

Sweden

Dell Computer Corporation
9505 Arboretum Blvd.
Austin, TX 78759 USA
Products: Computers and computer peripherals
Recruiter: **Bill McBride**
Director, International Recruitment
9505 Arboretum Blvd.
Auston, TX 78759
Tel: (512) 338-4400
Fax: (512) 339-5324

IMO Industries
3450 Princeton Pike
Lawrenceville, NJ 08648 USA
Products: Electronic controls, optical instruments
Recruiter: **David Christensen**
Director, Human Resources
3450 Princeton Pike
P.O. Box 6550
Lawrenceville, NJ 08648
Tel: (609) 896-7600
Fax: (609) 896-7688

Reliance Electric Company
6065 Parkland Blvd.
Cleveland, OH 44124 USA
Products: Industrial automation equipment
Recruiter: **Dave Burke**
Manager, Human Resources
6065 Parkland Blvd.
Cleveland, OH 44124
Tel: (216) 266-7000
Fax: (216) 266-7666

Thomas & Betts
1001 Frontier St.
Bridgewater, NJ 08807 USA
Products: Electrical connectors
Recruiter: **Susan Kelly**
Human Resources Representative
1001 Frontier St.
Bridgewater, NJ 08807
Tel: (908) 685-1600
Fax: (908) 707-2056

Switzerland

Bio-Rad Laboratories
1000 Alfred Nobel Dr.
Hercules, CA 94547 USA
Products: Diagnostic instruments
Recruiter: **Joe Hardy**
Manager, Human Resources Services
1000 Alfred Nobel Dr.
Hercules, CA 94547
Tel: (415) 724-7000
Fax: (415) 724-0423

The Dexter Corporation
One Elm St.
Windsor Locks, CT 06096 USA
Products: Adhesives, specialty coatings, medical products
Recruiter: **Kevin Lake**
Corporate Director, Human Resources
One Elm St.
Windsor Locks, CT 06096
Tel: (203) 292-7678
Fax: (203) 627-9713

Gannett Company, Inc.
1100 Wilson Blvd.
Arlington, VA 22209 USA
Products: News and information services
Recruiter: **Thomas Bates**
Personnel Division, International
535 Madison Ave., 27th Fl.
New York, NY 10022
Tel: (212) 715-5427
Fax: (212) 207-8982

Pitney Bowes, Inc.
World Headquarters
Stamford, CT 06926 USA
Products: Office equipment and services
Recruiter: **Gus Stepp, Jr.**
Employment Director
World Headquarters
Stamford, CT 06926
Tel: (203) 356-5000
Fax: (203) 351-7681

Taiwan

American President Companies, Ltd.
1800 Harrison St.
Oakland, CA 94612 USA
Products: Container transportation by rail, sea, and truck
Recruiter: **Mike Mahr**
Personnel Director
1800 Harrison St.
Oakland, CA 94612
Tel: (415) 272-8000
Fax: (510) 272-8679

EG & G, Inc.
45 William St.
Wellesley, MA 02181 USA
Products: Technical research, services, and advanced scientific products
Recruiter: **Peter Murphy**
Corp. Director, Training & Development
45 William St.
Wellesley, MA 02181
Tel: (617) 237-5000
Fax: (617) 431-4114

Mattel, Inc.
333 Continental Blvd.
El Segundo, CA 90245 USA
Products: Games, toys, hobbies
Recruiter: **Trent Ready**
Human Resources
333 Continental Blvd.
El Segundo, CA 90245
Tel: (310) 524-2000
Fax: (310) 524-3537

Siliconix
2201 Laurelwood Rd.
Santa Clara, CA 95056-0591 USA
Products: Semiconductor components
Recruiter: **Diane Berg**
Human Resources Manager
2201 Laurelwood Rd.
Santa Clara, CA 95056-0591
Tel: (408) 988-8000
Fax: (408) 970-3950

Thailand

Bandag, Inc.
Bandag Center
Muscatine, IA 52761-5886 USA
Products: Rubber equipment and supplies for retreading
Recruiter: **Mel Hershey**
Personnel Department
Bandag Center
Muscatine, IA 52761-5886
Tel: (319) 262-1400
Fax: (319) 262-1344

National Semiconductor Corporation
2900 Semiconductor Dr.
Santa Clara, CA 95052 USA
Products: Semiconductors
Recruiter: **David Schoof**
Director of Staffing & Placement
2900 Semiconductor Dr., MS-14-175
Santa Clara, CA 95052
Tel: (408) 721-5000
Fax: (408) 730-1520

J. C. Penney Company, Inc.
6501 Legacy Dr.
Plano, TX 75024-3698 USA
Products: Household, personal, and consumer products
Recruiter: **Gale Duff-Bloom**
Director, Corp. Personnel/Administration
6501 Legacy Dr.
Plano, TX 75024-3698
Tel: (214) 431-1000
Fax: (214) 431-1315

Turkey

General Dynamics Corporation
3190 Fairview Park Dr.
Falls Church, VA 22042-4523 USA
Products: Weapons systems, defense contracting
Recruiter: **Robert Keller**
Corporate Personnel
P.O. Box 760
Troy, MI 48099-0760
Tel: (313) 244-7000
Fax: (313) 244-7001

International Data Group, Inc.
Five Speen St.
Framingham, MA 01701 USA
Products: Computer magazine publishing
Recruiter: **Mary Cornetta**
Human Resources
Five Speen St.
Framingham, MA 01701
Tel: (508) 875-5000
Fax: (508) 935-4680

James River Corporation
120 Tredegar St.
Richmond, VA 23219 USA
Products: Packaging products, paper
Recruiter: **Larry Olszewski**
Director, Human Resources
120 Tredegar St.
Richmond, VA 23219
Tel: (804) 649-4430
Fax: (804) 649-4340

Standard Commercial Corporation
2201 Miller Rd.
P.O. Box 450
Wilson, NC 27893 USA
Products: Tobacco and wool products
Recruiter: **Keith H. Merrick**
Treasurer
2201 Miller Rd.
Wilson, NC 27893
Tel: (919) 291-5507
Fax: (919) 237-1109

United Kingdom

Airborne Express
3101 Western Ave.
Seattle, WA 98111 USA
Products: Air cargo services

Recruiter: **Darby Langdon**
International Recruitment
3101 Western Ave.
Seattle, WA 98111
Tel: (206) 285-4600
Fax: (206) 282-2104

Burns International Security Services
Two Campus Dr.
Parsippany, NJ 07054 USA
Products: Security consulting and services

Recruiter: **Barry Kingman**
Training & Development
Two Campus Dr.
Parsippany, NJ 07054
Tel: (201) 397-2000
Fax: (201) 397-2493

Dayco Products, Inc.
P.O. Box 1004
Dayton, OH 45401-1004 USA
Products: Auto products

Recruiter: **Tim Albrecht**
Director, Human Resources
P.O. Box 1004
Dayton, OH 45401-1004
Tel: (513) 226-7000
Fax: (513) 226-4689

Knoll International
655 Madison Ave.
New York, NY 10021 USA
Products: Furniture and plastic foam products

Recruiter: **Marcia Thompson**
Director, Human Resources
Water St.
East Greenville, PA 18041
Tel: (215) 679-7991

Pepsico Foods International
7701 Legacy Dr.
Plano, TX 75024 USA
Products: Beverages and snack foods

Recruiter: **Matthew J. Durfee**
Director, Human Resources
7701 Legacy Dr.
Plano, TX 75024
Tel: (214) 334-3733
Fax: (214) 334-3609

10
100 Non-U.S. Employers in 25 Job Areas

All the following employers are huge, in terms of gross revenues, numbers of employees, and types of careers available. As you would expect, these companies primarily employ workers from their base country. But it is also true that these corporate giants all pursue *talent*, wherever it is found, to compete in the global marketplace. If you can convince them that you can help them acquire or use new technologies and gain market share, they are willing to work with or around work permit requirements to hire you as a non-native worker.

Many of these company names are virtual icons around the world. But if other corporate names are unfamiliar to you, do not assume they are backwater operations. These less familiar businesses may not advertise widely in the U.S. or "make the news" on a regular basis. You can tell, however, from the number of employees cited for each company that these are indeed business giants worth your consideration in your international job search. The great majority of these mammoth companies have branches and subsidiaries throughout the world. Do not assume, therefore, that the site specified for company headquarters in the following list is the only location in which you might work for the company. (Complete information on company products, financial data, and work locations can be found in *Principal International Business, The International Corporate 1000, Hoover's Handbook of World Business,* and the *American Encyclopedia of International Information,* all standard reference guides available in most libraries.)

Aerospace and Armaments

Airbus Industrie
Headquarters: 1 Rond Point Maurice Bellonte
F-31707 Blagnac Cedex, France
Tel: +33-61-93-34-31
Fax: +33-61-93-49-55
Contact: Thierry Schutte, Vice President, Human Relations

Principal business: Aircraft manufacturing
Approximate number of employees: 1,400

British Aerospace
Headquarters: Warwick House, P.O. Box 87
Farnsborough Aerospace Center
Farnsborough, Hampshire
GU14 6YU, UK
Tel: +44-(01) 252-373-232
Fax: +44-(01) 252-383-000
Contact: Frank Sterrett, Director of Human Resources

Principal business: Defense contracting, Rover vehicles, property development
Approximate number of employees: 88,000

Rolls-Royce PLC
Headquarters: 65 Buckingham Gate
London SW1E 6AT, UK
Tel: +44-(01) 72-222-9029
Fax: +44-(01) 72-233-1733
Contact: Tom Dale, VP Human Resource Administration

Principal business: Jet engines, power plants
Approximate number of employees: 46,000

Airlines

British Airways PLC
Headquarters: Speedbird House, Heathrow Airport
Houslow, Middlesex TW6 2JA, UK
Tel: +44-(01) 81-759-5511
Fax: +44-(01) 81-897-1889
Contact: Valerie Scoular, Director of Human Resources

Principal business: International airline
Approximate number of employees: 49,000

KLM Royal Dutch Airlines
Headquarters: Koninklijke Luchtvaart Maatschappij N.V.
Amsterdamseweg 55, Amstelveen
The Netherlands
Tel: +31-20-649-91-23
Fax: +31-20-648-80-69
Contact: P. F. Hartman, Executive Vice President of Personnel

Principal business: International airline
Approximate number of employees: 25,000

Qantas Airways Limited
Headquarters: Qantas Center, 203 Coward St.
Mascot, N.S.W. 2020, Australia
Tel: +61-2-691-3636
Fax: +61-2-236-3339
Contact: Carl Feil, Manager of Personnel Services

Principal business: International airline
Approximate number of employees: 27,000

Singapore Airlines Limited
Headquarters: Airline House, 25 Airline Rd.
Singapore 1781
Tel: +65-542-3333
Fax: +65-545-5034

Contact: Syn Chung Wah, Director of Personnel
Principal business: International airline
Approximate number of employees: 25,000

Banks

Barclay's PLC
Headquarters: Johnson Smirke Building, 4 Royal Mint Court London EC3N 4HJ, UK
Tel: +44-(0) 71-626-1567
Fax: +44-(0) 71-696-2811
Contact: J. W. G. Cotton, Director of Personnel
Principal business: Banking and loans
Approximate number of employees: 98,000

Credit Lyonnais
Headquarters: 19, Boulevard des Italiens
75002 Paris, France
Tel: +33-1-42-95-70-00
Fax: +33-1-42-95-30-40
Contact: Joseph Musseau, Head of Personnel
Principal business: Banking and loans
Approximate number of employees: 72,000

Dai-Ichi Kangyo Bank, Ltd.
Headquarters: 1-5, Uchisaiwaicho 1-chome, Chiyoda-ku
Tokyo 100, Japan
Tel: +81-3-3596-1111
Fax: +81-3-3596-2179
Contact: Yoshiharu Mani, Managing Director
Principal business: Banking and loans
Approximate number of employees: 20,000

Deutsche Bank AG
Headquarters: Deutsche Bank Aktiengesellschaft
Taunusanlage 12, D-60262
Frankfurt am Main, Germany
Tel: +49-69-7150-0000
Fax: +49-69-7150-4225
Contact: Douglas Byers, Head of Personnel
Principal business: Banking and loans
Approximate number of employees: 74,000

Union Bank of Switzerland
Headquarters: Bahnhofstrasse 45
8021 Zurich, Switzerland
Tel: +41-1-234-1111
Fax: +41-1-234-3415
Contact: Benno Stotz, Senior Vice President of Human Resources
Principal business: Banking and loans
Approximate number of employees: 28,000

Business Services and Advertising

Dentsu, Inc.
Headquarters: 1-11 Tsukiji, Chuo-ku
Tokyo 204, Japan
Tel: +81-3-5551-5599
Fax: +81-3-5551-2013
Contact: Diane Dennis, Director of Administration
Principal business: Advertising
Approximate number of employees: 6,000

Quebecor, Inc.
Headquarters: 612 Saint-Jacques St.
Montreal, Quebec H3C 4M8, Canada
Tel: (514) 877-9777
Fax: (514) 877-9757

Contact: Marc Shapiro, Vice President of Human Resources
Principal business: Commercial printing, magazine production
Approximate number of employees: 21,000

Saatchi & Saatchi Company PLC
Headquarters: 83/89 Whitfield St. London W1A 4XA, UK
Tel: +44-(01) 71-436-4000
Fax: +44-(01) 71-436-1998
Contact: Simon Goode, Human Resources Director

Principal business: Advertising and business consulting
Approximate number of employees: 12,000

Construction Materials and Furniture

Fletcher Challenge Ltd.
Headquarters: Fletcher Challenge House, 810 Great South Rd., Penrose Auckland, New Zealand
Tel: +64-9-525-9000
Fax: +64-9-525-0559
Contact: Edward Zabinski, Vice President of Human Resources

Principal business: Forest products and construction
Approximate number of employees: 22,000

Compagnie de Saint-Gobain SA
Headquarters: Les Miroirs, 18, Avenue d'Alsace
F924000, Courbevoie, France
Tel: +33-1-47-62-30-00
Fax: +33-1-47-78-45-03
Contact: Dennis Baker, Vice President Human Resources

Principal business: Building materials, glass, ceramics, and pipe
Approximate number of employees: 93,000

Chemicals

BASF Group
Headquarters: Carl-Bosch St. 38 67056 Ludwigshafen, Germany
Tel: +49-621-600
Fax: +49-621-604-2525
Contact: Helmut Glassen, Head of Human Resources

Principal business: Plastics, fibers, oil products
Approximate number of employees: 113,000

Formosa Plastics Corporation
Headquarters: 201 Tun Hwa North Rd.
Taipei, Taiwan
Tel: +886-(0) 2-712-2211
Fax: +886-(0) 2-717-5287
Contact: George Karliss, Director of Personnel

Principal business: PVC resin and acrylic fibers, polyester, circuit boards
Approximate number of employees: 3,500

Hoechst AG
Headquarters: D-65926 Frankfurt am Main, Germany
Tel: +49-69-3050
Fax: +49-69-303-665
Contact: Charles M. Langston, Vice President Human Resources

Principal business: Dyes, plastics, paints, and industrial gases
Approximate number of employees: 175,000

Rhone-Poulenc S.A.
  Headquarters: 25, quai Paul Doumer
  92408 Courbevoie, Cedex, France
  Tel: +33-1-47-68-12-34
  +33-1-47-68-19-11
  Contact: Pene Penisson, Vice President Human Resources
Principal business: Specialty chemicals and agrochemicals
Approximate number of employees: 82,000

Shanghai Petrochemical Co., Ltd.
  Headquarters: Jinshanwei, Shanghai 200540, China
  Tel: +86-21-794-3143
  Fax: +86-21-794-0050
  Contact: Zhou Yunnong, Vice President Administration and Personnel
Principal business: Benzene, ethylene, oil products
Approximate number of employees: 39,000

Computer Equipment

Compagnie des Machines Bull
  Headquarters: 1 Place Carpeaux, Tour Bull, Paris-la-Defense 92800, Puteaux, France
  Tel: +33-1-46-96-90-90
  Fax: +33-1-46-96-90-92
  Contact: Kathleen McGirr, Vice President Human Resources
Principal business: Computer equipment, data processing services
Approximate number of employees: 32,000

Fujitsu Ltd.
  Headquarters: 61, Marunouchi 1-chome, Chiyoda-ku
  Tokyo 100, Japan
  Tel: +81-3-3216-7955
  Fax: +81-3-3216-9352
  Contact: Mikio Ohtsuku, Executive Vice President
Principal business: Mainframe and personal computers, computer chips
Approximate number of employees: 164,000

Olivetti Group
  Headquarters: Via Jervis 77
  I-10015 Ivrea, Italy
  Tel: +39-125-522-639
  Fax: +39-125-523-884
  Contact: Kelle Adams, Manager Human Resources
Principal business: Computers, computer networks, office equipment
Approximate number of employees: 36,000

Consumer Appliances

Matsushita Electric
  Headquarters: 1006, Oaza Kadoma, Kadoma City
  Osaka, Japan
  Tel: +81-6-908-1121
  Fax: +81-6-908-2351
  Contact: Ted Takahaski
Principal business: Multimedia, camcorders, stereos, televisions
Approximate number of employees: 255,000

Nintendo Co., Ltd.
  Headquarters: 60 Fukuine Kamitakamatsu-cho, Higashiyama-ku
  Kyoto 605, Japan
  Tel: +81-75-451-6111
  Fax: +81-75-531-9577

Contact: John Bauer, Vice President Administration and Human Resources
Principal business: Video games
Approximate number of employees: 800

Philips Electronics N.V.
Headquarters: Groenewoudseweg 1, 5621 BA Eindhoven
The Netherlands
Tel: +31-40-786022
Fax: +31-40-785486

Contact: James R. Miller, Manager Human Relations
Principal business: Cassette tapes, VCRs, CD players
Approximate number of employees: 253,000

Sanyo Electric Co., Ltd.
Headquarters: 5-5 Keihan Hondori 2-chome
Moriguchi City, Osaka 570, Japan
Tel: +81-6-991-1181
Fax: +81-6-991-6566

Contact: Yoshinobu Nakatani, Vice President Human Resources
Principal business: Refrigeration equipment, video and audio products, microwave ovens, semiconductors
Approximate number of employees: 60,000

Sony Corporation
Headquarters: 7-35, Kitashinagawa 6-chome, Shinagawa-ku
Tokyo 141, Japan
Tel: +81-3-5448-2111
Fax: +81-3-5448-2244

Contact: Tsunao Hashimoto, Executive Deputy President of Finance and Personnel
Principal business: Radios, CDs, televisions, movies
Approximate number of employees: 130,000

Electronic Equipment

Alcatel Alsthom
Headquarters: 54, Rue la Boetie
75008 Paris, France
Tel: +33-1-40-76-10-10
Fax: +33-1-40-76-14-00

Contact: Stephane Dacquin
Principal business: Power plants, batteries, cables
Approximate number of employees: 198,000

Hitachi, Ltd.
Headquarters: 6, Kanda-Surugadai 4-chome, Chiyoda-ku
Tokyo 101, Japan
Tel: +81-3-3258-1111
Fax: +81-3-3258-2375

Contact: Iwao Hara, Vice President Personnel
Principal business: Electrical machinery, semiconductors, home electronics
Approximate number of employees: 330,000

NEC Corporation
Headquarters: 71, Shiba 5-chome, Minato-ku
Tokyo 108-01, Japan
Tel: +81-3-3454-1111
Fax: +81-3-3454-1519

Contact: Hirokaru Akiyama, Senior Vice President, Personnel
Principal business: PCs, semiconductors, electronic components
Approximate number of employees: 148,000

Oki Electric Industry Co., Ltd.
Headquarters: 7-12, Toranomon 1-chom, Minato-ku
Tokyo 105, Japan
Tel: +81-3-3501-3111
Fax: +81-3-3581-5522

Contact: Hiroshi Yamazaki, Director of Human Resources

Principal business: Data processing systems, electronic devices, ATM machines

Approximate number of employees: 23,000

Siemens AG

Headquarters: Wittelsbacherplatz 2 D-80333 Munich, Germany

Tel: +49-89-2340

Fax: +49-89-234-4242

Contact: Werner Maly, Corporate Human Resources

Principal business: Nuclear energy technologies, medical engineering, power plants, automotive systems

Approximate number of employees: 375,000

Toshiba Corporation

Headquarters: 1-1, Shibaura 1-chome, Minato-ku Tokyo 105-01, Japan

Tel: +81-3-3457-2105

Fax: +81-3-3456-4776

Contact: Takaaki Tanak, Vice President Human Resources

Principal business: Portable computers, electronic products, memory chips

Approximate number of employees: 175,000

Food and Beverage Products

Cadbury Schweppes PLC

Headquarters: 25 Berkeley Square London W1X 6HT, UK

Tel: +44-(01) 71-490-1313

Fax: +44-(01) 71-830-5200

Contact: John Soi, Vice President Human Resources

Principal business: Soft drin

Approximate number of em 40,000

Groupe Danone

Headquarters: 7, Rue de Teheran 75008 Paris, France

Tel: +33-1-44-35-20-20

Fax: +33-1-42-25-67-16

Contact: Richard Corcoran, Director of Personnel

Principal business: Dairy products, pasta, beer, sauces, condiments

Approximate number of employees: 57,000

Guinness PLC

Headquarters: 39 Portman Square London W1H 9HB, UK

Tel: +44-(01) 71-486-0288

Fax: +44-(01) 71-486-4968

Contact: Richard Martonchik, Vice President, Human Resources

Principal business: Alcoholic beverages, hotels, publishing

Approximate number of employees: 24,000

Kirin Brewery Co., Ltd.

Headquarters: 26-1, Jingumae 6-chome, Shibuya-ku Tokyo 150-11, Japan

Tel: +81-3-3499-6111

Fax: +81-3-3499-6151

Contact: James Tate, General Manager Administration and Personnel

Principal business: Beer, tea, coffee, fruit juices

Approximate number of employees: 9,000

Nestlé, Ltd.

Headquarters: Ave. Nestlé 55 CH-1800 Vevey, Switzerland

Tel: +41-21-924-2111

Fax: +41-21-921-1885

Contact: Cam Starrett, Executive Vice President, Human Resources
Principal business: Food products, chocolate, beverages
Approximate number of employees: 210,000

Tate & Lyle, PLC
Headquarters: Sugar Quay, Lower Thames St.
London EC3R 6DQ, UK
Tel: +44-(01) 71-626-6525
Fax: +44-(01) 72-623-5213
Contact: John Walker, Managing Director

Principal business: Sugar, sweeteners, monosodium glutamate
Approximate number of employees: 16,000

Freight and Shipping

Evergreen Group
Headquarters: 166, Minsheng E. Rd., Sec. 2
10444 Taipei, Taiwan
Tel: +886-2-505-7766
Fax: +886-2-505-5255
Contact: Kuo-Hua Chang, Vice President

Principal business: Shipping, hotels, construction
Approximate number of employees: 1,600

General Merchandise

Carrefour
Headquarters: 6, Avenue Raymond Poincare
75116 Paris, France
Tel: +33-1-53-70-19-00
Fax: +33-1-53-70-86-16
Contact: Michel Pinot, Member of the Executive Board

Principal business: Groceries, clothing, consumer goods for supermarkets
Approximate number of employees: 86,000

Cifra, S.A.
Headquarters: Jose Ma. Castorena 470, Delegacion Cuajimalpa
05200 Mexico, D.F., Mexico
Tel: +52-5-327-9211
Fax: +52-5-327-9259
Contact: Jose Maria Garcia Perez

Principal business: Retail consumer products sales
Approximate number of employees: 40,000

Daiei, Inc.
Headquarters: Minatojima, Nakamachi, Chuo-ku
Kobe 650, Japan
Tel: +81-78-302-5001
Fax: +81-78-302-5572
Contact: Hiromitsu Kameyama

Principal business: Supermarket chain, hotels, restaurants
Approximate number of employees: 19,000

Ito-Yokado Co., Ltd.
Headquarters: 1-4, Shibakoen 4-chome, Minato-ku
Tokyo 105, Japan
Tel: +81-3-3459-2111
Fax: +81-3-3434-8378
Contact: Hiroei Masukawa, Executive Vice President, Personnel

Principal business: Clothing, supermarkets, discount stores, restaurants
Approximate number of employees: 94,000

Vendex International, N.V.
Headquarters: P.O. Box 7997, 1088 AD Amsterdam
The Netherlands
Tel: +32-30-5490500
Fax: +32-20-6461954

100 Non-U.S. Employers in 25 Job Areas

Contact: J. A. H. Lempers, Head of Personnel
Principal business: Supermarkets, department stores, employment agencies
Approximate number of employees: 81,000

Hotels and Restaurants

Allied Domecq PLC
Headquarters: 24 Portland Pl. London W1N 4BB, UK
Tel: +44-(01) 71-323-9000
Fax: +44-(01) 72-323-1742
Contact: Peter F. Macfarlane, Group Director

Principal business: Alcoholic beverages, food products
Approximate number of employees: 72,000

Club Mediterranée SA
Headquarters: 25 Rue Vivienne, Place de la Bourse F-75088 Paris Cedex 02, France
Tel: +33-1-42-86-4000
Fax: +33-1-42-86-4616
Contact: Jean-Michel Landau, Executive Vice President

Principal business: Resorts
Approximate number of employees: 9,000

Rank Organization PLC
Headquarters: 6 Connaught Pl. London W2 2EZ, UK
Tel: +44-(01) 72-706-111
Fax: +44-(01) 71-262-9886
Contact: Richard C. Snodgrass, Vice President, Human Resources

Principal business: Media products, casinos, resorts
Approximate number of employees: 41,000

Household Produc

L'Oreal SA
Headquarters: 41, Rue Martre, 92117 Clichy, France
Tel: +33-1-47-56-70-00
Fax: +33-1-47-56-80-02
Contact: Francois Vachey, Vice President, Human Resources

Principal business: Cosmetics, pharmaceuticals
Approximate number of employees: 33,000

Reckitt & Colman PLC
Headquarters: One Burlington Lane London W42RW, UK
Tel: +44-81-994-6464
Fax: +44-81-994-8920
Contact: Colin C. C. Brown, Group Director

Principal business: Condiments, cleaning products, pharmaceuticals
Approximate number of employees: 22,000

Shiseido Company, Ltd.
Headquarters: 7-5-5, Ginza, Chuo-ku Tokyo 104-10, Japan
Tel: +82-3-3572-5111
Fax: +81-3-3289-4849
Contact: Sadao Abe, Director International Operations

Principal business: Cosmetics, toiletries
Approximate number of employees: 3,900

Waterford Wedgwood PLC
Headquarters: Kilbarry Waterford, Ireland
Tel: +353-517-3311
Fax: +353-517-8539
Contact: George Stonier, Director, Human Resources

Principal business: Crystal, porcelain, lamps, figurines
Approximate number of employees: 8,000

Insurance

Allianz AG Holding
Headquarters: Koeniginstrasse 28,
Pstfach 44 01 24
D-80802 Munich, Germany
Tel: +49-89-3-80-00
Fax: +49-89-34-99-41
Contact: Herbert Hansmeyer, Member of the Board of Management, Business Administration

Principal business: Property and casualty insurance
Approximate number of employees: 70,000

Lloyd's of London
Headquarters: One Lime St.
London EC3M 7HA, UK
Tel: +44-(01) 71-623-7100
Fax: +44-(01) 71-626-2389
Contact: Geoff Morgan, Director, Human Resources

Principal business: Property and casualty insurance
Approximate number of employees: 2,500

Tokio Marine and Fire
Headquarters: 2-1, Marunouchi
1-chome, Chiyoda-ku
Tokyo 100, Japan
Tel: +81-3-3212-6211
Fax: +81-3-5223-3100
Contact: Masakazu Nakanishi

Principal business: Property and casualty insurance
Approximate number of employees: 15,000

Medical Products, Including Pharmaceuticals

Novo Nordisk A/S
Headquarters: Novo Alle
DK-2880 Bagsvaerd, Denmark
Tel: +45-44-42-6468
Fax: +45-44-98-03-27
Contact: Connich Fryland, Executive Vice President, Corporate Development

Principal business: Insulin, industrial enzymes
Approximate number of employees: 12,000

Roche Group
Headquarters: POB CH-4002
Basel, Switzerland
Tel: +41-61-688-8888
Fax: +41-62-691-0014
Contact: Martin F. Spadler, Senior Vice President, Human Resources

Principal business: Pharmaceuticals, vitamins, perfumes
Approximate number of employees: 57,000

Sandoz Ltd.
Headquarters: Lichtstrasse 35
CH-4002 Basel, Switzerland
Tel: +41-61-324-11-11
Fax: +41-61-342-80-01
Contact: Alexandre F. Jetzer, Senior Officer, Management Resources and International Coordination

Principal business: Pharmaceuticals, chemicals, baby foods
Approximate number of employees: 53,000

SmithKline Beecham PLC
Headquarters: New Horizons Court
Brentford, Middlesex TW8 9EP, UK
Tel: +44-(01) 81-975-2000
Fax: +44-(01) 81-975-2090
Contact: Dan Phelan, Group Personnel Director

Principal business: Over-the-counter drugs, biotechnology
Approximate number of employees: 52,000

Metals and Mining

Fried. Krupp AG Hoesch-Krupp
Headquarters: D-45117 Essen, Germany
Tel: +49-201-188-1
Fax: +49-201-188-4100
Contact: Mike Dowell, Director, Human Resources

Principal business: Steel, automotive products, construction
Approximate number of employees: 79,000

Inco Ltd.
Headquarters: Royal Trust Tower, Toronto-Dominion Centre
Toronto, Ontario M5K 1N4, Canada
Tel: (416) 361-7511
Fax: (416) 361-7781
Contact: Lorne M. Ames, Vice President, Human Resources

Principal business: Nickel, copper, sulfuric acid, platinum, silver
Approximate number of employees: 17,000

Nippon Steel Corporation
Headquarters: 6-3, Otemachi 2-chome, Chiyoda-ku
Tokyo 100-71, Japan
Tel: +81-3-3242-4111
Fax: +81-3-3275-5607
Contact: Takao Katsumata, Executive Vice President, Personnel

Principal business: Steel, civil engineering, restaurants, amusement parks
Approximate number of employees: 51,000

Zambia Consolidated Copper Mines
Headquarters: 5309 Dedan Kimathi Rd., P.O. Box 30048
Lusaka 10101, Zambia
Tel: +260-1-229115
Fax: +260-1-221057
Contact: Bannie M. Lombe, Director of Human Resources

Principal business: Copper, cobalt
Approximate number of employees: 61,000

Office Equipment

Canon, Inc.
Headquarters: 30-2, Shimomaruko 3-chome, Ohta-ku
Tokyo 146, Japan
Tel: +81-3-3758-2111
Fax: +81-3-5482-5130
Contact: Annette Colarusso, Director of Personnel

Principal business: Business machines, cameras, printers, workstations
Approximate number of employees: 65,000

Moore Corporation Ltd.
Headquarters: One First Canadian Pl., P.O. Box 78
Toronto, Ontario M5X 1G5, Canada
Tel: (416) 364-2600
Fax: (416) 364-1667
Contact: Matthew R. Bove, Director of Human Resources

Principal business: Business forms, management services
Approximate number of employees: 23,000

Ricoh Company, Ltd.
Headquarters: 15-5, Minami-Aoyama 1-chome, Minato-ku
Tokyo 107, Japan
Tel: +81-3-3479-3111
Fax: +81-3-3403-1578
Contact: Tatsuo Hirakawa, Executive Managing Director

Principal business: Copiers, fax machines, office machines
Approximate number of employees: 49,000

Sharp Corporation
  Headquarters: 22-22 Nagaike-cho, Abeno-ku
  Osaka 545, Japan
  Tel: +81-6-621-1221
  Fax: +81-6-628-1667
  Contact: Yutaka Wada, Senior Executive Vice President, International Business

Principal business: Calculators, televisions, computer monitors, camcorders, refrigerators
Approximate number of employees: 45,000

Oil and Gas

British Petroleum Co., PLC
  Headquarters: Britannic House, One Finsbury Circus
  London EC2M 7BA, UK
  Tel: +44-(0) 71-496-4000
  Fax: +44-(0) 71-496-4570
  Contact: Felix Strater, Vice President, Human Resources

Principal business: Oil exploration, petroleum products, chemicals
Approximate number of employees: 85,000

Elf Aquitaine
  Headquarters: Tour Elf Cedex 45
  92078 Paris La Defense, France
  Tel: +33-1-47-44-45-46
  Fax: +33-1-47-44-75-94
  Contact: Lowell Williams, Senior Vice President, Personnel

Principal business: Hydrocarbons, chemicals, health products
Approximate number of employees: 95,000

Petrofina SA
  Headquarters: 52, Rue de l'Industrie
  B-1040 Brussels, Belgium
  Tel: +32-2-288-9111
  Fax: +32-2-288-3445
  Contact: Jose G. Rebelo, Director, Human Resources

Principal business: Oil, gas, chemicals
Approximate number of employees: 15,000

Petroleos de Venezuela
  Headquarters: Torre Este, Av. Libeertador, La Campina, Apartado Postal 169
  Caracas 1010-A, Venezuela
  Tel: +58-2-708-4111
  Fax: +58-2-708-4661
  Contact: Nelson E. Olmedillo

Principal business: Oil exploration, petroleum products, natural gas, coal
Approximate number of employees: 50,000

Royal Dutch/Shell Group
  Headquarters: 30 Carel van Bylandtlaan
  2596 HR The Hague
  The Netherlands
  Tel: +31-70-377-9111
  +31-70-377-3115
  Contact: B. W. Levan, Vice President, Human Resources

Principal business: Petroleum products, chemicals, polymers, insecticides, coal
Approximate number of employees: 119,000

TOTAL
  Headquarters: 24 Cours Michelet
  92800 Puteaux, France
  Tel: +33-1-41-35-40-00
  +33-1-41-35-64-65
  Contact: Scott Topham, Vice President, Human Resources

Principal business: Retail gas stations, oil, gas, inks, paints
Approximate number of employees: 50,000

Paper and Lumber Products

MacMillan Bloedel Ltd.
Headquarters: 925 W. Georgia St.
Vancouver, British Columbia
V6C3L2, Canada
Tel: (604) 661-8000
Fax: (604) 661-8377
Contact: G. H. Johncox, Vice President, Human Resources

Principal business: Lumber, plywood, paper products, packaging materials
Approximate number of employees: 13,000

Photographic Equipment

Fuji Photo Film Co., Ltd.
Headquarters: 26-30, Nishiazabu 2-chome, Minato-ku
Tokyo 106, Japan
Tel: +81-3-3406-2844
Fax: +81-3-3406-2193
Contact: S. Akaishi, Personnel Manager

Principal business: Film, cameras, office machines, medical technologies
Approximate number of employees: 26,000

Minolta Co., Ltd.
Headquarters: 3-13, Azuchi-machi 2-chome, Chuo-ku
Osaka 541, Japan
Tel: +81-6-271-2251
Fax: +81-6-266-1010
Contact: Thomas R. McVeigh, Director Human Resources

Principal business: Cameras, office equipment
Approximate number of employees: 7,000

Publishing and Information Services

Bertelsmann AG
Headquarters: Carl-Bertelsmann-Strasse 270, Postfach 111 D-33311
Guetersloh, Germany
Tel: +49-52-41-80-0
Fax: +49-52-41-7-51-66
Contact: Berhnard von Minckwitz, President, Bertelsmann Publishing Group International

Principal business: Books, sheet music, paper products, records
Approximate number of employees: 52,000

Havas S.A.
Headquarters: 136, Avenue Charles-de-Gaulle
92522 Neuilly-sur-Seine Cedex, France
Tel: +33-1-47-47-30-30
Fax: +33-1-47-47-3223
Contact: Jean-François Meaudre, Executive Vice President

Principal business: Business and trade publishing, advertising, book publishing, multimedia products
Approximate number of employees: 19,000

Reuters Holdings PLC
Headquarters: 85 Fleet St.
London EC4 4AJ, UK
Tel: +44-(01) 72-250-1122
Fax: +44-(01) 71-510-4064
Contact: Patrick A. V. Mannix

Principal business: News services, financial information services
Approximate number of employees: 230,000

The Thomson Corporation
Headquarters: Toronto Dominion Bank Tower, P.O. Box 24, Toronto-Dominion Centre
Toronto, Ontario M5K 1A1, Canada

Tel: (416) 360-8700
Fax: (416) 360-8812
Contact: Gerald D. Tenser, Vice President, Human Resources
Principal business: Book publishing, information services, newspaper publishing
Approximate number of employees: 47,000

Telecommunications

BCE, Inc.
Headquarters: 1000, Rue de La Gauchetière Ouest, Bureau 3700 Montreal, Quebec H3B 4Y7, Canada
Tel: (514) 397-7000
Fax: (514) 397-7223
Contact: Derek H. Burney, Executive Vice President International
Principal business: Standard telephone service and products, mobile telephone services, telecommunications consulting, directory publication
Approximate number of employees: 120,000

British Telecommunication PLC
Headquarters: BT Centre
81 Newgate St.
London EC1A 7AJ, UK
Tel: +44-71-356-4008
Fax: +44-71-356-5520
Contact: Michael L. Hepher, Group Managing Director
Principal business: Telephone service
Approximate number of employees: 160,000

Hong Kong Telecommunications, Ltd.
Headquarters: 26th Fl., Office Tower, Convention Plaza, One Harbour Rd. Wanchai, Hong Kong
Tel: +852-888-2888
Fax: +852-877-8877
Contact: M. Hayton, Director, Personnel
Principal business: Telecommunications services
Approximate number of employees: 17,000

Nippon Telegraph and Telephone Corp.
Headquarters: 1-6, Uchisaiwai-cho 1-chome, Chiyoda-ku Tokyo 100-19, Japan
Tel: +81-3-3509-5111
Fax: +81-3-3509-4598
Contact: Toshihiro Inamura, Vice President, Human Relations
Principal business: Telecommunications services
Approximate number of employees: 250,000

Telefonica de Espana, S.A.
Headquarters: Gran Via 28, 28013 Madrid, Spain
Tel: +34-1-556-8753
Fax: +34-1-584-7582
Contact: Oscar Maraver Sanchez-Valdepeñas, Deputy General Manager, Human Resources
Principal business: Telecommunications services
Approximate number of employees: 75,000

Telefonos de Mexico, S.A.
Headquarters: Parque Via 198, Oficina 508, Colonia Cuauhtemoc 06599 Mexico, D.F., Mexico
Tel: +52-5-703-3990
Fax: +52-5-254-5955
Contact: Francisco Sanchez y Garcia, Director, Human Resources and Labor Relations
Principal business: Telecommunications products and services
Approximate number of employees: 64,000

Teleglobe, Inc.
Headquarters: 1000 de la
Gauchetière St. West
Montreal, Quebec H3B 4X5, Canada
Tel: (514) 868-8124
Fax: (514) 868-7234
Contact: Lucia Valente, Director,
Human Resources
Principal business:
Telecommunications services
Approximate number of employees:
2,200

Utilities

Tokyo Electric Power Co., Inc.
Headquarters: 1-3, Uchisaiwai-cho
1-chome, Chiyoda-ku
Tokyo 100, Japan
Tel: +81-3-3501-8111
Fax: +81-3-5511-8436
Contact: Kiyoshi Ishii, Managing
Director
Principal business: Electric utility
service
Approximate number of employees:
42,000

Vehicle and Parts Manufacturing, Including Tires

Bayerische Motoren Werke AG
Headquarters: Petruelring 130,
BMW Haus, Postfach 40 02 40
W-8000 Munich 40, Germany
Tel: +49-98-3-59-36-87
Fax: +49-89-3-59-36-22
Contact: John F. Cagnina, Manager,
Human Relations
Principal business: BMW automobile
production, servicing
Approximate number of employees:
67,000

Daimler-Benz Aktiengesellschaft
Headquarters: D-70546 Stuttgart 80,
Germany
Tel: +49-711-1-7-22-87
Fax: +49-711-1-79-41-09
Contact: Janice Simonson, Director
of Human Resources
Principal business: Mercedes
production, servicing
Approximate number of employees:
368,000

Fiat SPA
Headquarters: Corso Marconi 10
Turin, Italy
Tel: +39-(0) 11-686-1111
Fax: +39-(0) 11-686-3400
Contact: Giovanni Berthod, Vice
President, Human Resources
Principal business: Fiat vehicles, railway
systems, chemicals, financial services
Approximate number of employees:
270,000

Honda Motor Co., Ltd.
Headquarters: 1-1, 2-chome,
Minami-Aoyama, Minato-ku
Tokyo 107, Japan
Tel: +81-3-3423-1111
Fax: +81-3-3423-0511
Contact: Hiroyuki Yoshino,
Executive Vice President
Principal business: Honda
automobiles, motorcycles
Approximate number of employees:
92,000

PSA Peugeot Citroen
Headquarters: 75 Rue de la Grande-
Armée
75116 Paris, France
Tel: +33-1-40-66-37-60
Fax: +33-1-40-66-51-99
Contact: Cheryl Sugalski, Manager,
Human Resources
Principal business: Peugeot
automobiles, mopeds
Approximate number of employees:
145,000

Pirelli SPA
Headquarters: Viale Sarca 202
I-20126 Milan, Italy
Tel: +39-2-64421
Fax: +39-2-644233000
Contact: Carlo Buora, General Manager, Administration

Principal business: Tires, conveyor belts, cables
Approximate number of employees: 43,000

Saab-Scania Holdings Group
Headquarters: S-581 88 Linkoeping, Sweden
Tel: +46-13-18-00-00
Fax: +46-13-18-18-02
Contact: Tom Reis, Director, Human Resources

Principal business: Auto, truck, aircraft, and armament products
Approximate number of employees: 27,000

AB Volvo
Headquarters: S-405 08 Göeteborg, Sweden
Tel: +46-31-59-00-00
Fax: +46-31-54-79-59
Contact: Keld Alstrup, Vice President, Human Relations

Principal business: Cars, trucks, buses, commercial engines
Approximate number of employees: 74,000

Yamaha Corporation
Headquarters: 10-1, Nakazawa-cho Hamamatsu, Shizuoka Pref. 430 Japan
Tel: +81-53-460-2850
Fax: +81-53-456-1109
Contact: Don Patrick, Division Manager, Corporate Personnel

Principal business: All-terrain vehicles, golf carts, marine and auto engines, motorcycles, snowmobiles
Approximate number of employees: 11,000

11
Eight Areas for Temporary International Employment

Child/Elder Care and Domestic Work

Advertisements for these positions can be found readily in newspapers. Positions are often live-in, and wages tend to be relatively low. On the positive side, caregivers often find themselves traveling to interesting places with the family. It's also common, over time, to build up an extended network of friends through the family. These contacts often lead to other job experiences.

Here are ten agencies that may be helpful in your efforts to locate a child/elder care position:

The Au Pair Company
50 Avenue Rise
Bushey, Hertshire, England WD2 3AS
Tel: 01-950-3125

Childcare Agency
40 Uppleby Road
Parkstone, Poole, Dorset, England
BH12 3DE
Tel: 0202 737171

Euro-Pair Agency
28 Derwent Ave.
Pinner, Middlesex, England HA5 4QJ
Tel: 01-421 2100

London Au Pair & Nanny Agency
23 Fitzjohn's Avenue, Hampstead,
London
England NW3 5JY
Tel: 01-435 3891

Interlingua Centre
Torquay Road, Foxrock
Dublin 18, Ireland
Tel: 01-893876

Okista
Turkenstrasse 4
1090 Vienna IX, Austria
Tel: 23 75 26

Pro Filia
14B Ave. du Mail
1205 Geneva, Switzerland
Tel: 22 29 84 62

Relaciones Culturales Internacionales
Calle Ferraz No. 82
Madrid, Spain 28008
Tel: 479 64 46

Relations Internationales
20 rue de l'Exposition
75007 Paris, France
Tel: 45 50 23 23

Universal Care
Chester House
9 Windsor End
Beconsfield, Buckshire HP9 2JJ
Tel: 04946 78811

Agriculture

Casual work in this area usually requires stamina and the nerve to approach a farmer in the field. Jobs frequently are not advertised at all. You simply present yourself at a harvest, planting, shearing, etc. If you look strong, you have a good chance of getting a day or two of work. If that goes well, you'll be taken on as a regular—often without a handshake or a contract of any kind. Agricultural workers frequently find themselves traveling from harvest to harvest. Earnings for an extended summer of hard work can be substantial.

Bulletin boards in pubs and rural markets are often good places to look for agricultural work.

Contacts for Short-Term Agricultural Work

Inter-Exchange
161 Sixth Ave.
New York, NY 10013
Tel: (212) 924-0446
Fax: (212) 924-0575

Agricultural work throughout Europe for US jobseekers aged 18–30. This private agency also provides placement in au pair, hotel, and English tutoring positions.

Willing Workers on Organic Farms (WWOOF)
Buchan, Victoria, 3885, Australia
Tel: 051-550-218

Contact this organization for information on summer and short-term positions working on organic farms throughout Australia.

Nature et Progres
B.P. 6, F-69921 Oullins Cedex, France
Tel: 72-39-04-36
Fax: 78-50-53-47
This organization will send you publications listing openings for temporary agricultural workers in Europe.

S.C.A. Soldive
17, Ave. de la Cooperation
86200 Loudun, France
Tel: 49-22-40-63
Fax: 49-22-40-37

A major employer of harvest workers, packers, and mechanics.

Atlantis Youth Exchange
Rolf Hofmosgate 18
N-0655, Oslo, Norway
Tel: 226-70043
Fax: 226-86808
This organization places noncitizen workers aged 18–30 on Norwegian farms for paid positions.

Teaching English

In many countries, the most direct route to a better paying job is to learn English. The demand for English-speaking tutors is therefore high, and wages are often quite good. For bona fide positions within companies and established language schools, register with the TESOL Job Placement Service, 1118 22nd St. NW, Suite 205, Washington, D.C. 20037. For a subscription fee of $18 you will receive bi-monthly listings of English teaching jobs around the world. A 1988 book, *Teaching Abroad*, is available from the Institute of International Education, 809 United Nations Plaza, New York, NY 10017. The cost at the time of publication was $22.

More casual positions as an English tutor can be found by watching ads in foreign newspapers or, just as good, placing an ad of your own. If you are willing to provide a bit of childcare along with your tutoring, you may find yourself advantageously employed by a family. You will also want to check directly with private language schools, which will probably appraise you much more on the professionalism of your appearance and quality of your speaking than on academic preparation. Bring along a briefcase (that omnipresent symbol of capability) and a neatly typed resume. Especially in Asian countries, carry a business card that you can leave behind. Often your best employment contacts will come from call-backs.

Contacts for Positions in English Teaching and Tutoring

Two Japanese agencies are particularly prominent in providing local orientation and placement for English teachers and tutors:

Universal Language Institute
Kinoshita Royal Building, 5th Fl.
4-5-7 Koenji Minami
Suginami-ku
Tokyo 166, Japan
Tel: 03-5377-3801

Tokyo Language Institute
Jishido Building, 6th Fl.
Higashi-Ikebukoro 2-56-2
Toshima-ku
Tokyo 170, Japan

Write to these organizations (in English) for full information about their programs and placement opportunities.

The largest supplier of English teachers to South Korea is English Language School International, Personnel Recruitment, 4761 Buckingham Parkway, Culver City, CA 90230, Tel: (800) 468-8978. Contact this group for their current requirements and openings.

The Hess Language School hires English teachers and tutors for their 42 branches in Taiwan. Contact Hess Language School, 83 Poae Rd., 2nd Fl., Taipei, Taiwan, Tel: 02-382-5440 or their U.S. office, Hess Language School, 105 Lower Dix Ave., Glens Falls, NY 12804, Tel: (518) 793-6128.

Worldwide English teaching positions in American schools throughout the world can be obtained through International School Services, 15 Roszel Rd., P.O. Box 5910, Princeton, NJ 08543 and the Department of Defense, Office of Dependents Schools, 2461 Eisenhower Ave., Alexandria, VA 22331. Contact is requested by mail only.

Shops and Selling

Particularly in tourist areas, your ability to speak English and your bright, healthy appearance may land you a casual job in a shop or as an outside salesperson for a manufacturer or distributor. These jobs are found through newspaper ads and by approaching shopkeepers directly. It is not uncommon for these people to offer you a percentage of your total sales during the day. You may want to give yourself a week to see what sort of numbers you're able to achieve on such a commission basis. Your grooming and dress will be a major factor in a shopkeeper's or manufacturer's decision to let you represent his or her products.

Manual Labor

If you don't object to a ten-hour day of grueling and often dirty work, stand around a construction site until the boss takes your interest in work seriously or asks you to leave. Wages, when compared to domestic work or childcare, can be good. But expect to do hard time: wheeling loads of wet concrete up ramps, carrying heavy bricks and construction blocks to bricklayers, and digging trenches in rocky ground.

You'll often be paid cash for your labor at the end of each day. Be sure to get a reference letter before you leave the job. The letter will make it much easier to get your next manual labor job, and may place you a bit higher in the pecking order of workers.

Military Installations

Throughout the world, the United States maintains military bases that can be a nirvana for those seeking nonpermit work. Military employment officers are often willing to bend the rules a bit to accommodate an earnest (and hungry) face from home. It's necessary, however, to obtain a visitor's pass to get past the gate guard. Ask by phone or in person how to get the pass, then present yourself and your story to the officer in charge of casual labor. Be flexible in what you're willing to do. Typical military base jobs include cleaning, kitchen work, gardening, and language tutoring.

Yachts, Cruise Lines, Fishing Boats, and Commercial Shipping

If you have your sea legs (or want them), check harbor areas for opportunities at sea. You may find yourself swabbing decks, preparing meals, cleaning staterooms, baiting hooks, or performing more prestigious duties. If you have entertainment skills, be sure to mention them and be prepared to demonstrate them. Cruise lines are often looking for nighttime dancers and singers who are also willing to do manual work by day.

Contacts for Yacht, Cruise, Hotel, Tour Guide, and Resort Employment

Casterbridge Tours, Ltd.
Casterbridge Hall
Bowden Rd.
Templecombe, Somerset, BA OLB
Tel: 01963-370753
Fax: 01963-371220

Opportunities for tour guides and assistants to countries in Europe, Scandinavia, Africa, Asia, and South America.

Euro Disney
Service de Recrutement-Casting
BP 110, F-7777 Marne-la-Vallée
Cedex 4, France
Tel: 149-31-19-99

A wide range of opportunities in Disney's 47 restaurants, 5,200 hotel rooms, 45 shops, and theme park.

Hotel Sofitel
BP 258, F-73155 Val D'Isère Cedex, France

Use this contact to gain access to opportunities in this large chain of worldwide hotels.

Eurocamp Summer Jobs
P.O. Box 170
Liverpool L70 1ES

Camp counselor and supervisor opportunities through Sunsites, Eurocamp Travel, and French Country Camping.

Club Mediterranée
106 Brompton Rd.
London SW3 1JJ

Staffing opportunities for Club Meds in Europe and North Africa.

Marriott Corporation
One Marriott Dr.
Washington, DC 20058

Openings in Marriott's 700 hotels worldwide.

Hyatt International Corporation
200 W. Madison St.
Chicago, IL 60606
Tel: (312) 750-1234

Hyatt owns resort hotels in 18 foreign countries, with hundreds of job opportunities of all kinds.

American Canadian Caribbean Line
P.O. Box 368
Warren, RI 02885
Tel: (401) 247-0955

Cruise ship travel to various ports-of-call throughout Central America and the Caribbean.

Resort Work

This broad category includes opportunities for ski instructors, divers, exercise leaders, maintenance workers, security guards, ticket takers, food servers, and many others. The key to finding such employment seems to hinge on getting past the written job application. You have to meet the person doing the hiring face to face. You then have a minute or two to make your best case. If you can impress him or her with your enthusiasm and presentability, you'll probably get the job. Experience (of almost any kind) can be very helpful in your application. If possible, carry letters of reference with you from previous work experiences.

Appendix A
State-by-state U.S. Employers with Foreign Offices

The following company names and descriptions are offered for investigation by those seeking international positions. The list is selective, to feature a wide range of companies and potential occupations. No recommendation or endorsement is implied by this selection. The inclusion of a company name here does not imply current solicitation of job applications by the company or the company's willingness to supply job-related information to applicants.

In some cases, the regional office of a company has been listed. Often, jobseekers have better luck beginning with a company location in their home state, where they can meet company personnel and learn about operations. This approach is often preferable to simply sending a resume to a distant corporate home office. If necessary, the regional office will refer you to national headquarters for further information.

Alabama

Allied Corporation/Birmingham
P.O. Box 593
Fairfield, AL 35064
Tel: (205) 787-8605
Contact: Manager
An area producer of coal tar pitch, creosote and coal tar solutions, and refined tars. Parent company, Allied Signal Corporation, serves a broad spectrum of industries through its more than 40 strategic businesses, which are grouped into five sectors: Aerospace; Automotive; Chemical; Industrial and Technology; and Oil and Gas. Allied Signal is one of the nation's largest industrial organizations, and has 115,000 employees in over 30 countries. Corporate headquarters location: Morristown, NJ. International:

Australia, Belgium, Canada, England, Hong Kong, Mexico, New Zealand, Switzerland, Venezuela.

Quantegy, Inc.
2111 Marvin Pkwy.
Opelika, AL 36803-0190
Tel: (334) 749-7678

Contact: Ken Brown, Personnel Manager

A world leader in professional audio-video systems and recording tape. Also engaged in the manufacture of computer peripheral and instrumentation technology. Introduced the first audio tape recorder in the U.S. and developed the first successful video cassette recorder. Company has designed products for the broadcast industry: video tape and disc recorders, computer graphics, special effect systems, editing and switching systems for television and mastering and mix-down audio recorders for the music business. Common positions include: Accountant; Buyer; Chemist; Computer Programmer; Draftsperson; Chemical Engineer; Electrical Engineer; Industrial Engineer; Mechanical Engineer; Operations/Production Manager. Principal educational backgrounds sought: Accounting; Chemistry; Computer Science; Engineering; Finance. Company benefits include: Medical insurance; dental insurance; pension plan; life insurance; tuition assistance; disability coverage; employee discounts; savings plan. Corporate headquarters located in Redwood City, CA. Operations at this facility include: Manufacturing.

International: Argentina, Australia, Bahamas, Belgium, Brazil, Colombia, Canada, England, France, Germany, Greece, Hong Kong, Israel, Italy, Japan, Mexico, Netherlands, Spain, Sweden.

SCI Systems, Inc.
2101 W. Clinton
Huntsville, AL 35805
Tel: (205) 882-4601

Contact: Francis K. Henry, Vice President, Personnel

Designs and develops electronic products for government and commercial clients. Corporate headquarters location. International: Scotland, Singapore.

Sinclair International
2200 Industrial St.
P.O. Box 7284
East Mobile, AL 36607
Tel: (334) 661-0736

An area producer of specialty printing inks and coatings, press chemicals, and printing supplies. Parent company, Allied Signal Corporation, serves a broad spectrum of industries through its more than 40 strategic businesses, which are grouped into five sectors: Aerospace; Automotive; Chemical; Industrial and Technology; and Oil and Gas. Allied Signal is one of the nation's largest industrial organizations, and has 115,000 employees in over 30 countries. Corporate headquarters location: Morristown, NJ. International: Canada, Colombia, Germany, Mexico, Netherlands.

Alaska

**Atlantic Richfield Company/
Alaska Region**
P.O. Box 100360
Anchorage, AK 99510
Tel: (907) 276-1215
Contact: Jane E. Crane, Vice President, Human Resources

A major energy and natural resources firm with operations in petroleum, natural gas, and exploration. Corporate headquarters location: Los Angeles, CA. Numerous area facilities. International: Argentina, Australia, Belgium, China, Colombia, England, France, Germany, Greece, Italy, Ivory Coast, Japan, Mexico, Singapore, Switzerland, Zimbabwe.

Xerox Corporation
4341 B St.
Anchorage, AK 99503
Tel: (907) 561-8200
Contact: Personnel Coordinator

Offers a wide range of office products, as well as sales and service operations. Products include copiers and telecommunications equipment, as well as office and printing systems. Other Alaska facilities include: Fairbanks, Juneau, Kenai, Prudhoe Bay and Valdez. Corporate headquarters location: Stamford, CT. International: Australia, Austria, Belgium, Colombia, Denmark, England, France, Germany, Hong Kong, Ireland, Italy, Japan, Kenya, Malaysia, Netherlands, New Zealand, Nigeria, Norway, Portugal, Singapore, Spain, Sweden, Switzerland, Venezuela.

Arizona

Ameron Pipe Division/Southwest
P.O. Box 20505
Phoenix, AZ 85036
Tel: (602) 252-7111
Contact: Alan L. Rhea, Personnel Manager

Produces a wide range of pipe products, including concrete reinforced steel pipe, concrete pipe, and reinforced concrete pipe for drainage and irrigation. Nationally, company is engaged principally in four produce areas: pipe products, construction products, steel products, and corrosion control products. Pipe products include concrete and steel pressure and non-pressure pipe for water transmission and storm, industrial waste water, and sewage control. Construction products include ready-mix cement, steel reinforced concrete pipe, welded wire mesh and various other construction materials. Steel products include carbon and alloy steel rod and wire products, such as wire and cold-heading products. Corrosion control produces coatings to prevent or control corrosion during repair, construction and maintenance of facilities in the marine, sanitation, chemical, petrochemical and nuclear industries. International operations. Corporate headquarters location: Monterey Park, CA. New York Stock Exchange. International: Brazil,

Colombia, France, Germany, Hong Kong, Mexico, Netherlands, Saudi Arabia, Spain.

Burr-Brown Corporation
6730 S. Tucson Blvd.
Tucson, AZ 85706
Tel: (602) 746-1111
Contact: Seth Slaughter, Director, Human Resources

A leading supplier of precision microelectronic devices and microcomputer-based systems for use in data acquisition, signal conditioning, and industrial control. Operates in five market segments: Instrumentation (including electronic test, analytical, and medical); Industrial (including process control, factory data collection, and environmental/geophysical measurement); Military/Aerospace (including navigation/guidance/control, radar/ sonar/ECM, and test and measurement); Computers (including industrial measurement and control systems, peripheral equipment, and graphics and image processing equipment); and Communications (including data communications, telecommunications, and audio/visual signal processing). Operating divisions are: Industrial Systems Products Division, Military Products Division, Micro Technology Division, and International. International: Austria, England, France, Germany, Holland, Japan, Scotland.

Allied Signal Corporation
P.O. Box 52170
Phoenix, AZ 85072
Tel: (602) 231-1000

Contact: Lupe Alvarez, Personnel

Provides spare parts and aftermarket services to the aviation industry. Allied Signal Corporation serves a broad spectrum of industries through its more than 40 strategic business, which are grouped into five sectors: Aerospace, Automotive; Chemical; Industrial and Technology; and Oil and Gas. Allied Signal is one of the nation's largest industrial organizations, and has 115,000 employees in over 30 countries. Common positions include: Accountant; Administrator; Commercial Artist; Computer Programmer; Customer Service Representative; Aerospace Engineer; Electrical Engineer; Mechanical Engineer; Technical Writer/Editor. International: Australia, Brazil, Canada, England, France, Germany, Ireland, Japan, Singapore, Spain, Sweden, Switzerland.

Packard-Hughes Interconnect
P.O. Box 679
Fort Defiance, AZ 86504
Tel: (520) 729-5711
Contact: Sylvia L. Hunt, Director, Personnel

Manufactures printed circuit board assemblies, harness assemblies, and related electronic components. Nationally, company is a major diversified corporation with manufacturing interests in aircraft, space systems, missiles, ships, electronics, mining, tanks, and other military equipment. Corporate headquarters location: St. Louis, MO. New York Stock Exchange. International: Australia, Belgium, Denmark, Egypt, Germany, Greece,

Israel, Japan, Korea, Netherlands, Norway, Spain.

Revlon, Inc.
4301 W. Buckeye Rd.
Phoenix, AZ 85043
Tel: (602) 352-5000
Contact: Stanley Gray, Director, Personnel

Produces a wide variety of cosmetics, toiletries, and perfumes. Nationally, company is engaged in the manufacture of a diverse range of products, including beauty products, health care products, ethical pharmaceuticals, and optical products. Corporate headquarters location: New York, NY. New York Stock Exchange. International: Argentina, Australia, Belgium, Bermuda, Canada, England, France, Germany, Hong Kong, Ireland, Israel, Italy, Japan, Mexico, New Zealand, Singapore, Spain, Venezuela.

Arkansas

International Paper Pine Bluff Mill
P.O. Box 7069
Pine Bluff, AR 71611
Tel: (501) 541-5600
Contact: Ray Halloway, Personnel

A major paper mill producing coated publication papers and bleached board. Common positions include: Accountant; Chemical Engineer; Civil Engineer; Electrical Engineer; Mechanical Engineer. Principal educational backgrounds sought: Accounting; Engineering. Company benefits include: Medical, dental, and life insurance; pension plan; tuition assistance; savings plan. Corporate headquarters location: Purchase, NY. Operations at this facility include: Manufacturing. New York Stock Exchange. International: Greece, Israel, Japan, Spain, Switzerland.

Whirlpool Corporation
6400 S. Jenny Lind
Fort Smith, AR 72903
Tel: (501) 648-2000
Contact: Chuck Knapp, Director of Personnel

A major manufacturer of refrigerators and freezers. Divisional headquarters location. Corporate headquarters location: Benton Harbor, MI. New York Stock Exchange. Common positions include: Accountant; Chemist; Electrical Engineer; Industrial Engineer; Mechanical Engineer. Principal educational background sought: Engineering. Company benefits include: Medical insurance; dental insurance; pension plan; life insurance; tuition assistance; disability coverage; profit sharing; employee discounts; savings plan. International: Brazil, Canada.

California

Bell & Howell Company
819 Cowan Rd.
Burlingame, CA 94010
Tel: (415) 692-4550
Contact: Mrs. A. Gilly, Office Manager

Parent company is a diversified corporation doing business in three major areas: Specialized Business Equipment, which produces items such as microfilm recorders, readers, jackets, and services, as well as micropublishing, and office collation and mailing machines; Learning and Materials, which operates technical training schools in electronics and computer science, publisher textbooks, and produces a variety of instructional materials at all levels; and Instrumentation, which produces measuring and recording equipment, magnetic tape instrumentation, and a variety of semi-conductor compounds, optics equipment, and photoplates for integrated circuits. This facility is part of the Specialized Business Equipment Group, and produces microfilm goods while providing related services. Corporate headquarters location: Chicago, IL. New York Stock Exchange. International: Australia, Belgium, Canada, England, France, Germany, Ireland, Japan.

Brunswick Corporation/Defense Division
3333 Harbor Blvd.
Costa Mesa, CA 92628
Tel: (714) 546-8030
Contact: Joan McGary, Personnel Director

A division of Brunswick Corporation. Primarily engaged in scientific, engineering, and manufacturing projects serving the United States military and its supporting defense operations. Products include tactical weapons and aerospace systems. Other plants located in Nebraska, Virginia, and Ohio. Operations include: Manufacturing; research/development. Corporate headquarters location: Skokie, IL. New York Stock Exchange. Common positions include: Accountant; Attorney; Buyer; Commercial Artist; Draftsperson; Engineer; Aerospace Engineer; Electrical Engineer; Industrial Engineer; Mechanical Engineer; Personnel and Labor Relations Specialist; Physicist; Systems Analyst; Technical Writer/Editor; Materials Engineer. Principal educational backgrounds sought: Business Administration; Computer Science; Engineering; Physics. Company benefits include: Medical, dental and life insurance; pension plan; tuition assistance; disability coverage; employee discounts. International: Argentina, Belgium, Brazil, Canada, Guatemala, Japan, Korea, Mexico, Switzerland.

Carnation Company
5045 Wilshire Blvd.
Los Angeles, CA 90036
Tel: (213) 932-6000
Contact: Frank Slohn, Manager/Personnel and Recruiting

A major firm that manufactures and sells a wide range of food products, pet foods, containers, and dietary products. Among many major products are Coffee-Mate, Instant Breakfast, hot cocoa mix, Contadina tomato products, Trio and Chef-Mate food service products, dairy items, metal containers and Friskies, Fancy Feast and Mighty Dog pet foods. Common positions include: Accountant; Computer Programmer; Agricultural Engineer; Chemical Engineer; Electrical Engineer; Industrial Engineer; Mechanical Engineer; Financial Analyst; Management Trainee; Operation/Production Manager; Marketing Specialist; Purchasing Agent; Quality Control Supervisor; Sales Representative; Statistician; Systems Analyst; Transportation and Traffic Specialist. Principal educational backgrounds sought: Accounting; Business Administration; Communications; Computer Science; Economics; Engineering; Finance; Marketing. Company benefits include: Medical, dental and life insurance; pension plan; tuition assistance; disability coverage; profit sharing. Parent company: Nestlé. International: Australia, Belgium, Dominican Republic, France, Germany, Greece, Jamaica, Japan, Mexico, Netherlands, Peru, Philippines, Singapore, Spain, Thailand.

Computer Sciences Corporation
2100 E. Grand
El Segundo, CA 90245
Tel: (310) 615-0311
Contact: Scott Sharpe, Vice President of Corporate Personnel

A major provider of computer services and consultation to industry and government. Works primarily in two operations areas: Contract Services, offering such capabilities as the development of custom-designed computer systems; and Data Systems, handling the firm's INFONET service, which provides remote data processing and value-added services via an international data communications network. Corporate headquarters location. New York Stock Exchange. International: Belgium, Canada, England, Germany, Netherlands.

Firestone Tire and Rubber Company
25375 Cabot #210
Hayward, CA 94545
Tel: (415) 786-0420
Contact: Personnel Department

Primarily engaged in the sale of a broad line of tires for the original equipment and replacement markets of the world. Manages its business through three primary operating groups: the World Tire Group is responsible for the design, development, testing, and manufacturing of tires throughout the world; the Sales and Marketing Group is a nationwide sales network which includes dealer outlets and automotive service centers; and the Corporate Development Group has the responsibility for corporate strategic planning activities. Employs approximately 60,000 people worldwide. Considers people for whole region, which includes California, Washington, Oregon, Montana, Idaho, Wyoming, Arizona, Utah, and Hawaii. Corporate headquarters location: Akron, OH. New York Stock Exchange. International: Argentina, Belgium, Brazil, Chile, Costa Rica, France, Ghana, Haiti, Italy, Ivory Coast, Japan, Kenya, Liberia, Monaco, Netherlands, New Zealand, Philippines, Portugal, Switzerland, Thailand, Tunisia, Uruguay, Venezuela.

Fluor Corporation
3353 Michelson Dr.
Irvine, CA 92730
Tel: (714) 975-2000
Contact: Charles J. Bradley, Jr., Director, Personnel

Primarily engaged in engineering and construction, as well as the production of various natural resources. Provides worldwide engineering and related services to energy, natural resource, industrial, commercial, utility, and government clients. International: France, Ivory Coast, Netherlands, Singapore.

Garrett Airesearch
2525 W. 190th St.
Torrence, CA 90509
Tel: (213) 776-1010

Contact: Jon Hansen, Manager, Employment

Engaged primarily in the design and manufacture of systems, products, and components for the aerospace industry, as well as such related fields as surface transportation. An Allied Signal Company. Common positions include: Accountant; Computer Programmer; Draftsperson; Aerospace Engineer; Ceramics Engineer; Chemical Engineer; Electrical Engineer; Industrial Engineer; Mechanical Engineer; Metallurgical Engineer; Financial Analyst; Industrial Designer; Operations/Production Manager; Physicist; Purchasing Agent; Quality Control Supervisor; Systems Analyst; Technical Writer/Editor. Principal educational backgrounds sought: Accounting; Business Administration; Computer Science; Economics; Engineering; Liberal Arts; Physics. Company benefits include: Medical insurance; dental insurance; pension plan; life insurance; tuition assistance; disability coverage; profit sharing; vacations and holidays. Corporate and divisional headquarters location. Parent company: Garrett Corporation. Operations at this facility include: Manufacturing; research/development; administration. Allied Signal is listed on the New York Stock Exchange. International: Australia, Brazil, Canada, England, France, Germany, Ireland, Japan, Singapore, Spain, Sweden, Switzerland.

Getz Brothers Company, Inc.
150 Post Rd.
Suite 500
San Francisco, CA 94108
Tel: (415) 772-5500

Contact: Tracy Moore, Manager, Human Resources

Getz Brothers specializes in worldwide marketing and distribution services. Knowledge of a foreign language will prove helpful for applicants. International: Australia, Hong Kong, Philippines, Singapore, United Kingdom.

Hewlett-Packard Company
3000 Hanover St.
Department 20AC
Palo Alto, CA 94304
Tel: (415) 857-1502

Contact: F. R. Peterson, Vice President, Personnel

Mailed inquiries only. A worldwide firm engaged in the design, manufacture, marketing, and servicing of a broad array of precision electronics instruments and systems for measurement, analysis, and computation. Company's line of over 10,000 products are used in business, industry, science, education, and medicine. The company employs approximately 84,000 people in 24 U.S. cities, Europe, Japan, Canada, Australia, the Far East and Latin America. Common positions include: Accountant; Administrator; Attorney; Blue-Collar Worker Supervisor; Buyer; Chemist; Computer Programmer; Customer Service Representative; Chemical

Engineer; Electrical Engineer; Industrial Engineer; Mechanical Engineer; Financial Analyst; Industrial Designer; Operations/Production Manager; Marketing Specialist; Personnel and Labor Relations Specialist; Physicist; Public Relations Worker; Purchasing Agent; Quality Control Supervisor; Sales Representative; Systems Analyst; Technical Writer/Editor. Principal educational backgrounds sought: Accounting; Business Administration; Communications; Computer Science; Engineering; Finance; Marketing; Mathematics; Physics. Company benefits include: Medical, dental and life insurance; pension plan; tuition assistance; disability coverage; profit sharing; employee discounts; savings plan; flexible work hours; credit union; income protection plan; recreational activities. Corporate headquarters location. Operations include: Administration. New York Stock Exchange. International: Argentina, Australia, Austria, Belgium, Brazil, France, Hong Kong, Ireland, Italy, Japan, Korea, Lebanon, Luxembourg, Malaysia, Mexico, Netherlands, New Zealand, Norway, Scotland, Singapore, Spain, Sweden, Switzerland, Taiwan, Venezuela.

Lockheed Martin Corporation
P.O. Box 551
Burbank, CA 91520-9044
Tel: (818) 847-4734

Contact: Professional Staffing

Other area facilities include: Ontario. A major aerospace corporation. Conducts aerospace research and development and produces advanced aircraft and aerospace systems; also constructs and repairs ships, and provides aircraft maintenance and modification and other related technical support. Most business is conducted in four industry segments: Missiles, Space and Electronics, including activities in space exploration, weaponry, and communications; Aircraft and Related Services, maintaining operations in such diverse areas as strategic airlifters, tactical reconnaissance aircraft, and software services; Aerospace Support, encompassing the fields of aircraft modification and aviation services; and Shipbuilding, including operations in new ship construction and ship overhaul. United States Government is a major client. New York Stock Exchange. Corporate headquarters location. International: Australia, Bahrain, Canada, China, England, France, Hong Kong, Ivory Coast, Japan, Kenya, Lebanon, Singapore, Spain, Switzerland.

SRI International
333 Ravenswood Ave.
Menlo Park, CA 94025
Tel: (415) 326-6200

Contact: Michael Patrick (Engineering) or Beth Solomon (Sciences)

A multi-disciplinary research, development, and consulting organization engaged in government and private industry research. Corporate headquarters location. Common positions include: Biochemist; Biologist; Chemist; Economist; Biomedical Engineer; Chemical Engineer; Electrical Engineer; Mechanical Engineer; Financial Analyst; Personnel and

Labor Relations Specialist; Physicist; Systems Analyst; Technical Writer/Editor. Principal educational backgrounds sought: Biology; Business Administration; Chemistry; Communications; Computer Science; Economics; Engineering; Finance; Mathematics; Physics. Company benefits include: Medical, dental and life insurance; pension plan; tuition assistance; disability coverage; employee discounts. International: Australia, Canada, England, France, Germany, Italy, Japan, Netherlands, Philippines, Saudi Arabia, Singapore, Sweden, Switzerland, Taiwan.

Colorado

Dana Corporation/Engine Products Division
P.O. Box 666
Pueblo, CO 81002
Tel: (719) 948-3311

Contact: Personnel Department

A manufacturer of aluminum pistons and bell housings. Common positions in this facility include: Accountant; Blue-Collar Worker Supervisor; Computer Programmer; Industrial Engineer; Mechanical Engineer; Operations/Production Manager; Personnel and Labor Relations Specialist; Quality Control Supervisor. Principal educational backgrounds sought: Accounting; Engineering. Company benefits include: Medical insurance; dental insurance; pension plan; life insurance; tuition assistance; disability coverage; savings plan. Corporate headquarters location: Toledo, OH. Operations at this facility include: Manufacturing.

New York Stock Exchange. International: Brazil, India.

Paine Webber
370 17th St., Suite 4100
Denver, CO 80202
Tel: (303) 436-9000

Contact: Ms. Billy Battiato, Director, Personnel

Denver office of the well-known financial stock-brokerage firm. International: England, France, Hong Kong, Japan, Switzerland.

Ralston Purina Company
4555 York St.
Denver, CO 80216
Tel: (303) 295-0818

Contact: Office Manager

Produces a nationally-advertised line of dog foods, cat foods, and feed for other domestic animals. Overall, company is the world's largest producer of dog and cat foods, commercial livestock feeds, cereals, canned goods (tuna and mushrooms), soybean meal, and soybean oil. Also involved in various diversified businesses. Employs more than 63,000 people worldwide at 250 facilities. Corporate headquarters location: St. Louis, MO. New York Stock Exchange. International: Australia, Belgium, Brazil, Canada, Colombia, France, Germany, Guatemala, Italy, Japan, Korea, Mexico, Netherlands, Panama, Peru, Spain.

Connecticut

Amax
Amax Center
Greenwich, CT 06836-1700
Tel: (203) 861-6660

Contact: Joe Pereira, Supervisor Employee Relations

A diversified minerals and energy development company with worldwide operations. The company explores for, mines, refines, and sells a wide variety of minerals and metals, and has interests in coal, petroleum, and natural gas. Principal products are molybdenum, coal, zinc, petroleum and natural gas, potash, tungsten, silver, gold, and magnesium. Through Alumax, Inc., company is also involved in the production of aluminum and the fabrication and marketing of aluminum products. Common positions include: Accountant; Computer Programmer; Financial Analyst. Principal educational backgrounds sought: Accounting; Finance. Company benefits include: Medical, dental, and life insurance; pension plan; tuition assistance; disability coverage; profit sharing; savings plan. Corporate headquarters location. Operations at this facility include: Administration; sales. New York Stock exchange. International: Canada, England, Netherlands.

Amphenol Corporation
358 Hall Ave.
Wallingford, CT 06492
Tel: (203) 265-8900

Contact: Wayne Simms, Director, Personnel

An area producer of flat ribbon cable. Parent company, Allied Signal Corporation, serves a broad spectrum of industries through its more than 40 strategic businesses, which are grouped into five sectors: Aerospace; Automotive; Chemical; Industrial and Technology; and Oil and Gas. Allied Signal is one of the nation's largest industrial organizations, and has 115,000 employees in over 30 countries. Corporate headquarters location: Morristown, NJ. International: Austria, Canada, England, France, Germany, Hong Kong, India, Italy, Japan, Netherlands, Sweden.

Gerber Scientific
83 Gerber Rd. W.
South Windsor, CT 06074
Tel: (203) 644-1551

Contact: Anthony Pagliuco, Personnel Manager

A company engaged in the manufacture of high tech drafting equipment such as photo plotters. International: Belgium, England, Finland, Germany, Sweden.

The Stanley Works
1000 Stanley Dr.
New Britain, CT 06053
Tel: (203) 225-5111

Contact: Barbara W. Bennett, Personnel Manager

Several area locations, including Farmington, New Britain and Plantsville, CT. A worldwide marketer and manufacturer of quality tools for do-it-yourselfers and professionals, including carpenters, mechanics, electricians, plumbers, and industrial maintenance engineers. Manufactures hardware and complementary products for the home, the factory, and the building industry. Its industry segments are: Consumer Products, including hand tools, fasteners, home hardware, garage door openers, and residential entry doors for the do-it-yourself market; Builders' Products, which provides products to the professional construction industry, including architectural and residential hardware, pedestrian power-operated doors, insulated steel entry doors, garage doors and openers, and automatic parking gates and commercial doors; and Industrial products, which includes products sold to industrial and automotive customers, including professional hand tools, 'MAC' mechanics' tools, air tools, hydraulic tools, industrial storage systems, and industrial hardware and stampings. Plants are located throughout the United States (significant Connecticut operations), and in more than 30 foreign countries. Corporate headquarters location. New York Stock Exchange. International: Australia, Belgium, Brazil, Canada, Colombia, Denmark, England, Finland, France, Germany, Greece, Hong Kong, Italy, Mexico, Netherlands, New Zealand, Norway, Philippines, Portugal, Singapore, Taiwan.

Delaware

Chrysler Corporation
500 S. College Ave.
Newark, DE 19713-1302
Tel: (302) 453-5113

Contact: Mrs. Delores Perna, Personnel Administrator

An auto assembly warehouse plant for the major manufacturer of automobile parts for Chrysler dealers. Corporate headquarters location: Detroit, MI. International: Canada, England, Israel, Japan, Mexico, Switzerland.

E.I. Du Pont de Nemours and Company
1007 Market St.
Wilmington, DE 19898
Tel: (302) 774-1000

Contact: D. John Ogren, Senior Vice President, Human Resources

A major corporation whose diverse activities include the manufacture of biomedical products; the manufacture of industrial and consumer products, such as photographic, data-recording and video devices; the production of man-made fiber products, with applications in a variety of consumer and commercial industries; the production of polyier products, such as plastic resins, elastomers and films; the production of agricultural and industrial chemicals, such as herbicides and insecticides, and pigments, fluorochemicals, petroleum additives and mineral acids; the exploration for and production of crude oil and natural gas, internationally; the refining, marketing and downstream transportation of petroleum; and the mining and distribution of steam and metallurgical coals, exported mainly to overseas steel producers. Corporate headquarters location. International: Argentina, Australia, Belgium, Brazil, Canada, Colombia, England, Finland, Germany, Guatemala, Hong Kong, Ireland, Japan, Mexico, Netherlands, New Zealand, Norway, Peru, Singapore, Spain, Sweden, Switzerland, Taiwan, Thailand, Venezuela.

J.C. Penney Co.
5000 Dover Mall
Dover, DE 19901
Tel: (302) 674-4200
Contact: Patricia Collins, Personnel Assistant

A national company that operates a chain of department stores and thrift drug stores, and that also provides banking services. Area locations in Wilmington [(302) 998-1131] and Newark [(302) 366-7680]. International: Belgium, Italy.

District of Columbia

Carlton Hotel [a Sheraton property]
923 16th St. NW
Washington, DC 20006
Tel: (202) 638-2626
Contact: Personnel Director

A major downtown hotel facility, with 250 rooms and complete dining facilities. Part of the international ITT hotel chain, offering hotel, dining, convention, and meeting facilities at major metropolitan locations throughout the world. Corporate headquarters: ITT Corporation, New York, NY. Common positions include: Accountant; Administrator; Computer Programmer; Credit Manager; Customer Service Representative; Electrical Engineer; Mechanical Engineer; Hotel Manager/Assistant Manager; Department Manager; General Manager; Management Trainee; Personnel and Labor Relations Specialist; Public Relations Worker; Purchasing Agent; Sales Representative; Systems Analyst. Principal educational backgrounds sought: Accounting; Business Administration; Communications; Computer Science; Economics; Engineering; Finance; Liberal Arts; Marketing; Mathematics. International: Argentina, Australia, Austria, Bahamas, Bahrain, Belgium, Bermuda, Bolivia, Brazil, Cameroon, Canada, Chile, China, Colombia, Costa Rica, Cyprus, Denmark, Dominican Republic, Ecuador, Egypt, El Salvador, England, Finland, France, Germany, Greece, Guatemala, India, Italy, Mexico, Spain, Sweden, Thailand, Venezuela, and others.

Florida

Walt Disney World
P.O. Box 10000
Lake Buena Vista, FL 32830-1000
Tel: (407) 824-2222
Contact: Professional Staffing Department

Corporate office for the internationally renowned theme park. International: Belgium, Canada, Denmark, England, France, Germany, Italy, Japan, Portugal, Spain.

Motorola Radio Products Group
8000 W. Sunrise Blvd.
Plantation, FL 33322
Tel: (305) 723-5700
Contact: Jerry Vetter, Staffing Manager

Manufacturers of two-way radios, special applications products and pagers for commercial and government markets. Common positions include: Accountant;

Computer Programmer; Chemical Engineer; Electrical Engineer; Industrial Engineer; Mechanical Engineer; Metallurgical Engineer; Financial Analyst; Industrial Designer; Marketing Specialist; Personnel and Labor Relations Specialist; Purchasing Agent; Systems Analyst; Technical Writer/Editor. Principal educational backgrounds sought: Accounting; Chemistry; Computer Science; Engineering; Finance; Marketing. Company benefits include: Medical, dental, and life insurance; pension plan; tuition assistance; disability coverage; profit sharing; employee discounts; savings plan. Corporate headquarters location: Schaumburg, IL. Operations at this facility include: Divisional headquarters; manufacturing; research/development; administration. New York Stock Exchange. International: Australia, Austria, Belgium, Canada, Costa Rica, Denmark, England, France, Germany, Hong Kong, Ireland, Japan, Korea, Malaysia, Mexico, Netherlands, Norway, Philippines, Singapore, Spain, Sweden, Switzerland, Taiwan.

Ryder Systems, Inc.
3600 NW 82nd Ave.
Miami, FL 33166
Tel: (305) 593-4396

Contact: Sam Hines, Manager, Staffing

Ryder is a well-known worldwide supplier of highway transportation services, including commercial truck rentals. Through its Caledonian Airmotive and Aviall divisions, Ryder provides jet engine maintenance service for major carriers and is a leading distributor of aviation parts. International: Canada, Germany, Mexico, United Kingdom.

Sensormatic Electronics Corporation
500 NW 12th Ave.
Deerfield Beach, FL 33442
Tel: (305) 420-2000

Contact: Larry Smith, Director, Human Resources. Mailed inquiries only.

Manufacturing and engineering of electronic article surveillance equipment and sensor vision. Common positions include: Accountant; Blue-Collar Worker Supervisor; Buyer; Computer Programmer; Customer Service Representative; Draftsperson; Electrical Engineer; Industrial Engineer; Mechanical Engineer; Financial Analyst; Industrial Designer; Department Manager; Management Trainee; Operations/Production Manager; Personnel and Labor Relations Specialist; Purchasing Agent; Quality Control Supervisor; Sales Representative; Systems Analyst. Principal educational backgrounds sought: Accounting; Business Administration; Communications; Computer Science; Engineering; Finance; Marketing. Company benefits include: Medical insurance; dental insurance; pension plan; life insurance; tuition assistance; disability coverage; profit sharing. Corporate headquarters location. Operations at this facility include: Manufacturing; research/development; administration; service; sales. International: Austria, Belgium,

France, Germany, Spain, Switzerland.

Georgia

The Coca-Cola Company
P.O. Drawer 1734
Atlanta, GA 30301
Tel: (404) 676-2121

Contact: Michael W. Walters, Vice President, Human Resources

One of the world's leading producers of soft drinks; among the world's largest citrus processors; and the third largest wine company in the United States. Company operates nationwide in two primary areas: Soft Drink Sector (Coca-Cola, Tab, Sprite, Fresca, and many others); and Food and Wine Sector (Minute Maid orange juice, Hi-C drinks, Presto plastic wraps and films, Taylor wines, Sterling wines, Great Western sparkling wines, and other products). Corporate headquarters location. International: Argentina, Australia, Bahamas, Belgium, Bermuda, Brazil, Cameroon, China, Colombia, Costa Rica, Denmark, Ecuador, Finland, Greece, Guatemala, Hong Kong, India, Italy, Japan, Kenya, Korea, Mexico, Morocco, Netherlands, New Zealand, Norway, Pakistan, Panama, Peru, Philippines, Spain, Sweden, Switzerland, Thailand, Tunisia, Turkey, Uruguay, Venezuela, Zimbabwe.

Container Corporation of America
5853 E. Ponce de Leon Ave.
Stone Mountain, GA 30083
Tel: (770) 469-4111

Contact: Jim Logan, Employee Relations Manager

Produces corrugated and fiber boxes. Nationally, company is one of the world's largest producers of paperboard packaging, with major manufacturing facilities located throughout the United States and throughout the world. Some major products include shipping containers, folding cartons, composite cans, plastic drums, and many others. A major operating subsidiary of Mobil Corporation (New York, NY). International: Colombia, Italy, Mexico, Netherlands, Spain, Venezuela.

Hawaii

Chevron USA (Hawaii Division)
1001 Bishop St.
Pauahi Tower, Suite 1000
Honolulu, HI 96813
Tel: (808) 527-2700

Contact: Liz Ayau, Personnel Specialist

Parent company, Chevron Corporation, refines and sells petroleum. Chevron Chemical (Ortho gardening and home products) is a subsidiary. International: Saudi Arabia, Uruguay.

Dillingham Construction Pacific Rim
P.O. Box 4088
Honolulu, HI 96812
Tel: (808) 735-3211

Contact: Evelyn Kuniyoshi, Vice President, Human Resources and Communication

A general construction contractor. Parent company, Dillingham Construction, is in Pleasanton, CA. Other subsidiaries include: Dillingham Construction Guam,

Dillingham Construction (H.K.), Hawaiian Dredging & Construction, HD&C Glass, Hawaiian Bitumuls & Paving, Hawaiian Rock Products. Common positions include: Civil Engineer; Mechanical Engineer; Construction Engineer. Principal educational background sought: Engineering. Company benefits include: Medical, dental and life insurance; pension plan; tuition assistance; disability coverage; profit sharing; savings plan. Corporate headquarters location: Pleasanton, CA. Operations at this facility include: Divisional headquarters. International: Guam.

Idaho

Boise Cascade Corporation
One Jefferson Sq.
Boise, ID 83728-0001
Tel: (208) 384-6161

Contact: Alice E. Hennessey, Senior Vice President, Human Resources

An integrated forest products company, engaged principally in the manufacture, distribution and sale of paper, office products, and building products and in the management of timberland resources to support these operations. Common positions include: Accountant; Computer Programmer; Chemical Engineer; Electrical Engineer; Mechanical Engineer; Financial Analyst; Forester; Management Trainee; Operations/Production Manager; Marketing Specialist; Sales Representative. Principal educational backgrounds sought: Accounting; Business Administration; Computer Science; Engineering; Finance; Marketing.

Company benefits include: Medical, dental, and life insurance; pension plan; tuition assistance, disability coverage; profit sharing; savings plan. Operations at this facility: divisional headquarters; administration. New York Stock Exchange. International: Austria, Canada, France, Germany.

Sears, Roebuck & Company
300 N. Milwaukee
Boise, ID 83788
Tel: (208) 322-5100

Contact: Mitzi Holt, Personnel Director

Formerly known primarily for its chain of department stores, Sears, Roebuck & Company is a leader in merchandising, insurance (Allstate), real estate, and financial services (Dean Witter). Corporate headquarters: Hoffman Estates, IL. International: Canada, Mexico, Japan, Germany.

Illinois

Brunswick Corporation
One N. Field Ct.
Lake Forest, IL 60045-4811
Tel: (708) 735-4700

Contact: Patrick J. Gannon, Director, Human Resources

Several area locations including: Niles, Morton Grove, Libertyville, St. Charles. A multi-industry firm engaged primarily in four industry segments: Technical Group, including manufacturing facilities in Niles, Morton Grove, and St. Charles (Vapor Division), Skokie (Defense Division and Technetics Division), and Libertyville (Ozite Division); Medical Group (manufactures disposable equipment, industrial gloves, diagnostic equipment, and other products—no Illinois facilities); Marine Power Group (inboard and outboard motors, marine accessories—no Illinois facilities); and the Recreation Group, with headquarters for more than 250 recreation centers (bowling alleys) located in Skokie, as well as the group's Brunswick and Consumer Divisions, which produce a variety of bowling products, billiard tables, and other recreational products. The Technical Group's Vapor Division produces process control products; Defense Division manufactures products such as motor cases and pressure vessels, fire detection systems, launch and weapons systems, honeycomb and metal-bonded structures, camouflage, and others; Technetics produces industrial filters, valves, jet engine seals, metal fiber products, golf club shafts, and other products; Ozite Division produces residential and commercial carpets, and specialty automotive and industrial coverings. Corporate headquarters location. New York Stock Exchange. International: Argentina, Belgium, Brazil, Canada, Guatemala, Japan, Korea, Mexico, Switzerland.

Caterpillar, Inc.
100 NE Adams St.
Peoria, IL 61629-7310
Tel: (309) 675-1000

Contact: Wayne M. Zimmerman, Vice President, Human Resources

A multinational company that designs, manufactures and markets earthmoving equipment, materials handling equipment, and diesel engines. Common positions include: Blue-Collar Worker Supervisor; Electrical Engineer; Metallurgical Engineer (company has current hiring freeze). Principal educational backgrounds sought: Accounting; Computer Science; Engineering. Company benefits include: Medical insurance; dental insurance; pension plan; life insurance; tuition assistance; disability coverage; profit sharing; savings plan. Operations at this facility include: Manufacturing. Corporate headquarters location: Peoria, IL. New York Stock Exchange. International: Australia, Belgium, Brazil, Canada, England, France, Hong Kong, India, Japan, Mexico, Scotland, Singapore, Switzerland.

Mead Container
7601 S. 78th Ave.
Bridgeview, IL 60455
Tel: (708) 458-8100

Contact: Beverly Grybas, Administrative Manager.

Several area locations including: Chicago (2) and Hillside. A multi-industry firm with segments operating primarily in the forest products industry (paper, pulp, lumber, etc.), but also in such areas as balance-engineered castings, molded rubber parts, distribution of piping and electrical supplies, and the manufacture of advanced digital information systems. Forest products segment includes two major subsidiaries: Brunswick Pulp and Paper, and Northwood Forest Industries. Bridgeview facility produces corrugated shipping containers; facility at 9540 S. Dorchester Ave., Chicago (60628) produces folding cartons; subsidiary facility (Birmingham and Prosser) at

125 Fencl Ln., Hillside (60162) is responsible for distributing paper products; and subsidiary Ft. Dearborn Paper Company, 2901 W. 36th Pl., Chicago (60632) produces and converts paper. Parent company is divided into five operating segments: Paper, Paperboard, Consumer and Distribution, Industrial Products, and Advanced Systems. Corporate headquarters location: Dayton, OH. International: Canada, England, France, Germany, Italy, Japan, Netherlands, Switzerland.

Owens-Illinois, Inc./Machine Division
315 Tolle Ln.
Godfrey, IL 62035
Tel: (618) 466-8811

Contact: Personnel Department

One of several area division of the well-known diversified manufacturer of packaging products. Company's principal products are glass containers, although the company also produces and sells containerboard, corrugated containers, printing plates and ink, plywood and dimension lumber, blown plastic containers, plastic beverage bottles, plastic drums, metal and plastic closures, tamper-resistant closures, plastic and glass prescription containers, pharmaceutical items, labels, and multipack plastic carriers for containers. Specialized glass products made and sold by the company include Libbey Tumblers, stemware, and decorative glassware, television bulbs for picture tubes, and Kimble scientific and laboratory ware. Some overseas affiliates also manufacture flat glass and related products. International: Australia, Brazil, Canada, Colombia, Germany, Italy, Japan, Singapore, Switzerland, Venezuela.

Ozite Corporation
1755 Butterfield Rd.
Libertyville, IL 60048
Tel: (708) 362-8210

Contact: Beverly Mangan, Chief Personnel Manager

Manufactures commercial, automotive, and industrial carpeting and wall covering. Corporate headquarters location. Common positions include: Accountant; Administrator; Bank Officer/Manager; Blue-Collar Worker Supervisor; Buyer; Chemist; Claim Representative; Computer Programmer; Credit Manager; Customer Service Representative; Industrial Engineer; Personnel and Labor Relations Specialist; Purchasing Agent; Quality Control Supervisor; Sales Representative. Principal educational backgrounds sought: Accounting; Business Administration; Engineering; Liberal Arts; Marketing. Company benefits include: Medical insurance; dental insurance; pension plan; life insurance; tuition assistance; disability coverage; profit sharing; employee discounts; savings plan. International: Canada, Saudi Arabia.

Sara Lee
Three First National Plaza
70 W. Madison
Chicago, IL 60602
Tel: (312) 726-2600

Contact: Toni Lang, Vice President, Human Resources

The corporate office of the cake, cake-mix, and dessert snacks producer. International: Australia, France, Netherlands.

Skil-Bosch Corporation
4300 W. Peterson Ave.
Chicago, IL 60646
Tel: (312) 286-7330

Contact: George Pike, Manager of Human Resources

Several area locations including: Skokie and Elk Grove Village. Manufacturers of hand and power tools. A subsidiary of Emerson Electric Company. Corporate headquarters location. International: Australia, Austria, Mexico, Netherlands, Sweden, Switzerland.

Indiana

Bristol-Myers U.S. Pharmaceutical and Nutrition
400 W. Lloyd Expwy.
Evansville, IN 47721
Tel: (812) 429-5000

Contact: Employment Office

Engaged in the research, manufacture, and marketing of pharmaceutical and nutritional products for the consumer and pharmaceutical markets. Operations include administration, marketing, and research at the Bristol Myers USPNG Research Center. Common positions include: Accountant; Biochemist; Chemist; Computer Programmer; Biomedical Engineer; Chemical Engineer; Electrical Engineer; Industrial Engineer; Mechanical Engineer; Financial Analyst; Personnel and Labor Relations Specialist; Quality Control Supervisor; Sales Representative; Statistician; Systems Analyst; Technical Writer/Editor. Principal educational backgrounds sought: Accounting; Chemistry; Computer Science; Engineering; Marketing (MBA). Company benefits include: Medical insurance; dental insurance; life insurance; tuition assistance; disability coverage; employee discounts; savings plan; pension plan. Corporate headquarters located in New York, NY. New York Stock Exchange. International: Egypt, Hong Kong, Italy, Japan, Panama, Spain, Venezuela.

Eli Lilly and Company
Lilly Corporate Center
Indianapolis, IN 46285
Tel: (317) 276-2000

Contact: Pedro P. Granadillo, Vice President, Human Resources

A major researcher and producer of pharmaceuticals, cosmetics, medical instrument systems and animal health products. International: Argentina, Australia, Austria, Belgium, Brazil, Canada, Chile, Colombia, Denmark, England, France, Germany, Greece, Guatemala, Italy, Japan, Korea, Malaysia, Mexico, Netherlands, New Zealand, Peru, Philippines, Singapore, Switzerland, Taiwan, Thailand, Venezuela.

Stewart-Warner Corp./South Wind Division
5701 Fortune Circle S., Suite J
Indianapolis, IN 46221-5534
Tel: (317) 243-7367

Contact: Manager of Personnel

Develops, manufactures and markets heat transfer and combustion heating equipment. Primary customers include commercial and military aircraft manufacturers, truck, off-the-road, and bus manufacturers. Divisional headquarters. Operations include: Manufacturing; research/development; administration; sales. Corporate headquarters location. Common positions include: Accountant; Computer Programmer; Industrial Engineer; Mechanical Engineer; Financial Analyst; Department Manager; Operations/Production Manager; Marketing Specialist; Sales Representative; Systems Analyst. Principal educational backgrounds sought: Accounting; Business Administration; Computer Science; Engineering; Finance; Marketing. Company benefits include: Medical insurance; pension plan; life insurance; tuition assistance; credit union. International: Australia, England, Germany, India, Italy, Mexico.

Iowa

Matco
811 E. Main
Marshalltown, IA 50158
Tel: (515) 752-4291

Contact: Dick White, Personnel

Manufacturer of commercial steam and hot water systems and components. Corporate headquarters location: West Hartford, CT. Operations include: Manufacturing; service; sales. Common positions include: Accountant; Administrator; Advertising Worker; Blue-Collar Worker Supervisor; Buyer; Draftsperson; Engineer; Industrial Engineer; Mechanical Engineer; Manager; Branch Manager; Department Manager; General Manager; Management Trainee; Operations/Production Manager; Marketing Specialist; Personnel and Labor Relations Specialist; Purchasing Agent. Principal educational backgrounds sought: Accounting; Business Administration; Engineering; Marketing. Company benefits include: Medical insurance; pension plan; life insurance; tuition assistance; disability coverage; employee discounts; savings plan. International: Canada, England, Germany.

Norplex Division/Allied Signal
P.O. Box 977
N.E. Country Rd.
Postville, IA 52162
Tel: (319) 864-7321

Contact: Personnel Director

Engaged in the manufacture of copper clad and unclad plastic laminates. Parent company, Allied Signal Corporation, serves a broad spectrum of industries through its more than 40 strategic businesses, which are grouped into five sectors: Aerospace; Automotive; Chemical; Industrial and Technology; and Oil and Gas. Allied Signal is one of the nation's largest industrial organizations, and has 115,000 employees in over 30 countries. Corporate headquarters location: Morristown, NJ. International: Brazil, China, France, Japan.

Rockwell International/Avionics Group
400 Collins Rd. NE
Cedar Rapids, IA 52498
Tel: (800) 835-9355

Contact: John P. Gorman, Professional Staffing Specialist

Operates three divisions—Collins Air Transport Division, Collins General Aviation Division, and Collins Government Avionics

Division—which provide aviation electronics products, systems and services to the air transport, business and general aviation, and military and government aircraft markets worldwide. Common positions include: Electrical Engineer; Mechanical Engineer; Marketing Specialist. Principal educational backgrounds sought: Computer Science; Engineering. Company benefits include: Medical insurance; dental insurance; pension plan; life insurance; tuition assistance; disability coverage; employee discounts; savings plan; company pharmacy; child care center; recreation center. Corporate headquarters location: El Segundo, CA. Parent company: Rockwell International. Operations at this facility include: Group headquarters; manufacturing; research/development; administration; service; sales. New York Stock Exchange. International: Australia, Belgium, Brazil, Canada, Egypt, England, France, Germany, Hong Kong, Israel, Italy, Japan, Korea, Mexico, Philippines, Saudi Arabia, Singapore, Spain, Taiwan.

BTR Sealing Systems
P.O. Box 2230
3200 Main St.
Keokuk, IA 52632
Tel: (319) 524-2806

Contact: Darlene Busey, Employment/Training Supervisor.

A diversified manufacturer serving the auto, industrial, and consumer markets. Produces automotive equipment and aftermarket parts. Corporate headquarters location: Toledo, OH. Operations include: Manufacturing. New York Stock Exchange. Common positions include: Accountant; Blue-Collar Worker Supervisor; Chemist; Computer Programmer; Draftsperson; Engineer; Electrical Engineer; Industrial Engineer; Mechanical Engineer; Financial Analyst; Management Trainee; Operations/Production Manager; Personnel and Labor Relations Specialist; Quality Control Supervisor; Statistician; Transportation and Traffic Specialist. Principal educational backgrounds sought: Accounting; Business Administration; Chemistry; Computer Science; Engineering; Finance; Liberal Arts. Company benefits include: Medical insurance; dental insurance; life insurance; pension plan; tuition assistance; disability coverage; profit sharing; employee discounts; savings plan. International: Canada, England, France, Mexico.

Kansas

Cessna Aircraft Company
P.O. Box 7704
Wichita, KS 67277
Tel: (316) 941-6000

Contact: Dick Quattlebaum, Personnel

Engaged in the engineering, fabrication, assembly, and marketing of light commercial and business aircraft. Primary customers are corporations with limited sales to individuals. Common positions include: Accountant; Buyer; Computer Programmer; Draftsperson; Aerospace Engineer; Electrical Engineer; Industrial Engineer; Mechanical Engineer;

Personnel and Labor Relations Specialist; Systems Analyst; Technical Writer/Editor. Principal educational backgrounds sought: Accounting; Computer Science; Engineering; Marketing. Company benefits include: Medical, dental, and life insurance; pension plan; tuition assistance; disability coverage; savings plan. Corporate headquarters location. Parent company: General Dynamics. Operations at this facility include: Divisional headquarters; manufacturing; research/development; administration; service; sales. International: France, Scotland.

Shullep International, Inc.
Box 1287
County Rd. 319
McPherson KS 67460
Tel: (316) 241-6260

Contact: Georgeanne Peterson, Personnel Director

A manufacturer and distributor of fiberglass insulation products. International: Argentina, Australia, Belgium, Bermuda, Canada, England, France, Germany, Italy, Japan, Mexico, Saudi Arabia, Singapore, Spain, United Arab Emirates, Venezuela, Zaire.

Drew Industrials
3155 Fiberglass Rd.
Kansas City, KS 06115
Tel: (913) 621-6410

Contact: Ronald W. Major, Director/Personnel and Safety

A water treatment company. A subsidiary of Olin Corporation (Stamford, CT). Divisional headquarters. New York Stock Exchange. Common positions include: Accountant; Computer Programmer; Department Manager; General Manager; Marketing Specialist; Purchasing Agent; Sales Representative. Principal educational backgrounds sought: Chemistry; Marketing. Company benefits include: Medical, dental and life insurance; pension plan; tuition assistance; disability coverage; employee discounts; savings plan. International: Australia, Belgium, Colombia, England, France, Germany, Ireland, Japan, Mexico, New Zealand, Singapore, Spain, Taiwan, Venezuela.

Kentucky

Ashland, Inc.
1000 Ashland Dr.
Russell, KY 41169
Tel: (606) 329-3333

Contact: Philip W. Block, Vice President, Human Resources

Ashland Oil, the 60th largest industrial company in the United States, is a large diversified corporation with a strong base in its traditional refining, marketing, and transportation businesses and an equally strong group of nonrefining operations. These operations include: Retail marketing, motor oil marketing, chemicals, engineering and construction, and oil and gas exploration and production. Common positions include: Accountant; Attorney; Chemist; Computer Programmer; Chemical Engineer; Civil Engineer; Electrical Engineer; Industrial Engineer; Sales Representative; Systems Analyst.

Principal educational backgrounds sought: Accounting; Business Administration; Chemistry; Computer Science; Engineering; Marketing. Company benefits include: Medical insurance; dental insurance; pension plan; life insurance; tuition assistance; disability coverage; savings plan; employee stock ownership plan; credit union. Corporate headquarters location. Operations at this facility include: Divisional headquarters; manufacturing; research/development. Company is listed on the New York Stock Exchange. International: England, India.

Brown & Williamson Tobacco Corporation
P.O. Box 35090
Louisville, KY 40232
Tel: (501) 568-7000

Contact: Office of Human Resources

Researches, develops, manufactures, and markets tobacco products, principally cigarettes. Emphasis is on research, development, and engineering; finance; management information systems; and marketing. Division of BATUS, subsidiary of British American Industries, London, England. Corporate headquarters location. Common positions include: Accountant; Attorney; Buyer; Chemist; Computer Programmer; Engineer; Chemical Engineer; Civil Engineer; Electrical Engineer; Industrial Engineer; Mechanical Engineer; Food Technologist; Marketing Specialist; Physicist; Statistician; Systems Analyst. Principal educational backgrounds sought: Business Administration; Chemistry; Computer Science; Engineering; Finance; Marketing; Mathematics. Company benefits include: Medical, dental, and life insurance; pension plan; tuition assistance; disability coverage; profit sharing; savings plan. International: Costa Rica, Turkey.

Sargent & Greenleaf, Inc.
P.O. Box 930
Nicholasville, KY 40340-0930
Tel: (606) 885-9411

Contact: Ms. Shirlean Herron, Industrial Relations Manager

Produces high security locks, access controls and devices. Corporate headquarters location. Operations include: Manufacturing; research/development; administration; service; sales. Common positions include: Accountant; Blue-Collar Worker Supervisor; Buyer; Computer Programmer; Credit Manager; Customer Service Representative; Draftsperson; Engineer; Industrial Engineer; Mechanical Engineer; Financial Analyst; Industrial Designer; Department Manager; General Manager; Operations/Production Manager; Marketing Specialist; Personnel and Labor Relations Specialist; Purchasing Agent; Quality Control Supervisor; Sales Representative; Systems Analyst. Principal educational backgrounds sought: Accounting; Business Administration; Engineering; Finance; Marketing. Company benefits include: Medical insurance; pension plan; life insurance; tuition assistance; disability coverage. International: England, Switzerland.

Louisiana

Allied Chemical/Menickens
P.O. Box 2830
Baton Rouge, LA 70821
Tel: (504) 383-5222
Contact: Personnel Director

An area producer of chemicals, including genetron, muriatic acid, zinc, hydrofluoric acid, sulfuric acid, oleum, and calcium chloride. Parent company, Allied Signal Corporation, serves a broad spectrum of industries through its more than 40 strategic businesses, which are grouped into five sectors: Aerospace; Automotive; Chemical; Industrial and Technology; and Oil and Gas. Allied Signal is one of the nation's largest industrial organizations, and has 115,000 employees in over 30 countries. Corporate headquarters location: Morristown, NJ. International: Australia, Belgium, Canada, England, Hong Kong, Mexico, New Zealand, Switzerland, Venezuela.

Grace Offshore
701 Poydras, Suite 4700
New Orleans, LA 70139
Tel: (504) 584-9600
Contact: Personnel Department

Engaged in offshore oil well workover and completion services. Parent company, W. R. Grace & Co., is a diversified worldwide enterprise consisting of specialty and agricultural chemicals, energy production and services, retailing, restaurants, and other businesses; the firm operates over 2,500 facilities in 47 states and 42 foreign countries and employs 80,000 people. Corporate headquarters location: New York, NY. International: Argentina, Australia, Brazil, Canada, Denmark, England, Finland, France, Germany, Greece, Guatemala, Hong Kong, Ivory Coast, Japan, Malaysia, Mexico, New Zealand, Norway, Philippines, Portugal, Singapore, Spain, Sweden, Switzerland, Venezuela.

Maine

Burnham & Morrill Division/ IC Industries
One Beanpot Circle
Portland, ME 04104
Tel: (207) 772-8341
Contact: Mindy Geisser, Personnel

A manufacturer of a variety of food products, including brown bread, puddings, and baked beans. Corporate headquarters location: Chicago, IL. International: Australia, China, Colombia, India, Italy, Malaysia, Mexico, New Zealand, Philippines, Switzerland, Venezuela.

Maryland

The Black & Decker Corporation
701 E. Joppa Rd.
Towson MD 21286
Tel: (410) 716-3900
Contact: Leonard A. Strom, Vice President, Human Resources

Engaged in manufacturing, selling, and servicing electric, pneumatic, and gasoline-powered tools, including accessories generally used in homes and home workshops, for lawn care and maintenance, in timbering, in the service and maintenance trades, and on farms. International: Argentina, Australia, Austria, Belgium, Brazil, Canada, China, Colombia, Costa Rica, Denmark, Ecuador, El Salvador, England, Finland, Germany, Greece, Hong Kong, India, Ireland, Israel, Italy, Kenya, Korea, Mexico, Netherlands, New Zealand, Nigeria, Norway, Panama, Portugal, Singapore, Spain, Sweden, Switzerland, Taiwan, Venezuela, Yugoslavia, Zambia.

Dresser Industries, Inc./ Wayne Division
P.O. Box 1859
124 W. College Ave.
Salisbury, MD 21801
Tel: (301) 546-6623

Contact: Linas Orentas, Human Resources Administrator

Develops, manufacturers, markets and services Globe automobile hoists and Wayne gasoline dispensing systems for the domestic and export markets. Common positions include: Accountant; Administrator; Advertising Worker; Blue-Collar Worker Supervisor; Buyer; Computer Programmer; Credit Manager; Customer Service Representative; Draftsperson; Economist; Industrial Engineer; Mechanical Engineer; Operations/Production Manager; Marketing Specialist; Personnel and Labor Relations Specialist; Public Relations Worker; Purchasing Agent; Quality Control Supervisor; Sales Representative; Systems Analyst; Technical Writer/Editor; Tool Engineer; Design Engineer; Inventory Control; Export Personnel. Principal educational backgrounds sought: Accounting; Business Administration; Communications; Computer Science; Economics; Engineering; Finance; Liberal Arts; Marketing; Mathematics; Physics. Company benefits include: Medical insurance; dental insurance; pension plan; life insurance; tuition assistance; disability coverage; savings plan. Corporate headquarters location: Dallas, TX. Operations at this facility include: Divisional headquarters; manufacturing; research/development; administration; service; sales. New York Stock Exchange. International: Argentina, Australia, Belgium, Brazil, Canada, Chile, Colombia, China, England, Germany, Greece, Hong Kong, Indonesia, Italy, Japan, Kuwait, Luxemborg, Mexico, Netherlands, Nigeria, Norway, Peru, Saudi Arabia, Scotland, Singapore, Spain, Sweden, Switzerland, Thailand, Taiwan, USSR, Venezuela.

National Can Corporation
2010 Reservoir Rd.
Sparrows Point, MD 21219
Tel: (301) 477-3131

Contact: Contact Personnel

Produces metal cans, including sanitary containers, and beverage and other containers. Nationally, company is one of the world's leading manufacturers of packaging products, manufacturing and marketing aluminum and steel cans, glass and plastic blow-molded containers, steel crowns, aluminum closures, and metal and plastic caps for a variety of end-uses. Operates more than 70 manufacturing and support facilities in 10 countries and Puerto Rico. Principal markets include the beer, soft drink, and food processing industries around the world. Corporate headquarters location: Chicago, IL. New York Stock Exchange. International: England, Greece.

Weyerhauser
3400 E. Biddle St.
Baltimore, MD 21213
Tel: (410) 327-7376

Contact: Office of Human Resources

Manufactures corrugated fiber cartons. Nationally, company is an international firm specializing in the manufacture of high-quality papers for communications, packaging, and high-technology applications. Products include packaging for both industrial and consumer markets, and envelopes (where company is among the world's largest producers). Other area facilities in Luke, Baltimore, Pasadena, and Laurel, MD. Corporate headquarters location: New York, NY. International: Australia, Belgium, Brazil.

Massachusetts

Borg-Warner Corporation/ New Bedford Gear
Theodore Rice Blvd.
Industrial Park
New Bedford, MA 02745
Tel: (508) 995-2616

Contact: Paul Humason, Personnel Manager

The New Bedford Gear Division specializes in metal cutting, primarily for transmission gears and timing sprockets for automobiles. Nationally, the company is a $2.7 billion diversified manufacturing and services firm, with some 50 divisions operating in 20 countries on six continents. Most products are made for manufacturers serving the transportation, construction, consumer products, machinery, agribusiness, and energy markets. The company also has extensive operations that provide financial and protective services for business. The company's major divisions are: Air Conditioning, primarily through subsidiary York Air Conditioning; Chemicals and Plastics, including a family of engineering thermoplastics designed for abuse-resistance in hundreds of consumer products, as well as other resin and chemical products; Financial Services, primarily operating through Borg-Warner Acceptance Corporation, one of the leading independent finance companies in the United States; Protective Services, which operates through subsidiary Baker Industries, parent company of Wells Fargo armored, alarm, and guard services, and Pony Express courier service; Energy and Industrial Equipment, whose major products include centrifugal pumps for power generating plants, pipelines, water plants, and irrigation, precision seals for pumps and compressors, valves, automotive and industrial chain, bearings, and a wide range of power transmission products, as well as other products; and Transportation Equipment, supplied to original equipment manufacturers and the automotive aftermarket, including automatic and manual transmissions and transmission components, carburetion and ignition equipment, clutches, four-wheel drive units, axles, emission controls, and radiators. These components are supplied for passenger cars, trucks, and off-highway vehicles and equipment. Corporate headquarters location: Chicago, IL. New York Stock Exchange. International: Argentina, Australia, Austria, Belgium, Brazil, Canada, England, France, Germany, Italy, Japan, Mexico, Netherlands, New Zealand, Panama, Scotland, Singapore, Spain, Venezuela.

Arthur D. Little, Inc.
25 Acorn Pk.
Cambridge, MA 02140
Tel: (617) 498-5000

Contact: A. Friedman, Senior Vice President, Human Resources

A worldwide contract research, engineering, and management consulting organization whose business is to help industry, institutions, and governments manage the problems and opportunities created by change. Professional staff includes some 1,400 members, representing experts in hundreds of different disciplines and industries; also has approximately 450 specialized consultants, drawn largely from universities and colleges. Affiliated business units include: Arthur D. Little Systems (Burlington), which specializes in the development of computer software, computer systems design, and implementation; Delphi Associates (Lowell—a subsidiary of ADL Systems); Pilgrim Health Applications (Lowell), which processes medical claims for third-party payment; and a wide range of other companies providing diverse consulting services. Corporate headquarters location. International: Belgium, Brazil, Canada, England, France, Germany, Greece, Portugal, Saudi Arabia, Spain.

Raytheon Company
141 Spring St.
Lexington, MA 02173
Tel: (617) 862-6600

Contact: Christopher L. Hoffman, Senior Vice President, Human Resources

A major high-technology electronics firm, actively engaged in the conception, development, manufacture, and sale of electronic systems and subsystems, equipment, and components for government and commercial use. Corporate headquarters location. New York Stock Exchange. International: Argentina, Australia, Belgium, Brazil, Canada, Chile, Denmark, Egypt, England, France, Germany, Hong Kong, Israel, Italy, Japan, Kenya, Mexico, Netherlands, New Zealand, Saudi Arabia, Singapore, Spain, Switzerland, Taiwan, Turkey, Venezuela.

Stone & Webster Engineering
P.O. Box 2325
Boston, MA 02107
Tel: (617) 589-5111

Contact: Nancy Chamberlain, Professional Employment Representative

Provides a wide range of engineering consulting services, including design and construction, on large-scale projects, primarily for the power generation industry. Also provides consulting services for other industries, including petrochemicals, industrial manufacturing, and others. Offices located throughout the United States and in some international locations. Employs 12,000 people worldwide. Corporate headquarters location. International: Canada, England, France, Indonesia, Korea, Malaysia, Mexico, Saudi Arabia, United Arab Emirates.

Michigan

Emhart Corporation/Warren Division
P.O. Box 868
Mount Clemens, MI 48403
Tel: (810) 949-0440

Contact: Mr. Morris, Director of Human Resources

A leading area manufacturer of plastic products. Employs 500. International: Argentina, Australia, Austria, Belgium, Brazil, Canada, Chile, Denmark, Egypt, Finland, France, Germany, Hong Kong, Ireland, Italy, Japan, Mexico, Netherlands, New Zealand, Norway, Portugal, Singapore, Spain, Sweden, Switzerland, Taiwan.

Johnson Control, Inc. Automotive Systems Group
2455 S. Industrial Way, Ste. C
Ann Arbor, MI 48108
Tel: (313) 769-7979

Contact: Mike Cercone, Director, Personnel

Engaged in the manufacture of automotive seating and body systems for the automotive industry. Employs over 5,000. Common positions include: Accountant; Administrator; Chemist; Computer Programmer; Customer Service Representative; Draftsperson; Industrial Engineer; Mechanical Engineer; Financial Analyst; Industrial Designer; Department Manager; General Manager; Personnel and Labor Relations Specialist; Purchasing Agent; Sales Representative; Systems Analyst. Principal educational backgrounds sought: Accounting; Business Administration; Chemistry; Computer Science; Engineering; Marketing; Mathematics. Company benefits include: Medical, dental, and life insurance; pension plan; tuition assistance; disability coverage; employee discount; savings plan. Corporate headquarters location: Milwaukee, WI. Operations at this facility include: Divisional headquarters; research/development; administration; sales. New York Stock Exchange.

Parke Davis-Rochester
870 Parkdale Rd.
Rochester MI 48307
Tel: (313) 651-9081

Contact: Debbie Sullivan, Personnel

A major Southeastern Michigan manufacturer of pharmaceutical products. Employs 600. International: Argentina, Australia, Brazil, Ecuador, Egypt, England, Germany, Hong Kong, India, Italy, New Zealand, Nigeria, Pakistan, Panama, Peru, Portugal, Saudi Arabia, Spain, Sweden, Taiwan, Thailand, Venezuela.

Steelcase, Inc.
910 44th St. SE
Grand Rapids, MI 49508
Tel: (616) 247-2710
Contact: Dan Wiljanen, Personnel Director

A large manufacturer of furniture. International: Canada, England, France, Germany, Japan.

Minnesota

GAF Corporation
50 Lowry Ave. N.
Minneapolis, MN 55411
Tel: (612) 529-9121
Contact: Jan Steffan, Personnel Director

Regional production facility of the well-known chemicals, building materials, photographic and reprographic products manufacturer. A grocery store chain. International: Australia, Austria, Belgium, Brazil, Canada, England, France, Germany, Italy, Japan, Mexico, Netherlands, New Zealand, Singapore, Spain, Sweden, Switzerland.

Maico Hearing Instruments, Inc.
7375 Bush Lake Rd.
Minneapolis, MN 55435
Tel: (612) 835-4400
Contact: Tammy Tester, Personnel Director

A producer of audiometers and hearing aids. Common positions include: Accountant; Administrator; Advertising; Worker; Buyer; Credit Manager; Customer Service Representative; Draftsperson; Electrical Engineer; Mechanical Engineer; General Manager; Operations/Production Manager; Marketing Specialist; Personnel and Labor Relations Specialist; Purchasing Agent; Quality Control Supervisor; Sales Representative; Technical Writer/Editor; Assembler; Principal educational backgrounds sought: Accounting; Business Administration; Communications; Engineering; Marketing. Company benefits include: Medical insurance; dental insurance; pension plan; life insurance; tuition assistance; disability coverage. Corporate headquarters location. Parent company: Gfeller, US. Operations at this facility include: Manufacturing; research/development; administration; service; sales. International: Uruguay.

Northern Telecom, Inc.
9701 Data Park
Minnetonka, MN 55343
Tel: (800) 676-4636
Contact: Human Resources

A major manufacturer of computers and telephones. International: Australia, Belgium, Canada, France, Germany, Ireland, Italy, Netherlands, Spain, Switzerland.

Pillsbury Company
Pillsbury Center
Mail Station 0110
Minneapolis, MN 55402
Tel: (612) 330-4960
Contact: Jeff Johnson, Personnel Director

Manufactures and markets food products for consumer, industrial, and international markets. Corporate headquarters location. International: Canada, England, France, Germany, Guatemala, Mexico, Venezuela.

Mississippi

Colt Industries/Holley Carburetor Division
P.O. Drawer 727
Walter Valley, MS 38965
Tel: (601) 473-3100

Contact: Personnel Director

Manufactures carburetors, pistons. Employs 1,000. International: Canada, England, France.

Genesco, Inc.
1208 Bethdale Dr.
Iuka, MS 38852
Tel: (601) 423-3254

Contact: Terry Harrell, Personnel Manager/Safety Coordinator

Manufactures men's and women's leather shoes. Corporate headquarters location: Nashville, TN. Operations include: Manufacturing. New York Stock Exchange. Common positions include: Blue-Collar Worker Supervisor; Buyer; Industrial Engineer; Department Manager; Operations/Production Manager; Personnel and Labor Relations Specialist; Maintenance Manager; Plant Superintendent. Principal educational backgrounds sought: Engineering; Management; Personnel Management. Company benefits include: Medical insurance; pension plan; life insurance; tuition assistance; disability coverage; employee discounts; savings plan; credit union. International: Canada.

Missouri

Anheuser-Busch Companies, Inc.
One Busch Pl.
St. Louis, MO 63118
Tel: (314) 577-2000

Contact: Charles DiMercurio Manager/Recruiting Services and College

A diversified corporation whose products include beer, agricultural operations and products, and family entertainment complexes. Corporate headquarters location. International: England, Japan.

Emerson Electric Co.
8100 W. Florissant
St. Louis, MO 63136
Tel: (314) 553-2000

Contact: C. T. Kelly, Vice President, Human Resources

The Government and Defense Group (Electronics and Space Division) is engaged in the design and manufacturing of electro-mechanical armaments for aircraft, ships and ground vehicles; automatic test equipment; and electronic warfare equipment. A subsidiary of Emerson Electric Company, the major worldwide electronics and manufacturing firm (same location). Divisional headquarters location. Operations include: Manufacturing. Common positions include: Accountant; Computer Programmer; Engineer; Electrical Engineer; Systems Analyst; Technical Writer/Editor.

Principal educational background sought: Engineering. Company benefits include: Medical, dental, and life insurance; pension plan; tuition assistance; disability coverage; employee discounts; savings plan. International: Belgium, Japan, Saudi Arabia.

The Hertz Corporation
10278 Natural Bridge Rd.
St. Louis, MO 63134
Tel: (314) 426-7555
Contact: Lynn Skelton, Personnel Director

Area offices for one of the nation's leading transportation services organization. Company operates nationally through several divisions: Rent-A-Car Division (car rental services); Car Leasing Division; and Equipment Rental and Leasing Division. Also engaged in joint venture truck leasing operations with Penske Corporation (Hertz Penske Truck Leasing) at 600 locations. A major subsidiary of RCA Corporation (New York, NY). Corporate headquarters location: New York, NY. International: Australia, Austria, Japan, Denmark, England, Germany, Ireland, Israel, Italy, Japan, Netherlands, Panama, Portugal, Spain, Switzerland.

Pinkerton's, Inc.
9666 Olive St., Suite 710
St. Louis, MO 63132
Tel: (314) 997-7801
Contact: Karen Beasky, Personnel Administrator

St. Louis office of the oldest and largest nongovernmental security service organization in the world today, operating for over 130 years. Principal business is providing high-quality security, investigative, and consulting services to a multitude of commercial, industrial, institutional, governmental, and residential clients. Operates from 129 offices in the United States, Canada, and Great Britain. Major services include: Industrial plant security, retail security, nuclear plan security, institutional security, commercial and residential building security, construction security, patrol and inspection service, courier service, inventory service, community security, sports and special events service, K9 patrol service, investigation service, security consultation, and equipment evaluation. Employs more than 35,000 people worldwide. International: Canada, England.

Montana

Conoco, Inc.
P.O. Box 2548
Billings, MT 59103
Tel: (406) 255-2500
Contact: Personnel Director

A refinery that processes asphalt, diesel fuel, gasoline, Jet 50, and propane. Corporate headquarters location: Houston, TX. International: Argentina, Australia, Austria, Bahrain, Belgium, Brazil, Chad, Egypt, England, France, Germany, Indonesia, India, Italy, Japan, Netherlands, Nigeria, Norway, Scotland, Singapore, Spain, Sweden, Switzerland, Tunisia, United Arab Emirates.

Nebraska

Campbell Soup Company
P.O. Box 778
Omaha, NE 68101
Tel: (402) 342-8118

Contact: Joseph Hilke, Manager of Human Resources

The Omaha division of the well-known food producer manufactures frozen convenience meals. Common positions include: Accountant; Blue-Collar Worker Supervisor; Buyer; Chemist; Computer Programmer; Draftsperson; Electrical Engineer; Industrial Engineer; Mechanical Engineer; Food Technologist; Personnel and Labor Relations Specialist; Purchasing Agent; Quality Control Supervisor; Statistician; Systems Analyst. Principal educational backgrounds sought: Accounting; Biology; Business Administration; Chemistry; Computer Science; Engineering. Company benefits include: Medical insurance; dental insurance; pension plan; life insurance; tuition assistance; disability coverage; employee discounts; savings plan. Corporate headquarters location: Camden, NJ. Operations at this facility include: Manufacturing. New York Stock Exchange. International: Argentina, Australia, Belgium, Canada, England, France, Germany, Hong Kong, Italy, Japan, Mexico, Netherlands.

Conagra
One Conagra Dr.
Omaha, NE 68102-5001
Tel: (402) 595-4000

Contact: L. B. Thomas, Personnel Director

A diversified family of companies operating across the food chain. Products range from supplies farmers need to grow crops to prepared food items. ConAgra operates in three segments of the food chain: Agriculture, Trading and Processing, and Prepared Foods. The company has major business in agricultural chemicals, animal feed, fertilizer, specialty trading, grain processing, beef, pork, lamb, poultry, processed meats, dairy products, seafood and frozen prepared foods. International: Spain.

Mutual/United of Omaha Insurance Co.
Mutual of Omaha Plaza
Omaha, NE 68175
Tel: (402) 342-7600

Contact: Employment Manager

Mutual of Omaha offers a full portfolio of (insurance) coverages and services with $25.4 billion paid in benefits to policy holders. United of Omaha Life Insurance Company ranks among the top 2% of all life insurance companies in the United States with more than $53 billion of life insurance in force. Common positions include: Accountant; Actuary; Attorney; Claim Representative; Computer Programmer; Customer Service Representative; Financial Analyst; Marketing Specialist; Personnel and Labor Relations Specialist; Systems Analyst; Underwriter. Principal educational backgrounds sought: Accounting; Business Administration; Computer Science; Finance; Liberal Arts; Marketing; Mathematics. Company benefits include: Medical, dental, and life insurance; pension plan; tuition assistance; disability coverage; employee discounts; savings plan. Corporate headquarters location. Operations at this facility include: Regional headquarters; divisional headquarters; administration; service. International: Canada, Panama.

Union Pacific Corporation
1416 Dodge St., Suite 400
Norchem Building
Omaha, NE 68179
Tel: (402) 271-3643
Contact: J. A. Hale, Jr., Director/Audit Personnel and Planning
Principal industry areas are energy, transportation, and natural resources. Divisional headquarters location. Corporate headquarters location: New York, NY. New York and American Stock Exchanges. Common positions include: Accountant; Auditor. Principal educational backgrounds sought: Accounting; Business Administration; Computer Science. Company benefits include: Medical insurance; dental insurance; pension plan; life insurance; tuition assistance; disability coverage; profit sharing. International: Canada.

Nevada

Wackenhut Services, Inc.
2950 S. Highland Dr., Suite E
Las Vegas, NV 89109
Tel: (702) 295-3575
Contact: Personnel Department
A leading Nevada detective agency. Employs 400. International: Argentina, Bermuda, Canada, Chile, Colombia, Costa Rica, Dominican Republic, Ecuador, England, Germany, Hong Kong, Japan, Korea, Mexico, Panama, Philippines, Saudi Arabia, Scotland, Venezuela.

New Hampshire

Osram Sylvania, Inc.
Portsmouth Ave.
Exeter, NH 03833
Tel: (603) 772-4331
Contact: Human Resources Manager
Operations in the following divisions: Coated Coil operation, which involves production of tungsten filaments coated with high performance insulator aluminum oxide used in television electron guns; Special Refractory Products, which manufactures products made from refractory metals that are used as furnace hardware; Ceramics Department, which produces various types of steatite ceramic electrical insulators used in bases of light bulbs; and the Quartz Department, which produces and finishes quartz crucibles for use by the semiconductor industry. Divisional headquarters location. Corporate headquarters location: Stamford, CT. Operations include: Manufacturing. New York Stock Exchange. Common positions include: Accountant; Computer Programmer; Customer Service Representative; Ceramics Engineer; Metallurgical Engineer. Principal educational backgrounds sought: Engineering; Marketing. Company benefits include: Medical

insurance; dental insurance; pension plan; life insurance; tuition assistance; disability coverage; employee discounts; savings plan; 401K plan. International: Argentina, Australia, Belgium, Brazil, Canada, England, France, Germany, India, Italy, Japan, Kenya, Mexico, Switzerland, Thailand.

Markem Corporation
150 Congress St.
Keene, NH 03431
Tel: (603) 352-1130, ext. 230

Contact: Manager, Human Resources Division

An international firm providing complete in-plant printing systems to industry throughout the world. Specialized in the design, manufacturing, sales and service of printing elements, various in-line and independent printing mechanisms and the accompanying chemical supplies. Corporate and regional headquarters. Operations include: Manufacturing; research/development. Common positions include: Accountant; Advertising Worker; Buyer; Commercial Artist; Computer Programmer; Customer Service Representative; Draftsperson; Engineer; Chemical Engineer; Electrical Engineer; Mechanical Engineer; Management Trainee; Marketing Specialist; Personnel and Labor Relations Specialist; Sales Representative; Technical Writer/Editor. Principal educational backgrounds sought: Business Administration; Computer Science; Engineering; Liberal Arts; Marketing. Company benefits include: Medical insurance; pension plan; life insurance; tuition assistance; disability coverage; profit sharing; employee discounts; savings plan; in-plant library, bank, cafeteria, greenhouse; training. International: Canada, England, France, Germany, Italy, Japan, Mexico, Netherlands, Sweden.

MPB Corporation
P.O. Box 547
Keene, NH 03431
Tel: (603) 352-0310

Contact: Robert Rooney, Personnel Director

A stand-alone company owned by a group of investors headed by Harold S. Geneen. Common positions include: Accountant; Administrator; Blue-Collar Worker Supervisor; Buyer; Computer Programmer; Customer Service Representative; Draftsperson; Aerospace Engineer; Industrial Engineer; Mechanical Engineer; Metallurgical Engineer; Department Manager; General Manager; Operations/Production Manager; Personnel and Labor Relations Specialist; Purchasing Agent; Quality Control Supervisor; Systems Analyst. Educational backgrounds sought include: Business Administration; Engineering. Company benefits include: Medical insurance; dental insurance; pension plan; life insurance; tuition assistance; disability coverage; profit sharing; employee discounts; savings plan. Corporate headquarters location: Keene, NH. Operations at this facility include: Manufacturing. International: Germany.

New Jersey

American Cyanamid Company
One Cyanamid Plaza
Wayne, NJ 07470
Tel: (201) 831-3081
Contact: Leo J. Medicus, Manager/College Relations and Professional Placement

Several area locations, including Princeton, NJ; Pearl River, NY; and Stamford, CT. A diversified, multinational organization, engaged in the research, development, manufacture, and marketing of agricultural, chemical, consumer, and medical products. Operates 17 research laboratories and nearly 100 plants nationwide; offers 2,500 products in more than 135 countries. Medical business consists of both prescription and nonprescription pharmaceutical products and hospital products, made and marketed by Lederle Laboratories Division (in United States). Agricultural business consists of animal feed and health products; insecticides, fungicides, herbicides and plant regulators; and fertilizers. Chemical business consists of more than 5,000 organic and inorganic chemicals and related products in six operating divisions: Chemical Products; Polymer Products; Glendale Optical Company; Fibers; and Industrial Products. Consumer products operates in three divisions: Shulton, Inc./USA makes and markets personal care and grooming products (brand names such as 'Old Spice,' 'Breck,' and others); and household maintenance and cleaning aids (including 'Pine Sol' cleaner); Jacqueline Cochran, Inc., which makes and markets men's and women's prestige fragrances; and Shulton International, which manufactures and markets the above products internationally. Corporate headquarters location. New York Stock Exchange. Common positions include: Biochemist; Chemist; Engineer; Agricultural Engineer; Chemical Engineer; Industrial Engineer; Mechanical Engineer; Metallurgical Engineer; Mining Engineer; Petroleum Engineer; Marketing Specialist; Statistician; Systems Analyst. Principal educational backgrounds sought: Business Administration; Chemistry; Computer Science; Engineering; Marketing. International: Australia, Austria, Belgium, Brazil, Canada, Colombia, Denmark, Egypt, England, France, Germany, Greece, Guatemala, Hong Kong, India, Italy, Japan, Kenya, Korea, Mexico, Netherlands, New Zealand, Nigeria, Pakistan, Peru, Philippines, Portugal, Spain, Sweden, Switzerland, Taiwan, Turkey, Venezuela.

Curtiss-Wright Corporation
1200 Wall St. W.
Lyndhurst, NJ 07071
Tel: (201) 896-8400
Contact: Mr. Cap W. Orr, Corporate Director of Labor Relations

A diversified multinational manufacturing concern. The corporation manufactures and markets products and provides services to industrial customers and under Government contracts in four broad areas: Aerospace; Flow

Control and Marine; Industrial; and Electrical Generating. Aerospace segment produces jet engine and reciprocating engine parts, control and actuation components and systems, shot-peening and peen-forming services, and custom extruded shapes and shafts, for U.S. Government agencies, foreign governments, commercial/military/general aviation airframe manufacturers, commercial/military helicopter manufacturers, jet aircraft engineer manufacturers, and commercial airlines. Flow Control and Marine segment produces globe, gate, solenoid and safety relief valves, and custom extruded shapes and seamless alloy pipe for U.S. Navy propulsion systems, commercial power systems, and U.S. Navy shipbuilders. Industrial segment produces precision spring clutches, manual impact wrenches, and aircraft windshield wiper systems for the office machine, industrial/military hand tool and general aviation markets, custom extruded shapes and seamless alloy pipe for the shipbuilding, oil/petrochemical/chemical construction industries, shot-peening and heat treating for the general metal working, and oil and gas drilling and exploration industries, the industrial compressor industry, and U.S. Government agencies. Canadian operation manufactures air compressors and distributes small reciprocating engines for commercial/industrial, and lawn and garden uses. Area subsidiaries include Curtiss-Wright Flight Systems, Inc., a manufacturer of aerospace control and actuation components and systems (300 Fairfield Rd., Fairfield, NJ 07006); Metal Improvement Company, which performs shot-peening, peen-forming, and heat-treating services (10 Forest Ave., Paramus, NJ 07652); and Target Rock Corporation, a manufacturer of flow control valves (East Farmingdale, NY 11735). Common positions include: Accountant; Administrator; Attorney; Computer Programmer; Draftsperson; Aerospace Engineer; Electrical Engineer; Industrial Engineer; Mechanical Engineer; Metallurgical Engineer; Financial Analyst; Operations/Production Manager; Personnel and Labor Relations Specialist; Quality Control Supervisor; Systems Analyst. Principal educational backgrounds sought: Accounting; Business Administration; Engineering; Finance. Company benefits include: Medical, dental, and life insurance; pension plan; tuition assistance; disability coverage; savings plan. Corporate headquarters location. New York Stock Exchange. International: Australia, Canada, England, France, Germany, India, Israel, Kuwait, Netherlands.

Owens-Illinois, Inc.
Park 80
Plaza W. One
Saddle Brook, NJ 07662
Tel: (201) 845-5030

Contact: Mrs. S. L. Donovan, Sales Service Manager

Multiple area locations, including Bridgeton, East Brunswick, Edison, Wayne, Glassboro, and Vineland, NJ; Brockport and Volney, NY; Milford, CT. One of the world's

State-by-state U.S. Employers with Foreign Offices

leading and most diversified manufacturers of packaging products. The company produces and sells glass containers, multiwall paper and plastic shipping sacks, plastic shrink and stretch film, printing plates and ink, plywood and dimension lumber, blown plastic containers, plastic beverage bottles, plastic drums, metal and plastic closures, tamper-resistant closures, plastic and glass prescription containers, pharmaceutical items, labels, and multipack plastic carriers for containers. Specialized glass products made and sold by the company include 'Libbey' tumblers, stemware, and decorative glassware, television bulbs for picture tubes, 'Kimble' scientific and laboratory ware, and 'SUNPAK' evacuated glass tubes for use in solar energy collectors. Some overseas affiliates also manufacture flat glass and related products. Operates through five segments: Glass Container Group (facilities in Bridgeton, NJ; Brockport and Volney, NY; and many other domestic and international locations); Forest Products Group (no area facilities); Plastics & Closure Group (facilities in East Brunswick and Edison, NJ; Milford, CT; and in other domestic and international locations); Consumer Products Group (no area facilities); and Health Care Group (plant located in Vineland, NJ). This is a major sales facility for the company's complete line of products. Corporate headquarters location: Toledo, OH. New York Stock Exchange. International: Austria, Brazil, Canada, Colombia, Germany, Italy, Japan, Singapore, Switzerland, Venezuela.

Schering-Plough Corporation
One Giralda Farms
Madison, NJ 07940
Tel: (201) 882-7000
Contact: Gordon C. O'Brien, Senior Vice President, Human Resources

Several area locations, including Kenilworth. A worldwide company primarily engaged in the discovery, development, manufacturing, and marketing of pharmaceutical and consumer products. Pharmaceutical products include prescription drugs, over-the-counter medicines, eye-care products, and animal-health products promoted to the medical and allied professions. The consumer products group consists of proprietary medicines, toiletries, cosmetics, and foot-care products marketed directly to the public. Well-known products include 'Coricidin' cough/cold medicines; 'Maybelline' eye, face, lip, skin-care, and nail-color products; 'Wesley-Jessen' vision-care products; 'Coppertone' sun care products; 'Dr. Scholl' foot-care products; and 'St. Joseph's' line of children's over-the counter analgesics. Corporate headquarters location: Madison, NJ. New York Stock Exchange. International. Operations include: Manufacturing, research/development; administration; service; sales. New York Stock Exchange. Common positions include: Accountant; Administrator; Advertising Worker; Attorney; Biochemist; Biologist; Blue-Collar Worker Supervisor; Buyer; Chemist; Computer

Programmer; Credit Manager; Customer Service Representative; Draftsperson; Economist; Biomedical Engineer; Chemical Engineer; Electrical Engineer; Industrial Engineer; Mechanical Engineer; Financial Analyst; Branch Manager; Department Manager; General Manager; Management Trainee; Operations/Production Manager; Marketing Specialist; Personnel and Labor Relations Specialist; Physicist; Programmer; Public Relations Worker; Purchasing Agent; Quality Control Supervisor; Reporter/Editor, Sales Representative; Statistician; Systems Analyst; Technical Writer/Editor. Principal educational backgrounds sought: Accounting; Biology; Business Administration; Chemistry; Communications; Computer Science; Economics; Engineering; Finance; Marketing; Mathematics; Pharmacy; Physics; Nursing. Company benefits include: Medical insurance; dental insurance; pension plan; life insurance; tuition assistance; disability coverage; profit sharing; employee discounts; savings plan; employee stock ownership. International: Argentina, Australia, Brazil, Canada, France, India, Ireland, Japan, Kenya, Peru.

New Mexico

Digital Equipment Corporation
P.O. Box 499
Albuquerque, NM 87103
Tel: (505) 343-7000

Contact: Human Resources Department

Designs, manufactures, sells, and services computers and associated peripheral equipment and related software and supplies. Applications and programs include: Scientific research, computation, communications, education, data analysis, industrial control, time sharing, commercial data processing, graphic arts, word processing, health care, instrumentation, engineering, and simulation. Employs 63,000 people in the United States and 37 foreign countries. Albuquerque facility produces computers. Corporate headquarters location: Maynard, MA. New York Stock Exchange. International: Australia, Austria, Denmark, England, France, Germany, Japan, Ireland, Switzerland, Taiwan.

Motorola, Inc.
4800 Alameda Blvd. NE
Albuquerque, NM 87113
Tel: (505) 822-8801

Contact: Liz Hill, Personnel Manager

One of the world's leading manufacturers of electronic equipment and components, engaged in the design, manufacture, and sale of a diversified line of products, including two-way radios and other electronic communications systems; semiconductors, including integrated circuits; electronic engine controls; digital appliance controls; automobile radios; citizens' band radios, and other automotive and industrial electronic equipment; and data communications products for a wide range of users, including low-, medium-, and high-speed modems, multiplexors, and network processors. Albuquerque facility produces ceramic products for electronics applications, including optics and audio uses. Corporate headquarters location: Chicago, IL. New York Stock Exchange. International: Australia, Austria, Belgium, Canada, Costa Rica, Denmark, England, France, Germany, Hong Kong, Ireland, Italy, Japan, Korea, Malaysia, Mexico, Netherlands, Norway, Philippines, Singapore, Spain, Sweden, Switzerland, Taiwan.

New York

American Home Products Corporation
685 3rd Ave.
New York, NY 10017
Tel: (201) 660-5000
Contact: Employment Specialist

A leading manufacturer and marketer of prescription drugs and medical supplies, packaged medicines, food products, and household products and housewares. Prescription Drugs and Medical Supplies segment operates through the following subsidiaries: Wyeth Laboratories (produces ethical pharmaceuticals, biologicals, and nutritional products); Ayers Laboratories (produces ethical pharmaceuticals, over-the-counter antacids, vitamins, and sunburn remedies); Ives Laboratories (ethical pharmaceuticals); Fort Dodge Laboratories (veterinary pharmaceuticals and biologicals); Sherwood Medical (medical devices, diagnostic instruments, test kits, bacteria identification systems); and Corometrics Medical Systems (medical electronic instrumentation for obstetrics and neonatology). Packaged Medicines segment operates through subsidiary Whitehall Laboratories (produces analgesics, cold remedies, and other packaged medicines). Food Products segment operates through subsidiaries American Home Foods (canned pasta, canned vegetables, specialty foods, mustard, popcorn); and E. J. Brach & Sons (assorted chocolates, novelties, and other general line candies). Household Products and Housewares segment operates through subsidiaries Boyle-Midway (cleaners, insecticides, air fresheners, waxes, polishes, and other items for home, appliance, and apparel care); Dupli-Color Products (touch-up, refinishing, and other car-care and shop-use products); Ekco Products (food containers, commercial baking pans, industrial coatings, food handling systems, foilware, plasticware; Ekco Housewares (cookware, cutlery, kitchen tools, tableware and accessories, padlocks); and Prestige Group (cookware, cutlery, kitchen tools, carpet sweepers, pressure cookers). Corporate headquarters location. International: Argentina, Australia, Belgium, Brazil, Canada, Chile, Colombia, England, France, Germany, Greece, Guatemala, Italy, Japan, Kenya, Mexico, New Zealand, Nigeria, Pakistan, Peru, Portugal, Spain, Sweden, Switzerland, Turkey, Uruguay, Venezuela.

Northrop Grumman Corporation
S. Oyster Bay Rd.
Bethpage, NY 11714
Tel: (516) 575-7558
Contact: Human Resources Department

One of the nation's largest diversified high-technology manufacturers, operating more than 110 manufacturing plants, field offices, and test sites, as well as 75 sales offices and other small facilities in the United States and around the world. Employs more than 28,000 people worldwide. Company is one of the United States' ten largest defense contractors, and a major developer of military aircraft and spacecraft (including craft used in moon landings). Operates through several divisions, including Grumman Aerospace Corporation, Grumman Allied Industries, Grumman Data Systems Corporation, Grumman Credit Corporation, and Grumman International. Grumman Aerospace manufactures various military aircraft, including the F-14 Tomcat, the A-6E Intruder, the EA-6B Prowler, the E-2C Hawkeye, the EF-111A Tactical Jamming System, and many other related systems and components. Grumman Allied Industries manufactures buses, energy systems, aluminum trucks, fire-trucks, yachts, canoes, boats, and temperature-controlled trucks. Grumman Data Systems provides computer services to government, business, and industry, as well as to other Grumman subsidiaries. Grumman International performs marketing and sales activities for Grumman products and services overseas, and initiates collaborative programs with foreign industries. Corporate headquarters location. New York Stock Exchange. International: France, Kuwait.

The McGraw-Hill Companies, Inc.
1221 Avenue of the Americas
New York, NY 10020-1095
Tel: (212) 512-2000

Contact: Frank Durante, Manager, Corporate Staffing

Founded in 1889, McGraw-Hill publishes a wide variety of magazines, books, and newsletters and is a major provider of online information through computer networks, software, videotapes, and compact discs. International: Australia, Belgium, Brazil, Canada, Germany, Hong Kong, Japan, Mexico, Switzerland, United Kingdom.

Philip Morris Companies, Inc.
120 Park Ave.
New York, NY 10017
Tel: (212) 880-5000

Contact: Director/Employee Relations

The number one tobacco products company worldwide, Philip Morris also is a major producer of beer (Miller Brewing) and food products (General Foods and Kraft). Particularly well-known brand names are Marlboro, Post, and Breyer. International: Argentina, Bulgaria, Dominican Republic, France, Germany, Japan, Netherlands, Poland, Romania, Russia, Switzerland, Turkey, and Venezuela.

Salomon, Inc.
Seven World Trade Center
New York, NY 10048
Tel: (212) 783-7000

Contact: Ed Weihenmayer, Managing Director, Human Resources

An international investment banking, market making, and research firm, serving corporations, state and local governments, sovereign and provincial governments and their agencies, supranational organizations, central banks, and other financial institutions. A major operating subsidiary of Phibro-Salomon, Inc. Corporate headquarters location. International: England, Hong Kong, Japan.

Stone & Webster, Incorporated
250 W. 34th St.
New York, NY 10119
Tel: (212) 290-7500
Contact: Darlene Lucas, Director, Human Resources

Provides a wide range of engineering consulting services, including design and construction, on large-scale projects, primarily for the power generation industry. Also provides consulting services for other industries, including petrochemicals, industrial manufacturing, and others. Offices located throughout the United States and in some international locations. Employs 12,000 people worldwide. Corporate headquarters: Boston, MA. International: Canada, England, France, Indonesia, Korea, Malaysia, Mexico, Saudi Arabia, United Arab Emirates.

John Wiley & Sons, Inc.
605 3rd Ave.
New York, NY 10158
Tel: (212) 850-6000
Contact: Susan Fisher, Personnel Recruiter

Several area locations, including Somerset, NJ. An independent publisher of educational, business, and professional books, reference works, journals, and related materials. A new subsidiary, Wilson Learning Corporation (Eden Prairie, MN), produces adult learning programs for industry. Company's publications and programs are edited, produced, and marketed worldwide through a diversified group of domestic and international subsidiaries, foreign affiliates, and overseas sales offices. Company's Educational, Professional, Medical, and International Groups are all located in New York. Corporate headquarters location. International: Australia, England, India, Singapore.

North Carolina

Resistoflex Company/Division of Crane Company
P.O. Box 1449
Marion, NC 28752
Tel: (704) 724-9524
Contact: Human Resources

Manufactures thermoplastic products, including thermoplastic line pipe and flexible hoses. A subsidiary of Crane Company. Corporate headquarters location: New York, NY. Operations include: Manufacturing; research/development; administration; sales. New York Stock Exchange. Common positions include: Accountant; Administrator; Blue-Collar Worker Supervisor; Buyer; Customer Service Representative; Draftsperson; Industrial Engineer; Mechanical Engineer; Financial Analyst; Operations/Production Manager; Marketing Specialist; Personnel and Labor Relations Specialist; Programmer; Purchasing Agent; Quality Control Supervisor; Systems

Analyst. Principal educational backgrounds sought: Accounting; Business Administration; Computer Science; Engineering; Finance; Marketing; Mathematics. Company benefits include: Medical insurance; dental insurance; pension plan; life insurance; tuition assistance; disability coverage; savings plan. International: Belgium, Canada, England, Spain.

North Dakota

Amoco Oil Company
P.O. Box 500
Mandan, ND 58554
Tel: (701) 667-2400
Contact: Leif Peterson, Personnel Director

An operating facility of the major petroleum firm. Corporate headquarters location: Chicago, IL. International: England, Hong Kong, Switzerland.

Ohio

Allen-Bradley/Systems Division
One Allen Bradley Dr.
Mayfield Heights, OH 44124
Tel: (216) 949-6700
Contact: Department of Human Resources

Engaged in the design and production of distributed process and numerical control equipment for industrial automation. Also involved in the design of automation systems. Operations at this facility include: Research/development; administration. Corporate headquarters location: Milwaukee, WI. Common positions include: Accountant; Draftsperson; Biomedical Engineer; Electrical Engineer; Mechanical Engineer; Industrial Designer; Marketing Specialist; Physicist; Programmer; Purchasing Agent; Quality Control Supervisor; Statistician; Systems Analyst; Technical Writer/Editor; Test Engineer; Quality/Reliability Engineer. Principal educational backgrounds sought: Accounting; Computer Science; Engineering; Finance; Marketing; Mathematics; Physics. Company benefits include: Medical, dental, and life insurance; pension plan; tuition assistance; disability coverage; employee discounts; savings plan. International: Australia, Belgium, Brazil, Canada, England, France, Germany, India, Italy, Japan, Mexico, Saudi Arabia, Spain.

Beatrice/Hunt-Wesson, Inc.
P.O. Box 450
29180 Glenwood Rd.
Perrysburg, OH 43551
Tel: (419) 666-2134
Contact: Personnel Manager

A manufacturer of food and tomato products. Corporate headquarters location: Fullerton, CA. Common positions include: Accountant; Buyer; Electrical Engineer; Industrial Engineer; Mechanical Engineer; Department Manager; Operations/Production Manager; Personnel and Labor Relations Specialist; Purchasing Agent; Quality Control Supervisor. Principal educational backgrounds sought: Accounting; Business Administration; Engineering; Finance. Company benefits include:

Medical insurance; dental insurance; pension plan; life insurance; tuition assistance; disability coverage; 401K. International: Australia, Belgium, Canada, Colombia, England, France, Germany, Ireland, Jamaica, Japan, Malaysia, Mexico, Netherlands, Norway, Peru, Singapore, Spain, Switzerland, Thailand, Venezuela.

The B.F. Goodrich Company
3925 Embassy Pkwy.
Department 0007
Akron, OH 44333
Tel: (216) 374-3985

Contact: Harold D. Mason, Director, Human Resources

A diversified manufacturer of plastics, specialty chemicals, and products for the aerospace and defense industries. Common positions include: Accountant; Attorney; Buyer; Claim Representative; Computer Programmer; Editor; Financial Analyst; Personnel Specialist; Purchasing Agent; Systems Analyst. Principal educational backgrounds sought: Accounting; Business Administration; Communications; Computer Science; Finance; Human Resources; Law; Liberal Arts. Company benefits include: Medical insurance; pension plan; life insurance; tuition assistance; disability coverage; employee discounts; savings plan; stock purchase plan; prescription drug plan; 401K plan. Corporate headquarters location. Operations at this facility include: Administration. New York Stock Exchange. International: Australia, Brazil, Hong Kong, India, Italy, Mexico, Netherlands, Philippines, Thailand.

White Consolidated Industries, Inc.
11770 Berea Rd.
Cleveland, OH 44111
Tel: (216) 252-3700

Contact: Director of Personnel

A diversified manufacturer of products for both consumer and industrial markets worldwide. Products include: Washers and dryers. Corporate headquarters location. New York Stock Exchange. International: Canada, England, Japan, Mexico.

Oklahoma

TDK, Inc.
5900 N. Harrison
Shawnee, OK 74801
Tel: (405) 275-2100

Contact: Ron Benefee, Human Resources

Produces ceramic magnets for PM motor applications and ferrite components for electronic, communications and computer applications. Common positions include: Accountant; Chemist; Customer Service Representative; Ceramics Engineer; Electrical Engineer; Mechanical Engineer; Operations/Production Manager; Personnel and Labor Relations Specialist; Purchasing Agent; Quality Control Supervisor; Systems Analyst; Sales Engineers (Electrical Engineer). Principal educational backgrounds sought: Accounting; Chemistry; Engineering; and Marketing. Company benefits include: Medical insurance; dental insurance; pension plan; life insurance; tuition assistance; disability coverage; and savings plan. Divisional headquarters. Corporate headquarters location: Milwaukee, WI. Parent company is Rockwell International, Pittsburgh, PA. Operations at this facility include manufacturing, research and development, administration and sales. International: Australia, Belgium, Brazil, Canada, England, France, Germany, India, Italy, Japan, Mexico, Saudi Arabia, Spain.

Memorex/Telex Computer Products, Inc.
6422 E. 41st St.
Tulsa, OK 74135
Tel: (918) 627-1111

Contact: Peg O'Neil, Director, Personnel

A major manufacturer of computers and related information management products, including magnetic tape products and printers. Employs over 2,000 people. Established 1965. International: England.

The Williams Companies, Inc.
One Williams Center
Tulsa, OK 74172
Tel: (918) 588-2000

Contact: John C. Fischer, Vice President, Human Resources

Engaged in three essential industries: energy, fertilizer, and metals. Operates through six companies: Northwest Energy Company (interstate natural gas pipeline systems), Williams Pipe Line Company (gas pipelines), Williams Natural Gas Company (gas pipelines), Williams Gas Marketing and Williams Telecommunications Group.

Corporate headquarters location. Common positions include: Accountant; Attorney, Claim Representative; Commercial Artist; Computer Programmer; Customer Service Representative; Draftsperson; Electrical Engineer; Mechanical Engineer; Mining Engineer; Financial Analyst; Marketing Specialist; Personnel and Labor Relations Specialist; Reporter/Editor; Sales Representative; Systems Analyst. Principal educational backgrounds sought: Accounting; Business Administration; Computer Science; Engineering; Finance; Marketing. Company benefits include: Medical insurance; dental insurance; pension plan; life insurance; tuition assistance; disability coverage; profit sharing; savings plan. Corporate headquarters location. Operations at this facility include: Administration. International: Australia, England.

Oregon

ESCO Corporation
2141 NW 25th Ave.
Portland, OR 97210
Tel: (503) 228-2141

Contact: Manager of Personnel

A manufacturer of a variety of equipment for a wide range of industries, including mining, food processing, nuclear energy developing, and logging. Products include: Dredge cutters; tractor and dozer equipment; chain conveying systems; and custom castings. Corporate headquarters location. Operations at this facility include: Manufacturing; service; sales. Common positions include:

Accountant; Administrator; Advertising Worker; Attorney; Blue-Collar Worker Supervisor; Buyer; Chemist; Computer Programmer; Credit Manager; Customer Service Representative; Draftsperson; Ceramics Engineer; Industrial Engineer; Mechanical Engineer; Metallurgical Engineer; Financial Analyst; Branch Manager; Department Manager; General Manager; Management Trainee; Operations/Production Manager; Marketing Specialist; Personnel and Labor Relations Specialist; Programmer; Public Relations Worker; Purchasing Agent; Quality Control Supervisor; Sales Representative; Systems Analyst. Principal educational backgrounds sought: Accounting; Business Administration; Computer Science; Engineering. Company benefits include: Medical insurance; dental insurance; pension plan; life insurance; tuition assistance; disability coverage; employee discounts; savings plan. International: France.

General Foods Corporation
P.O. Box 2705
Portland, OR 97208
Tel: (503) 771-4790

Contact: Betty Jackson, Personnel Director

Nationally, the firm is one of the world's largest processors and marketers of food and beverage products; operates in such areas as packaged convenience foods, processed meats, coffee, and foodservice products. Facilities are located throughout the United States and abroad. Positions available at this location:

Department Manager; Sales Representative (4-year degree required). Company benefits include: Medical, dental, and life insurance; pension plan; tuition assistance; profit sharing; savings plan. Regional and divisional headquarters. Operations at this facility include: Administration; service; sales. Corporate headquarters location: White Plains, NY. New York Stock Exchange. International: Belgium, Brazil, Canada, Colombia, Denmark, England, France, Germany, Hong Kong, Ireland, Italy, Japan, Korea, Mexico, Panama, Philippines, Singapore, Spain, Switzerland.

Blount/Oregon Cutting Systems Division
4909 SE International Way
Portland, OR 97210
Tel: (503) 653-8881

Contact: Richard Lindsay, Director, Personnel

A leading manufacturer of equipment for harvesting timber and pulpwood, and of expendable products for gun-sportsmen and do-it-yourselfer hobbyists. The company is also a major supplier of chainsaw blades to original equipment manufacturers. Corporate headquarters location. International: Australia, Belgium, Brazil, Canada, England, France, Germany, Japan, Sweden.

Wang Laboratories, Inc.
Five Centerpointe Dr., Suite 300
Lake Oswego, OR 97035
Tel: (503) 230-0411

Contact: Personnel

A major producer of office automation systems; products

include a wide variety of computers and CRT word processing equipment, systems, and subsystems. Corporate headquarters location: Lowell, MA. International: Australia, Austria, Belgium, Canada, Egypt, Germany, Hong Kong, Israel, Japan, Netherlands, New Zealand, Singapore, Switzerland.

Pennsylvania

Aluminum Company of America
425 6th Ave.
Alcoa Building
Pittsburgh, PA 15219

Contact: Paul H. O'Neill, Executive Vice President, Human Resources

The world's leading producer of aluminum products. Employs more than 45,000 people in 150 operating locations and sales offices worldwide. The company's principal operations are in the mining of bauxite, refining it into alumina, smelting the alumina into aluminum, processing aluminum and aluminum alloys into milled and finished products, as well as recycling used aluminum products. Operations include manufacturing products from other metals, producing chemicals, and selling engineering and construction services. The firm is engaged in large research and development projects. Other Pennsylvania plans are located in Lebanon and Alcoa Center. Common positions include: Accountant; Ceramics Engineer; Electrical Engineer; Industrial Engineer; Mechanical Engineer; Metallurgical Engineer; Sales Representative; Business Analyst; Systems Analyst; Marketing Specialist; Personnel and Labor Relations Specialist; Financial/EDP Auditor. Principal educational backgrounds sought include: Accounting; Business Administration; Computer Science; Engineering; Marketing. Company benefits include: Medical, dental and life insurance; pension plan; tuition assistance; disability coverage; savings plan; profit sharing. Corporate regional, and divisional headquarters. New York Stock Exchange. International: Australia, Belgium, Jamaica, Japan, Mexico, Norway, Spain, Surinam.

Fruehauf Corporation
P.O. Box 110
Middletown, PA 17057
Tel: (171) 944-7491

Contact: Steve Horney, Personnel Manager

Engaged in the manufacture, sale, leasing, financing, distribution, and servicing of transportation equipment. Operates in three segments: Trailer Operations, Auto Operations, and Maritime and Aerospace Operations. Corporate headquarters location: Detroit, MI. Second major Pennsylvania facility, producing liquid bulk trailers, is located in Uniontown. New York Stock Exchange. International: Australia, Belgium, Canada, England, France, Mexico, Netherlands.

Occidental Chemical PVC Divisions
P.O. Box 699
Pottstown, PA 19464
Tel: (610) 317-6400

Contact: Human Resources Manager

Manufacturers a wide range of PVC resins, compounds, and fabricated products as a division of Occidental Chemical Corporation, which is a part of Occidental Petroleum Company, a natural resources company engaged in the exploration for and development of oil and natural gas in the United States. Corporate headquarters location: Los Angeles, CA. International: Belgium, Bermuda, Bolivia, Brazil, Canada, Colombia, England, Germany, India, New Zealand, Pakistan, Peru, Saudi Arabia, Scotland, Spain, Switzerland, Tunisia, USSR, United Arab Emirates, Venezuela.

Playskool, Inc.
110 Pitney Rd.
Lancaster, PA 19046
Tel: (800) 752-9755

Contact: Rose Bleacher, Personnel Manager

Well-known manufacturer of child guidance, infant and preschool toys. A subsidiary of Hasbro. International: Switzerland.

SPS Technologies
Highland Ave.
Jenkintown, PA 19046
Tel: (215) 572-3400

Contact: Employment Department

Engaged in the design, manufacturing, and marketing of high-technology fastener products, including precision components and high-technology fastener products, including precision components and assembly tools, and material-handling products such as storage systems, steel shelving, shop equipment, and automated material-handling products such as storage systems, steel shelving, shop equipment, and automated material-handling systems. Maintains more than 15 manufacturing plants and sales offices located throughout the world, including Great Britain, Mexico, and Australia. Divisional headquarters location. Operations at this facility include: Manufacturing; research/ development; administration; service; sales. International: Australia, Belgium, Canada, England, France, Germany, India, Ireland, Italy, Japan, Mexico.

Rhode Island

A.T. Cross Company
One Albion Rd.
Lincoln, RI 02865
Tel: (401) 333-1200

Contact: Director, Personnel

A.T. Cross Company is a major international manufacturer of fine writing instruments. These products are sold to the consumer gift market through selected jewelry, department, stationery, gift and book stores, and sold to the business gift market via a network of companies specializing in recognition programs. International: Ireland.

South Carolina

Cooper Air Tools/Division of Cooper Industries
670 Industrial Dr.
P.O. Box 1410
Lexington, SC 29072
Tel: (803) 359-1200

Contact: Manager/Employment and Training

A manufacturer of pneumatic hand tools, air motors, airfeed drills, and hoists. Divisional headquarters location. Operations include: Manufacturing; research/development; administration; service; sales. Corporate headquarters location: Houston, TX. New York Stock Exchange. Common positions include: Accountant; Advertising Worker; Blue-Collar Worker Supervisor; Buyer; Commercial Artist; Computer Programmer; Customer Service Representative; Draftsperson; Industrial Engineer; Mechanical Engineer; Metallurgical Engineer; Financial Analyst; Industrial Designer; Department Manager; Marketing Specialist; Personnel and Labor Relations Specialist; Purchasing Agent; Quality Control Supervisor; Sales Representative; Systems Analyst. Principal educational backgrounds sought: Accounting; Business Administration; Computer Science; Engineering; Finance; Liberal Arts; Marketing; Mathematics. Company benefits include: Medical, dental, and life insurance; pension plan; tuition assistance; disability coverage; employee discounts; savings plan. International: Canada, Mexico, Netherlands.

Riegel Textile Corporation
P.O. Box 3478
Greenville, SC 29602
Tel: (802) 233-4151

Contact: Dan Scott, Manager of Public Relations

A diversified, integrated company serving many different markets: apparel, industrial, interior furnishings, kitchen textiles, traditional infants' products, disposable diapers, personal care products, and data processing services. Company is decentralized into operating divisions and subsidiaries which are autonomous profit centers, each responsible for its own operation. Corporate headquarters location. New York Stock Exchange. Common positions include: Accountant; Blue-Collar Worker Supervisor; Buyer; Chemist; Computer Programmer; Credit Manager; Customer Service Representative; Electrical Engineer; Industrial Engineer; Mechanical Engineer; Financial Analyst; Marketing Specialist; Personnel and Labor Relations Specialist; Quality Control Supervisor; Sales Representative; Systems Analyst. Principal educational backgrounds sought: Accounting; Business Administration; Chemistry; Computer Science; Engineering; Finance; Marketing. Company benefits include: Medical insurance; dental insurance; pension plan; life insurance; tuition assistance; disability coverage; employee discounts; savings plan. International: Canada, France, Ivory Coast, Morocco.

South Dakota

Amoco Foam Products Company
3803 N. 4th Ave.
Sioux Falls, SD 57104
Tel: (605) 335-5521

Contact: Bruce Lake, Personnel Director

Manufactures plastic food containers. Corporate headquarters location: Worthington, MN. International: England, Hong Kong, Switzerland.

Tennessee

Holiday Inns Worldwide
3796 Lamar
Memphis, TN 38195
Tel: (903) 521-9349

Contact: Pat Ferguson, Director of General Employment

The world's largest hospitality company, operating in two businesses; hotels and hotel/casinos. With some 1,600 properties worldwide, its Holiday Inn hotel system is nearly three times the size of its nearest chain competitor. Three other hotel brands and a casino gaming company round out Holiday's diversified product portfolio. Its other hotel brands are: Embassy Suites, an all-suite full-service hotel chain; Hampton Inn, a limited service, moderately priced chain; and Home Wood Suites, a new extended-stay hotel product introduced early in 1988. Together, the company's four hotel brands comprise more than 1,800 hotels and 353,000 rooms worldwide. Common positions include: Accountant; Architect; Attorney; Computer Programmer; Customer Service Representative; Draftsperson; Mechanical Engineer; Hotel Manager/Assistant Manager; General Manager; Personnel and Labor Relations Specialist; Systems Analyst. Principal educational backgrounds sought: Accounting; Business Administration; Communications; Computer Science; Engineering; Finance; Marketing. Company benefits include: Medical, dental, and life insurance; pension plan; tuition assistance; disability coverage; profit sharing; employee discounts; savings plan. Corporate headquarters location. Operations at this facility include: Regional headquarters; divisional headquarters; research/development; administration; service; sales. New York Stock Exchange. International: Australia, Belgium, Bolivia, Brazil, Canada, Dominican Republic, France, Germany, Greece, Hong Kong, Italy, Japan, Netherlands, Philippines, Spain, Switzerland, Taiwan, Thailand, United Arab Emirates, Venezuela, Yugoslavia.

Texas

Bell Helicopter/Textron
P.O. Box 482
Department 19, Plant 1
Fort Worth, TX 76101
Tel: (817) 280-2011

Contact: Manager of Technical Staffing

Engaged in the manufacture of a variety of commercial and civilian helicopters, as well as extensive research and development activities. International: Australia, Belgium, Canada, England, France, Germany, Mexico, Singapore, Spain, Switzerland.

Hobart Corporation
8120 Jetstar Dr., Suite 100
Irving, TX 75063
Tel: (214) 915-6887

Contact: Gene Ettli, Office Manager

Manufactures food equipment for restaurants and supermarkets such as: slicers, mixers, scales, fryers, food cutters, toasters. Parent company: Dart and Kraft. Common positions include: Accountant; Electrical and Mechanical

Technician; Sales Representative. International: Australia, Belgium, Canada, France, Italy, Mexico, Netherlands, Switzerland.

Hunt Consolidated, Inc.
1445 Ross
Dallas, TX 75202
Tel: (214) 978-8000

Contact: Chuck Mills

A petroleum and natural gas refinery and distributor. Common positions include: Accountant; Computer Programmer; Petroleum Engineer; Geologist, Geophysicist; Purchasing Agent. Principal educational backgrounds sought include: Accounting; Engineering; Geology. Company benefits include: Medical, dental and life insurance; pension plan; tuition assistance; disability coverage; employee discounts; savings plan. Corporate headquarters location. Operations at this facility include: Research and development; administration; services; sales. International: England.

M.W. Kellogg Company
Three Greenway Plaza E.
Houston, TX 77046
Tel: (713) 690-2222

Contact: Mr. Jim Wilhite, Manager of Personnel

A full service design, engineering, procurement, and construction management firm. Company serves the process and energy industries worldwide. Primarily involved in hydrocarbon-processing plants, including oil refining units, petrochemical manufacturing plants, ammonia and fertilizer plants, and gas processing units. Employs approximately 3,200 persons. A Signal Company. International: Argentina, Canada, Chile, England, Hong Kong, Indonesia, Saudi Arabia, Singapore, Spain, United Arab Emirates.

Tenneco, Inc.
P.O. Box 2511
Houston, TX 77252
Tel: (713) 757-2131

Contact: Steve Smith, Senior Vice President

For information on professional hiring contact Howard Spiegel, Director, Human Resources at P.O. Box 2511, Houston, TX 77252.

A diversified, multinational corporation engaged in a wide range of industries, including oil, natural gas pipelines, construction, and farm equipment, shipbuilding, agriculture and land management, automotive, packaging, and insurance. Operates through the following groups: Tenneco Oil, Tennessee Gas Transmissions, J. I. Case, Newport News Shipbuilding, Tenneco West, Tenneco Automotive, Packaging Corporation of America, Philadelphia Life Insurance Company, Southwestern Life Insurance Company, and Southern General Life Insurance Company. Corporate headquarters location. New York Stock Exchange. International: Brazil, England, France, Malagasy, Spain.

Zale Corporation
901 W. Walnut Hill Ln.
Irving, TX 75038
Tel: (214) 580-4000

Contact: A. Herschel Krantz, Personnel Manager

Corporate offices for one of the nation's largest specialty retailing firms and the world's largest retailer of fine jewelry, operating more than 1,100 stores worldwide. Operating divisions: Fine Jewelers Guild Division, which operates carriage trade jewelry stores; Diamond Park Division, which operates leased departments. Company manages its operations in 48 states, and in international locations. Corporate headquarters location: Dallas, TX. Common positions include: Accountant; Buyer; Computer Programmer; Management Trainee; Marketing Specialist; Sales Representative; Store Manager. Principal educational backgrounds sought: Accounting; Business Administration; Computer Science; Marketing; Retail Management. Company benefits include: Medical; dental; life insurance; pension plan; tuition assistance; disability coverage; profit sharing; employee discounts; savings plan. Corporate headquarters location. Divisional headquarters. Operations at this facility include: Administration. International: Belgium, England, Japan, Switzerland.

Utah

AMSCO
P.O. Box 25368
Salt Lake City, UT 84125
Tel: (801) 972-6444
Contact: Howard Smith, Office Manager
Produces a broad range of building products. Corporate headquarters location. International: Canada, Hong Kong.

The Coleman Company
597 N. 1500 W.
Cedar City, UT 84720
Tel: (801) 586-9437
Contact: Personnel Director
Manufactures a broad range of sleeping bags and tents. Nationally, the company manufactures the following classes of products: Outing Sports Products; 'Hobie Cat' and 'O'Brien' Marine Products; 'Coleman' Camping Trailers; 'Crosman' Airguns; Home Heating and Air Conditioning Products; and Recreational Vehicle Products. Operates internationally through Coleman Canadian Sales and Coleman Foreign Sales. Specific products include lanterns, camp stoves, sleeping bags, tent, sailboats, waterskis, camping trailers, air rifles, and air conditioners. Corporate headquarters location: Wichita, KS. International: Australia, Canada, England, Germany, Japan, Netherlands.

Georgia-Pacific Corporation
2875 S. 300 W.
Salt Lake City, UT 84115
Tel: (801) 486-9281
Contact: Manager
Nationally, a leading manufacturer and distributor of a wide range of forest products, operating over 200 manufacturing and production facilities located throughout the United States and Canada, and internationally. One of the top producers of softwood, plywood, pulp, paper and paperboard. Also manufactures ammonia, methanol, cumene, acetone, and chlorine. Conducts extensive research and development. Corporate

headquarters location: Atlanta, GA. International facilities. New York Stock Exchange. International: Brazil, Canada, Indonesia.

Varian Eimac
1678 S. Pioneer Rd.
Salt Lake City, UT 84104
Tel: (801) 972-5000
Contact: John Gray, Personnel Manager

Produces electron tubes for use in company products. Nationally, company is engaged in the research, development, manufacture, and marketing of various products and services in the fields of communications, industrial equipment, medicine, scientific research, and defense. Operates in four industry segments: Electron Devices, Analytical Instruments, Industrial Equipment, and Medical Equipment. Corporate headquarters location: Palo Alto, CA. New York Stock Exchange. International: Australia, Belgium, Brazil, Canada, England, France, Germany, Ireland, Israel, Italy, Japan, Mexico, Netherlands, Sweden, Switzerland.

Vermont

Boise Cascade Corporation/ Specialty Paperboard Division/Pressboard Products
Brudie Rd.
P.O. Box 498
Brattleboro, VT 05301
Tel: (802) 257-0365
Contact: Jim Barker, Personnel Director

A manufacturer of types I, II, and III genuine and imitation pressboard, pattern board, jacquard board, electrical insulating paper and board, guide stock, tube stock, trunk board, and cover stock. Trade names include: Guidex, Norval, Fiberlec, Press-Guard, Press-Mate, Genuine Pressboard. Home office: One Jefferson Square, Boise, ID 83728. International: Austria, Canada, France, Germany.

Virginia

Inland Motor/Kollmorgen Corporation
501 1st St.
Radford, VA 22102
Tel: (703) 639-9045
Contact: John Clark, Personnel Director

Manufacturers DC torque motors, amplifiers, electromechanical actuators and controllers, magnetic bearings, and other advanced motion control products. Divisional headquarters location. Operations include: Manufacturing. Corporate headquarters location: Hartford, CT. New York Stock Exchange. Common positions include: Accountant; Buyer; Computer Programmer; Draftsperson; Engineer; Electrical Engineer; Industrial Engineer; Mechanical Engineer; Department Manager; General Manager; Operations/Production Manager; Personnel and Labor Relations Specialist; Purchasing Agent; Quality Control Supervisor. Principal educational backgrounds sought: Engineering. Company benefits include: Medical insurance; dental insurance; pension plan; life insurance; tuition assistance; disability coverage; profit sharing; savings plan. International: Ireland.

Pitney Bowes, Inc.
6100 Lincolnia Rd.
Alexandria, VA 22312
Tel: (703) 750-1200
Contact: Mark Cassanda, Sales Manager

Commercial sales and service facility for the world's largest producer of postage meters and other mailing equipment products, including mailing machines, postage scales, modular mailroom furniture, collators, addresser-printers, embossing machines, folding and inserting equipment, mail openers, counting and imprinting machines, and tax stamping equipment. Also a leading producer of copiers and copier supplies, retail price-marking equipment, and customer identification systems. Corporate headquarters location: Stamford, CT. New York Stock Exchange. International: Australia, Brazil, Canada, England, France, Germany, Switzerland.

Washington

Olin Defense Systems Group
11441 Willows Rd.
Redmond, WA 98052
Tel: (206) 885-5000
Contact: John Knapp, Employment Manager

A division of a major corporation engaged in manufacturing of rocket engines and gas generators, aviation power supplies and avionics. Also involved in high energy pulse power systems and their use in nuclear weapons effect testing. Common positions include: Electrical Engineer; Mechanical Engineer; Physicist. Principal educational backgrounds sought: Engineering; Physics. International: Australia, Belgium, Colombia, England, France, Germany, Ireland, Japan, Mexico, New Zealand, Singapore, Spain, Taiwan, Venezuela.

Sundstrand Data Control, Inc.
15001 N.E. 36th St.
P.O. Box 97001
Redmond, WA 98703
Tel: (206) 885-3711
Contact: Manager/Employee Relations

Engaged in the production of aircraft equipment and parts including temperature control components, digital recorders, and a variety of instrumentation systems. Employs over 1,000 people. Group headquarters location. Operations at this facility include: Manufacturing; administration; service; sales. Common positions include: Accountant; Administrator; Computer Programmer; Customer Service Representative; Engineer; Aerospace Engineer; Electrical Engineer; Industrial Engineer; Mechanical Engineer; Financial Analyst; Manager; Department Manager; General Manager; Operations/Production Manager; Personnel and Labor Relations Specialist; Programmer; Purchasing Agent; Quality Control Supervisor Systems Analyst; Technical Writer/Editor. Principal educational backgrounds sought: Accounting;

Business Administration; Computer Science; Engineering; Finance; Mathematics. Company benefits include: Medical insurance; dental insurance; pension plan; life insurance; tuition assistance; savings plan. International: Belgium, France, Japan, Singapore, Switzerland.

Weyerhaeuser Company
33663 32nd Dr. S.
Tacoma, WA 98477
Tel: (206) 924-2345

Contact: Effenus Henderson, Director, International Administration

Send resume with cover letter. One of the world's largest forest products companies. Products include lumber, plywood, pulp, shipping, and milk cartons, specialty papers, and panel products. Also engaged in real estate development and the management of nurseries and ornamentals. Corporate headquarters location. Operations at this facility include: Manufacturing; research/development; administration; service; sales. New York Stock Exchange. Common positions include: Accountant; Computer Programmer; Economist; Engineer; Chemical Engineer; Electrical Engineer; Industrial Engineer; Mechanical Engineer; Financial Analyst; Forester; Management Trainee; Sales Representative. Principal educational backgrounds sought: Accounting; Biology; Computer Science; Engineering; Finance; Marketing. Company benefits include: Medical insurance; dental insurance; pension plan; life insurance; tuition assistance; disability coverage. International: Australia, Belgium, Canada, Hong Kong, Japan, Switzerland.

West Virginia

FMC Corporation Spring Hill Plant
3200 MacCorkle Ave.
South Charleston, WV 25303
Tel: (304) 746-1500

Contact: Personnel Director

Produces hydrogen peroxide for use in the pulp and paper, textile, semiconductor, and food industries. Corporate headquarters location: Chicago, IL. Common positions include: Chemist; Chemical Engineer. Principal educational backgrounds sought: Chemistry; Engineering. Company benefits include: Medical insurance; pension plan; dental insurance; tuition assistance; life insurance; disability coverage; savings plan. Operations at this facility include: Manufacturing. New York Stock Exchange. International: Australia, Austria, Brazil, Colombia, Costa Rica, Germany, Greece, Hong Kong, Ireland, Italy, Korea, Netherlands, Philippines, Singapore, Spain, Switzerland.

Manville Sales
2905 3rd Ave.
P.O. Box 5130
Vienna, WV 26105
Tel: (304) 295-9361

Contact: Manager/Employee Relations

Manufactures glass and fiberglass for automotive and commercial industries. Operations include: Manufacturing. Corporate headquarters location: Denver, CO. New York Stock Exchange. Common positions include: Accountant; Computer Programmer; Customer Service Representative; Draftsperson; Ceramics Engineer; Electrical Engineer; Industrial Engineer; Mechanical Engineer; Department Manager; Personnel and Labor Relations Specialist; Quality Control Supervisor; Department Manager; Operations/Production Manager. Principal educational backgrounds sought: Accounting; Business Administration; Engineering; Finance; Industrial/Labor Relations; Organizational Development. Company benefits include: Medical insurance; dental insurance; pension plan; life insurance; tuition assistance; disability coverage; employee discounts; savings plan; prescription plan, accident insurance. Corporate headquarters location: Denver, CO. Operations at this facility include: Manufacturing. New York Stock Exchange. International: Australia, Austria, Belgium, Canada, England, France, Germany, Italy, Japan, Mexico, Saudi Arabia, Singapore, Spain, United Arab Emirates, Venezuela, Zaire.

PPG Industries
P.O. Box 191
New Martinsville, WV 26155
Contact: C. K. Willis, Employment Manager

Mailed inquiries only. Major manufacturer of industrial and specialty chemicals. Common positions include: Chemical Engineer; Mechanical Engineer. Principal educational backgrounds sought: Chemistry; Computer Science; Engineering. Company benefits include: Medical insurance; dental insurance; pension plan; life insurance; tuition assistance; disability coverage; profit sharing; employee discounts; savings plan. Parent Company: PPG Industries, Inc. (Pittsburgh, PA). Operations at this facility include: Manufacturing. New York Stock Exchange. International: Canada, France, Israel, Japan, Mexico, Switzerland, Taiwan, Venezuela.

Wisconsin

Briggs & Stratton Corporation
12301 W. Wirth St.
Wauwatusa, WI 53222
Tel: (414) 259-5333
Contact: Gerald E. Zitzer, Vice President, Human Resources

Briggs & Stratton is best known as the world's largest manufacturer of small air-cooled gasoline engines, powering equipment in more than 85 countries on all seven continents. In addition, the company is a major producer of automotive locking devices. Common positions include: Accountant; Blue-Collar Worker Supervisor; Buyer; Chemist; Computer Programmer; Customer Service Representative; Draftsperson; Electrical Engineer; Industrial Engineer; Mechanical Engineer; Metallurgical Engineer; Personnel and Labor Relations Specialist; Purchasing Agent; Quality Control Supervisor; Sales Representative; Statistician; Systems Analyst; Technical Writer/Editor. Principal educational backgrounds sought: Accounting; Business Administration; Communications; Engineering. Company benefits include: Medical insurance; dental insurance; pension plan; life insurance; tuition assistance; disability coverage; profit sharing; savings plan. Corporate headquarters location. Operations at this facility include: Regional and divisional headquarters; manufacturing; research/development; administration; service; sales. New York Stock Exchange. International: Germany.

Harley-Davidson, Inc.
3700 W. Juneau Ave.
Milwaukee, WI 53208
Tel: (414) 342-4680

Contact: C. William Gray, Vice President, Human Resources

A motorcycle manufacturer. Corporate headquarters location. Operations include: Manufacturing; research/development; administration; service; sales. Common positions include: Accountant; Buyer; Claim Representative; Computer Programmer; Customer Service Representative; Draftsperson; Mechanical Engineer; Electrical Engineer; Financial Analyst; Department Manager; General Manager; Marketing Specialist; Personnel and Labor Relations Specialist; Sales Representative; Technical Writer/Editor. Principal educational backgrounds sought: Accounting; Business Administration; Engineering; Finance; Marketing. Company benefits include: Medical, dental, and life insurance; pension plan; tuition assistance; disability coverage; employee discounts; savings plan. International: Germany.

Oscar Mayer Foods Corporation
910 Mayer Ave.
Madison, WI 53704
Tel: (608) 241-6853

Contact: Mr. Kwame S. Salter, Manager, Human Resources

Primarily involved in the manufacture and distribution of processed meat and poultry products. A subsidiary of General Foods Corporation. Employs approximately 12,500. Corporate headquarters location. Common positions include: Accountant; Computer Programmer; Biochemist; Chemist; Chemical Engineer; Civil Engineer; Electrical Engineer; Industrial Engineer; Mechanical Engineer; Food Technologist. Principal educational backgrounds sought: Accounting; Biology; Business Administration; Chemistry; Computer Science; Economics; Engineering; Finance; Marketing; Liberal Arts. Company benefits include: Medical, dental, and life insurance; pension plan; tuition assistance; disability coverage; profit sharing; savings plan. Corporate headquarters location. Operations at this facility include: Regional headquarters, divisional headquarters, research/development, administration. International: Japan, Switzerland, Venezuela.

Rayovac Corporation
601 Rayovac Dr.
Madison, WI 53711
Tel: (608) 275-3340

Contact: Personnel Manager

Manufactures primary batteries and battery-operated lighting devices. Corporate headquarters location. Common positions include:

Accountant; Buyer; Chemist; Computer Programmer; Draftsperson; Engineer; Chemical Engineer; Mechanical Engineer; Financial Analyst; Marketing Specialist; Sales Representative; Systems Analyst. Principal educational backgrounds sought: Accounting; Business Administration; Chemistry; Computer Science; Engineering; Finance; Marketing. Company benefits include: Medical, dental, and life insurance; tuition assistance; pension plan; disability coverage; profit sharing; employee discounts; savings plan. International: Brazil, Canada, England, Hong Kong, Japan, Mexico, Netherlands, Peru.

Wyoming

Marathon Oil
P.O. Box 2690
Cody, WY 82414
Tel: (307) 587-4961

Contact: Employee Relations Manager

Production and exploration office for the Rocky Mountain region. Common positions include: Accountant; Draftsperson; Petroleum Engineer; Geologist; Geophysicist. Principal educational backgrounds sought: Accounting; Business Administration; Engineering; Geology. Company benefits include: Medical insurance; dental insurance; pension plan; life insurance; tuition assistance; disability coverage; savings plan. Corporate headquarters location: Findlay, OH. Regional headquarters location. International: Brazil, Egypt, England, Germany, Indonesia, Ireland, Nigeria, Scotland, Singapore, Syria, Tunisia.

Safeway Stores
6106 Yellowstone, Suite E
Cheyenne, WY 82009
Tel: (307) 634-3591

Contact: District Manager

District office for the major supermarket chain. Corporate headquarters location: Denver, CO. International: Australia, Canada, England, Germany.

Appendix B
Selected Foreign-based Companies with U.S. Offices

The following companies, taken together, employ well over four million people worldwide and have offices in more than 100 countries. As might be expected from such corporate giants, virtually every occupation is represented, ranging from secretaries to assemblers to accountants to salespeople. To inquire about current international employment possibilities, write to the company's U.S. office, as listed.

BASF
Based in Ludwigshafen, West Germany.
Major product lines: paints, inks, chemicals, industrial products
Write to: BASF Corp.
200 Park Ave.
New York, NY 10166
Tel: (212) 682-1784

Bayer
Based in Leverkusen, West Germany
Major product lines: industrial and scientific chemicals, herbicides, pesticides, photographic chemicals and equipment
Write to: Bayer USA
500 Grant St.
Pittsburgh, PA 15219-2502
Tel: (412) 394-5554

Bridgestone
Based in Tokyo, Japan
Major product lines: bicycles, tires, rubber products
Write to: Bridgestone
2000 W. 190th St.
Torrance, CA 90504
Tel: (213) 320-6020

Casio
Based in Tokyo, Japan
Major product lines: electronic calculators, computers, watches, measurement devices
Write to: Casio, Inc.
15 Gardner Rd.
Fairfield, NJ 07006
Tel: (201) 575-7400

Club Méditerranée
Based in Paris, France
Major product lines: hotels, tourist industry promotions
Write to: Club Méditerranée
40 W. 57th St.
New York, NY 10019
Tel: (212) 944-2100

Daimler-Benz
Based in Stuttgart, West Germany
Major product lines: diesel engines and products, trucks, buses, automobiles, defense industry contracting
Write to: Mercedes-Benz of North America
One Mercedes Dr.
Montvale, NJ 07645
Tel: (201) 573-0600

Fiat
Based in Turin, Italy
Major product lines: automobiles and automobile parts, trucks, tractors
Write to: Fiat USA
375 Park Ave.
New York, NY 10152
Tel: (212) 486-3300

Heineken
Based in Amsterdam, The Netherlands
Major product lines: soft drinks, beer
Write to: Van Munching & Company
1270 Avenue of the Americas
New York, NY 10020
Tel: (212) 265-2685

Hitachi
Based in Tokyo, Japan
Major product lines: computer chips, consumer electronics, computers, TVs, construction, and chemicals
Write to: Hitachi America Ltd.
50 Prospect Ave.
Tarrytown, NY 10591
Tel: (914) 332-5800

F. Hoffmann-La Roche
Based in Basel, Switzerland
Major product lines: perfume, pharmaceuticals, vitamins, chemical laboratories, and laboratory products
Write to: F. Hoffmann-La Roche
840 Kingsland St.
Nutley, NJ 07110
Tel: (201) 235-5000

Hyundai
Based in Seoul, Korea
Major product lines: ships, automobiles, construction, computer products, musical instruments, furniture
Write to: Hyundai
One Bridge Plaza N.
Fort Lee, NJ 07024
Tel: (201) 592-7766

Kikkoman
Based in Noda, Japan
Major product lines: food condiments, wine, soy products
Write to: Kikkoman International
50 California St.
San Francisco, CA 94111
Tel: (415) 956-7550

Matsushita
Based in Osaka, Japan
Major product lines: consumer electronics, TVs, VCRs, laser products, FAX, copiers
Write to: Matsushita
One Panasonic Way
Secaucus, NJ 07904
Tel: (201) 348-7000

Michelin
Based in Paris, France
Major product lines: tires, rubber products, tourist guides
Write to: Michelin
Patewood Industrial Park
P.O. Box 19001
Greensville, SC 29602

Selected Foreign-based Companies with U.S. Offices

NEC
Based in Tokyo, Japan
Major product lines: telecommunication equipment, satellite components, computers, consumer electronics, monitors
Write to: NEC America
8 Old Farm Rd.
Melville, NY 11747
Tel: (516) 753-7060

Nestlé
Based in Vevey, Switzerland
Major product lines: coffee, chocolate, infant formula, food products
Write to: Nestlé
100 Blommingdale Rd.
White Plains, NY 10605
Tel: (914) 251-3000

Pearson
Based in London, England
Major product lines: magazines, newspapers, dishes, food products, textbooks
Write to: Pearson
c/o Lazard Frères
One Rockefeller Plaza
New York, NY 10020
Tel: (212) 489-6600

Perrier
Based in Paris, France
Major product lines: bottled water, fitness systems
Write to: Perrier
Great Waters of France
777 W. Putnam Ave.
Greenwich, CN 06830
Tel: (203) 531-4100

Philips
Based in Eindhoven, The Netherlands
Major product lines: general industrial products, consumer electronics, light bulbs, TVs, medical equipment

Write to: North American Philips
100 E. 42nd St.
New York, NY 10017
Tel: (212) 697-3600

Siemens
Based in Munich, West Germany
Major product lines: medical equipment, telecommunications, dental equipment, lighting products
Write to: Siemens
767 5th Ave.
New York, NY 10153
Tel: (212) 832-6601

Sony
Based in Tokyo, Japan
Major product lines: radio, TV, consumer electronics, compact discs, motion pictures
Write to: Sony Corporation of America
9 W. 57th St.
New York, NY 10019
Tel: (212) 371-5800

Thyssen
Based in Duisberg, West Germany
Major product lines: steel, heavy industrial products, shipping, pipes
Write to: Thyssen, c/o Budd Company
3155 W. Bay Beaver Rd.
Troy, Michigan 48084
Tel: (313) 643-3520

Toshiba
Based in Tokyo, Japan
Major product lines: nuclear products, lighting, computer products, TVs
Write to: Toshiba America
82 Totowa Ave.
Wayne, NJ 07470

Unilever
Based in London, England and Rotterdam, The Netherlands
Major product lines: food products, soaps, hygiene products

Write to: Unilever
10 E. 53rd St.
New York, NY 10022
Tel: (212) 688-6000

Yamaha
Based in Hamamatsu, Japan
Major product lines: consumer electronics, musical instruments, recreational vehicles, boats, sports equipment, computers
Write to: Yamaha International
P.O. Box 6600
Buena Park, CA 90622
Tel: (714) 522-9011

Appendix C
Using a World Trade Center in the Job Search

The World Trade Centers Association is an organization comprised of 115 member groups in 45 nations. Founded in 1968, the purpose of the association is to encourage the expansion of world trade and to promote international business relationships.

You can use a World Trade Center to receive information about business opportunities, meet influential foreign business people, and broaden your horizons with regard to the kinds of career possibilities available internationally. For a job candidate beginning to build foreign contacts and acquire useful information about international trade, a visit to a World Trade Center is an extremely worthwhile investment of time.

Australia

Melbourne
 World Trade Center Melbourne
 Cnr Flinoers and Spencer Sts.
 P.O. Box 4721
 Melbourne, Victoria, Australia 3001
 Tel: 611 1999

Bahrain

Bahrain
 World Trade Center Bahrain
 P.O. Box 669
 Bahrain, Arabian Gulf
 Tel: 243425

Belgium

Antwerp
 N.V. The World Trade Center of Belgium
 Braderijstreat 12-14-16
 B-2000 Antwerpen, Belgium
 Tel: 031/31-80-71 and 72

Brugge
 De Brugse Henze
 Internationale Club of West Flanders
 Steenstraat 96
 800 Brugge, Belgium
 Tel: 050/33-47-99

Brussels
World Trade Center Association
Brussels
162 Blvd. Emile Jacqmain
1000 Brussels, Belgium
Tel: 018-05-49

Ghent
International Club of Flanders
Sint-Pietersplein 11
9000 Ghent, Belgium
Tel: 091-22-96-68

Luxembourg
World Trade Center Luxembourg
Three Square Baron Bouvier
Brussels 1060, Belgium
Tel: 02537-71-56

Brazil

Rio de Janeiro
World Trade Center do Rio de Janeiro
Rua Mexico, 111/Gr. 1504—15 andar
Rio de Janeiro, Brazil 20031
Tel: (021) 224-3065

Sao Paulo
World Trade Center de Sao Paulo
Serviease S.A.
Rua Estado Unido, 1093
01427 Sao Paulo—SP—Brazil
Tel: (011) 280-4811

Bulgaria

Sofia
Bulgarian Chamber of Commerce and Industry
11A, Stambolilski Blvd.
Sofia, Bulgaria
Tel: 87-26-31

Canada

Calgary
World Trade Centre Calgary
Stock Exchange Tower
609 Granville St., Suite 1900
Vancouver, B.C. Canada V7Y 1A7
Tel: (604) 688-0211

Edmonton
World Trade Center Edmonton
7300—116 Ave.
Box 1480
Edmonton, Alberta, Canada T5J 2N5
Tel: (403) 471-7283

Halifax
World Trade and Convention Center—Halifax
1800 Argyle St.
P.O. Box 955
Halifax, Nova Scotia, Canada B3J 2V9
Tel: (902) 421-8686

Montreal
World Trade Centre Montreal
Montreal Chamber of Commerce
772 West Sherbrooke St.
Montreal, Quebec, Canada H3A 1G1
Tel: (514) 288-9090

Ottawa
World Trade Centre Ottawa
W.T.C. World Trade Centres of Canada, Ltd.
1191 Mountain St.
Montreal, Quebec, Canada H3Q 1Z2
Tel: (514) 866-1352

Quebec
Centre de Commerce International de l'Est du Quebec
17 Rue St. Louis
Quebec City, Quebec, Canada GIR 3Y8
Tel: (481) 692-3853

Toronto
World Trade Centre Toronto
Toronto Harbour Commissioners
60 Harbour St.
Toronto, Ontario, Canada M5J 1B7
Tel: (416) 863-2154

Vancouver
World Trade Center Vancouver
The Vancouver Board of Trade
1177 W. Hastings St., Suite 500
Vancouver, B.C. Canada V6E 2K3
Tel: (604) 681-2111

Winnipeg
World Trade Center Winnipeg
c/o W.T.C. World Trade Centers of
Canada, Ltd.
1191 Mountain St.
Montreal, Quebec, Canada H3Q 1Z2
Tel: (514) 866-1352

Colombia
Bogota
World Trade Center Bogota
P.O. Box 6005
Bogota, Colombia
Tel: 2184411

Congo
Pointe-Noire
Chamber of Commerce of Pointe-Noire
3 Ave. du General de Gaulle
P.O. Box 665
Pointe-Noire, People's Republic of Congo
Tel: 94-12-80

Cuba
Havana City
Chamber of Commerce of the
Republic of Cuba
661 21st St.
Vedado, Havana City, Cuba
c/o Ramon Sanchez Parodi
Cuban Interests Section
2630 16 St. NW
Washington, DC 20009 U.S.A.
Telex: 511752 CAMAR CU

Cyprus
Cyprus Chamber of Commerce and Industry
Evagoras Ave.
Hadjisavvas Building, 6th Fl.
P.O. Box 1455
Nicosia, Cyprus
Tel: 63212-49500

Denmark
Copenhagen
World Trade Center Copenhagen
International House
Bella Center A/S
Center Blvd.
DK-2300 Copenhagen S. Denmark
Tel: (01) 51-88-11

Dubai
Dubai International Trade Centre
Trade Center Management Co., Ltd.
P.O. Box 9292
Dubai, United Arab Emirates
Tel: 472200

Egypt
Cairo
Cairo World Trade Center
Arab International Bank
35 Abdel Khalek Sarwat St.
P.O. Box 1563
Cairo, Egypt
Tel: 926120 and 926233

Port Said
World Trade Center Port Said
Arab International Bank
35 Abdel Khalek Sarwat St.
P.O. Box 1563
Cairo, Egypt
Tel: 926233

France
Le Havre
World Trade Center Le Havre
Quai George V
76600 Le Havre, France
Tel: (35) 21-43-41

Marseille
Mediterranean World Trade Center
2, Rue Henri-Barbusse
13241 Marseille, Cedex 01, France
Tel: (91) 08-60-02

Nantes
   Atlantic World Trade Center
   Chamber of Commerce and Industry
   18X—44040 Nantes, Cedex, France
   Tel: (40) 89-30-00
Paris
   World Trade Center of Paris
   Chamber of Commerce and Industry
   2 Rue de Viarmes
   75000 1 Paris, France
   Tel: (1) 508-36-00
Strasbourg
   Maison du Commerce International
   de Strasbourg
   Immeuble "Le Concorde"
   4 Quai Kleber
   F 67056 Strasbourg Cedex, France
   Tel: (88) 32-48-90

Hong Kong

Hong Kong
   World Trade Centre Hong Kong
   c/o World Trade Centre Club
   Hong Kong
   2/M and 3/F World Trade Centre
   Causeway Bay, Hong Kong
   Tel: 5-779528

Hungary

Budapest
   Hungarian Chamber of Commerce
   Kossuth Lajos Ter 6-8
   Budapest, Hungary 1389
   Tel: 533-333

India

Bombay
   World Trade Center, Bombay
   M. Vivesvaraya Industrial Research
   and Development Centre
   Cuffe Parade
   Colaba, Bombay-5, India
   Tel: 21-44-34-21-73-96

Chandigarh
   World Trade Center Chandigarh
   Bhatia and Associates
   1532, Sector 34-D
   Chandigarh—160 022
   India Cable: "WORLDTRADE"
   Chandigarh
New Delhi
   Trade Development Authority
   Bank of Baroda Building
   16, Sansad Marg
   P.O. Box 767
   New Delhi, 110001, India
   Tel: 312819

Indonesia

Jakarta
   World Trade Center of Indonesia
   P.T. Jakarta Land
   Level 10, Wisma Metropolitan
   Jalan, Sudiman, Jakarta
   P.O. Box 3164/JKT
   Jakarta, Indonesia
   Tel: 584801, 584802, 584803

Israel

Tel-Aviv
   World Trade Center Israel
   Industry House
   29 Hamered St.
   P.O. Box 50029
   Tel-Aviv, Israel
   Tel: 03-65-01-20

Italy

Genoa
   Compagnia Sanbergnigno S.p.A.
   Chamber of Commerce
   Via Garibaldi, 4
   16124 Genoa, Italy
   Tel: (010) 20-941

Milan
World Trade Center Italy
Palazzo WTC
Centro Direzionale Milanofiori
20090 Asago (Milan) Italy
Tel: 8244086

Japan

Tokyo
The World Trade Center of Japan, Inc.
P.O. Box 57
World Trade Center Building
No. 4-1, 2-chome, Hamamatsu-cho
Minato-ku, Tokyo, 105 Japan
Tel: (03) 435-5651

Ivory Coast

Abidjan
World Trade Center Abidjan
P.O. Box V.68
Abidjan, Ivory Coast
Tel: 32-38-69/32-37-87/32-38-74

Malaysia

Kuala Lumpur
Putra World Trade Centre
Rahim and Co., Chartered
Surveyors SDN BHD
International Real Estate Consultant
Wisma Jayanita
64 Jalan Raja Muda
P.O. Box 11215
Kuala Lumpur, Malaysia
Tel: 03-919922

The Netherlands

Amsterdam
World Trade Center Amsterdam
Prinses Irenestraat
P.O. Box 7030
1007 JA Amsterdam, The
Netherlands
Tel: (01) 20-5759111

Eindhoven
World Trade Center Electronics
Fellenoord 51
P.O. Box 2085
5600 CB Eindhoven, The Netherlands
Tel: (040) 442575

Leiden
World Flower Trade Center
P.O. Box 9324
2300 PH Leiden, The Netherlands
Tel: 31 (72) 31-2031

Rotterdam
World Trade Center Rotterdam
Meent 134
P.O. Box 30055
3001 DB Rotterdam, The
Netherlands
Tel: (010) 333611

Nigeria

Lagos
World Trade Center of Nigeria, Ltd.
Western House, 8th Fl.
8/10 Broad St.
P.O. Box 4466
Lagos, Nigeria
Tel: 635128

People's Republic of China

Beijing
World Trade Centre Beijing
Fua Hua Enterprises Ltd.
c/o World Trade Centre Club Hong Kong
World Trade Centre
Causeway Bay, Hong Kong
Tel: 5-779528

Nanjing
Jiansu Provincial Travel and
Tourism Corp., P.R.C.
North Zhong Shan Rd.
Nanjing, P.R.C.
Tel: 34121, 44141

Shanghai
The Preparatory Office of Shanghai
World Trade Centre
c/o CCPIT Shanghai Sub-Council
33 Zhong Shan Dong yi Lu
Shanghai, P.R.C.
Tel: 232348

Shenzhen
Convention Center of Shenzhen
Parker Hill
Shenzhen, P.R.C.
Tel: 22834

Portugal

Lisbon
World Trade Center Lisbon
Av. do Brasil, N.1
1700 Lisbon, Portugal
Tel: 733871-733571

Porto
World Trade Center Porto
Av. da Boavista N. 1203—5-sala 505
Porto, Portugal
Tel: (2) 62095

Saudi Arabia

Jeddah
Jeddah World Trade Center
Saudi Economic and Development
Co., Ltd.
P.O. Box 4384
Jeddah, Kingdom of Saudi Arabia
Tel: (02) 644-0920-1

Singapore

Singapore
World Trade Center Singapore
One Maritime Square, No. 02-11
World Trade Centre
Singapore 0490
Republic of Singapore
Tel: 271221, Ext. 2791

South Africa

Johannesburg
The South African Foreign Trade
Organization
P.O. Box 9039
Johannesburg, 2000
South Africa

South Korea

Seoul
World Trade Center Korea
Korean Traders Association
10-1, 2-Ka Hoehyon-dong, Chung-Ku
C.P.O. Box 1117
Seoul, Korea
Tel: 771-41

Spain

Barcelona
Spanish Federation of Importers and
Exporters
Trafalgar, 4, 4-A
06010 Barcelona, Spain
Tel: 317-95-86-317-95-90

Madrid
World Trade Center Madrid, S.A.
Jose Ortega Y Gasset 22,7
28006 Madrid, Spain
Tel: (1) 4359393

Valencia
World Trade Center Valencia S.A.
Eduarbo Bosca, 33
46023 Valencia, Spain
Tel: 6-360-46-77

Sweden

Gothenburg
Scandinavian World Trade Center
AB
Storgatan 26
S-411 38 Goetborg, Sweden
Tel: 031/177660

Switzerland

Basel
World Trade Center Basel
c/o Swiss Industries Fair, Basel
Isteinerstrasse 51
CH-4021 Basel, Switzerland
Tel: 061-26-2029

Geneva
World Trade Center Geneva
P.O. Box 306
CH 1215 Geneva—Airport 15
Switzerland
Tel: (022) 989-989

Zurich
FIATA
29 Brauerstrasse
POB 177
CH-8026 Zurich, Switzerland
Tel: 241-80-45

Taiwan

Taipei
Taipei World Trade Center, Ltd.
Sung Shan Airport Terminal
340 Tun Hwa N. Rd.
Taipei, Taiwan
Tel: (02) 715-1551

Thailand

Bangkok
World Trade Center Bangkok Co., Ltd.
8th Fl. Sinthon Building
132 Wireless Rd. Patumwam
10500, Bangkok, Thailand
Tel: 2501801-7

Turkey

Istanbul
Istanbul World Trade Center, Inc.
Istanbul Ticaret Odaai
Ragip Gumuspala Cad.
Eminomu, Istanbul
P.O. Box 377, Turkey
Tel: (00901) 526-62-15

United Kingdom

London
World Trade Centre London
International House
St. Katharine-by-the-Tower
London, E1 9UN
United Kingdom
Tel: 01-488-2400

Manchester
The Manchester Chamber of
Commerce and Industry
56 Oxford St.
King St.
Manchester, M60 7HJ
United Kingdom
Tel: (061) 236-3210

United States

Atlanta
World Trade Club of Atlanta, Inc.
240 Peachtree St., Suite 2200
Atlanta, GA 30303 U.S.A.
Tel: (404) 525-4144

Baltimore
The World Trade Center Baltimore
Baltimore, MD 21202 U.S.A.
Tel: (301) 659-4544

Baltimore
The Merchants Club
206 East Redwood St.
Baltimore, MD 21202 U.S.A.
Tel: (301) 742-6467

Boston
International Business Center of
New England
22 Batterymarch St.
Boston, MA 02210 U.S.A.
Tel: (617) 542-0426

Chicago
Club International
The Drake Hotel
140 E. Walton Pl.
Chicago, IL 60611 U.S.A.
Tel: (312) 787-2200

Colorado Springs
Rocky Mountain World Trade Center
Red Rock Canyon Project
3221 W. Colorado Ave.
Colorado Springs, CO 80904 U.S.A.
Tel: (303) 633-9041

Columbus
World Trade and Technology Center
of Columbus
10793 State Rt. 37 W.
Sunbury, OH 43074 U.S.A.
Tel: (614) 965-2974

Des Moines
Iowa World Trade Center Des
Moines
3200 Ruan Center
666 Grand Ave.
Des Moines, IA 50390 U.S.A.
Tel: (515) 245-2555

Ft. Lauderdale
World Trade Center Fort
Lauderdale, Florida
P.O. Box 13066
1800 Eller Dr.
Port Everglades, FL 33316 U.S.A.
Tel: (305) 523-5307

Greensboro
World Trade Center—North
Carolina
P.O. Box 19290
Greensboro, NC 27419 U.S.A.
Tel: (929) 854-0078

Honolulu
Hawaii International Services
Branch
Department of Planning and
Economic Development
P.O. Box 2359
Honolulu, HI 96804 U.S.A.
Tel: (808) 548-3048

Houston
World Trade Center Houston
1520 Texas Ave., Suites 1D and 1E
Houston, TX 77002 U.S.A.
Tel: (713) 225-0968

Jacksonville
Jacksonville International Trade
Association
Jacksonville Chamber of Commerce
Three Independent Dr.
P.O. Box 329
Jacksonville, FL 32201 U.S.A.
Tel: (904) 353-0300

Long Beach
The Port of Long Beach
925 Harbor Plaza
P.O. Box 570
Long Beach, CA 92801 U.S.A.
Tel: (213) 437-0041

Miami
Execucentre International
444 Brickell Ave., Suite 650
Miami, FL 33131 U.S.A.
Tel: (305) 374-8300

New Orleans
International House—WTC
611 Gravier St.
New Orleans, LA 70230 U.S.A.
Tel: (504) 522-3591

New York
World Trade Center New York
The Port Authority of New York and
New Jersey, Suite 63 W
One World Trade Center
New York, NY 10048 U.S.A.
Tel: (212) 466-8380

Norfolk
World Trade Center Norfolk
600 World Trade Center
Norfolk, VA 23510 U.S.A.
Tel: (804) 623-8000

Orlando
World Trade Center Orlando
P.O. Box 1234
Orlando, FL 32801 U.S.A.
Tel: (305) 425-1234

Pomona
Inland Pacific World Trade Institute
422 W. 7th St., Suite 302
Los Angeles, CA 90014 U.S.A.
Tel: (213) 627-6738

Portland
Columbia World Trade Center Corp.
121 S.W. Salmon
Portland, OR 97204 U.S.A.
Tel: (503) 220-3067

San Francisco
World Trade Center of San
Francisco, Inc.
1170 Sacramento St.
Penthouse B
San Francisco, CA 92108 U.S.A.
Tel: (415) 928-3438

Santa Ana
World Trade Center Association of
Orange County
200 E. Sandpointe Ave.
Santa Ana, CA 92707 U.S.A.
Tel: (714) 549-8151

Sarasota
World Trade Council of Southwest
Florida
P.O. Box 911
Sarasota, FL 33578 U.S.A.
Tel: (813) 366-4060

Seattle
Seattle World Trade Center Corp.
500 Union St., Suite 840
Seattle, WA 96101 U.S.A.
Tel: (206) 622-4121

St. Paul
Minnesota World Trade Center
1300 Conwed Tower
444 Cedar St.
St. Paul, MN 55101 U.S.A.
Tel: (612) 297-1580

Tacoma
World Trade Center Tacoma
P.O. Box 1837
Tacoma, WA 96401 U.S.A.
Tel: (206) 383-5841, Ext. 321

Tampa
Tampa Bay International Trade
Council
P.O. Box 420
Tampa, FL 33601 U.S.A.
Tel: (813) 228-7777, Ext. 234

Toledo
Toledo World Trade Center
136 N. Summit St.
P.O. Box 2087
Toledo, OH 43603 U.S.A.
Tel: (419) 255-7226

Washington, DC
World Trade Center Washington
1000 Connecticut Ave., NW, Suite 707
Washington, DC 20036 U.S.A.
Tel: (202) 955-6164

Wales

Cardiff
World Trade Centre Cardiff
16 Cathedral Rd.
Cardiff, South Glamorgan, Wales
Tel: Cardiff 44191

West Germany

Ruhr Valley
World Trade Center Ruhrbebiet
Verein pro Ruhrgebiet e.V.
Kronprinzenstrasse 35
D 4300 Essen 1, W. Germany
Tel: 2069-318

Yugoslavia

Ljubijana
Business Association MAGOS
Titova 118
6113 Ljubijana, Yugoslavia
Tel: 961/347-756

Appendix D
Obtaining Information and Applications from Embassies

The Washington embassies of foreign countries are, collectively, a treasure-house of information and potential contacts for international jobseekers. Needless to say, embassies are not employment offices. They can, however, furnish you with detailed information about work permit procedures, types of business and industry in the country, and the culture and geography of the country.

To ask for this kind of information, simply write to the country's ambassador, as in this sample letter:

Date

Your Address

The Honorable Ambassador
Embassy of Sweden
600 New Hampshire Ave. NW
Washington, DC 20007

Dear Ambassador:

   I am planning a trip to Sweden in the near future, and would deeply appreciate whatever literature or information you can furnish on [specify your interests here—visa information, work permits, contact with trade organizations, general cultural information about Sweden and its people]. By way of introduction, I am [introduce yourself briefly—what you do, what your background is, what your goals are].

I'm eager to learn as much as possible about Sweden before beginning my trip. Thank you for assisting me.

Sincerely,
(signature)
Your Name

Type this letter on quality stationery. The response you receive will be in direct relation to the professionalism of your letter.

When you receive a response from the ambassador, send a brief thank-you note. It's a contact you'll want to nurture.

Embassy of Afghanistan
2341 Wyoming Ave. NW
Washington, DC 20008
Tel: (202) 234-3770

Embassy of Algeria
2118 Kalorama Rd. NW
Washington, DC 20008
Tel: (202) 265-2800

Embassy of Argentina
1600 New Hampshire Ave. NW
Washington, DC 20009
Tel: (202) 939-6400

Embassy of Australia
1601 Massachusetts Ave. NW
Washington, DC 20036
Tel: (202) 797-3000

Embassy of Austria
3524 International Ct. NW
Washington, DC 20008
Tel: (202) 895-6700

Embassy of the Bahamas
2220 Massachusetts Ave. NW
Washington, D.C. 20008
Tel: (202) 319-2660

Embassy of Bangladesh
2201 Wisconsin Ave. NW
Washington, DC 20007
Tel: (202) 342-8372

Embassy of Barbados
2144 Wyoming Ave. NW
Washington, DC 20008
Tel: (202) 939-9200

Embassy of Belgium
3330 Garfield St. NW
Washington, DC 20008
Tel: (202) 333-6900

Embassy of Belize
2535 Massachusetts Ave. NW
Washington, DC 20008
Tel: (202) 332-9636

Embassy of the People's Republic of Benin
2737 Cathedral Ave. NW
Washington, DC 20008
Tel: (202) 232-6656

Embassy of Bolivia
3014 Massachusetts Ave. NW
Washington, DC 20008
Tel: (202) 483-4410

Embassy of Brazil
3006 Massachusetts Ave. NW
Washington, DC 20008
Tel: (202) 745-2700

Embassy of Brunei Darussalm
2600 Virginia Ave. NW
Washington, DC 20007
Tel: (202) 342-0159

Embassy of Burkina Faso
2340 Massachusetts Ave. NW
Washington, DC 20008
Tel: (202) 332-5577

Embassy of the Union of Burma
2300 S. St. NW
Washington, DC 20008
Tel: (202) 332-9044

Embassy of the United Republic of Cameroon
2349 Massachusetts Ave. NW
Washington, DC 20008
Tel: (202) 265-8790

Embassy of Canada
501 Pennsylvania Ave. NW
Washington, DC 20001
Tel: (202) 682-1740

Embassy of Cape Verde
3415 Massachusetts Ave. NW
Washington, DC 20007
Tel: (202) 965-6820

Embassy of Chad
2002 R St. NW
Washington, DC 20009
Tel: (202) 462-4009

Embassy of Chile
1732 Massachusetts Ave. NW
Washington, DC 20036
Tel: (202) 785-1746

Embassy of Colombia
2118 Leroy Pl. NW
Washington, DC 20008
Tel: (202) 387-8338

Embassy of Costa Rica
1825 Connecticut Ave. NW
Washington, DC 20009
Tel: (202) 234-2945

Embassy of Cyprus
2211 R St. NW
Washington, DC 20008
Tel: (202) 462-5772

Embassy of Czech Republic
3900 Spring of Freedom St. NW
Washington, DC 20008
Tel: (202) 274-9100

Embassy of Denmark
3200 Whitehaven Ave. NW
Washington, DC 20008
Tel: (202) 234-4300

Embassy of The Dominican Republic
1715 22nd St. NW
Washington, DC 20008
Tel: (202) 332-6280

Embassy of Ecuador
2535 15th St. NW
Washington, DC 20009
Tel: (202) 234-7200

Embassy of Egypt
3521 International Ct. NW
Washington, DC 20008
Tel: (202) 895-5400

Embassy of El Salvador
2308 California St. NW
Washington, DC 20008
Tel: (202) 265-3480

Embassy of Ethiopia
2134 Kalorama Rd. NW
Washington, DC 20008
Tel: (202) 234-2281

Embassy of Fiji
2233 Wisconsin Ave. NW
Washington, DC 20007
Tel: (202) 337-8320

Embassy of Finland
3216 New Mexico Ave. NW
Washington, DC 20016
Tel: (202) 298-5800

Embassy of France
4101 Reservoir Rd. NW
Washington, DC 20007
Tel: (202) 944-6000

Embassy of The Republic of Gabon
2034 20th St. NW, Ste. 200
Washington, DC 20009
Tel: (202) 797-1000

Embassy of German Federal Republic
4645 Reservoir Rd. NW
Washington, DC 20007
Tel: (202) 298-4000

Embassy of Greece
2221 Massachusetts Ave. NW
Washington, DC 20008
Tel: (202) 939-5800

Embassy of Grenada
1701 New Hampshire Ave.
Washington, DC 20009
Tel: (202) 265-2561

Embassy of Guatemala
2220 R St. NW
Washington, DC 20008
Tel: (202) 745-4952

Embassy of New Guinea
2112 Leroy Pl. NW
Washington, DC 20008
Tel: (202) 483-9420

Embassy of Guyana
3490 Tracy Pl. NW
Washington, DC 20008
Tel: (202) 265-6900

Embassy of Honduras
3007 Tilden St. NW
Washington, DC 20008
Tel: (202) 966-7702

Embassy of Hungary
3910 Shoemaker St. NW
Washington, DC 20008
Tel: (202) 362-6730

Embassy of Iceland
1156 15th St. NW, Ste. 1200
Washington, DC 20005
Tel: (202) 265-6653

Embassy of India
2107 Massachusetts Ave. NW
Washington, DC 20008
Tel: (202) 939-7000

Embassy of The Republic of Indonesia
2020 Massachusetts Ave. NW
Washington, DC 20036
Tel: (202) 775-5200

Embassy of Iraq
1801 P St. NW
Washington, DC 20036
Tel: (202) 483-7500

Embassy of Ireland
2234 Massachusetts Ave. NW
Washington, DC 20008
Tel: (202) 462-3939

Embassy of Israel
3514 International Dr. NW
Washington, DC 20008
Tel: (202) 364-5500

Embassy of Italy
1601 Fuller St. NW
Washington, DC 20009
Tel: (202) 328-5500

Embassy of Jamaica
1850 K St. NW
Washington, DC 20006
Tel: (202) 452-0660

Embassy of Japan
2520 Massachusetts Ave.
Washington, DC 20008
Tel: (202) 939-6700

Embassy of Jordan
3504 International Dr. NW
Washington, DC 20008
Tel: (202) 966-2664

Embassy of Kenya
2249 R St. NW
Washington, DC 20008
Tel: (202) 387-6101

Embassy of Kuwait
3500 International Dr. NW
Washington, DC 20008
Tel: (202) 364-2100

Embassy of The Lao People's Democratic Republic
2222 S St. NW
Washington, DC 20008
Tel: (202) 332-6416

Embassy of Lebanon
2560 28th St. NW
Washington, DC 20008
Tel: (202) 939-6300

Embassy of Luxembourg
2200 Massachusetts Ave NW
Washington, DC 20008
Tel: (202) 265-4171

Embassy of Madagascar
2374 Massachusetts Ave. NW
Washington, DC 20008
Tel: (202) 265-5525

Embassy of Malawi
2408 Massachusetts Ave. NW
Washington, DC 20008
Tel: (202) 797-1007

Embassy of Malaysia
2401 Massachusetts Ave. NW
Washington, DC 20008
Tel: (202) 328-2700

Embassy of The Republic of Mali
2130 R St. NW
Washington, DC 20008
Tel: (202) 332-2249

Embassy of Malta
2017 Connecticut Ave. NW
Washington, DC 20008
Tel: (202) 462-3611

Embassy of Mauritius
4301 Connecticut Ave. NW
Washington, DC 20008
Tel: (202) 244-1491

Embassy of Mexico
1911 Pennsylvania Ave. NW
Washington, DC 20006
Tel: (202) 728-1600

Embassy of Morocco
2601 21st St. NW
Washington, DC 20009
Tel: (202) 462-7979

Embassy of Mozambique
1990 M St. NW, Ste. 570
Washington, DC 20036
Tel: (202) 293-7146

Embassy of Nepal
2131 Leroy Pl. NW
Washington, DC 20008
Tel: (202) 667-4550

Embassy of The Netherlands
4200 Wisconsin Ave. NW
Washington, DC 20016
Tel: (202) 244-5300

Embassy of Nicaragua
1627 New Hampshire Ave. NW
Washington, DC 20009
Tel: (202) 939-6570

Embassy of Niger
2204 R St. NW
Washington, DC 20008
Tel: (202) 483-4224

Embassy of Nigeria
1333 16th St. NW
Washington, DC 20036
Tel: (202) 986-8400

Embassy of Norway
2720 34th St. NW
Washington, DC 20008
Tel: (202) 333-6000

Embassy of Oman
2535 Belmont Rd. NW
Washington, DC 20008
Tel: (202) 387-1980

Embassy of Pakistan
2315 Massachusetts Ave. NW
Washington, DC 20008
Tel: (202) 939-6200

Embassy of Panama
2868 McGill Terrace NW
Washington, DC 20008
Tel: (202) 483-1407

Embassy of Papua New Guinea
1615 New Hampshire Ave. NW
3rd Fl.
Washington, DC 20009
Tel: (202) 745-3680

Embassy of Paraguay
2400 Massachusetts Ave. NW
Washington, DC 20008
Tel: (202) 483-6960

Embassy of the Peoples' Republic of China
2300 Connecticut Ave. NW
Washington, DC 20008
Tel: (202) 328-2500

Embassy of Peru
1700 Massachusetts Ave. NW
Washington, DC 20036
Tel: (202) 833-9860

Embassy of Portugal
2125 Kalorama Rd. NW
Washington, DC 20008
Tel: (202) 328-8610

Embassy of Qatar
600 New Hampshire Ave. NW
Washington, DC 20037
Tel: (202) 338-0111

Embassy of Romania
1607 23rd St. NW
Washington, DC 20008
Tel: (202) 332-4846

Embassy of Russia
1125 16th St. NW
Washington, DC 20036
Tel: (202) 628-7551

Embassy of Rwanda
1714 New Hampshire Ave. NW
Washington, DC 20009
Tel: (202) 232-2882

Embassy of Saudi Arabia
601 New Hampshire Ave. NW
Washington, DC 20037
Tel: (202) 342-3800

Embassy of Senegal
2112 Wyoming Ave. NW
Washington, DC 20008
Tel: (202) 234-0540

Embassy of Sierra Leone
1701 19th St. NW
Washington, DC 20009
Tel: (202) 939-9261

Embassy of Singapore
3501 International Pl. NW
Washington, DC 20008
Tel: (202) 537-3100

Embassy of Somali Democratic Republic
600 New Hampshire Ave. NW
Washington, DC 20037
Tel: (202) 342-1575

Embassy of South Africa
3051 Massachusetts Ave. NW
Washington, DC 20008
Tel: (202) 232-4400

Embassy of Spain
2375 Pennsylvania Ave. NW
Washington, DC 20037
Tel: (202) 728-2340

Embassy of Sri Lanka
2148 Wyoming Ave. NW
Washington, DC 20008
Tel: (202) 483-4025

Embassy of St. Kitts and Nevis
3216 New Mexico Ave. NW
Washington, DC 20016
Tel: (202) 833-3550

Embassy of St. Lucia
3216 New Mexico Ave. NW
Washington, DC 20016
Tel: (202) 463-7378

Embassy of Sudan
2210 Massachusetts Ave. NW
Washington, DC 20008
Tel: (202) 338-8565

Embassy of The Kingdom of Swaziland
3400 International Dr. NW
Washington, DC 20008
Tel: (202) 362-6683

Embassy of Sweden
1501 M St. NW
Washington, DC 20005
Tel: (202) 467-2600

Embassy of Switzerland
2900 Cathedral Ave. NW
Washington, DC 20008
Tel: (202) 745-7900

Embassy of Syria
2215 Wyoming Ave. NW
Washington, DC 20008
Tel: (202) 232-6313

Embassy of Tanzania
2139 R St. NW
Washington, DC 20008
Tel: (202) 939-6125

Embassy of Togo
2208 Massachusetts Ave. NW
Washington, DC 20008
Tel: (202) 234-4212

Embassy of Trinidad and Tobago
1708 Massachusetts Ave. NW
Washington, DC 20036
Tel: (202) 467-6490

Embassy of Tunisia
1515 Massachusetts Ave. NW
Washington, DC 20005
Tel: (202) 862-1850

Embassy of Turkey
1714 Massachusetts Ave. NW
Washington, DC 20036
Tel: (202) 659-8200

Embassy of Uganda
5911 16th St. NW
Washington, DC 20011
Tel: (202) 726-7100

Embassy of Uruguay
1918 F St. NW
Washington, DC 20006
Tel: (202) 331-1313

Embassy of The United Arab Emirates
3000 K St. NW, Ste. 600
Washington, DC 20007
Tel: (202) 338-6500

Embassy of Venezuela
1099 30th St. NW
Washington, DC 20007
Tel: (202) 342-2214

Embassy of the SFR of Yugoslavia
2410 California St. NW
Washington, DC 20008
Tel: (202) 462-6566

Embassy of The Republic of Zaire
1800 New Hampshire Ave. NW
Washington, DC 20009
Tel: (202) 234-7690

Embassy of The Republic of Zambia
2419 Massachusetts Ave. NW
Washington, DC 20008
Tel: (202) 265-9717

Embassy of Zimbabwe
1608 New Hampshire Ave. NW
Washington, DC 20009
Tel: (202) 332-7100

Appendix E
Finding International Jobs with Councils, Associations, and Government Agencies

You may already belong to one or more organizations that regularly send employees to foreign posts. Each of the following agencies and associations will provide you with complete information about its mission, geographic scope of operations, and staffing. It's a good idea to write for general information before asking about specific job openings. The presence of an organization on this list does not imply that it currently advertises international job openings.

AFL-CIO
Department of International Affairs
815 16th St. NW
Washington, DC 20006

Agency for International Development
International Development Intern Recruitment
Office of Personnel and Management
320 21st St. NW
Washington, DC 20523

Agricultural Development Council
1290 Avenue of the Americas
New York, NY 10020

AIESEC-US (Association internationale des etudiants en sciences economiques et commerciales)
14 W. 23rd St.
New York, NY 10010

Appendix E

American Council on Education
One Dupont Circle NW
Washington, DC 20036

American Field Service
313 E. 43rd St.
New York, NY 10017

American Graduate School of International Management
Glendale, AZ 85306

Asian Development Bank
2330 Roxas Blvd.
Pasay City, Philippines

Association for International Practical Training
American City Building, Suite 217
Columbia, MD 21044

Association of Teachers of English as a Second Language (TESOL)
1860 19th St. NW
Washington, DC 20009

Bureau of International Aviation
Civil Aeronautics Board
1825 Connecticut Ave. NW
Washington, DC 20428

Bureau of International Labor Affairs
Department of Labor
200 Constitution Ave. NW
Washington, D.C. 20210

Business Council for International Understanding
420 Lexington Ave.
New York, NY 10170

Carnegie Endowment for International Peace
30 Rockefeller Plaza
New York, NY 10020

Central Intelligence Agency
Washington, DC 20505

Chamber of Commerce of the United States
1615 H Street NW
Washington, DC 20006-4902

Committee for Economic Development
477 Madison Ave.
New York, NY 10022

Congressional Budget Office
National Security and International Affairs Division
Washington, DC 20515

Congressional Research Service
Library of Congress
10 First St. SE
Washington, DC 20540

Council on International Educational Exchange
205 E. 42nd St.
New York, NY 10017

Ford Foundation
320 E. 43rd St.
New York, NY 10017

Foreign Agriculture Service
Personnel Division
U.S. Department of Agriculture
Washington, DC 20007

Foreign Commercial Service
Commerce Department Building
Washington, DC 20230

Foster Parents Plan International
Box 400
Warwick, RI 02887

General Accounting Office (GAO)
International Division
441 G St. NW
Washington, DC 20548

General Services Administration (GSA)
18th and F Sts. NW
Washington, DC 20405

Institute of International Education
809 United Nations Plaza
New York, NY 10017

Inter-American Development Bank
808 17th St. NW
Washington, DC 20577

Finding Jobs with Councils, Associations, and Government Agencies

International Atomic Energy Agency
P.O. Box 100
A-1400 Vienna, Austria

International Association for the Exchange of Students for Technical Experience
American City Building
Columbia, MD 21044

International Development Cooperation Agency
320 21st St. NW
Washington, DC 20523

International Fund for Agricultural Development
Via del Serafico 107
EUR 00142 Rome, Italy

International Institute for Studies and Training
15-3 Kamiide
Fujinomiya-shi
Shizuoka-ken, Japan

International League for Human Rights
236 E. 46th St.
New York, NY 10017

International Schools Association
CTC Case 20
CH-1211 Geneva 20, Switzerland

International Schools Services
P.O. Box 5910
Princeton, NJ 08540

International Monetary Fund
Economists Program
700 19th St. NW
Washington, DC 20431

International Trade Administration
Commerce Dept. Building
Washington, DC 20230-0002

Maritime Administration
U.S. Department of Transportation
400 7th St. SW
Washington, DC 20590

Modern Language Association
62 5th Ave.
New York, NY 10011

National Association for Foreign Student Affairs
1860 19th St. NW
Washington, DC 20009

National Association of Foreign Trade Zones
Commerce Tower, Suite 1020
911 Main St.
Kansas City, MO 64105

National Foreign Trade Council
100 E. 42nd St.
New York, NY 10017

National Geographic Society
17th and M Sts. NW
Washington, DC 20036

National Science Foundation
Division of International Programs
1800 G St. NW
Washington, DC 20550

Office of International Health
Department of Health and Human Services
200 Independence Ave. SW
Washington, DC 20201

Operation Crossroads Africa
150 5th Ave.
New York, NH 10011

Organization of American States
Constitution Ave. and 17th St. NW
Washington, DC 20006

Overseas Education Association
1201 16th St. NW
Washington, DC 20036

Peace Corps
806 Connecticut Ave. NW
Washington, DC 20526

Rockefeller Foundation
1133 Avenue of the Americas
New York, NY 10020

Save the Children
50 Wilton Rd.
Westport, CT 06880

Sister Cities International
1625 I St. NW, Suite 424
Washington, DC 20006

Society for International Development
777 UN Plaza
New York, NY 10017

Teacher of English to Speakers of Other Languages (TESOL)
202 DC Transit Building
Georgetown University
Washington, DC 20057

United Board for Christian Higher Education in Asia
475 Riverside Dr.
New York, NY 10027

United Nations
Recruitment Prorammes Section
New York, NY 10017

United Nations Children's Fund
866 UN Plaza
New York, NY 10017

U.S. Civil Service Commission
1900 E St. NW
Washington, DC 20415

U.S. Department of Commerce
14th and E Sts., NW
Washington, DC 20230

U.S. Committee for UNICEF
331 E. 38th St.
New York, NY 10016

U.S. Customs Service
1301 Constitution Ave. NW
Washington, DC 20002-6419

U.S. Department of Agriculture
14th St. and Independence Ave. SW
Washington, DC 20250

U.S. Department of Defense
The Pentagon
Washington, DC 20301-0999

U.S. Department of State
Bureau of Economic and Business Affairs
Office of Business and Export Affairs
2201 C St. NW
Washington, DC 20520

U.S. Department of Transportation
Assistant Secretary for Policy and International Affairs
400 7th St. SW
Washington, DC 20590

United States Information Agency
301 4th St. SW
Washington, DC 20547

U.S. Immigration and Naturalization Service
425 I St. NW
Washington, DC 20001-2542

U.S. International Trade Commission
Office of Administration
701 E St. NW
Washington, DC 20436

U.S. Student Travel Service
801 2nd Ave.
New York, NY 10017

Voice of America
Office of Personnel and Recruitment
3300 Independence Ave. SW
Washington, DC 20547

World Health Organization
20 Ave. APPIA
CH-1211 Geneva 27, Switzerland

World Tourism Organization
Calle Capitan Haya 42
E-Madrid 20, Spain

World Trade Centers Association
One World Trade Center, 63W
New York, NY 10048

Appendix F
Using Federal Information Centers in Your Job Search

The federal government sends thousands of employees abroad each year, in capacities ranging from the Peace Corps to diplomatic service to civilian support staff for military installations. To learn about current federal job openings, contact the Federal Job Information Center nearest you.

Alabama
Federal Job Information Center
806 Governors Dr. SW
Huntsville, AL 35801

Alaska
Federal Job Information Center
P.O. Box 22
Anchorage, AK 99513

Arizona
Federal Job Information Center
522 N. Central Ave.
Phoenix, AZ 85004

Arkansas
Federal Job Information Center
700 W. Capital Ave.
Little Rock, AR 72201

California
Federal Job Information Center
845 S. Figueroa
Los Angeles, CA 90017

Federal Job Information Center
880 Front St.
San Diego, CA 92188

Federal Job Information Center
1029 J St., Room 202
Sacramento, CA 91028

Federal Job Information Center
450 Golden Ave.
San Francisco, CA 94102

Colorado
Federal Job Information Center
1845 Sherman St.
Denver, CO 80298

Connecticut
Federal Job Information Center
450 Main St.
Hartford, CN 06103

Delaware
Federal Job Information Center
844 King St.
Wilmington, DE 19801

District of Columbia
Federal Job Information Center
1900 E St. NW
Washington, DC 20415

Florida
Federal Job Information Center
80 N. Hughey Ave.
Orlando, FL 32801

Georgia
Federal Job Information Center
75 Spring St. SW
Atlanta, GA 30303

Hawaii
Federal Job Information Center
300 Ala Moana Blvd.
Honolulu, HI 96850

Illinois
Federal Job Information Center
219 S. Dearborn St.
Chicago, IL 60604

Indiana
Federal Job Information Center
46 E. Ohio St., Room 123
Indianapolis, IN 46204

Iowa
Federal Job Information Center
210 Walnut St., Room 191
Des Moines, IA 50309

Kansas
Federal Job Information Center
230 S. Market St.
Wichita, KS 67202

Kentucky
Federal Job Information Center
600 Federal Pl.
Louisville, KY 40202

Louisiana
Federal Job Information Center
610 South St., Room 103
New Orleans, LA 70130

Maine
Federal Job Information Center
Federal Building, Room 611
Sewall St. and Western Ave.
Augusta, ME 04330

Maryland
Federal Job Information Center
101 W. Lombard St.
Baltimore, MD 21201

Massachusetts
Federal Job Information Center
Three Center Plaza
Boston, MA 02108

Michigan
Federal Job Information Center
477 Michigan Ave., Room 595
Detroit, MI 48226

Minnesota
Federal Job Information Center
Ft. Snelling
Twin Cities, MN 55111

Mississippi
Federal Job Information Center
100 W. Capitol St.
Jackson, MS 39201

Missouri
Federal Job Information Center
601 E. 12th St.
Kansas City, MO 64106

Montana
Federal Job Information Center
301 S. Park, Room 153
Helena, MT 59626

Nebraska
Federal Job Information Center
215 N. 17th St.
Omaha, NE 68102

Nevada
Federal Job Information Center
P.O. Box 3296
Reno, NV 89505

Using Federal Information Centers in Your Job Search **243**

New Hampshire
Federal Job Information Center
Daniel and Penhallow Sts.
Portsmouth, NH 07102

New Mexico
Federal Job Information Center
421 Gold Ave. SW
Albuquerque, NM 87102

New York
Federal Job Information Center
590 Grand Concourse
Bronx, NY 10451

North Carolina
Federal Job Information Center
310 New Bern Ave.
Raleigh, NC 27611

North Dakota
Federal Job Information Center
657 2nd Ave. N.
Fargo, ND 58102

Ohio
Federal Job Information Center
1240 E. 9th St.
Cleveland, OH 44199

Oklahoma
Federal Job Information Center
200 NW 5th St.
Oklahoma City, OK 73102

Oregon
Federal Job Information Center
1220 SW 3rd St.
Portland, OR 97204

Pennsylvania
Federal Job Information Center
600 Arch St.
Philadelphia, PA 19106

Rhode Island
Federal Job Information Center
Federal and Post Office Building
Providence, RI 02903

South Carolina
Federal Job Information Center
334 Meeting St.
Charleston, SC 29403

South Dakota
Federal Job Information Center
515 9th St.
Rapid City, SD 57701

Tennessee
Federal Job Information Center
167 N. Main St.
Memphis, TN 38103

Texas
Federal Job Information Center
1100 Commerce St.
Dallas, TX 75202

Utah
Federal Job Information Center
1234 S. Main St.
Salt Lake City, UT 84101

Vermont
Federal Job Information Center
P.O. Box 489
Burlington, VT 05402

Virginia
Federal Job Information Center
200 Granby Mall
Norfolk, VA 23510

Washington
Federal Job Information Center
915 2nd Ave.
Seattle, WA 98174

Wisconsin
Federal Job Information Center
161 W. Wisconsin Ave.
Milwaukee, WI 53203

Wyoming
Federal Job Information Center
2120 Capital Ave.
Cheyenne, WY 82001

Appendix G
Obtaining Country and Business Information from the U.S. Department of Commerce

The U.S. Department of Commerce has hundreds of publications, fact sheets, and profiles on international trade and business opportunities. When you contact one of the following offices, request their current catalog of publications and specify the country or region of your particular interest.

Alabama

Birmingham—Patrick T. Wall (Dir.)
 Medical Forum Building, 7th Fl.
 950 22nd St. N., ZIP: 35203
 Tel: (205) 731-1331
 Fax: (205) 731-0076

Alaska

Anchorage—Charles Becker (Dir.)
 World Trade Center
 421 W. 1st St., ZIP: 99501
 Tel: (907) 271-6237
 Fax: (907) 271-6242

*Denotes Trade Specialist at a Branch Office

**Denotes a U.S. Export Assistance Center

***Office with managerial and administrative oversight responsibilities (offers no direct business counseling)

Arizona

Phoenix—Frank Woods (Dir.)
Tower One, Suite 970
2901 N. Central Ave., ZIP: 85012
Tel: (602) 640-2513
Fax: (602) 640-2518

Arkansas

Little Rock—Lon J. Hardin (Dir.)
TCBY Tower Building, Suite 700
425 W. Capitol Ave., ZIP: 72201
Tel: (501) 324-5794
Fax: (501) 324-7380

California

Los Angeles—Stephen Morris (Dir.)
11000 Wilshire Blvd., Room 9200
ZIP: 90024
Tel: (310) 235-7104
Fax: (310) 235-7220

(*) Newport Beach
3300 Irvine Ave., Suite 305
ZIP: 92660
Tel: (714) 660-1688
Fax: (714) 660-8039

(**) Long Beach USEAC—
Joe Sachs (Dir.)
US&FCS Manager—Maria Solomon
One World Trade Center, Suite 1670
ZIP: 90831
Tel: (310) 980-4551
Fax: (310) 980-4561

Ontario—Fred Latuperissa (Dir.)
3281 E. Gausti Rd., Suite 100
ZIP: 91761
Tel: (909) 390-5650
Fax: (909) 390-5759

San Diego—Mary Delmege (Dir.)
6363 Greenwich Dr., Suite 230
ZIP: 92122
Tel: (619) 557-5395
Fax: (619) 557-6176

San Francisco—James S. Kennedy
(Acting Dir.)
250 Montgomery St., 14th Fl.
ZIP: 94104
Tel: (415) 705-2300
Fax: (415) 705-2297

(*) Santa Clara
5210 Great Amer. Pkwy., #456
ZIP: 95054
Tel: (408) 970-4610
Fax: (408) 970-4618

Colorado

Denver—Neil Hesse (Dir.)
1625 Broadway, Suite 680
ZIP: 80202
Tel: (303) 844-6622
Fax: (303) 844-5651

Connecticut

Hartford—Carl Jacobsen (Dir.)
450 Main St., Room 610B, ZIP: 06103
Tel: (203) 240-3530
Fax: (203) 240-3473

Delaware

Served by the Philadelphia District Office

District of Columbia

Served by the Baltimore USEAC

*Denotes Trade Specialist at a Branch Office

**Denotes a U.S. Export Assistance Center

***Office with managerial and administrative oversight responsibilities (offers no direct business counseling)

Florida

(**) Miami USEAC—
Peter B. Alois (Dir.)
P.O. Box 590570, ZIP: 33159
5600 N.W. 36th St., Suite 617
ZIP: 33166
Tel: (305) 526-7425
Fax: (305) 526-7434

(*) Clearwater
128 N. Osceola Ave.
ZIP: 34615
Tel: (813) 461-0011
Fax: (813) 449-2889

(*) Orlando
Eola Park Centre, Suite 1270
200 E. Robinson St., ZIP: 32801
Tel: (407) 648-6235
Fax: (407) 648-6756

(*) Tallahassee
107 W. Gaines St., Room 366G
ZIP: 32399
Tel: (904) 488-6469
Fax: (904) 487-1407

Georgia

Atlanta—George T. Norton, Jr. (Dir.)
Plaza Square N., Suite 310
4360 Chamblee Dunwoody Rd.
ZIP: 30341
Tel: (404) 452-9101
Fax: (404) 452-9105

Savannah—Barbara Prieto (Dir.)
120 Barnard St., Room A-107
ZIP: 31401
Tel: (912) 652-4204
Fax: (912) 652-4241

Hawaii

Honolulu—George B. Dolan (Dir.)
P.O. Box 50026
300 Ala Moana Blvd., Room 4106
ZIP: 96850
Tel: (808) 541-1782
Fax: (808) 541-3435

Idaho

(*) Boise—Portland District Office
700 W. State St., 2nd Fl.
ZIP: 83720
Tel: (208) 334-3857
Fax: (208) 334-2783

Illinois

(**) Chicago USEAC—
Brad Dunderman (Dir.)
Stanley Bokota, US&FCS Dir.
Xerox Center
55 W. Monroe St., Suite 2440
ZIP: 60603
Tel: (312) 353-8040
Fax: (312) 353-8098

(*) Wheaton
c/o Illinois Institute of
Technology
201 E. Loop Rd., ZIP: 60187
Tel: (312) 353-4332
Fax: (312) 353-4336

(*) Rockford
P.O. Box 1747
515 N. Court St., ZIP: 61110
Tel: (815) 987-8123
Fax: (815) 963-7943

---

*Denotes Trade Specialist at a Branch Office

**Denotes a U.S. Export Assistance Center

***Office with managerial and administrative oversight responsibilities (offers no direct business counseling)

Indiana

Indianapolis—Andrew Thress (Dir.)
Penwood One, Suite 106
11405 N. Pennsylvania St.
Carmel, IN 46032
Tel: (317) 582-2300
Fax: (317) 582-2301

Iowa

Des Moines—Randall J. LaBounty (Dir.)
Federal Building, Room 817
210 Walnut St., ZIP: 50309
Tel: (515) 284-4222
Fax: (515) 284-4021

Kansas

(*) **Wichita**—Kansas City District Office
151 N. Volutsia, ZIP: 67214
Tel: (316) 269-6160
Fax: (316) 683-7326

Kentucky

Louisville—John Autin (Dir.)
601 W. Broadway, Room 634B
ZIP: 40202
Tel: (502) 582-5066
Fax: (502) 582-6573

Louisiana

New Orleans—Paul K. Rees (Acting Dir.)
Hale Boggs Federal Building
501 Magazine St., Room 1043
ZIP: 70130
Tel: (504) 589-6546
Fax: (504) 589-2337

Maine

(*) **Augusta**—Vacant
40 Western Ave., Suite 506A
ZIP: 04333
Tel: (207) 622-8249
Fax: (207) 626-9156

Maryland

(**) **Baltimore USEAC**—
Roger Fortner (Dir.)
World Trade Center, Suite 2432
401 Pratt St., ZIP: 21202
Tel: (410) 962-4539
Fax: (410) 962-4529

Massachusetts

Boston—Frank J. O'Connor (Dir.)
164 Northern Ave.
World Trade Center, Suite 307
ZIP: 02210
Tel: (617) 424-5990
Fax: (617) 424-5992

Michigan

Detroit—Dean Peterson (Dir.)
1140 McNamara Building
477 Michigan Ave., ZIP: 48226
Tel: (313) 226-3650
Fax: (313) 226-3657

(*) **Grand Rapids**
300 Monroe NW, Room 406
ZIP: 49503
Tel: (616) 456-2411
Fax: (616) 456-2695

*Denotes Trade Specialist at a Branch Office

**Denotes a U.S. Export Assistance Center

***Office with managerial and administrative oversight responsibilities (offers no direct business counseling)

Minnesota

Minneapolis—Ronald E. Kramer (Dir.)
108 Federal Building
110 S. 4th St., ZIP: 55401
Tel: (612) 348-1638
Fax: (612) 348-1650

Mississippi

Jackson—Mark E. Spinney (Dir.)
201 W. Capitol St., Suite 310
ZIP: 39201
Tel: (601) 965-4388
Fax: (601) 965-5386

Missouri

St. Louis—Sandra Gerley (Dir.)
8182 Maryland Ave., Suite 303
ZIP: 63105
Tel: (314) 425-3302
Fax: (314) 425-3381

Kansas City—Rick Villalobos (Dir.)
601 E. 12th St., Room 635, ZIP: 64106
Tel: (816) 426-3141
Fax: (816) 426-3140

Montana

Served by the Boise Branch Office

Nebraska

Omaha—Des Moines District Office
11135 "O" St., ZIP: 68137
Tel: (402) 221-3664
Fax: (402) 221-3668

Nevada

Reno—James K. Hellwig (Dir.)
1755 E. Plumb Ln., Suite 152
ZIP: 89502
Tel: (702) 784-5203
Fax: (702) 784-5343

New Hampshire

(*) **Nashua**—Attila Gyenis, Mgr.
547 Amherst St., 2nd Fl.
ZIP: 03063
Tel: (603) 598-4315
Fax: (603) 598-4323

(*) **Portsmouth**—Susan Berry, Mgr.
601 Spaulding Tpke., Suite 29
ZIP: 03801
Tel: (603) 334-6074
Fax: (603) 334-6110

New Jersey

Trenton—Rod Stuart (Dir.)
3131 Princeton Pike, Building #6,
Suite 100, ZIP: 08648
Tel: (609) 989-2100
Fax: (609) 989-2395

New Mexico

(*) **Sante Fe**—Denver District Office
c/o New Mexico Dept. of
Economic Development
1100 St. Francis Dr., ZIP: 87503
Tel: (505) 827-0350
Fax: (505) 827-0263

*Denotes Trade Specialist at a Branch Office

**Denotes a U.S. Export Assistance Center

***Office with managerial and administrative oversight responsibilities (offers no direct business counseling)

New York

Buffalo—George Buchanan (Dir.)
1304 Federal Building
111 W. Huron St., ZIP: 14202
Tel: (716) 846-4191
Fax: (716) 846-5290

(*) Rochester—James C. Mariano
111 E. Ave., Suite 220, ZIP: 14604
Tel: (716) 263-6480
Fax: (716) 325-6505

New York—Joel W. Barkan (Dir.)
26 Federal Plaza, Room 3718
ZIP: 10278
Tel: (212) 264-0634
Fax: (212) 264-1356

North Carolina

Greensboro—Samuel P. Troy (Dir.)
400 W. Market St., Suite 400
ZIP: 27401
Tel: (910) 333-5345
Fax: (910) 333-5158

North Dakota

Served by the Minneapolis District Office

Ohio

Cincinnati—John M. McCaslin (Dir.)
550 Main St., Room 9504, ZIP: 45202
Tel: (513) 684-2944
Fax: (513) 684-3200

Cleveland—Toby T. Zettler (Dir.)
Bank One Center
600 Superior Ave. E., Suite 700
ZIP: 44114
Tel: (216) 522-4750
Fax: (216) 522-2235

Oklahoma

Oklahoma City—
Ronald L. Wilson (Dir.)
6601 Broadway Ext., Room 200
ZIP: 73116
Tel: (405) 231-5302
Fax: (405) 231-4211

(*) Tulsa
440 S. Houston St., Room 505
ZIP: 74127
Tel: (918) 581-7650
Fax: (918) 581-2844

Oregon

Portland—Denny Barnes (Dir.)
One World Trade Center, Suite 242
121 S.W. Salmon, ZIP: 97204
Tel: (503) 326-3001
Fax: (503) 326-6351

Pennsylvania

Philadelphia—Henry LeBlanc (Acting Dir.)
660 American Ave., Suite 201
King of Prussia, PA 19406
Tel: (610) 962-4980
Fax: (610) 962-4989

---

*Denotes Trade Specialist at a Branch Office

**Denotes a U.S. Export Assistance Center

***Office with managerial and administrative oversight responsibilities (offers no direct business counseling)

Pittsburgh—John A. McCartney (Dir.)
2002 Federal Building
1000 Liberty Ave., ZIP: 15222
Tel: (412) 644-2850
Fax: (412) 644-4875

Puerto Rico

San Juan (Hato Rey)—
J. Enrique Vilella (Dir.)
Federal Building, Room G-55
Chardon Ave., ZIP: 00918
Tel: (809) 766-5555
Fax: (809) 766-5692

Rhode Island

(*) Providence—
Raimond Meerbach, Mgr.
Seven Jackson Walkway, ZIP: 02903
Tel: (401) 528-5104
Fax: (401) 528-5067

South Carolina

Columbia—Jane Woodward (Dir.)
Strom Thurmond Federal Building,
Suite 172
1835 Assembly St., ZIP: 29201
Tel: (803) 765-5345
Fax: (803) 253-3614

(*) Charleston—Ann Watts, Mgr.
P.O. Box 975, ZIP: 29402
81 Mary St., ZIP: 29403
Tel: (803) 727-4051
Fax: (803) 727-4052

South Dakota

(*) Sioux Falls
Des Moines District Office
200 N. Phillips Ave., Commerce
Center, Suite 302, ZIP: 57102
Tel: (605) 330-4264
Fax: (605) 330-4266

Tennessee

Nashville—Jim Charlet (Dir.)
Parkway Towers, Suite 114
404 James Robertson Pkwy.
ZIP: 37219
Tel: (615) 736-5161
Fax: (615) 736-2454

(*) Memphis
22 N. Front St., Suite 200, ZIP: 38103
Tel: (901) 544-4173
Fax: (901) 575-3510

(*) Knoxville
301 E. Church Ave., ZIP: 37915
Tel: (615) 545-4637
Fax: (615) 545-4435

Texas

Dallas—Bill Schrage (Acting Dir.)
P.O. Box 58130
2050 N. Stemmons Fwy., Suite 170
ZIP: 75258
Tel: (214) 767-0542
Fax: (214) 767-8240

(*) Austin
P.O. Box 12728
1700 Congress, 2nd Fl., ZIP: 78701
Tel: (512) 482-5939
Fax: (512) 482-5940

*Denotes Trade Specialist at a Branch Office

**Denotes a U.S. Export Assistance Center

***Office with managerial and administrative oversight responsibilities (offers no direct business counseling)

Houston—James D. Cook (Dir.)
One Allen Center, Suite 1160
500 Dallas, ZIP: 77002
Tel: (713) 229-2578
Fax: (713) 229-2203

Utah

Salt Lake City—Stephen P. Smoot (Dir.)
324 S. State St., Suite 105, ZIP: 84111
Tel: (801) 524-5116
Fax: (801) 524-5886

Vermont

(*) Montpelier—James Cox
(Branch Mgr.)
109 State St., 4th Fl., ZIP: 05609
Tel: (802) 828-4508
Fax: (802) 828-3258

Virginia

Richmond—Philip A. Ouzis (Dir.)
700 Centre
704 E. Franklin St., Suite 550
ZIP: 23219
Tel: (804) 771-2246
Fax: (804) 771-2390

Washington

Seattle—Lisa Kjaer-Schade (Dir.)
3131 Elliott Ave., Suite 290
ZIP: 98121
Tel: (206) 553-5615
Fax: (206) 553-7253

(*) Tri-Cities
320 N. Johnson St., Suite 350
Kennewick, WA 99336
Tel: (509) 735-2751
Fax: (509) 783-9385

West Virginia

Charleston—W. Davis Coale, Jr. (Dir.)
405 Capitol St., Suite 807, ZIP: 25301
Tel: (304) 347-5123
Fax: (304) 347-5408

Wisconsin

Milwaukee—Paul D. Churchill (Dir.)
517 E. Wisconsin Ave., Room 596
ZIP: 53202
Tel: (414) 297-3473
Fax: (414) 297-3470

Wyoming

Served by the Denver District Office

Regional Offices

(***) Region I, Philadelphia
Paul Walters, Regional Director
660 American Ave., Suite 202
King of Prussia, PA 19406
Tel: (610) 962-4990
Fax: (610) 962-1326

(***) Region II, Atlanta
LoRee Silloway, Regional Director
Plaza Square N., Suite 405
4360 Chamblee Dunwoody Rd., 30341
Tel: (404) 455-7860
Fax: (404) 455-7865

*Denotes Trade Specialist at a Branch Office

**Denotes a U.S. Export Assistance Center

***Office with managerial and administrative oversight responsibilities (offers no direct business counseling)

(***) **Region III, Cincinnati**
Gordon Thomas, Regional Director
9504 Federal Building
550 Main St., ZIP: 45202
Tel: (513) 684-2947
Fax: (513) 684-3200

(***) **Region IV, St. Louis**
Donald R. Loso, Regional Director
8182 Maryland Ave., Suite 305
ZIP: 63105
Tel: (314) 425-3300
Fax: (314) 425-3375

(***) **Region V, San Francisco**
Michael Liikala, Regional Director
250 Montgomery St., 14th Fl.
ZIP: 94104
Tel: (415) 705-2310
Fax: (415) 705-2299

*Denotes Trade Specialist at a Branch Office

**Denotes a U.S. Export Assistance Center

***Office with managerial and administrative oversight responsibilities (offers no direct business counseling)

Appendix **H**

An Entrepreneur's Directory to Foreign Service Officers

Doing Business Overseas—
Your First Point of Contact

If you are planning a trip overseas or need information about doing business overseas, your first point of contact should be the nearest U.S. Department of Commerce District Office.

There are 44 District Offices and 24 Branch Offices in cities throughout the United States and Puerto Rico staffed by trade specialists from the United States and Foreign Commercial Service (US&FCS). These District Offices provide information on foreign markets, agent/distributor location services, trade leads, and counseling on business opportunities.

All District Offices have access to the National Trade Data Bank, a "one-stop" computerized source for current export promotion and country-specific trade data collected by 17 U.S. Government agencies. U.S. Export Assistance Centers, which combine the export promotion and trade finance services of the Department of Commerce, the Export-Import Bank, the Small Business Administration, and the Agency for International Development, now are open in Miami, Chicago, Long Beach, and Baltimore.

It is strongly recommended that business representatives inform the District Office of their plans to travel overseas. The District Office will notify Commercial Sections in overseas posts of the upcoming visit to ensure that they are adequately prepared to help.

The *Key Officers Guide* lists key officers at Foreign Service posts with whom American business representatives would most likely have contact. All embassies, missions, consulates general, and consulates are listed.

At the head of each U.S. diplomatic mission are the Chief of Mission (with the title of *Ambassador, Minister,* or *Charge d' Affaires*) and the Deputy Chief of Mission. These officers are responsible for all components of the U.S. Mission within a country, including consular posts.

A *Chief of Mission Secretary* is responsible for the scheduling of appointments for that official. In addition to other duties, this secretary may also assist businesspersons by directing inquiries to the appropriate Mission office.

Commercial Officers advise U.S. business on local trade and tariff laws, government procurement procedures, and business practices; identify potential importers, agents, distributors, and joint venture partners; provide information on local government tenders; and assist with resolution of trade and investment disputes. At smaller posts, commercial interests are represented by Economic/Commercial Officers from the Department of State.

Commercial Officers for Tourism promote the U.S. travel and tourism industry.

Economic Officers advise U.S. business on the local investment climate and economic trends; negotiate trade and investment agreements to open markets and level the playing field; and analyze and report on macroeconomic trends and trade policies and their potential impact on U.S. interests.

Resource Officers counsel U.S. business on issues related to natural resources, including minerals, oil and gas and energy; and analyze and report on local natural resource trends and trade policies and their potential impact on U.S. interests.

Agricultural Officers promote the export of U.S. agricultural products and report on agricultural production and market developments in their area.

Animal and Plant Health Inspection Service Officers are responsible for animal and plant health issues as they impact U.S. trade and in protecting U.S. agriculture from foreign pests and diseases. They expedite U.S. exports in the area of technical sanitary and phytosanitary (S&P) regulations.

Environment, Science and Technology (EST) Officers analyze and report on EST developments and their potential impact on U.S. policies and programs.

Financial Attaches analyze and report on major financial developments.

Consular Officers extend to U.S. citizens and their property abroad the protection of the U.S. Government. They maintain lists of local attorneys, act as liaison with police and other officials, and have the authority to notarize documents. The Department recommends that business representatives residing overseas register with the consular officer; in troubled areas, even travelers are advised to register.

Immigration and Naturalization Service Officers are responsible for enforcing the laws regulating the admission of foreign-born persons (i.e., aliens) to the United States and for administering various immigration benefits, including the naturalization of resident aliens.

Regional Security Officers are responsible for providing physical, procedural, and personnel security services to U.S. diplomatic facilities and personnel; they also provide local in-country security briefings and threat assessments to business executives.

AID Mission Directors are responsible for AID programs, including dollar and local currency loans, grants, and technical assistance.

Political Officers advise U.S. business executives on the local political climate and analyze and report on political developments and their potential impact on U.S. interests.

Labor Officers follow the activities of labor organizations to supply such information as wages, nonwage costs, social security regulations, labor attitudes toward American investments, etc. They advise U.S. business on local labor laws and practices and analyze and report on activities of local labor organizations, labor laws and practices, and their potential impact on U.S. interests.

Administrative Officers are responsible for normal business operations of the post, including purchasing for the post and its commissary.

Security Assistance Officers are responsible for Defense Cooperation in Armaments and foreign military sales to include functioning as primary in-country point of contact for U.S. Defense Industry.

Information Systems Managers are responsible for the post's unclassified information systems, database management, programming, and operational needs. They provide liaison with appropriate commercial contacts in the information field to enhance the postal system's integrity.

Communications Programs Officers are responsible for the telecommunications, telephone, radio, diplomatic pouches, and records management programs within the diplomatic mission. They maintain close contact with the host government's information/communications authorities on operational matters.

Public Affairs Officers are the press and cultural affairs specialists and maintain close contact with the local press.

Legal Attaches serve as representatives to the U.S. Department of Justice on criminal matters.

U.S. Department of State and Commerce Country Desk Officers

Both the Departments of State and Commerce have country desk officers based in Washington, DC who have comprehensive, up-to-date information on particular countries and can advise U.S. companies of the political and economic climate.

International Economic Policy (IEP) country desk officers in the Department of Commerce collect information on individual country regulations, tariffs, business practices, economic and political developments, trade data, and market size and growth, keeping a finger on the pulse of the potential markets for U.S. products, services, and investments.

IEP has several regional business information centers that focus on new opportunities for trade and investment in various parts of the world: the former Soviet Union, Eastern Europe, Japan, Latin America and the Caribbean, and the European Community.

For a specific country desk officer or regional business center, call (202) 482-3022.

Country desk officers at the Department of State maintain regular contact with overseas diplomatic missions and can provide country-specific economic and political analysis for U.S. companies.

For a specific State Department country desk officer, call (202) 647-4000.

The Department of State, Bureau of Diplomatic Security, can also provide current data on the security situation to interested persons planning trips abroad. American business representatives desiring this information should contact the Overseas Security Advisory Council at (202) 663-0533.

Department of State Coordinator for Business Affairs

The Coordinator for Business Affairs coordinates the Department's advocacy for U.S. companies overseas competing in international bids; problem-solving assistance to U.S. companies; dialogue with the U.S. private sector to ensure that business concerns are appropriately factored into foreign policy; and programs and practices to improve the Department's support for business. You should consider the Coordinator for Business Affairs a resource for business concerns within the Department of State. Tel: (202) 647-1625; Fax: (202) 647-3953.

Trade Information Center

For general information about U.S. Government export promotion programs, you should contact the Trade Information Center. It provides information on Federal programs and activities that support U.S. exports, information on overseas markets and industry trends, and a computerized calendar of U.S. Government-sponsored domestic and overseas trade events. The center's nationwide toll-free number is 1-800-USA-TRADE (1-800-872-8723).

A special line is available for those who are deaf or hearing-impaired: TDD 1-800-833-8723.

Examples of Accepted Forms for Addressing Mail
(Addresses Are Examples Only)

Posts with APO/FPO Numbers:

APO/FPO Address*
 Name
 Organization
 PSC or Unit number, Box number
 APO AE 09080 or APO AA 34038 or
 APO AP 96337

International Address**
 Name of Person/Section
 American Embassy
 P.O. Box 26431***
 Manama, Bahrain

Posts without APO/FPO Numbers:

Diplomatic Pouch Address*
 Name of Person/Section
 Name of Post
 Department of State
 Washington, DC 20521—plus four-digit add-on

International Address**
 Name of Person/Section
 American Embassy
 Jubilaeumstrasse 93***
 3005 Bern, Switzerland

NOTE: Do not combine any of the above forms (e.g., international plus APO/FPO addresses). This will only result in confusion and possible delays in delivery. Mail sent to the Department for delivery through its pouch system for posts with APO/FPO addresses cannot be accepted and will be returned to the sender.

 *Use domestic postage.
 **Use international postage.
 ***Use street address only when P.O. Box is not supplied.

> **Addresses:** for clarity, street and mailing addresses are separated by a bullet (•). Also **see** Accepted Forms for Addressing Mail on page 259.
>
> **Telephones:** country codes in brackets [ ] and city codes in parentheses ( ) must be dialed with all telephone and fax numbers when calling from the United States. **e-Mail:** DOSNET e-mail addresses can be found in the address list of each user's desktop mail system (Wang Office, MS Mail, Banyan Mail). DOSNET users can be addressed from the Internet, and their Internet e-mail addresses can be determined using the instruction sheets available from their local e-mail administrator.

Albania

Tirana (E)
Tirana Rruga E. Elbansanit 103
• PSC 59, Box 100 (A)
APO AE 09624
Tel: 355-42-32875, 33520
Fax: 32222

AMB:	Joseph E. Lake
AMB SEC:	Estelle R. Aubin
DCM:	Douglas R. Smith
POL:	Carl R. Siebentritt
ECO/COM:	Steve Hall
CON:	Susan Lively
ADM:	Ellen Sullivan
IPO:	Richard Emond
GSO:	Alaina Teplitz
ODA:	Ltc. Stephen Bucci, USA
PAO:	Charles Walsh
AID:	Dianne Blane
AGR:	Holly Higgins (resident in Milan)
FAA:	Steven B. Wallace (resident in Rome)
IRS:	Larry J. Legrand (resident in Rome)

Algeria

Algiers (E)
Four Chemin Cheikh Bachir El-Ibrahimi
• B.P. Box 549
(Alger-Gare) 16000
Tel: [213] (2) 69-12-55, 69-11-86, 69-18-54, 69-38-75
Fax: 69-39-79
COM Tel: 69-23-17
Fax: 69-18-63
USIS Tel: 69-19-40
Fax: 69-14-88

AMB:	Ronald E. Neumann
AMB SEC:	Joan Szabados
DCM:	Albert W. Dalgliesh, Jr.
POL/PAO:	Nancy Johnson
CON/COM/ECO:	Robert Ford
COM:	(Vacant)
ADM:	Ellen Engels
RSO:	Scott E. McHugh
ODA:	Col. Byron S. Paul III, USAF
IPO:	Rudolph Szabados
AGR:	Evans "Duffy" Browne (resident in Tunis)
FAA:	J. Stuart Jamison (resident in Brussels)
IRS:	Frederick D. Pablo (resident in Paris)

Angola

Luanda (E)
Rua Houari Boumedienne No. 32
Miramar, Luanda

An Entrepreneur's Directory to Foreign Service Officers 261

- International Mail: Caixa Postal 6484 Luanda, Angola or
- Pouch: American Embassy Luanda Department of State Washington, DC 20521-2550

INMARSAT: Int'l Operator: 873-151-7430
Tel: [244] (2) 346-418/345-481
Fax: 396-924, 347-884
ODA Fax: 347-217
Admin/Consular Annex: Casa Inglesa
Rua Major Kanhangula No. 132/135 Angola or use above pouch address
ADMIN Tel: 392-498
CON Tel: 396-927
Fax: 390-515

AMB:	Donald K. Steinberg
AMB SEC:	Sheila M. Jones
DCM:	James J. Hamilton
POL:	Douglas P. Climan
POL/MIL:	Dave Hollinger
ADM:	(Vacant)
ECO/COM:	Robert B. Murphy
CON:	Daniel L. Chase
IPO:	Antonio J. Gonzalez
RSO:	Randall D. Bennett
PAO:	Alfred F. Head
AID/OFDA:	Douglas Mercado
FAA:	Ronald L. Montgomery (resident in Dakar)
ODA:	Major Sherman Grandy
IRS:	Stanley Beesley (resident in London)
AGR:	James M. Benson (resident in Pretoria)

Argentina

Buenos Aires (E)
4300 Colombia, 1425
- Unit 4334, APO AA 34034

Tel: [54] (1) 777-4533 and 777-4534
Fax: 777-0197
COM Fax: 777-0673
Telex: 18156 AMEMBAR

AMB:	James R. Cheek
AMB SEC:	Nancy Graham
DCM:	Ronald D. Godard
POL:	William J. Brencick
ECO:	Peter D. Whitney
COM:	Arthur Alexander
CON:	Nicholas J. Ricciuti
ADM:	John M. Salazar
RSO:	James J. Walsh (resident in Montevideo)
PAO:	Alexander Almasov
IMO:	Robert Siletzky
EST:	Kenneth D. Cohen
AID:	Robert J. Asselin, Jr. (resident in Montevideo)
ODA:	Col. Wayne C. Fisher, USAF
MILGP:	Col. Jose A. Rodriguez
AGR:	Max F. Bowser
APHIS:	Thomas J. Andre, Jr.
LAB:	Randolph Marcus
FAA:	Santiago Garcia (resident in Rio de Janeiro)
FAA/CASLO:	Larry Bruce
IRS:	Charles Shea (resident in Caracas)

Armenia

Yerevan (E)
18 Gen Bagramian
Tel: 7-8852-151-144 or 524-661
Fax: 151-138
Telex: 243137 AMEMY

AMB:	Peter Tomsen
DCM:	Ted Nist
AMB SEC:	Judy Thiessen
POL:	Michael Scanlan
ECO:	Albert R. Fournier
ADM:	Ruben Alcantara
COM:	Frank Sparhawk
CON:	Patricia Lieberman

GSO: Winifred Grayson
IPO: Cal McQueen
AID: Fred Winch
PAO: John Quintus
RSO: Rebecca Dockery
(resident in Tbilisi)
FAA: Dennis B. Cooper
(resident in Moscow)
AGR: Mary Revelt
(resident in Moscow)
IRS: Joe D. Hook
(resident in Bonn)
PC: Robert McClendon

Australia

Canberra (E)
Moonah Pl.
Yarralumla, A.C.T. 2600
• APO AP 96549
Tel: [61] (6) 270-5000
Afterhours Tel: 270-5900
Telex: 62104, USAEMB
Fax: 270-5970

AMB: Edward J. Perkins
AMB SEC: Nancy R. Buss
DCM: Kaarn J. Weaver
POL: Roger McGuire
ECO: Ralph R. Moore
COM: John W. Bligh
(resident in Sydney)
CON: Michael John Mates
ADM: Marshall F. Atkins
GSO: Larry J. Kozak
RSO: John Henry Kaufmann
PAO: Shiela W. Austrian
IMO: Anthony Muse
ISO: Durwood L. Franke
EST: Zachary Z. Teich
ODA: Col. Stephen E.
Barneyback, USAF
MNL: John Michael Garner
AGR: James A. Truran
APHIS: Wesley H. Garnett, Jr.
FAA: Fred Laird
CUS: Donald K. Shruhan, Jr.
(resident in Singapore)
LAB: George S. Dragnich

Melbourne (CG)
553 St. Kilda Rd.
Melbourne, Victoria 3004
• P.O. Box 6722, Unit 11011
APO AP 96551-0002
Tel: [61] (3) 9526-5900
Fax: 9510-4646
COM Fax: 9510-4660
USIS Tel: 9526-5930
Fax: 9510-4686

CG: Ross Wilson
CG SEC: Jean C. Pedersen
POL/ECO: Edward V. O'Brien
COM: Kenneth L. Norton
CON: Steven A. Hardesty
ADM: Steven H. Kraft
BPAO: William F. Brent
IPO: Marc A. Beroud

Sydney (CG)
59th Fl, MLC Centre
19-29 Martin Pl.
Sydney N.S.W. 2000
• PSC 280, Unit 11026
APO AP 96554-0002
Tel: [61] (2) 373-9200
ADMIN Fax: 373-9125
COM Fax: 221-0573
CON Fax: 373-9184

CG: Jerome F. Tolson, Jr.
CG SEC: Margaret M. McDermott
POL: Kristine Pely
COM: John W. Bligh
CON: Teddy Gong
ADM: Lewis A. Lukens
BPAO: Hugh J. Ivory
IPO: Allan Friedbauer
IRS: Vivian L. Simon
USTTA: Daniel J. Young
FAA/CASLO:
Steve Earnest

Perth (CG)
13th Fl., 16 Georges Terr.
Perth, WA 6000
• APO AP 96530
Tel: [61] (9) 231-9400
Fax: 231-9444

CG: Nicholas A. Sherwood
CG SEC: Marian H. Primrose

An Entrepreneur's Directory to Foreign Service Officers   **263**

CON/ADM:
    Daniel P. Claffey
USN: Cdr. James P. Winter
Brisbane (C)
4th Fl., 383 Wickham Terr.
Brisbane, Queensland 4000
- APO AP 96529
Tel: [61] (7) 831-3330
Fax: 832-6247

Austria

Vienna (E)
Boltzmanngasse 16
A-1091, Vienna
Tel: [43] (1) 313-39
Fax: 310-06-82
CON: Gartenbaupromenade 2
4th Fl., A-1010 Vienna
Tel: 313-39
Fax: 513-43-51
COM Fax: 310-69-17

AMB:	Swanee G. Hunt
AMB SEC:	Susan B. Ray
DCM:	Joan E. Corbett
ECO/POL:	Timothy M. Savage
CON:	Guyle Cavin
COM:	Stephen Kaminski
ADM:	Joann M. Jenkins
RSO:	Edward F. Gaffney
PAO:	Helena Finn
IMO:	David L. Collins
ODA:	Col. John R. Miller, USA
AGR:	Francis J. Tarrant
LAB:	Eugene P. Tuttle
INS:	Jean Christiansen
LEGATT:	Julianne Slifco
CUS:	Ivan E. Taborsky
DEA:	Bohdan Mizak
FAA:	Steven B. Wallace (resident in Rome)
FAA/CASLO:	Amelia D. Fitzgibbons
IRS:	Joe D. Hook (resident in Bonn)

US Mission to International Organizations in Vienna (UNVIE)
Obersteinergasse 11
A-1190 Vienna
Tel: [43] (1) 313-39
Fax: 36-91-585 or
EXEC Tel: 36-92-095
IAEA Tel: 36-92-093
Fax: 36-83-92

US REP:	John B. Ritch III
SEC:	Theda Kettler
DCM:	Joseph Snyder
POL/ECO, UNDCP:	Raymond R. Snider
IAEA:	Leroy C. Simpkins
UNIDO, UNCITRAL, COPUS, UNRWA:	Henry Ensher
SR SCI ATT:	Marvin R. Peterson
SCI ATT:	Lisa Hilliard
NUC SAFETY ATT:	James Richardson
ISPO:	Susan Pepper

Organization on Security and Cooperation in Europe (OSCE)
Obersteinegasse 11/1
A-1190 Vienna
Tel: [43] (1) 313-39
Fax: 36-63-85

HEAD OF DELEGATION:	Samuel W. Brown, Jr.
SEC:	Anne Kirlian
DEP HEAD OF DELEGATION:	John Lekson
POL/ECO:	Mark A. Sigler
PAA:	Elizabeth B. Pryor
JCS:	Ltc. Michael Simone
ACDA:	Louis Sell
OSD:	(Vacant)
IPO:	Sebastian Failla

Azerbaijan

Baku (E)
Azadliq Prospekti 83
Tel: (9) (9412) 98-03-36, 98-03-37, 96-00-19, 93-64-80, and 96-36-21

INMARSAT: 008-73-151-2713
Fax: 98-37-55
Telex: 142110 AMEMB SU

AMB:	Richard D. Kauzlarich
DCM:	David Sedney
EXEC ASST:	Linda Wardman
CON:	Julie Ann Ruterbories
POL:	Arnold Horowitz
IPO:	David Bendt
ECO:	Jack Tucker
ADM:	Duane C. Butcher
PAO:	Donald Cofman
GSO:	Jennifer A. McIntyre
RSO:	Rebecca Dockery (resident in Tbilisi)
ODA:	Douglas Bruun
AGR:	Larry Panasuk (resident in Ankara)
FAA:	Dennis B. Cooper (resident in Moscow)
IRS:	Joe D. Hook (resident in Bonn)

Bahamas, The

Nassau (E)
Queen St.
• P.O. Box N-8197
Tel: (809) 322-1181 and 328-2206
Telex: 20-138 AMEMB NS138
Fax: 328-7838
Nonimmigrant Visa Section
Tel: 328-3496
COM Fax: 328-3495

AMB:	Sidney Williams
AMB SEC:	Vanessa Brooks
DCM:	John S. Ford
POL/ECO:	James P. McAnulty
ECO/COM:	Mary Eileen Earl
CON:	Vincent A. Principe
ADM:	Brian McIntosh
RSO:	Todd J. Brown
PAO:	Mary Eileen Earl (Acting)
APHIS:	David Tollett
IPO:	Elwood (Skip) Rische

NAU:	Matthew B. Kaplan
NLO:	LCdr. Michael C. Doles, USN
CGLO:	LCdr. James D. Maes, USCG
CUS:	Michael Fienberg
DEA:	Richard C. Stuart
FAA:	Celio Young (resident in Miami)
INS:	James M. Ward
IRS:	Louis Hobbie
LAB:	Ollie P. Anderson, Jr. (resident in Washington, DC)

Bahrain

Manama (E)
Building No. 979
Rd. 3119 (next to Al-Ahli Sports Club)
Zinj District
• FPO AE 09834-5100
International Mail: P.O. Box 26431
Switchboard Tel: (973) 273-300
Afterhours Tel: 275-126
Fax: 272-594
ECO/COM Fax: 256-717
USIS Tel: 276-180
Fax: 270-547
US OMC Tel: 276-962
Fax: 276-046

AMB:	David M. Ransom
DCM:	Joseph E. Le Baron
POL:	Andrew J. Schofer
POL/MIL:	James F. Sartain
ECO/COM:	Donald A. Roberts
CON:	Karen L. Enstrom
ADM:	Raul E. Chavera
RSO:	Michael Williams
PAO:	Dr. A. Chris Eccel
IPO:	Stephan D. Campos
OMC:	Col. Richard C. Groesch, USAF
AGR:	Edwin Porter (resident in Dubai)
FAA:	Dennis Beres (resident in Riyadh)

… An Entrepreneur's Directory to Foreign Service Officers **265**

FAA/CASLO:
          Ronald N. Reynolds
IRS: David Robison
          (resident in Riyadh)

Bangladesh
Dhaka (E)
Diplomatic Enclave
Madani Ave., Baridhara
• G.P.O. Box 323
Dhaka 1212
Tel: [880] (2) 884700-22
Telex: 642319 AEDKA BJ
Fax: 883-744
USIS Jiban Bima Bhaban,
5th Fl., 10 Dilkusha C.A.
Dhaka 1000
Tel: 862550 through 4
Fax: 833987
workweek: Sunday through Thursday

AMB: David N. Merrill
AMB SEC: Kathleen J. Alexander
DCM: Nancy J. Powell
POL: William H. Hill II
ECO/COM: Cornelia M. Weierback
CON: David R. Dreher
ADM: Lawrence Blackburn
RSO: William H. Lamb
PAO: Donald M. Bishop
IPO: Russell F. Himmelsbach
RMO: Richard A. Bienia
AID: Richard M. Brown
ODA: Ltc. James Dunn, USA
AGR: Thomas Pomeroy
               (resident in New Delhi)
FAA: David L. Knudson
               (resident in Singapore)
CUS: Donald K. Shruhan, Jr.
               (resident in Singapore)
IRS: Charles W. Landry
               (resident in Singapore)

Barbados
Bridgetown (E)
P.O. Box 302 or FPO AA 34055

Tel: (809) 436-4950
Fax: 429-5246
Telex: 2259 USEMB BG1 WB
Marine Sec. Guard
Tel: 436-8995
CON *Fax:* 431-0179
AID *Fax:* 429-4438
USIS *Fax:* 429-5316
MLO *Fax:* 427-1668
LEGATT *Fax:* 437-7772
Canadian Imperial Bank of Commerce Building
Broad St.

AMB: Jeanette W. Hyde
AMB SEC: Fran Wilson
DCM: Donald Holm
POL/ECO: Thomas R. Hutson
ECO: Carole Jackson
CON: Dale E. Shaffer
ADM: James D. McGee
RSO: John M. Davis
PAO: Tyrone W. Kemp
CPO: Karl J. Jarvis
AID: Mosina H. Jordan
ODA: Ltc. Clark Lynn, USA
MLO: Cdr. P. Tim Swanson, USN
RMO: Dr. LaRae W. Kemp
AGR: Larry Senger
               (resident in Caracas)
LAB: Peggy Zabriskie
LEGATT: Paul F. Nolan
IRS: Charles Shea
               (resident in Caracas)
FAA: Celio Young
               (resident in Miami)

Belarus
Minsk (E)
Starovilenskaya #46
Tel: [7] (0172) 31-50-00
Fax: 34-78-53
AMB: Kenneth S. Yalowitz
AMB SEC: Carole Crenshaw
DCM: John Boris

ADM: Gregory Slotta
CON: Catherine Shuman
GSO: Janine Boiarsky
IPO: Phillip Bunch
RSO: Michael Wilkins
PAO: Janet Demiray
AGR: Mary Revelt
(resident in Moscow)
FAA: Dennis B. Cooper
(resident in Moscow)
IRS: Joe D. Hook
(resident in Bonn)

Belgium

Brussels (E)
27 Boulevard du Regent
B-1000 Brussel
• PSC 82, Box 002
APO AE 09724
Tel: [32] (2) 508-2111
Fax: 511-2725
COM Fax: 512-6653

AMB: Alan J. Blinken
AMB SEC: Roberta E. Viggiano
DCM: Lange Schermerhorn
POL: Judith Rodes Johnson
ECO: Terry A. Breese
COM: Terrence Flannery
CON: Ted W. Halstead
ADM: Jim D. Mark
RSO: Douglas J. Rosenstein
PAO: Harriet L. Elam
ISM: Sherril L. Pavin
IMO: Richard J. Getze
ODA: Col. John R. Fairlamb, USA
ODC: Col. Richard I. Kearsley, USAF
AGR: Steven Yoder
(resident in The Hague)
FAA/ILO: Patrick M. Poe
LAB: Harry J. O'Hara
IRS: Frederick D. Pablo
(resident in Paris)

US Mission to the North Atlantic Treaty Organization (USNATO)
Autoroute de Zaventem
B-1110 Brussels
• APO AE 09724
Tel: [32] (02) 726-4580
Fax: 726-5796
USIS Fax: 726-9368

US PERM REP: Robert E. Hunter
PERM REP SEC: Mary Ann T. Silva
DEP PERM/REP/DCM: W. Robert Pearson
DEF ADV: Dr. Catherine Kelleher
POL/ADV: Douglas L. McElhaney
PUB AFF ADV: Robert Bemis
ADM ADV: Henry M. Reed II
EST ADV: Paul Rambaut
IMO: James R. Thompson

US Mission to the European Union (USEU)
40 Blvd. du Regent
B-1000 Brussels
• APO AE 09724
Tel: [32] (02) 508-2222
Fax: 505-8117

AMB: Stuart E. Eizenstat
AMB SEC: Carolyn W. Keene
DCM: Earl Anthony Wayne
POL: G. Jonathan Greenwald
ADM: Gail Roberts
ECO: Charles P. Ries
COM: Steven C. Arlinghaus
PAO: Stephen M. Dubrow
EST/TECH AFF: Stephen V. Noble
CUS: Robert Mall
TRADE POL OFF: Bennett M. Harman
TREAS: Gregory J. Berger
NAS: Brian R. Stickney
AGR: Bryant H. Wadsworth
APHIS: Ed L. Ayers, Jr.
LAB: (Vacant)

European Logistical Support Office (ELSO-Antwerp)
Noorderlaan 147, Bus 12A
B-2030 Antwerp
• APO AE 09724
Tel: [32] (03) 542-4775
Telex: 34964
Fax: 542-6567
DIR: Michael J. Adams
DEP DIR: Robert H. Cooper

SHAPE Belgium
B-7010
• APO NY 09088
Tel: (065) 445-000
POLAD: Vernon D. Penner

EURMAC
15 Klaverbladstraat
B-3560 Lummen, Belgium
• APO AE 09724
Tel: [32] (013) 531-071
Fax: 531-315
MGR: Larry D. Allen

Belize

Belize City (E)
Gabourel Lane and Hutson St.
• P.O. Box 286, Unit 7401
APO AA 34025
Tel: [501] (2) 77161 through 63
Fax: 30802
ADM Fax: 35321
ODA Fax: 32795
DEA Fax: 33856
PC Fax: 303451
VOA: [501] (7) 22127
MLO Tel: 25-2009/2019
Fax: 25-2553
USAID Tel: 31067
Fax: 30215
AMB: George C. Bruno
AMB SEC: Victoria L. Connerley
DCM: Gerard M. Gallucci
POL: John A Connerley
ECO/COM: Robert W. Merrigan
CON: Michael R. Schimmel
ADM: Sylvie L. Martinez
RSO: Martin T. Donnelly
(resident in Guatemala City)
IPO: Michael E. Lamberg
AID: Robert T. Dakan
VOA: Gaines R. Johnson
PAO: Mark Krischik
(resident in Tegucigalpa)
ODA: Col. William L. Brown, USAF
(resident in Tegucigalpa)
MLO: Ltc. Jose Rivera-Sanabria, USA
PC: Mattie M. Roter
(co-director)
Sandy N. Roter
(co-director)
DEA: Ruth Higgs
AGR: Grant A. Pettrie
(resident in Guatemala City)
FAA: Victor Ramariz
(resident in Miami)
LAB: Melvin R. Turner
(resident in Tegucigalpa)
IRS: Daniel R. Dietz
(resident in Mexico City)

Benin

Contonou (E)
Rue Caporal Bernard Anani
B.P. 2012
Tel: [229] 30-06-50, 30-05-13, 30-17-92
Fax: 30-14-39 and 30-19-74
workweek: Monday through Friday
AMB: Ruth A. Davis
AMB SEC: Diane E. McBride
POL/ECO: Alan R. Tousignant
CON: Ellen B. Thorburn
ADM: Lois A. Price
RSO: Charles Hartley
(resident in Lome)
PAO: Anthony Hutchinson

IPO: Carol Burris
AID: Thomas Cornell
ODA: Col. Kenneth Hibl, USA
(resident in Abidjan)
ATO: Maurice W. House
(resident in Lagos)
FAA: Ronald L. Montgomery
(resident in Dakar)

Bermuda
Hamilton (CG)
Crown Hill
16 Middle Rd.
Devonshire
• P.O. Box HM325
Hamilton HMBX, Bermuda
Tel: (809) 295-1342
Fax: 295-1592

CG: Robert A. Farmer
POL/ADM: Bruce Berton
CON: Edmund Leather
INS: Edward R. Moore
IRS: Louis Hobbie
(resident in Nassau)
RSO: Craig Daugherty
(resident in Ottawa)
USDA: Helena Gomez
CUS: Steve Vogelhaupt
APHIS: Helena Gomez
LAB: Ollie P. Anderson, Jr.
(resident in Washington, DC)
NASA: Steven Stompf

Bolivia
La Paz (E)
Ave. Arce No. 2780
• P.O. Box 425
La Paz, Bolivia
APO AA 34032
Tel: [591] (2) 430251
Fax: 433900

USAID Tel: 786355, 786544, 786147
Fax: 782325

AMB: Curt Warren Kamman
AMB SEC: Karen Smith Ruiz
DCM: Robert C. Perry
POL: Stephen G. Wesche
ECO/COM: Paul B. Larsen
CON: Jeanne L. Schulz
ADM: Lee R. Lohman
RSO: Andrew J. Colantonio
PAO: Phillip Parkerson
CPO: Lewis F. La Turner
IMC: Judith Chidester
ISM: Joseph Smith
FBO: Joseph W. Toussaint
AID: Lewis Lucke (Acting)
ODA: Col. Gregory Landers, USAF
MILGP: Col. Roger D. Slaughter, USA
PC: Diane S. Hibino
AGR: Richard B. Helm
(resident in Santiago)
FAA: Santiago Garcia
(resident in Rio de Janeiro)
LAB: Kenneth C. Keller
IAGS: Liam P. O'Brien
NAS: J. Richard Baca

Bosnia-Herzegovina
Sarajevo (E)
43 Ul. Dure Dakovica
Tel: [387] (71) 645-992, 445-700, 659-743

AMB: (Vacant)
ADM: Mathew Levey
POL: Philip Laidlaw
RSO: Peter Hargraves
IPO: Robert Jennings
PAO: (Vacant)
LAB: John W. Zerolis
(resident in Zagreb)
FAA: Steven B. Wallace
(resident in Rome)

AGR: William Huth (resident in Sofia)
IRS: Larry J. Legrand (resident in Rome)

Botswana

Gaborone (E)
P.O. Box 90
Tel: [267] 353-982
Fax: 356-947
Afterhours Tel: 357-111

AMB: Howard F. Jeter
AMB SEC: Margie Jeanne Douglas
DCM: Gillian M. Milovanovic
POL/ECO: Alexander M. Laskaris
POL/MIL: Stacey K. Kazacos
CON/COM: Theodore J. Craig
ADM: Alphonso G. Marquis
RSO: Thomas J. Colin
PAO: Dudley Sims
CPO: David E. Heil
AID: Howard R. Handler
AGR: Besa L. Kotati (resident in Pretoria)
FAA: Ronald L. Montgomery (resident in Dakar)
LAB: Thomas A. Shannon, Jr. (resident in Johannesburg)
ODC: Ltc. Rodney Low, USA
ODA: Col. Daniel Henk, USA (resident in Harare)
VOA: Dennis Brewer
IRS: Stanley Beesley (resident in London)

Brazil

Brasilia (E)
Avenida das Nacoes, Lote 3
• Unit 3500
APO AA 34030
Tel: [55] (61) 321-7272
Fax: 225-9136 (State)
FCS Fax: 225-9136
USIS Fax: 321-2833
Telex: 1091 and 61-2318

AMB: Melvyn Levitsky
AMB SEC: Claudia Romero
DCM: Mark Lore
DCM SEC: Betty Taylor
POL: Theodore Wilkinson
ECO: Paul H. Wackerbarth
COM: Robert Farris
CON: Layton Russell
ADM: Robert D. Austin, Jr.
RSO: John C. Murphy
PAO: Carl Howard
IMO: Nicodemo Romeo
SCI: Leroy C. Simpkins
ISM: Thomas Smith
AID: Edward Kadunc
ODA: Col. Layton Dunbar, USA
MLO: Col. Dennis J. McMahan, USAF
AGR: Shackford Pitcher
NAS: Norma V. Reyes
FAA: Santiago Garcia (resident in Rio de Janeiro)

Rio de Janeiro (CG)
Avenida Presidente Wilson
147 Castelo
Rio de Janeiro-RJ 20030-020
• Unit 3501
APO AA 34030
Tel: [55] (21) 292-7117
Fax: 220-0439
USIS Telex: 22831
Fax: 262-1820

CG: James Derham
CG SEC: Deborah K. Saunier
DPO/ECO: Robert Taylor
POL: Nadia Tongour
COM: Dar Jalane Pribyl
CON: Edwin R. Beffel
ADM: Roland Estrada
RSO: Jackson Booth

BPAO: Katherine Lee
IPO: Anthony J. Skok
ODA: Cdr. Mark Gabrynowicz
MLO: LCdr. Michael Rabang
RES: Curtis M. Stewart
AGR: Shackford Pitcher
(resident in Brasilia)
LAB: Patrick Del Vecchio
FAA: Santiago Garcia
LOC: James C. Armstrong

Sao Paulo (CG)
Rua Padre Joao Manoel
933, 01411
• P.O. Box 8063
APO AA 34030
Tel: [55] (11) 881-6511
Fax: 852-5154
USIS Telex: 31574
Fax: 852-1395

CG: Philip B. Taylor III
CG SEC: Delia Ozeta
DPO/ECO: Gilbert J. Donahue
POL: Bruce Williamson
CON: Linda L. Donahue
COM: Richard Ades
ADM: Herbert Brown
RSO: Kevin Durnell
BPAO: Susan Ann Clyde
IPO: James H. Porter
AGR: Alan D. Hrapsky
LAB: Patrick Del Vecchio
IRS: Charles Shea
(resident in Caracas)

Commercial Office (Trade Center)
Rua Estados Unidos
1812, Sao Paulo
S.P. 01427-002
Tel: (11) 853-2011/2411/2778
Fax: 853-2744
Telex: 011-25274
COM: Richard Ades

Porto Alegre (C)
Rua Coronel Genuino
421 (9th Fl.) Unit 3504
APO AA 34030

Tel: [55] (51) 226-4288, 226-4697, 222-1666
Fax: 221-2213
USIS Telex: 2292
Fax: 221-6212
PO: Brent E. Blaschke
CON: Lesslie C. Viguerie

Recife (C)
Rua Goncalves Maia, 163
• APO AA 34030
Tel: [55] (81) 421-2441 or 5723
Emergency Tel: 421-3551
Fax: 231-1906
USIS Fax: 421-5535
PO: Maria Sanchez-Carlo
CON: Katherine Farrell
BPAO: Dale Prince

Commercial and Agricultural offices are also located at:
Belo Horizonte (USIS and COM Branch)
AV Alvares Cabral
16003 Andar - Belo Horizonte
MG CEP 30170
Tel and Fax: [55] (31) 335-3250
Telex: 1817
USIS Fax: 335-3054
COM: Richard Ades
(resident in Sao Paulo)

Belem (CA and FCS Branch)
Rua Osvaldo Cruz 165
66017-090 Belem Para, Brazil
Tel: [55] (91) 223-0800 and 223-0613
Fax: 223-0413
CA: Christine Serrao
COM: Richard Ades
(resident in Sao Paulo)

Fortaleza (CA)
Tel: [55] (85) 221-5743
Fax: 252-1561
CA: Patricia Cavin

Manaus (CA)
Rua Recife 1010
Adrianopolis, CEP 69057-001

Manaus Amazonas, Brazil
Tel: [55] (92) 234-4546
Telex: 2183
Fax: (81) 231-1906
CA: James R. Rish

Salvador da Bahia (CA)
Av. Antonio Carlos Magalhaes
S/N-Ed. Cidadella Center 1
Sala 410
40275-440 Salvador
Bahia, Brazil
Tel: [55] (71) 358-9166 or 9195
Telex: 2780 EEVA
Fax: 351-0717
CA: Heather May Marques

Brunei

Bandar Seri Begawan (E)
3rd Fl. - Teck Guan Plaza
Jalan Sultan
• AMEMB Box B
APO AP 96440
Tel: [673] (2) 229-670
Telex: BU 2609 AMEMB
Fax: 225-293

AMB:	Theresa A. Tull
AMB SEC:	Glenda W. Wright
ECO/POL:	Anthony M. Kolankiewicz
ADM/CON:	Mary F. Martinez
RSO:	John L. Tello (resident in Kuala Lumpur)
PAO:	Nicholas Mele (resident in Kuala Lumpur)
IPO/GSO:	Mark F. Marrano
SAO:	Ltc. Dennis B. Fowler, USAF (resident in Singapore)
ODA:	Col. Richard D. Welker (resident in Singapore)
ATO:	Robert D. Fondahn (resident in Singapore)
FAA:	David L. Knudson (resident in Singapore)
CUS:	Donald K. Shruhan, Jr. (resident in Singapore)
IRS:	Charles W. Landry (resident in Singapore)

Bulgaria

Sofia (E)
1 Saborna St.
• Unit 1335
APO AE 09213-1335
Tel: [359] (2) 88-48-01 through 05
Fax: 80-19-77
CON Fax: 80-75-86
COM Fax: 80-38-50
AGR Fax: 80-35-68
AID Fax: 54-31-11
GSO Fax: 80-75-86
USIS Fax: 80-06-46

AMB:	William D. Montgomery
AMB SEC:	Anna J. Thomas
DCM:	Rose M. Likins
POL/ECO:	Ruth E. Hansen
COM:	Patrick Hughes
CON:	David A. Rollman
ADM:	Douglas B. Leonnig
RSO:	Mark T. Fogarty
IPO:	Allan K. Jeffries
ISO:	Christopher P. Graham
PAO:	Lawrence I. Plotkin
AID:	John A. Tennant
ODA:	Col. Jon Bell, USAF
AGR:	William P. Huth
FAA:	Steven B. Wallace (resident in Rome)
IRS:	Nina Crumbie
PC:	Lawrence Bartlett

Burkina Faso

Ouagadougou (E)
01 B.P. 35
Tel: [226] 30-67-23 through 25
Afterhours Tel: 31-26-60 and 31-27-07

Telex: AMEMB 5290 BF
Telex Fax: (State) 31-23-68
USAID Fax: 30-89-03
AMB: Donald J. McConnell
AMB SEC: Carol A. Duffy
DCM: John M. Jones
POL/MIL/ECO/COM:
    Liam J. Humphreys
CON: Lois E. Turner
ADM: Joseph A. Hilts
RSO: Raymond Lee Yates
    (resident in Niamey)
PAO: Patricia M. Hawkins
IPO: Charles H. Adams
AID: Jatinder Cheema
ODA: Col. Kenneth Hibl, USA
    (resident in Abidjan)
FAA: Ronald L. Montgomery
    (resident in Dakar)
LAB: Frederick B. Cook
    (resident in Washington, DC)
ISM: Catherine Volpe
    (resident in Abidjan)
    (resident in Dakar)
RETO: Timothy H. Robinson
    (resident in Dakar)
IRS: Charles W. Landry
    (resident in Singapore)

Burma

Rangoon (E)
581 Merchant St. (GPO 521)
• Box B
APO AP 96546
Tel: [95] (1) 82055, 82182
Telex: 083-21230 AMBYGN BM
Fax: 80409
AMB: (Vacant)
CHG: Marilyn A. Meyers
CHG SEC: Yolanda Norvell
PO:/ECO: Angus T. Simmons
COM: Laura J. Kirkconnell
CON: Martin B. Tatuch
ADM: Russell E. Morrow
GSO: Gary W. Mignano

RSO: Christopher J. St. Onge
PAO: Douglas M. Barnes
IPO: Jerry C. Oliver
AGR: Peter Kurz
    (resident in Bangkok)
ODA: Col. Danwill A. Lee, USA
FAA: David L. Knudson
    (resident in Singapore)
DEA: Gary L. Carter
IRS: Charles W. Landry
    (resident in Singapore)

Burundi

Bujumbura (E)
B.P. 1720
Avenue des Etats-Unis
Tel: [257] 22-34-54
Fax: 22-29-26
AID Tel: 22-59-51
Fax: 22-29-86
AMB: Robert C. Krueger
AMB SEC: Frances C. Wickes
DCM: Susan W. Zelle
ECO/COM/CON:
    Julie O'Reagan
ADM: Christa U. Griffin
RSO: Christopher W. Reilly
PAO: Gordon K. Duguid
CPO: Clyde J. Jackson
FAA: Ronald L. Montgomery
    (resident in Dakar)
AID: Myron Golden
ODA: Ltc. Thomas P. Odom, USA
    (resident in Kinshasa)
RETO: Timothy H. Robinson
    (resident in Dakar)
IRS: David Robison
    (resident in Riyadh)

Cambodia

Phnom Penh (E)
27 EO St. 240
• Box P

APO AP 96546
Tel: (855) 23-26436 or 26438
Fax: 23-26437

AMB:	Charles H. Twining, Jr.
AMB SEC:	Louise Ramirez
DCM:	Robert C. Porter, Jr.
POL:	Mary G. McGeehan
ECO/COM:	Helen Hudson
CON:	Kenneth L. Foster
ADM:	Robert W. Pons
IPO:	James A. Griffin
AID:	Joseph Goodwin
PAO:	Franklin E. Huffman
RSO:	Donald W. Weinberg
FAA:	David L. Knudson (resident in Singapore)
JTF/FA:	Maj. Scott A. Chavez
CINCPACREP:	
	Ltc. Barry Shapiro
IRS:	Charles Landry (resident in Singapore)

Cameroon

Yaounde (E)
Rue Nachtigal
B.P. 817
Tel: [237] 23-40-14
Pouch American Embassy DOS
Washington, DC 20521-2520
Telex: 8223 KN
Fax: 23-07-53

AMB:	Harriet W. Isom
AMB SEC:	Cherryl D. Busch
DCM:	Morris N. Hughes, Jr.
POL:	Peter A. O'Donohue
ECO/COM:	Aubrey V. Verdun
CON:	Michael John Murphy
ADM:	John O'Leary
RSO:	Michael H. Ross
PAO:	Gerald Huchel
CPO:	Todd D. Roe
ISM:	Robert L. Olson
ODA:	Ltc. James L. Cobb, USA
FAA:	Ronald L. Montgomery (resident in Dakar)
IRS:	Frederick D. Pablo (resident in Paris)

Canada

Ottawa, Ontario (E)
100 Wellington St.
K1P 5T1
• P.O. Box 5000
Ogdensburg, NY 13669-0430
Tel: (613) 238-5335 or 238-4470
Fax: 238-5720
COM Fax: 233-8511

AMB:	James Johnston Blanchard
AMB SEC:	Joanne P. Holliday
DCM:	James Donald Walsh
POL:	David T. Jones
ECO:	Marshall L. Casse
COM:	Dale V. Slaght
CON:	Nancy H. Sambaiew
ADM:	Ned W. Arcement
RSO:	Michael G. Considine
PAO:	Gail J. Gulliksen
CPO:	Steve A. Lauderdale
ISM:	W. A. Peter Bolton
EST:	Teresa Chin Jones
ODA:	Col. David W. Eberly
AGR:	Richard T. McDonnell
DEA:	Benny Mangor
LAB:	(Vacant)
CUS:	Richard Mercier
IRS:	Patricia Fong

Calgary, Alberta (CG)
Suite 1050, 615 Macleod Trail, SE
Calgary, Alberta, Canada T2G 4T8
Tel: (403) 266-8962
Fax: 264-6630
COM Fax: 264-6630

CG:	Richard V. Fisher
CON:	Robert S. Bagen
ADM/POL:	Deidre Warner

Halifax, Nova Scotia (CG)
Suite 910, Cogswell Tower
Scotia Sq.
Halifax, NS, Canada B3J 3K1
Tel: (902) 429-2480
Fax: 423-6861
COM *Fax:* 423-6861

CG: R. Bruce Ehrnman
CON: Laurence E. Tobey

Montreal, Quebec (CG)
P.O. Box 65
Postal Station Desjardins, H5B 1G1
• P.O. Box 847
Champlain, NY 12919-0847
Tel: (514) 398-9695
Fax: 398-0973, (514) 398-0711

CG: Eleanor W. Savage
CG SEC: Judith A. Brooks
ECO: Richard G. Johnson
COM: Andrew Tangalos
CON: Joan V. Smith
ADM: Elizabeth R. Beyene
BPAO: Susan E. Brandt
CPO: Arthur Pollik
USTTA: Andree Logan

US Mission to the International Civil Aviation Organization (ICAO)
1000 Sherbrooke St., W.
Room 753
Montreal, Quebec
• Box 847
Champlain, NY 12919
Tel: (514) 285-8304
Fax: 285-8021

US REP: Carol J. Carmody
ALT US REP: James H. Loos
ALT FIC/JSC REP:
 Gene Griffiths

Quebec, Quebec (CG)
Two Place Terrasse Defferin
C.P. 939, G1R 4T9
• P.O. Box 1547
Champlain, NY 12919-1547
Tel: (418) 692-2095
Fax: 692-4640

CG: Stephen Kelly
CON: W. Howie Muir

Toronto, Ontario (CG)
360 University Ave.
M5G 1S4
• P.O. Box 135
Lewiston, NY 14092-0135
Tel: (416) 595-1700
Fax: 595-0051, 595-5419
CON *Fax:* 595-5466

CG: G. Alfred Kennedy
CG SEC: Debra P. Tous
ECO: Michael J. Varga
COM: Dan A. Wilson
CON: Dean Dizikes
ADM: Wayne S. Salisbury
CPO: Edmund J. Gagliardi
BPAO: Patricia D. Norman
USTTA: Thomas Quinn
INS: John Garofano

Vancouver, British Columbia (CG)
1095 W. Pender St.
V6E 2M6
P.O. Box 5002
Point Roberts, WA 98281-5002
Tel: (604) 685-4311
Fax: 685-5285
COM *Fax:* 687-6095

CG: Michael F. Gallagher
CG SEC: Sally K. Macias
ECO: William T. Fleming, Jr.
COM: Jere Dabbs
CON: Barbara C. Cummings
BPAO: Karl H. Fritz

Republic of Cape Verde

Praia (E)
Rua Abilio Macedo 81
C.P. 201
Tel: [238] 61-56-16
Fax: 61-13-55

AMB: Joseph M. Segars
AMB SEC: Ruth Rust Walker
CON: Russell J. Hanks

ADM: Long N. Lee
RSO: Gary M. Gibson
(resident in Dakar)
AID: Barbara C. Kennedy
ODA: Ltc. Paul S. Cariker, USMC
(resident in Dakar)
LAB: Frederick B. Cook
(resident in Washington, DC)
ISM: Janet A. Cote
(resident in Dakar)
FAA: Ronald L. Montgomery
(resident in Dakar)
IMO: Terrence K. Williamson
(resident in Dakar)
IRS: Frederick D. Pablo
(resident in Paris)
RCON: Thomas E. Cairns
(resident in Dakar)

Central African Republic
Bangui (E)
Avenue David Dacko
B.P. 924
Tel: [236] 61-02-00, 61-02-10, 61-25-78
Telex: 5287 RC
Fax: 44-94

AMB: Robert E. Gribbin III
AMB SEC: Marilyn Y. Shaw
DCM: James F. Entwistle
ECO: Samuel C. Laeuchli
GSO/CON: Michael R. Keller
ADM: Rowena R. Cross-Najafi
RSO: Michael H. Ross
(resident in Yaounde)
PAO: (Vacant)
IPO: Michael C. Lawrence
FAA: Ronald L. Montgomery
(resident in Dakar)
IRS: Frederick D. Pablo
(resident in Paris)

Chad
N'Djamena (E)
Ave. Felix Eboue
B.P. 413
Tel: [235] (51) 40-09, 47-59, or 62-18
Telex: 5203 KD
Fax: 33-72 or 56-54

AMB: Laurence E. Pope II
AMB SEC: Patricia Reber
DCM: Douglas S. Kinney
POL/ECO: Stephanie Smith Kinney
POL/MIL: Donald J. Twombly
ADM: Joanne M. Thompson
IPO: Doyle R. Lee
RSO: Richard Chelune
PAO: Fawzi M. Freij
AID: Richard Fraenkel
ODA: Maj. Jean Luc Nash, USA
FAA: Ronald L. Montgomery
(resident in Dakar)
IRS: Frederick Pablo
(resident in Paris)

Chile
Santiago (E)
Av. Andres Bello 2800
Tel: [56] (2) 232-2600
Fax: 330-3710
COM Fax: 330-3172
AID Fax: 638-0931
FAS Fax: 330-3203
FBO Fax: 233-4108
CON: 330-3710

AMB: Gabriel Guerra-Mondragon
AMB SEC: Jill Johnston
DCM: Charles S. Shapiro
POL: Phillip T. Chicola
ECO: Anthony J. Interlandi
COM: Carlos F. Poza
CON: Richard S. Mann
ADM: Janice Ogden
RSO: Jeffrey L. Bozworth

PAO:	Barbara C. Moore	AMB:	(Vacant)
IMO:	Steven J. Valdez	AMB SEC:	(Vacant)
ODA:	Capt. Thomas L. Breitinger, USN	CHG:	Scott S. Hallford
		POL:	Neil E. Silver
MILGP:	Col. Steven E. Cady	ECO:	Jack L. Gosnell
AID:	Thomas Nicastro	COM:	Steven Hendryx
IRS:	Charles Shea (resident in Caracas)	CON:	Arturo S. Macias
		ADM:	Michael Boorstein
AGR:	Richard B. Helm	GSO:	Kenneth A. Cohen
APHIS:	James Mackley	RSO:	Donald P. Schurman
LAB:	Joseph G. McClean	PAO:	Frank Scotton
FAA:	Santiago Garcia (resident in Rio de Janeiro)	IMO:	Jerry Lester
		ES&T:	Marco Di Capua
		ODA:	BG Michael Brynes
		AGR:	William Brant
		ATO:	Scott Reynolds
		FAA:	Frederick Lee
		IRS:	Dennis Tsujimoto (resident in Tokyo)

China*

Beijing (E)
Xiu Shui Bei Jie 3, 100600
• PSC 461, Box 50
FPO AP 96521-0002
Tel: [86] (10) 532-3831
Telex: AMEMB CN 22701
EXEC CON Fax: 532-6422
POL/ES&T/RSO Fax: 532-6423
ESO/MSG Fax: 532-6421
GSO/Fax: 532-6057
Health Unit Fax: 532-6424
AGR FAS Fax: 532-2962
FAA Fax: 595-8094
USIS Fax: 532-2039
ACEE Fax: 501-5247
CON Fax: 532-3178
COM Fax: 532-3297
ADM/Travel Fax: 532-2483
American Center for Educational Exchange (ACEE)
Jing Guang Center
Tel: 501-5247
Federal Aviation Administration (FAA)
Jianguo Hotel, Rooms 128–130
No. 5 Jianguo St.
Tel: 595-8093

Guangzhou (CG)
No. 1 Shamian St. S.
Guangzhou 510133
• PSC 461, Box 100
FPO AP 96521-0002
Tel: [86] (20) 888-8911
Fax: 886-2341
COM Tel: 667-4011
Fax: 666-6409
AGR Tel: 667-7553
Fax: 666-0703
USIS Tel: 335-4269
Fax: 335-4764
American School of Guangzhou
Tel: 758-0001
Fax: 758-0002

CG:	G. Eugene Martin
CG SEC:	Genevieve DiMeglio
ECO/POL:	E. Mark Linton
POL:	Theodore Lyng
ECO:	Jeffery Zaiser
COM:	Robert Strotman
CON:	Edward McKeon
ADM:	Richard Nelson
RSO:	Brent Barker (resident in Shanghai)

*See Taiwan, page 345.

An Entrepreneur's Directory to Foreign Service Officers **277**

GSO: Ken Youngblood
BPAO: Leonard Korycki
IPO: Kanikar Daly
ATO: Ralph Gifford

Shanghai (CG)
1469 Huai Hai Middle Rd.
Shanghai 200031
• PSC 461, Box 200
FPO AP 96521-0002
(**Note:** Use Pouch address for official shipments, not FPO)
Tel: [86] (21) 433-6880
Fax: 433-4122
GSO Fax: 433-7595
CON Fax (VISAS/ACS): 437-5173
COM Fax: 433-1576
USIS Tel: 471-8689, 471-8690
Fax: 431-7630
Shanghai American School (SAS)
Tel: 252-1687
Fax: 251-1649

CG: Joseph J. Borich
EXEC SEC: Tess Johnston
POL: Bruce R. Nelson
ECO: Robert S. Wang
ADM: Boyd R. Doty
COM: David Murphy
CON: Robert D. Wilson
GSO: Alexander C. Fleming
BPAO: David E. Miller
RSO: Brent A. Barker
IPO: Robert A. Smith
ATO: Scott Reynolds

Shenyang (CG)
52, 14th Wei Rd.
Heping District 110003
• PSC 461, Box 45
FPO AP 96521-0002
Tel: [86] (24) 282-0068
Fax: 282-0074
USIS Fax: 282-0035

CG: Gerard R. Pascua
CG SEC: R. Karen Waddell
ECO: Patrick L. Chow
COM: (Vacant)
CON: Joanne M. Martin

POL: James R. Heller
ADM: Rosalyn H. Anderson
BPAO: Lisa C. Kennedy
IPO: Daniel E. Aguayo

Chengdu (CG)
Four Lingshiquan Rd.
Chengdu 610041
• PSC 461, Box 85
FPO AP 96521-0002
Tel: [86] (28) 558-2993, 558-9642
Fax: 558-3520
Telex: 60128 ACGCH CH
USIS Fax: 558-3792

CG: Cornelius M. Keur
POL/ECO: Jonathan Fritz
CON/POL: (Vacant)
ADM: James Leaf
FMS: John Moore
BPAO: Frank Neville

Colombia

Bogota (E)
Calle 38, No. 8-61
Apartado Aereo 3831
APO AA 34038
Tel: [57] (1) 320-1300
Fax: 288-5687
COM Fax: 285-7945

AMB: Myles R. R. Frechette
AMB SEC: Sheila M. Mullen
DCM: John B. Craig
POL: Thomas P. Hamilton
ECO: John L. Pitts
COM: Catherine Houghton
CON: Thomas L. Randall, Jr.
ADM: Thomas C. Tighe
RSO: Robert M. Brittian
PAO: L. W. Koengeter
IMO: Heywood Miller
AID: Lawrence J. Klassen
ODA: Col. William S. Justus, USA
MAAG: Col. Thomas R. Carstens, USA
AGR: Clyde Gumbmann

APHIS:	Gary T. Greene
FAA:	Victor Tamariz
	(resident in Miami)
LAB:	William L. Loftstrom
NAS:	Victor A. Abeyta
IRS:	Charles Shea
	(resident in Caracas)

Barranquilla (C)
Calle 77 Carrera 68
Centro Comercial Mayorista
Apartado Aereo 51565
• APO AA 34038
Tel: [57] (58) 45-8480/9067
Fax: 45-5216

PO:	(Vacant)
ADM/CON:	
	Patrick R. Quigley
POL/ECO:	Marvin S. Brown
IMO:	Heywood Miller
	(resident in Bogota)

Republic of the Congo

Brazzaville (E)
Avenue Amilcar Cabral
B.P. 1015
Tel: (242) 83-20-70
Telex: 5367 KG
Fax: 83-63-38

AMB:	William C. Ramsay
DCM:	Frances T. Jones
POL:	Gary S. Moe
CON:	Levon A. Eldemir
ECO:	Katherine K. Simonds
ADM:	Brent R. Bohne
RSO:	James P. Ennis
PAO:	Thomas J. Dougherty
IPO:	Griffith C. Murray
ODA:	Ltc. James F. Babbitt
FAA:	Ronald L. Montgomery
	(resident in Dakar)
RMO:	Dr. Ernest E. Davis
IRS:	Frederick D. Pablo
	(resident in Paris)

Costa Rica

San Jose (E)
Pavas, San Jose
• APO AA 34020
Tel: (506) 220-3939
Afterhours Tel: 220-3127
Fax: 220-2305
COM Fax: 231-4783

AMB:	Peter J. de Vos
AMB SEC:	Rosalie Natrop
DCM:	Joseph F. Becelia
DCM SEC:	Cornelia W. Molinaro
POL:	Mark Davison
ECO:	Ben F. Fairfax
COM:	Maria Galindo
CON:	Kenneth F. Sackett
ADM:	(Vacant)
RSO:	Nance B. Crawford
PAO:	Frances Sullinger
IPO:	Howard R. Charles
ISM:	David S. Fleming
AID:	Stephen C. Wingert
ODC:	Angel E. Pesante
AGR:	Scott Bleggi
APHIS:	Eric Hoffman
FAA:	Victor Tamariz
	(resident in Miami)
LAB:	John Mohanco
	(resident in Panama)
IRS:	Daniel R. Dietz
	(resident in Mexico City)

Cote D'Ivoire (formerly Ivory Coast)

Abidjan (E)
5 Rue Jesse Owens
01 B.P. 1712
Tel: (225) 21-09-79
Telex: 23660
Fax: 22-32-59

AMB:	Lannon Walker
AMB SEC:	Clayton Tolson
DCM:	Charles O. Cecil
POL:	Michele Sison

ECO: Kenneth H. Kolb
COM: Nikki Brajevic
COM rep to the AFDB:
           Margaret Hanson-Muse
CON: Andrew Passen
JAO: Kenneth M. Scott, Jr.
ADM: Edward Malcik
RSO: Joe D. Morton
PAO: Thomas Hart
IMO: Jim Rubino
AID/REDSO:
           Willard Pearson
ODA: Col. Kenneth Hibl, USA
AGR: Jonathan Gressel
FAA: Ronald L. Montgomery
           (resident in Dakar)
IRS: Frederick D. Pablo
           (resident in Paris)

African Development Bank/Fund
Ave., Joseph Anoma
01 B.P. 1387
Abidjan 01
Tel: (225) 20-40-15
Fax: 33-14-34
COM Tel: 21-46-16
Fax: 22-24-37

EXEC DIR: Alice Dear
ALT DIR: Daniel J. Duesterbereg
COM: (Vacant)

Croatia

Zagreb (E)
Andrije Hebranga 2
• Unit 1345
APO AE 09213-1345
Tel: [385] (1) 455-55-00
Afterhours Tel: 455-52-81
ADM Fax: 455-8585
USIS Fax: 440-235
COM Fax: 455-3126
CON Fax: 455-0774

AMB: Peter W. Galbraith
AMB SEC: Charlotte A. Stottman
DCM: Robert P. J. Finn
POL/ECO: Stephen H. Klemp

ECO: Thomas Mittnacht
COM: Damjam Bencic
ADM: Ronna S. Pazdral
PAO: Douglas Davidson
CPO: Ronald Grider
AID: Charles Aanenson
ODA: Ltc. John Sadler, USA
AGR: Frank J. Tarrant
           (resident in Vienna)
LAB: Thomas D. Mittnacht
FAA: Steven B. Wallace
           (resident in Rome)

Cuba

Havana (USINT)
Swiss Embassy
Calzada Between L and M Sts.
Vedado, Havana, USINT
Tel: 33-3551/9, 33-3543/7
Fax: 33-3700
CON Switchboard: 33-3546/7
Telex: 512206
Afterhours Marine Post: 1 33-3026
USIS Direct Line: 33-3967
Fax: 33-3869
FBO Direct Line: 33-4096/97
Fax: 33-3975

PO: Joseph G. Sullivan
DPO: Manuel Rocha
POL/ECO: Robert M. Witajewski
CON: Sandra Salmon
ADM: Fred Cook
RSO: Michael Kelly
PAO: Merrie Blocker
IMO: Steve Shinnick
FAA: Celio Young
           (resident in Miami)
FBO: James C. McQueen
LAB: John W. Zerolis

Cyprus

Nicosia (E)
Metochiou and Ploutarchou Sts.
Engomi, Nicosia, Cyprus

- P.O. Box 4536
FPO AE 09836
Tel: [357] (2) 476100
Afterhours Tel: 476-934
Telex: 4160 AMEMY CY
Fax: 465944
CON Fax: 465604
USIS Tel: 473143
Fax: 454003

AMB:	Richard A. Boucher
AMB SEC:	Valerie Mawdsley
DCM:	Alejandro Wolff
POL:	John Koenig
ECO/COM:	Patricia Nelson-Douvelis
CON:	Cynthia Stockbridge
ADM:	Mark Woerner
RSO:	Edwin J. Wood
PAO:	Marcelle Wahba
IMO:	Debra Wells
ODA:	Ltc. David N. Fetter (Army)
AGR:	Paul Hoffman (resident in Athens)
FAA:	Steven B. Wallace (resident in Rome)
IRS:	Larry J. Legrand (resident in Rome)

Czech Republic

Prague (E)
(Int'l) Trziste 15
11801 Prague 1
- Unit 1330
APO AE 09213-1330
Tel: [42] (2) 2451-0847
COM Tel: 2421-9844 or 2421-9846/7
Afterhours Marine Post 1 Tel: 531-200
Fax: 2451-1001
ADM Fax: 2451-1001
GSO Fax: 2451-0742
ECO Fax: 531-193
USIS and COM Address:
Hybernska 7A
117 16 Prague 1

COM Fax: 2421-9965
USIS Tel: 2423-1085
Fax: 2422-0983
AID Fax: 2451-0340
ODA Fax: 532988

AMB:	Jenonne R. Walker
AMB SEC:	Anissa Hanson
DCM:	Eric S. Edelman
POL/ECO:	Douglas Hengel
COM:	Daniel Harris
CON:	Robert Mustain, Jr.
ADM:	Carlos Perez
RSO:	David Schaeffer
PAO:	Leonard Williams
AID:	James Bednar
CPO:	Steve Curry
ISM:	Herbert Markowski
ODA:	Col. David Potts
AGR:	Frank J. Tarrant (resident in Vienna)
FAA:	Steven B. Wallace (resident in Rome)
PC:	William Piatt
EST:	Douglas B. McNeal
IRS:	Joe D. Hook (resident in Bonn)

Denmark

Copenhagen (E)
Dag Hammarskjolds Alle 24
2100 Copenhagen O
PSC 73
APO AE 09716
Tel: [45] (31) 42-31-44
Afterhours Tel: 42-92-70
Fax: [45] (35) 43-0223
Telex: 22216 AMEMB DK
USIS Fax: 42-72-73
FAS Fax: 43-02-78
USAF Fax: 25-51-08
COM Fax: 42-01-75

AMB:	Edward E. Elson
AMB SEC:	Hilda J. Wojahn
DCM:	Gregory L. Mattson
POL/ECO:	Patricia D. Hughes

COM:	Richard F. Benson	LAB:	Lois A. Arojan
EST:	Stephanie Smith Kinney		(resident in Nairobi)
FCS:	Richard F. Benso	IRS:	David Robison
CON:	Suella Pipal		(resident in Riyadh)
ADM:	Perry M. Adair		
RSO:	John W. Schilling		
PAO:	Stephan Strain		
IMO:	Glenn T. Jones		
ODA:	Capt. Terry W. Moore, USN		
ODC:	Col. Lawrence Haggenauer, USAF		
FAA:	Carl Burleson (resident in London)		
FAA/CASLO:	Donald G. Tyson		
AGR:	Margaret Dowling		
LAB:	Edward D. Keeton		
IRS:	Stanley Beesley (resident in London)		
FBI:	John E. Guido (resident in London)		

Republic of Djibouti

Djibouti (E)
Plateau du Serpent
Blvd. Marechal Joffre
B.P. 185
Tel: [253] 35-39-95
Fax: 35-39-40
Afterhours: 35-13-43

AMB:	Martin L. Cheshes
AMB SEC:	Julie Stinehart
DCM:	Joseph P. Gregoire
POL:	Peter R. Enzminger
POL/ECO:	(Vacant)
CON:	John F. Bates
ADM:	Michael A. Raynor
RSO/GSO:	John P. Davis
IPO:	Robert P. McCumber
USLO:	Maj. Peter W. Aubrey
ODA:	Col. Michael M. Ferguson, USA (resident in Addis Ababa)
FAA:	Dennis Beres (resident in Riyadh)

Dominican Republic

Santo Domingo (E)
Corner of Calle Cesar Nicholas
Penson & Calle Leopoldo Navarro
• Unit 5500
APO AA 34041
Tel: (809) 54-12171 or 54-18100
Telex: 3460013
Fax: 687-7437
COM Fax: 688-4838

ABM:	Donna Jean Hrinak
AMB SEC:	Beverly Oliver
DCM:	Cristobal Roberto Orozco
POL:	Dennis M. Linskey
ECO:	Milton K. Drucker
COM:	Robert J. Bucalo
CON:	Brooke C. Holmes
ADM:	Larry L. Palmer
RSO:	Thurron J. Mallory
PAO:	Cesar Beltran
CPO:	Charles E. Fleenor
ISM:	Jerry D. Helmick
AID:	Marilyn A. Zak
ODA:	Ltc. Jeffrey H. Kammerer, USN
MAAG:	Ltc. Michael F. Fukey, USAF
NAU:	Janice Elmore
AGR:	Susan Schayes
APHIS:	Carl W. Castleton
FAA:	Celio Young (resident in Miami)
IRS:	Louis Hobbie (resident in Nassau)

Ecuador

Quito (E)
Avenida 12 de Octubre y Avenida Patria
• APO AA 34039

Tel: [593] (2) 562-890
Afterhours Tel: 561-749
Voice Mail: 562-624
Fax: 502-052
COM Fax: 504-550

AMB:	Peter F. Romero
AMB SEC:	Susan Kamerick
DCM:	R. Susan Wood
POL:	David Randolph
ECO:	Paul E. Simons
COM:	Janice Corbett
CON:	Alfred Gonzales
ADM:	Charles B. Angulo
RSO:	Dennis Ravenscroft
PAO:	Guy Burton
IMO:	Charles D. Wisecarver
AID:	John A Sanbrailo
ODA:	Col. Ovidio E. Perez, USA
MILGP:	Col. Steven Hightower, USA
DMA:	James P. Hutchings
PC:	Jean Seigle
AGR:	Daryl Brehm
APHIS:	Raymond Carbajal
FAA:	Victor Tamariz (resident in Miami)
LAB:	James H. Benson
NAS:	Robert E. Snyder
IRS:	Charles Shea (resident in Caracas)

Guayaquil (CG)
9 de Octubre y Garcia Moreno
• APO AA 34039
Tel: [593] (4) 323-570
Afterhours Tel: 321-152
Fax: 325-286
COM Fax: 324-558

CG:	Daniel A. Johnson
CG SEC:	Deanna Cotter
COM:	Hector Raul Gomez
CON:	Larry D. Huffman
ADM:	Jeffrey C. Irwin
IPO:	John A. Montague

Egypt (Arab Republic of)
Cairo (E)
(North Gate) 8
Kamal El-Din Salah St.
Garden City
• Unit 64900
APO AE 09839-4900
Tel: [20] (2) 355-7371
Telex: 93773 AMEMB UN, 23227
AMEMB UN
Fax: 357-3200
ADM Fax: 355-4353
CON Fax: 357-2472
FCS Fax: 355-8368
AID Fax: 357-2233
USIS Fax: 357-3591
ODA Fax: 357-3049
FAS Fax: 356-3989
LOC Fax: 356-0233
FBO Fax: 356-2712
OMC Fax: 357-2273
POL Fax: 357-3491
RSO Fax: 357-2828
ECO Fax: 357-2181
workweek: Sunday through Thursday

AMB:	Edward S. Walker, Jr.
AMB SEC:	Mildred Tangney
DCM:	Edmund J. Hull
POL:	Jeffrey V. S. Millington
ECO:	Russell A. La Mantia
COM:	Laron L. Jensen
CON:	Nicholas Hahn
ADM:	(Vacant)
RSO:	Ronald A. Reams
PAO:	Marjorie A. Ransom
IMO:	Richard D. Rapier
ISO:	Otho N. Harbison
AID:	John R. Westley
ODA:	Col. Joseph P. Englehardt, USA
DEA:	Thomas M. Whiteside
OMC:	Mg. Otto K. Habedank, USA
AGR:	Forrest K. Geerken

An Entrepreneur's Directory to Foreign Service Officers   **283**

FAA: Dennis Beres
            (resident in Riyadh)
LAB: Barbara A. Leaf
FBO: William A. Smayda
LOC: E. Gene Smith
IRS: David Robison
            (resident in Riyadh)

Alexandria (BO)
3 El Faraana St.
• Unit 64900, Box 24
APO AE 09839–4900
USIS American Center
Tel: [20] (3) 472-1009
Fax: 483-3811
COM Tel: 482-5607 or 483-6330
COM Fax: 482-9199
Branch Office does not provide Consular services.

BPAO: Katherine Van De Vate
COM: Lauren L. Jensen
            (resident in Cairo)

El Salvador

San Salvador (E)
Final Blvd. Santa Elena
Antiguo Cuscatlan
• Unit 3116
APO AA 34023
Tel: (503) 278-4444
Fax: 278-6011
USAID Tel: 298-1666
USAID Fax: 298-0885
ECO/COM Fax: 298-2336
GSO Fax: 278-3347

AMB: Alan H. Flanigan
AMB SEC: Ingeborg Steinmetz
DCM: Gwen C. Clare
POL: James J. Carragher
ECO/COM: Christopher Lynch
CON: Robert T. Raymer
ADM: Joseph B. Schreiber
RSO: Arthur W. Jones
PAO: Francis B. Ward, III
IMO: Howard L. Keegan

CPO: Michael W. Meyers
IMC: Heywood Miller
ODA: Col. Carl G. Roe, USA
AID DIR: Carl Leonard
MILGP: Col. Joseph C. Fee
AGR: Grant A. Pettrie
            (resident in Guatemala)
PC: Donald B. Peterson
DEA: Thomas E. Detriquet
DOJ: Robert Loosle
APHIS: Steve C. Smith
FAA: Victor Tamariz
            (resident in Miami)
LAB: Simon Henshaw
IRS: Daniel R. Dietz
            (resident in Mexico City)

Equatorial Guinea

Malabo (E)
Calle de Los Ministros
• P.O. Box 597
Tel Direct Dial: [240] (9) 2185, 2406, 2507
Fax: 2164

AMB: Joseph O'Neill, CDA
POL/ECO/CON:
                Frank R. Adams
EXEC SEC: Judy J. Copenhaver
ADM: David W. Boyle
RSO: Stephen C. Meister
                (resident in Yaounde)
PAO: Gerald Huchel
                (resident in Yaounde)
CPO: Donald J. Connolly
AID: Peter Benedict
                (resident in Yaounde)
ODA: Ltc. Charles Vuckovic
                (resident in Yaounde)
RMO: Dr. Gretchen McCoy
                (resident in Lagos)
FAA: Ronald L. Montgomery
                (resident in Dakar)
IRS: Frederick D. Pablo
                (resident in Paris)
IPO: (Vacant)

Eritrea

Asmara (E)
34 Zera Yacob St.
• P.O. Box 211
Tel: [291] (1) 12-00-04
Fax: 12-75-84
USAID Tel: 12-18-95

AMB:	Robert G. Houdek
AMB SEC:	Frances L. Davey
POL/ECO:	Karl I. Danga
POL:	Christopher J. Bane
ADM:	Michael S. Hoza
GSO:	Richard A. Davey
CON:	Celio F. Sandate
COM:	Lian Hall-Hoza
PAO:	Christopher Datta
IPO:	Larry Bucher
AID:	George Jones
FAA:	Dennis Beres (resident in Riyadh)
ODA:	Col. Michael M. Ferguson, USA (resident in Addis Ababa)
RSO:	James W. Schnaible (resident in Addis Ababa)
LAB:	Lois Aroian (resident in Nairobi)

Estonia

Tallinn (E)
Kentmanni 20, EE 0001
Tel: [372] (6) 312-021 through 024
Cellular Tel: 5-244-091
Fax: 312-025

AMB:	Lawrence P. Taylor
AMB SEC:	Domenica P. Waller
DCM:	Jon Gunderson
POL:	Elo-Kai Ojamaa
ECO:	Ingrid Kollist
CON:	Robin L. Haase
ADM:	David Buss
AID:	Adrian DeGraffenreid
PAO:	Victoria S. Middleton
RSO:	Jeremy S. Zeikel (resident in Helsinki)
IPO:	Scott D. Ternus
ITO:	Kathleen M. Kilcullin
ODA:	Frederick E. Bush (resident in Helsinki)
AGR:	Thomas A. Hamby (resident in Stockholm)
FAA:	J. Stuart Jamison (resident in Brussels)
IRS:	Joe D. Hook (resident in Bonn)

Ethiopia

Addis Ababa (E)
Entoto St.
• P.O. Box 1014
Tel: [251] (1) 550-666
Telex: 21282
Fax: 552-191

AMB:	Irvin Hicks
AMB SEC:	Loyce Menard Rothin
DCM:	David M. Walker
POL/ECO:	Thomas C. Niblock, Jr.
ECO:	Eric P. Whitaker
COM:	Alan L. Patterson
CON:	Thomas J. Rice
ADM:	David C. Bennett
RP:	Michael L. Bajek
RSO:	James W. Schnaible
PAO:	Arlene R. Jacquette
IPO:	Eley M. Johnson
ISM:	Jean-Rene Chapoteau
RPO:	Jonita I. Whitaker
AID:	Margaret P. Bonner
ORA:	Christian C. Chatfield
ODA:	Col. Michael M. Ferguson, USA
LAB:	Lois A. Aroian (resident in Nairobi)
FAA:	Dennis Beres (resident in Riyadh)
IRS:	David Robison (resident in Riyadh)
RETO:	Timothy H. Robinson (resident in Dakar)

Fiji

Suva (E)
31 Loftu St.
• P.O. Box 218
Tel: [679] 314-466
Fax: 300-081
Exec. Off. Fax: 303-872
USIS Fax: 305-106

AMB:	(Vacant)
CHG:	Bruce N. Gray
POL:	Jane Miller Floyd
CON:	Nicholas C. H. MacNeil
ADM:	Dennis A. Droney
RSO:	John Henry Kaufmann (resident in Canberra)
PAO:	Charla Hatton
IPO:	Alan R. Haydt
ODA:	Ltc. Kip Naugle, USMC
FAA:	Fred Laird (resident in Tokyo)
IRS:	Vivian L. Simon (resident in Sydney)

Finland

Helsinki (E)
Itainen Puistotie 14A
FIN-00140
• APO AE 09723
Tel: [358] (0) 171931
Telex: 121644 USEMB SF
Fax: 174681
COM Fax: 635332
URSA: 379359

AMB:	Derek N. Shearer
AMB SEC:	Hortencia T. Gencalp
DCM:	Arma Jane Karaer
POL:	Richard DeVillafranca
ECO:	Michael J. Delaney
COM:	Maria Andrews
CON:	Charles L. Glatz, Jr.
ADM:	Thomas W. Ryan
RSO:	Jeremy S. Zeikel
PAO:	Phillipe I. Duchateau
CPO:	Paul A. Bialecki
ODA:	Michael C. Sheen, USAF
AGR:	Thomas A. Hamby (resident in Stockholm)
FAA:	Carl Burleson (resident in London)
LAB:	Kevin M. Johnson
IRS:	Stanley Beesley (resident in London)
URSA:	Johanna E. Schoeppl

France

Paris (E)
2 Avenue Gabriel
75382 Paris Cedex 08
• PSC 116
APO AE 09777
Tel: [33] (1) 43-12-22-22
Telex: 285319 and 285221 AMEMB
Fax: [33] (1) 4266-9783
AMB/AMB SEC: 42-12-27-00
DCM: 43-12-28-00
POL: 43-12-27-83
ECO: 43-12-26-54
COM: 43-12-23-83
Fax: 42-66-48-27
CON: 43-12-47-08
ADM: 43-12-20-09
RSO: 43-12-21-19
RAMC: 43-12-70-54
PAO: 43-12-48-98
IMO: 43-12-21-41
EST: 43-12-25-63
ODA: 43-12-21-33
ODC: 43-12-46-95
AGR: 43-12-22-77
LAB: 43-12-23-93
CUS: 43-12-73-55
FAA: 43-12-22-25
FAA/CASLO: 43-12-26-29
IRS: 43-12-45-60
USTTA: 43-12-27-70

AMB:	Pamela C. Harriman
AMB SEC:	Donna J. Dejban
DCM:	Avis T. Bohlen
POL:	William M. Bellamy

ECO:	John Medeiros		AID:	Lee Roussel
COM:	Peter G. Frederick		IND/COM:	Robin R. Layton
CON:	James L. Ward		INVES ADV:	
ADM:	Charles R. Allegrone			Kathleen M. Reddy
RSO:	Burley P. Fuselier, Jr.		ENERGY ADV:	
RAMC:	Kenneth Rosenberg			Wayne E. Neill II
PAO:	Christopher Snow		EST:	Coleman J. Nee
IMO:	Philip M. Tinney		STC:	Ronald D. Flack
EST:	Jerome J. Bosken		SEC/DEL/PAO:	
ODA:	Col. Daniel R. Larned, USA			Martin D. Murphy

US Observer Mission to the United Nations Educational, Scientific, and Cultural Organization (UNESCO)
2 Avenue Gabriel
75382, Paris CEDEX 08
• APO AE 09777
Tel: [33] (1) 43-12-20-16
Fax: 42-66-97-83

ODC:	Col. Richard A. Williams, USA
AGR:	George J. Pope
LAB:	Jean D. Gardner
CUS:	Paul D. Beaulieu
FAA:	J. Stuart Jamison (resident in Brussels)
FAA/CASLO:	
	David B. Hobbs
FIN:	Sara L. Paulson
IRS:	Frederick D. Pablo
USTTA:	Maximilian J. Ollendorf

OBSERVER: G. Dennise Mathieu

Bordeaux (CG)
22 Cours du Marechal Foch
33080 Bordeaux Cedex
• Unit 21551
APO AE 09777
Tel: [33] (56) 52-65-95
Telex: 540918 USCSUL
Fax: 51-60-42
COM: 51-60-42

US Mission to the Organization for Economic Cooperation and Development (USOECD)
19 Rue de Franqueville
75016 Paris
• PSC 116 (USOECD)
APO AE 09777
Tel: [33] (1) 45-24-74-77
Telex: 643964 F
Fax: 4524-7480
COM Fax: 4524-7410

CG:	Alan W. Eastham, Jr.
CON:	Robert R. Kiene

Marseille (CG)
12 Blvd. Paul Peytral
13286 Marseille Cedex 6
Paris Embassy (MAR)
• PSC 116
APO AE 09777
Tel: [33] (91) 549-200
Telex: 430597
Fax: 550-947
COM Fax: 550-947

AMB:	David L. Aaron
AMB SEC:	Marilyn H. Takacs
DCM:	Ann R. Berry
ECO/FIN:	James G. Wallar
ECO/SOC:	William A. Weingarten
COM:	Robin Layton
LAB/MAN/ADV:	
	Philip R. Wall
TRADE DIV:	
	Thomas P. Kelly
ADM:	Karlene G. Knieps
DOE:	Carol W. Lee

CG:	Jackson C. McDonald
DPO:	Donald F. Mulligan
CON:	Cynthia Kierscht
NCIS:	Geoffrey Yeowell

Strasbourg (CG)
15 Ave. D'Alsace
67082 Strasbourg CEDEX
• Unit 21551
APO AE 09777
Tel: [33] (88) 35-31-04
Fax: 24-06-95
Telex: 870907 AMERCON
COM *Fax:* 24-0695

CG: Shirley E. Barnes

US Commercial Office (Lyon)
45 Rue de la Bourse
• Unit 21551
APO AE 09777
Fax: [33] (16) 78-39-14-09

US Commercial Office (Nice)
Rue du Marechal Joffre
• Unit 21551
APO AE 09777
Tel: [33] (16) 93-88-89-55
Fax: 93-87-07-38

*COM: The Commerce Department/Foreign Commercial Service operates separate American Business Centers in these locations.

Gabon

Libreville (E)
Blvd. de la Mer
• B.P. 4000
Tel: [241] 762003/4, 743492
Fax: 745-507
Telex: 5250 GO

AMB:	Joseph C. Wilson IV
AMB SEC:	Rebecca J. Varner
DCM:	Michael A. Meigs
ECO/COM:	Peter X. Harding
CON:	Gregory Thome
ADM:	Frank J. Ledahawksy
GSO:	Pamela J. Mansfield
B&F:	Marilyn Mattke
RSO:	James P. Ennis (resident in Brazzaville)
PAO:	Judith Mudd Kaula

IPO:	Michael A. Cesena
ODA:	(Vacant)
FAA:	Ronald L. Montgomery (resident in Dakar)
IRS:	Frederick D. Pablo (resident in Paris)

Gambia, The

Banjul (E)
Fajara, Kairaba Ave.
P.M.B. 19, Banjul
Tel: (220) 392-856, 392-858, 391-970, 391-971
Fax: 392-475

AMB:	Andrew J. Winter
AMB SEC:	Maria K. Smith
POL/ECO:	James A. Knight
CON:	Thomas Cairns (resident in Dakar)
ADM:	Merritt C. Brown
RSO:	Gary Gibson (resident in Dakar)
IPO:	James W. Miles
AID:	Rose-Marie Depp
ODA:	Ltc. Paul S. Cariker, UMC (resident in Dakar)
LAB:	Frederick B. Cook (resident in Washington, DC)
FAA:	Ronald L. Montgomery (resident in Dakar)
IMO:	Terrence K. Williamson (resident in Dakar)
IRS:	Frederick D. Pablo (resident in Paris)

Georgia

Tbilisi (E)
25 Antoneli
SWBD 7-8832-989-967 or 933-803
Fax: 933-759
Satellite: (49) 5151-13057, ext. 165

Fax: 166 Voice

AMB:	Kent N. Brown
AMB SEC:	Linda Reiersgard
DCM:	Lawrence M. Kerr
POL/ECO:	Jessica LeCroy
ADM:	Alan Greefield
PAO:	James W. Hutcheson
CON:	Christopher G. Dunnett
RSO:	Rebecca Dockery
IPO:	Ronnie L. Martensen
ODA:	Ltc. Robert E. Lee
AID:	Christine M. Sheckler
FAA:	Dennis B. Cooper
	(resident in Moscow)
AGR:	Mary Revelt
	(resident in Moscow)
IRS:	Joe D. Hook
	(resident in Bonn)

Federal Republic of Germany

Bonn (E)
Deichmanns Aue 29
53170 Bonn
• Unit 21701, PSC 117
APO AE 09080
Tel: [49] (228) 3391
Fax: 339-2663
COM Fax: 334-649
ATO Tel: (40) 341-207
Fax: (40) 341-200

AMB:	Charles E. Redman
AMB SEC:	Victoria Jean DeLong
DCM:	J. D. Bindenagel
POL:	Robert D. Johnson
ECO:	Janice F. Bay
COM:	Robert A. Kohn
CON:	Michael W. Marine
ADM:	Donald S. Hays
RSO:	William D. Armor
RPSO:	Charles G. Krips
PAO:	Robert L. Earle
IMO:	Sandra Williams
ISM:	Susan Van Haften
FAA:	J. Stuart Jamison
	(resident in Brussels)

CUS:	Roger R. Urbanski
EST:	Richard R. Ries
ODA:	Col. Lawrence J. Kimmel, USA
ODC:	Col. Karl D. Horn, USA
AGR:	Gregg Young
LAB:	John J. Muth
FIN:	Carl J. Lohmann
IRS:	Joe D. Hook

Berlin (BO)
Neustaedtische Kirchstrasse 4-5
10117 Berlin
• PSC 120, Box 1000
APO AE 09265
Tel: [49] (30) 238-5174
Fax: 238-6290
COM Fax: 215-0246
CON address Clayallee 170
14169 Berlin
• PSC 120, Box 3000
APO AE 09265
Tel: 832-9233
CON Fax: 831-4926

PO:	James P. Covey
PO SEC:	Nancy J. Wilson
POL:	Kirk Augustine
ECO:	Lorraine Takahashi
COM:	James L. Joy
CON:	Edward Wehrli
ADM:	Michael Cutter
RSO:	John Beaudry
BPAO:	Joel L. Levy
IMO:	Fred Armand

Dusseldorf (CG)
Postal address: Kennedydamm 15–17
40476 Dusseldorf
Tel: (0211) 47061 203
Fax: 431-440
COM Tel: 46061 223
Fax: 431-431
POL/ECO Tel: 47061-206

CG:	Thomas L. Boam
COM:	Lee Boam
POL/ECO:	Kristina L. Scott

Frankfurt Am Main (CG)
Siesmayerstrasse 21
60323 Frankfurt
- PSC 115
APO AE 09213-0115
Tel: [49] (69) 7535-0
Fax: 748-938
COM Fax: 748-204

CG:	Janet S. Andres
CG SEC:	Diane Isaacson
DPO:	John A. Barcas
COM:	Donald Businger
CON:	Michael J. Hogan
ADM:	Mark J. Lijek
RSO:	Charles P. Bunn
BPAO:	Helena K. Finn
IMO:	Robert E. Coleman, Jr.
INS:	Jeffrey D. Trecartin
FAA/CASLO:	
	George Pfromm
USTTA:	Gert Lindenau
GAO:	Arthur R. Goldbeck
CDC:	William F. Simonsen

Hambrug (CG)
Alsterufer 27/28
20354 Hamburg
Tel: [49] (40) 41171-351
Afterhours Tel: 41171-211
FBU Fax: 443-004
ADM Fax: 417-665
COM Fax: 410-6598
USIS Tel: 450-104-0
Fax: 444-705

CG:	A. Daniel Weygandt
RSO:	John Beaudry
	(resident in Berlin)
POL/ECO:	George Frederick
COM:	Hans J. Amrhein
CON/ADM:	
	Cynthia Whittlesey
BPAO:	Lee James Irwin
ATO:	Andrew Burst

Leipzig (CG)
Wilhelm Seyfferth Strasse 4
04107 Leipzig
- PSC 120, Box 1000

APO AE 09235
Tel: [49] (341) 213-840
Fax: 213-8417
COM Tel: 213-8440
Fax: 213-8441
USIS Tel: 213-8420
Fax: 213-8432

CG:	Annette L. Veler
POL/ECO:	Brian J. Siler
COM:	James Joy
	(resident in Berlin)
ADM/CON:	
	Alessandra Vidotti
	(FSN)
BPAO:	Gregory L. Lynch
RSO:	John Beaudry
	(resident in Berlin)

Munich (CG)
Koeniginstrasse 5
80539 Muenchen
- Unit 24718
APO AE 09178
Tel: [49] (89) 28880
Fax: 283-047 or 280-2317
CON Fax: 280-5163
COM Fax: 285-261
JUS/CIV Fax: 282-230

CG:	Patrick J. Nichols
CG SEC:	Claire R. Sainz
POL/ECO:	Richard M. Dotson
COM:	Edward Ruse
CON:	Anthony Leggio
ADM:	Harold T. A. Burgess
GSO/PSO:	Louis J. Carlucci
IPPL:	Louis Escobedo, Jr.
RSO:	Charles P. Bunn
	(resident in Frankfurt)
BPAO:	William H. Graves
BOB/EUR:	Tadeusz Lipien
VOA/MRS:	William J. Connolly
JUS/CIV:	James A. Gresser
BIB:	Brian T. Conniff

Stuttgart (CG)
Urbanstrasse 7
70182 Stuttgart
- Unit 30607

APO AE 09154-0001
Tel: [49] (711) 2-10-08-0
Afterhours Tel: (69) 7535-3700
Fax: (711) 21008-20
Polad (USEUCOM, Patch Barracks, Stuttgart-Vaihingen)
Tel: (711) 680-4291
Fax: 680-8166
Polad (USAREUR, Campbell Barracks, Heidelberg)
Tel: [49] (6221) 57-6651
Fax: 57-8097

CG:	Michael A. Ceurvorst
POL/ECO:	Frank W. Ostrander
COM:	Camille E. Sailer
RSO:	Charles P. Bunn (resident in Frankfurt)
POLAD:	Jacques Paul Klein, USINCEUR (resident in Stuttgart-Vaihingen)
POLAD:	David A. Lange, CINCUSAREUR (resident in Heidelberg)

Ghana

Accra (E)
Ring Rd. E.
• P.O. Box 194
Tel: [233] (21) 775348
Tel Annex: 776601/2, 776944
Fax: 776008

AMB:	Kenneth L. Brown
AMB SEC:	M. Ruth Clifford
DCM:	James V. Ledesma
POL/LAB/MIL:	Peter Whaley
ECO/COM:	James F. Freund
CON:	Reginald J. McHugh
ADM:	Rosil A. Nesberg
GSO:	William P. O'Donnell
RSO:	Christian Schurman
ODA:	Col. Kenneth A. Hibl, USA (resident in Abidjan)
SAO:	Gale J. Ley
PAO:	Nicholas Robertson
IMO:	Eileen J. Nesberg
AID:	Barbara Sandoval
PC:	Harriett Lancaster
AGR:	Maurice W. House (resident in Lagos)
DEA:	Sam Gaye (resident in Lagos)
FAA:	Ronald L. Montgomery (resident in Dakar)
IRS:	Frederick D. Pablo (resident in Paris)

Greece

Athens (E)
91 Vasilissis Sophias Blvd.
10160 Athens
• PSC 108
APO AE 09842
Tel: [30] (1) 721-2951 or 721-8401
Fax: 645-6281
COM Fax: 721-8660
USIS Fax: 723-7332

AMB:	Thomas M. T. Niles
AMB SEC:	Dolores Montoya
DCM:	Thomas J. Miller
POL:	Robert W. Becker
ECO:	Basil G. Scarlis
COM:	John L. Priamou
CON:	Danny B. Root
ADM:	Michael McLaughlin
RSO:	Timothy Dixon
PAO:	Larry J. Ikels
IMO:	Raymond Norris
ISM:	Donald W. Newman
DEA:	George S. Carountzos
INS:	Anthony F. Lascaris
LEGATT:	Stephen Walker
ODA:	Capt. Will Gray, USN
ODC:	Col. Theodore R. Coberly, USA
AGR:	Paul Hoffman
FAA:	Steven B. Wallace (resident in Rome)
IRS:	Larry J. Legrand (resident in Rome)

Thessaloniki (CG)
59 Leoforos Nikis
GR-546-22 Thessaloniki
• PSC 108, Box 37
APO AE 09842
Tel: [30] (31) 242905
Fax: 242927, 242915
CG: Miriam Hughes
POL/ECO: David Shuler
BPAO: James Ellickson-Brown

Grenada

St. George's (E)
P.O. Box 54
St. George's, Grenada, W.I.
Tel: (809) 444-1173/8
Fax: 444-4820
AMB: Jeanette W. Hyde
 (resident in Bridgetown)
CHG: Dennis Carter
POL/ECO: Thomas R. Hutson
 (resident in Bridgetown)
CON: Dale E. Shaffer
 (resident in Bridgetown)
RSO: John M. Davis
 (resident in Bridgetown)
PAO: Tyrone W. Kemp
 (resident in Bridgetown)
ADM: James D. McGee
 (resident in Bridgetown)
AID: Mosina H. Jordan
 (resident in Bridgetown)
ODA: Ltc. Clark Lynn, USA
 (resident in Bridgetown)
MLO: Cdr. P. Tim Swanson, USN
 (resident in Bridgetown)
RMO: Dr. LaRae W. Kemp
 (resident in Bridgetown)
AGR: Larry Senger
 (resident in Caracas)
LAB: Peggy Zabriskie
 (resident in Bridgetown)
LEGATT: Paul F. Nolan
 (resident in Bridgetown)

FAA: Celio Young
 (resident in Miami)
IRS: Charles Shea
 (resident in Caracas)

Guatemala

Guatemala City (E)
7-01 Avenida de la Reforma
Zone 10
• APO AA 34024
Tel: [502] (2) 31-15-41
Fax: 31-88-85
AID Fax: 31-11-51
ROCAP Fax: 32-04-95
COM Fax: 31-73-73
AMB: Marilyn McAfee
AMB SEC: Carol A. Murphy
DCM: John F. Keane
POL: George A. Chester, Jr.
ECO: Geraldeen G. Chester
COM: Brian Brisson
CON: Charles F. Keil
ADM: Gary R. Alexander
RSO: Martin T. Donnelly
PAO: John D. Hamill
IMO: Michael J. Kovich
AID: William S. Rhodes
ROCAP: Irenemaree Castillo
ODA: Col. Dennis E. Keller, USA
MILGP: Col. Joe Haning, USA
AGR: Grant A. Pettrie
APHIS: Gordon Tween
NAS: David C. Becker
IAGS: Glenn T. Ramsey
PC: Peter A. Lara
FAA: Victor Tamariz
 (resident in Miami)
DEA: James R. White
LAB: John A. Cushing
IRS: Daniel R. Dietz
 (resident in Mexico City)

Guinea

Conakry (E)
Rue KA 038
B.P. 603
Tel: [224] 41-15-20 or 41-15-21
Fax: 41-15-22

AMB:	Joseph A. Saloom III
AMB SEC:	Theresa J. Everett
DCM:	John W. Limbert
POL:	Janice E. Mastorio-Worth
POL/MIL:	Bryan G. Lowe
POL/ECO:	Edward G. Stafford
ECO/CON:	Atul Keshap
RCON:	Thomas E. Cairns (resident in Dakar)
ADM:	Paul P. Pometto II
RSO:	John F. Rooney
GSO/CON:	James J. Hunter
PAO:	Gregory L. Garland
IPO:	Marvin L. Adams
ODA:	Ltc. Paul S. Cariker (resident in Dakar)
AID:	Wilbur G. Thomas
FAA:	Ronald L. Montgomery (resident in Dakar)
LAB:	Frederick B. Cook (resident in Washington, DC)
PC:	Jeffrey Page
RETO:	Timothy H. Robinson (resident in Dakar)
IRS:	Frederick D. Pablo (resident in Paris)

Guinea-Bissau

Bissau (E)
Bairro de Penha
Bissau, Guinea-Bissau
C.P. 297, 1067 Codex
Bissau, Guinea-Bissau
Tel: [245] 25-2273/6
Fax: 2282
Telex: 240 Publico Bi

USAID Tel: 1809, 20-1810
Fax: 20-1808
Peace Corps Tel: 25-2127
Fax: 25-2132
Medical Unit: 25-2133

AMB:	Roger A. McGuire
AMB SEC:	Diann M. Bimmerle
ADM:	Walter J. Hood
GSO:	Raymond Maxwell
POL/ECO/CON:	Apar S. Sidhu
RSO:	Gary M. Gibson (resident in Dakar)
IMO:	Terrence K. Williamson (resident in Dakar)
RMO:	Dr. Michael Nesemann (resident in Dakar)
IMS:	Noe Carbajal
ODA:	Ltc. Paul S. Cariker, USMC (resident in Dakar)
AID:	Michael Lukomski
PC:	Carol Herrera
FAA:	Ronald L. Montgomery (resident in Dakar)
LAB:	Frederick B. Cook (resident in Washington, DC)
RCON:	Thomas E. Cairns (resident in Dakar)
IRS:	Frederick Pablo (resident in Paris)

Guyana

Georgetown (E)
99-100 Young and Duke Sts.
Kingston, Georgetown, Guyana
• P.O. Box 10507
Tel: [592] (2) 54900-9 and 57960-9
Fax: 58497
USAID Fax: 57969
USIS Fax: 63636

AMB:	George F. Jones
AMB SEC:	Mary La Fleur

An Entrepreneur's Directory to Foreign Service Officers **293**

DCM: J. Christian Kennedy
POL: Edgar L. Embrey
ECO/COM: Chever X. Voltmer
CON: Rudolph F. Boone
ADM: Johney Brooks
RSO: Michael J. Eicher
PAO: Colleen A. Hoey
CPO: John M. Benton
USAID (DIR):
 Mosina Jordan
AID: Patrick M. McDuffie
ODA: Col. Michael J. Kenna, USAF
 (resident in Caracas)
AGR: Larry Senger
 (resident in Caracas)
LEGATT: Ralph Torres
 (resident in Caracas)
FAA: Celio Young
 (resident in Miami)
LAB: Peggy Zabriskie
 (resident in Bridgetown)
IRS: Charles Shea
 (resident in Caracas)

Haiti

Port-au-Prince (E)
 Harry Truman Blvd.
 • P.O. Box 1761
 Tel: [509] 22-0354, 22-0368, 22-0200, 22-0612
 Fax: 231641

AMB: William Lacy Swing
DCM: Vicki J. Huddleston
POL: Gene Christy
ECO/COM: John S. Creamer
CON: Charles R. Stephan III
ADM: James Griffin
RSO: David A. Akerman
PAO: Stanley Schrager
IMO: W. A. Peter Bolton
ISM: Roger Snider
AID: David Cohen
ODA: Ltc. Steven A. Lovasz, USA

MLO: Maj. Roland Lane
AGR: Susan Schayes
 (resident in Santo Domingo)
APHIS: (Vacant)
DEA: William Payne
FAA: Celio Young
 (resident in Miami)
IRS: Louis Hobbie
 (resident in Nassau)
INS: Olen Martin

The Holy See

Vatican City (E)
 Villa Domiziana
 Via Delle Terme Deciane 26
 00153 Rome, Italy
 • PSC 59
 APO AE 09624
 Tel: [396] 46741
 Fax: 575-8346 or 5730-0682

AMB: Raymond L. Flynn
AMB SEC: Sheila Dumas
DCM: Louis J. Nigro
POL: Damian R. Leader
ADM: Thomas D. Smitham
RSO: Stephen H. Jacobs
 (resident in Rome)
FAA: Steven B. Wallace
 (resident in Rome)

Honduras

Tegucigalpa (E)
 Avenida La Paz
 Apartado Postal No. 3453
 • APO AA 34022
 Tel: [504] 36-9320 or 38-5114
 Fax: 36-9037
 COM Fax: 38-2888
 USIS Fax: 36-9309
 USAID Fax: 36-7776

AMB: William T. Pryce
AMB SEC: Guadalupe Yameogo

DCM:	James C. Cason	ECO/POL:	Douglas G. Spelman
POL:	Thomas Ochiltree	COM:	David Katz
ECO:	Hugo L. Llorens	CON:	Wayne S. Leininger
COM:	Michael McGee	ADM:	Robert A. MacCallum
CON:	Fernando Sanchez	GSO:	Mark H. Jackson
ADM:	Peter Wood	RSO:	Paul T. Peterson
RSO:	Dale Karlen	PAO:	Patrick J. Corcoran
PAO:	Mark Krischik	IMO:	Timothy C. Lawson
IMO:	Harvey Eidenberg	ISM:	(Vacant)
ISO:	Larry Lopez	ODA:	Capt. James R. Glover, USN
AID:	Marshall Brown		
ODA:	Col. William Brown, USAF	ATO:	Laverne E. Brabant
		INS:	Richard B. Cravener
MILGP:	Col. Glenn Weidner, USA	CUS:	Patrick H. Sheridan
		DEA:	Richard C. Lamagna
DEA:	Max Pooley	FAA:	Frederick Lee (resident in Beijing)
AGR:	Grant A. Pettrie (resident in Guatemala City)		
		IRS:	Dennis Tsujimoto (resident in Tokyo)
INS:	Jerry Stuchiner		
APHIS:	James E. Novy		
FAA:	Victor Tamariz (resident in Miami)		
PC:	Donna Frago		
LAB:	Melvin R. Turner		
IRS:	Daniel R. Dietz (resident in Mexico City)		

Hong Kong

Hong Kong (CG)
26 Garden Rd.
• PSC 464, Box 30
FPO AP 96522-0002
Tel: [852] 2523-9011
CON Fax: 2845-4845
ADM Fax: 2845-1598
COM Fax: 2845-9800
ATO Address: 18th Fl.
St. John's Building, 33 Garden Rd.
Tel: 2841-2350
Fax: 2845-0943

CG:	Richard W. Mueller
CG SEC:	Jacqueline F. Carter
DPO:	Stephen Schlaikjer

Hungary

Budapest (E)
V. Szabadsag Ter 12
• Unit 1320
APO AE 09213-1320
Tel: [36] (1) 267-4400
Fax: 132-8934
Telex: 18048 224-222
Afterhours Tel: 111-2062
Fax: 132-8934
Commercial Devel Ctr Telex: 227136
USCDC H
USIS Tel: 142-4122, 142-3717, or 142-3156
Fax: 153-4274
COM Tel: 122-8600 or 122-1217
Fax: 142-2529
CON Fax: 153-0774

AMB:	Donald M. Blinken
AMB SEC:	Terri Lee Tedford
DCM:	James I. Gadsden
POL:	William H. Siefkin
ECO:	John L. Moran
COM:	John J. Fogarosi
CON:	Teddy B. Taylor

An Entrepreneur's Directory to Foreign Service Officers 295

PAO: Donna Culpepper
ADM: Mark S. Woerner
RSO: Patricia Hartnett-Kelly
ODA: Col. Arpad Szurgyi, USA
EST: Richard S. Taylor
IMO: David Patterson (Acting)
AID: Thomas Cornell
AGR: Francis J. Tarrant (resident in Vienna)
FAA: Steven B. Wallace (resident in Rome)
IRS: Larry J. Legrand (resident in Rome)

Iceland

Reykjavik (E)
Laufasvegur 21
• PSC 1003, Box 40
FPO AE 09728-0340
Tel: (354) 5629100
Fax: 5629139
USIS Tel: 5621020 and 5621022
Fax: 5529529

AMB: Parker W. Borg
AMB SEC: Prudence L. Hudson
DCM: Mark Tokola
POL: Michael Hammer
ECO/COM: David G. Wagner
CON: Craig M. White
ADM: David M. Robinson
RSO: John W. Schilling (resident in Copenhagen)
PAO: Richard C. Lundberg
IMO: Leonard M. Kraske, Jr.
FAA: Carl Burleson (resident in London)
IRS: Stanley Beesley (resident in London)

India

New Delhi (E)
Shanti Path
Chanakyapuri 110021
Tel: [91] (11) 600651
Telex: 031-82065 USEM IN
Fax: 687-2028
COM Fax: 687-2391
USIS Tel: 331-6841 or 4251
USIS Fax: 332-9499
USAID Tel: 686-5301
Fax: 686-8594

AMB: Frank G. Wisner
AMB SEC: Penelope R. O'Brien
DCM: Matthew P. Daley
POL: (Vacant)
ECO: Douglas A. Hartwick
COM: Jonathan M. Bensky
CON: Edwin P. Cubbison
ADM: William C. Kelly, Jr.
RSO: Robert R. Brand, Jr.
PAO: Thomas A. Homan
DEA: Michael Fredericks
IMO: Lyle H. Rosdahl
ISM: Alan L. Roecks
AID: Walter G. Bollinger
ODA: Col. Russell V. Olson, Jr.
EST: Dr. Paul C. Maxwell
AGR: Thomas Pomeroy
LAB: Eugene D. Price, Jr.
INS: William Bryan
DSA: Col. Walter T. Eastham, USAF
FAA: David L. Knudson (resident in Singapore)
IRS: Charles W. Landry (resident in Singapore)

Bombay (CG)
Lincoln House
78 Bhulabhai Desai Rd. 400026
Tel: [91] (22) 363-3611
Telex: 011-75425 ACON IN
Fax: 363-0350
COM Fax: 262-3850

CG: Louis B. Warren, Jr.
POL: Marilynn Gurian
ECO: Eden Brown
COM: John S. Wood
CON: Clyde Bishop
ADM: Burt F. English

BPAO: Joseph J. Brennig
DEA: Anthony Williams
ITO: Rodney C. Deaton

Calcutta (CG)
5/1 Ho Chi Minh Sarani
Calcutta 700071
Tel: [91] (33) 242-3611 through
242-3615, 242-2336 through 242-2337
Telex: 021-5982 ACON IN
CONGEN Fax: 242-2335
USIS Fax: 245-1616

CG: Robert K. Boggs, Jr.
COM: (Vacant)
CON: Helen M. Collings
ADM: Judith Grace
BPAO: Dino J. Caterini

Madras (CG)
220 Mount Rd., 600006
Tel: [91] (44) 827-3040/827-7542
Fax: 825-0240
USIS Fax: 826-3407
COM Bangalore: W-202, II Fl.
West Wing "Sunrise Chambers,"
22 Ulsoor Rd.
Bangalore 560042
Tel: (80) 558-1452
Fax: 558-3630

CG: Timothy P. Hauser
POL/ECO: James L. Huskey
COM: Michael Keaveny
CON: Laura L. Livingston
ADM: Lee M. Carter
BPAO: Miriam E. Guichard
IPO: Walter L. Myers

Indonesia

Jakarta (E)
Medan Merdeka Selatan 5
• Box 1
APO AP 96520
Tel: [62] (21) 360-360
Fax: 386-2259
Telex: 44218 AMEMB JKT
USIS Fax: 381-0243

COM Fax: 385-1632
AID Fax: 380-6694
FAS Fax: 380-1363
OMADP Fax: 372-518

AMB: Robert L. Barry
AMB SEC: (Vacant)
DCM: Barbara S. Harvey
POL: Barbara J. Schrage
ECO: Robert W. Fitts
COM: Michael Hand
CON: William H. Barkell
ADM: Maurice N. Gralnek
RSO: Bruce W. Tully
PAO: Wesley D. Stewart
IMO: Barbara J. Sullivan
AID: Charles F. Weden
AGR: Michael L. Humphrey
LAB: Thomas F. Murphy
GSO: Harlow J. Carpenter, Jr.
ODA: Col. Charles
 McFetridge, USA
OMADP: Col. Karl F. Eickemeyer,
 USA
FAA: David I. Knudson
 (resident in Singapore)
FAA/CAAG:
 Robert Salas
CUS: Donald K. Shruhan, Jr.
 (resident in Singapore)
EST: Sidney G. Smith
IRS: Charles W. Landry
 (resident in Singapore)

Medan (CG)
Jalan Imam Bonjol 13
• APO AP 96520
Tel: [62] (61) 552-200
Fax: 518-711
USIS Tel: 515-130
COM Tel: 519-590
Fax: 544-415

CG: Pamela Slutz
ECO: Leo Gallagher
ADM/CON:
 Kees C. Davison
BPAO: Martin Adler

Surabaya (CG)
Jalan Raya Dr. Sutomo 33
• Box 1, Unit 8131
APO AP 96520-0002
Tel: [62] (31) 582287 and 582288
Telex: 34331 AMCOSBIA
Fax: 574492
COM *Fax:* 577492

CG:	Mark C. Eaton
POL/ECO:	Brian D. McFeeters
ADM/CON:	Edward J. Fendley
BPAO:	Martha E. Estell

Iraq
Baghdad (E)
Opp. For. Ministry Club (Masbah Quarter)
• P.O. Box 2447
Alwiyah, Baghdad, Iraq
Tel: [964] (1) 719-6138/9, 7181840, 719-3791
Telex: 212287 USINT IK, 213966 USFCS IK
COM *Fax:* [964] (1) 718-9297

Operations have been suspended temporarily.

Ireland
Dublin (E)
42 Elgin Rd.
Ballsbridge
Tel: [353] (1) 6687122
Afterhours Tel: 6689612
Fax: 6689946
COM *Fax:* 682-840

AMB:	Jean Kennedy Smith
AMB SEC:	Edith D. Ferrante
DCM:	Dennis A. Sandberg
POL:	Richard B. Norland
ECO:	Madelyn E. Spirnak
COM:	Edward W. Cannon
CON:	Ann B. Sides
ADM:	Peter A. Prahar
RSO:	John M. Hampson
PAO:	Lynn L. Cassel
CPO:	Joseph P. Talbot
ODA:	Col. William T. Torpey
AGR:	Richard L. Barnes (resident in London)
INS:	Denis C. Riordan (resident in Shannon, Co. Clare)
CUS:	(Vacant) (resident in London)
FAA:	Carl Burleson (resident in London)
IRS:	Stanley Beesley (resident in London)

Israel*
*The Consulate General in Jerusalem is an independent US Mission, established in 1928, whose members are not accredited to a foreign government.

Tel Aviv (E)
71 Hayarkon St.
Tel Aviv
• PSC 98, Box 100
APO AE 09830
Tel: [972] (3) 517-4338
Afterhours Tel: 517-4347
Fax: 517-3227
ADM/GSO *Fax:* 510-2444
CON *Fax:* 516-0744
USIS *Fax:* 510-3830
COM *Tel:* 517-6161
Fax: 510-7215
AGR *Fax:* 510-2565

AMB:	Martin S. Indyk
DCM:	James A. Larocco
POL:	Bruce G. Burton
ECO:	(Vacant)
PAO:	David P. Good
COM:	Barry Friedman
CON:	Robert E. Tynes
ADM:	J. Robert Manzanares

RSO: William Gaskill
IMO: M. Audrey Anderson
ISO: Michael K. Haftel
ODA: Col. John V. Siebert, USAF
LAB: John Martin Hall
SCI: David W. Mulenex
AGR: Paul Hoffman
        (resident in Athens)
AID: Christopher D. Crowley
FAA: Steven B. Wallace
        (resident in Rome)
IRS: Larry J. Legrand
        (resident in Rome)
LEGATT: Stephen Walker
        (resident in Athens)

Jerusalem (CG)
18 Agron Rd.
Jerusalem 94190
• P.O. Box 290
PSC 98, Box 100
APO AE 09830
Tel: [972] (2) 253288 (via Israel)
Afterhours Tel: 253201
Fax: 259270
CON and USIS 27 Nablus Rd.
• P.O. Box 290
PSC 98, Box 100
APO AE 09830
CON Tel: 894748/894113
Afterhours Tel: 253201
Fax: 894198 (both offices via Israel)
USIS Tel: 895117
Fax: 894711
USAID Fax: 259484

CG: Edward G. Abington, Jr.
CG SEC: Pearlie A. White
POL: Maura Connelly
DPO: John H. Bargeron
ECO/COM: Paul Sutphin
CON: Kathleen A. Riley
ADM: Marcia L. Nye
RSO: Neil J. MacNeil
PAO: Karen L. Perez
CPO: Thomas H. Lien

FCS: Barry Friedman
        (resident in Tel Aviv)
AID: Christopher D. Crowley
        (resident in Tel Aviv)
IRS: Larry J. Legrand
        (resident in Rome)
LEGATT: Stephen Walker
        (resident in Athens)

Italy

Rome (E)
Via Veneto 119/A
00187-Rome
• PSC 59, Box 100
APO AE 09624
Tel: [39] (6) 46741
Telex: 622322 AMBRMA
USIS via Boncompagni 2
00187 Rome
Fax: 488-2672
COM Fax: 4674-2113
USIS Fax: 4674-2655

AMB: Reginald Bartholomew
AMB SEC: Karen Heitkotter
DCM: James F. Creagan
POL: Harry L. Coburn
POL/MIL: Angel M. Rabasa
ECO: Robert J. Smolik
COM: Keith R. Bovetti
CON: Michael M. Mahoney
ADM C: Anne M. Hackett
ADM O: Theodore E. Strickler
RSO: Stephen H. Jacobs
PAO: Cynthia J. Miller
IMO: Marvin A. Konopik
ISM: Valorie Strickler
EST: Gregory Dunn
ODA: Capt. Philip A. Bozzelli, USN
ODC: Col. Claude V. Christianson, USA
AGR: Frank A. Padovano
APHIS: Joseph F. Karpati
LAB: Charles R. Hare
CUS: Riccardo J. Olivieri

An Entrepreneur's Directory to Foreign Service Officers **299**

FAA: Steven B. Wallace
FAA/CASLO:
  Joseph Teixeira
FIN: Gay Sills Hoar
IRS: Larry J. Legrand
INS: Benedict J. Ferro

US Mission to the United Nations Agencies for Food and Agriculture (FODAG)
Via Sardegna 49
00187 Rome
• APO AE 0962
Tel: [39] (6) 4674-3500
Fax: 4788-7043

US REP: Thomas A. Forbord
DEP REP: John Egan McAteer
RELIEF AID:
  David J. Garms
DEV AID: Hugh I. Smith
AGR: Francis J. Vacca

Milan (CG), COM
Via Principe Amedeo
2 20121 Milan
Tel: 659-2260
Fax: 659-6561
USTTA: 659-5559
Fax: 659-5098

CG: Richard J. Shinnick
DPO/POL: Philo L. Dibble
POL: Thomas L. Delare
COM: Peter Alois
CON: Alma F. Engel
ADM: Michael L. Milligan
GSO: Megan Gaal
RSO: Christopher A. Baker
IPO: Harry M. Rivers
AGR: Holly S. Higgins
USTTA: Carol S. Ross
CUS: Albert Moy
DEA: Samuel C. Meale

US Information Service
Via Bigli 11/A
20121 Milano
Tel: [39] (2) 795051 2345
USIS Fax: 781-736

BPAO: Jeffrey C. Murray

Naples (CG)
Piazza della Republica 80122 Naples
• Box 18, PSC 810
FPO AE 09619-0002
Tel: [39] (81) 583-8111
Fax: 761-1869
USIS Fax: 664-207
COM Tel: 761-1592
Fax: 761-1869

CG: Clark N. Ellis
CG SEC: Ellen R. Ockey
POL/ECO: Cynthia R. Bunton
CON: Anthony C. Perkins
ADM: John D. Haynes
RSO: Stephen H. Jacobs
  (resident in Rome)
BPAO: Daniel A. Spikes
POLAD: James L. Clunan
  (resident in London)

Florence (CG)
Lungarno Amerigo Vespucci
38, 50123 Firenze
• APO AE 09613
Tel: [39] (55) 239-8276/7/8/9, 217-605
Fax: 284-088
COM Tel: 211-676
Fax: 283-780
USIS Tel: 216-531, 294-921
Fax: 288-338

CG: Sue H. Patterson
CON: Nereida M. Vazquez
RSO: Christopher A. Baker
  (resident in Milan)
BPAO: Carlos S. Bakota

US Commercial Office (Genoa)
Via Dante 2/43 (Palazzo Borsa)
16121 Genoa
Tel and Fax: [39] (10) 543-877

Ivory Coast—See Cote d'Ivoire

Jamaica

Kingston (E)
Jamaica Mutual Life Center
2 Oxford Rd., 3rd Fl.

Tel: (809) 929-4850 through 9
Fax: 926-6743
USIS Fax: 929-4850, ext. 1042

AMB:	J. Gary Cooper
AMB SEC:	Vianna Fieser
DCM:	John W. Vessey, III
ECO/POL:	George T. Boutin
COM:	Robert J. Bucalo (resident in Santo Domingo)
CON:	Dean L. Welty
ADM:	James B. Lane
RSO:	Douglas K. Roberts
PAO:	J. Michael Houhalan
IMO:	Rodney G. Painter
AID:	Dr. Carole H. Tyson
ODA:	Ltc. Norman Wiggins, USMC
MLO:	Ltc. Terry Derouchey, USA
AGR:	Susan Schayes (resident in Santo Domingo)
APHIS:	Lawrence H. Tengan
NAS:	Roy Sullivan
PC:	Janet P. Simoni
FAA:	Celio Young (resident in Miami)
LAB:	Janet Potash
IRS:	Louis Hobbie (resident in Nassau)
CPO:	Fredrick J. Vinson
ISM:	Anita D. Banks

Japan

Tokyo (E)
10-5, Akasaka 1-chome
Minato-ku (107)
• Unit 45004, Box 258
APO AP 96337-0001
Tel: [81] (3) 3224-5000
Fax: 3505-1862
CPU: 3224-5700
CPO: 3224-5691
COM Fax: 3589-4235

ATO Address: Tameike Tokyu Building
1-14 Akasaka 1-chome
Minato-ku, Tokyo 107
Tel: 3224-5115
Telex: J29180 ATO Tokyo
Fax: 3582-6429
USAID Tel: 3224-5015
Fax: 3224-5010

AMB:	Walter F. Mondale
DCM:	Rust M. Deming
POL:	Neil E. Silver
ECO:	John H. Penfold
COM:	George Mu
CON:	Wayne Griffith
ADM:	Lawrence R. Baer
RSO:	Nickolas W. Proctor
PAO:	Paul P. Blackburn
IMO:	James Vanderhoff
EST:	Gerald J. Whitman
ODA:	Capt. George R. McWilliams
MDO:	Col. Thomas L. Brown
AGR:	W. John Child
APHIS:	Ralph Iwamoto
ATO:	David Salmon
LAB:	James P. Dodd
IRS:	Dennis Tsujimoto
CUS:	John F. Markey
DOE:	Milton A. Eaton
USTTA:	Sandra T. Gamo
FAA:	Fred Laird
FIN:	Matthew P. Goodman
LEGATT:	Harry J. Godfrey III
AID/Tokyo:	Paul E. White

US Trade Center
7th Fl., World Import Mart
1-3 Higashi Ikebukuro 3-chome
Toshima-ku, Tokyo 170
Tel: [81] (3) 3987-2441
Fax: 3987-2447
COM Fax: 3987-2447

Naha, Okinawa (CG)
2564 Nishihara
Urasoe Cit Okinawa 90121
• PSC 556, Box 840, Unit 45

FPO AP 96386-0840
Tel: [81] (98) 876-4211
Fax: 876-4243

CG: Aloysius M. O'Neill III
POL/MIL: John Maher
ADM/CON:
  Janice L. Trickel

Osaka-Kobe (CG)
11-5, Nishitenma 2-chome
Kita Osaka 530
• Unit 45004, Box 239
APO AP 96337-0002
Tel: [81] (6) 315-5900
Telex: 5233037 AMCON
Fax: 361-5397
COM Fax: 361-5978
CON Fax: 315-5
ATO Address: Shima Office
Building, 3F
1-18, Kitaham chome
Chuo-Ku, Osaka 541
Tel: 208-0303
Telex: 523-3037
Fax: 208-0306

CG: David A. Pabst
CON: Charles E. Robertson
POL/ECO: Joyce S. Wong
COM: Todd Thurwachter
ADM: R. Douglas Brown
BPAO (Osaka):
  Warren Soiffer
BPAO (Kyoto):
  Dale Largent
ATO: Daniel K. Berman
IPO: George A. Hamic

Sapporo (CG)
Kita 1-Jo Nishi 28-chome
Chuo-ku, Sapporo 064
• Unit 45004, Box 276
APO AP 96337-0003
Tel: [81] (11) 641-1115/7
Fax: 643-1283
COM Fax: 643-0911

CG: Richard H. Gibson
CON: Daniel J. Kritenbrink
BPAO: Mark J. Davidson

Fukuoka (C)
5-26 Ohori 2-chome
Chuo-ku, Fukuoka 810
• Unit 45004, Box 242
APO AP 96337-0001
Tel: [81] (92) 751-9331/4
Telex: 725679
Fax: 713-9222
COM Fax: 713-922

PO: Jason P. Hyland
ECO: John Dyson
CON: Julie M. Gardner
BPAO: Judith L. Bryan

Nagoya (C)
Nishiki SIS Building, 6
10-33 Nishiki 3-chome Naka-ku
Nagoya 460
• c/o AMEMB Tokyo
Unit 45004, Box 280
APO AP 96337-0001
Tel: [81] (52) 203-4011
COM Tel: (direct) 203-4277
Fax: 201-4612

PO: Frank W. Stanley
COM: Henry Richard

Note: The Commerce Department/Foreign Commercial Service operates separate American Business Centers in these locations.

Jordan

Amman (E)
P.O. Box 354
Amman 11118 Jordan or
APO AE 09892-0200
Tel: [962] (6) 820-101
Direct line to Post 1: [962] (6) 820-148
USAID Office Tel: 820-101
EXEC/POL Fax: 820-159
ECO Fax: 820-146
COM Fax: 820-146
AID Fax: 820-143
USIS Fax: 820-121
MAP Fax: 820-160

AMB:	Wesley W. Egan, Jr.
AMB SEC:	June Ward
DCM:	Robert Beecroft
POL:	W. William Jordan
ECO/COM:	Douglas B. Neumann
CON:	Raymond E. Clore
ADM:	Joseph Huggins
RSO:	Steven Gleason
PAO:	Peter J. Kovach
CPO:	Robert Burkhart
ISM:	Sally Caldwell
AID:	William T. Oliver
ODA:	Col. Thomas F. Young, USA
AGR:	Forrest Geerken, Jr. (resident in Cairo)
IRS:	David Robison (resident in Riyadh)
FAA:	Dennis Beres (resident in Riyadh)

Kazakhstan

Almaty (E)
99/97 Furmanova St.
Almaty, Republic of Kazakhstan
480012
Tel: [7] (3272) 63-24-26, 63-13-75, 63-24-26
CPU and Afterhours Tel: [7] (3272) 63-39-05, ext. 116
INMARSAT: 02-00-873-151-2725
Fax: [7] (3272) 63-38-83
ADM Fax: 63-29-42

AMB:	William H. Courtney
DCM:	Jane B. Fort
POL/ECO:	Janet L. Bogue
ADM:	Jeffrey Vandreal
CON:	Lauren Catipon
GSO:	Russell A. Baum, Jr.
COM:	Susan Weidner
IPO:	Ritchie Miller
PAO:	Richard Lankford
AID:	Craig Buck
PC:	Mark Holt
RSO:	Robert W. Hanni
DATT:	Ltc. Daniel L. Perry

FAA:	Dennis B. Cooper (resident in Moscow)
AGR:	Mary Revelt (resident in Moscow)
IRS:	Joe D. Hook (resident in Bonn)
RMO:	Nancy Manahan

Kenya

Nairobi (E)
Moi/Haile Selassie Ave.
• P.O. Box 30137, Unit 64100
APO AE 09831
Tel: [254] (2) 334141
CPU STU-III 334122
Telex: 22964
Fax: 340838
COM Fax: [254] (2) 216-648

AMB:	Aurelia E. Brazeal
AMB SEC:	Christine E. Everhart
DCM:	Timberlake Foster
POL:	Marilyn F. Jackson
ECO:	Constance J. Freeman
COM:	Gene Harris
CON:	Marsha von Duerckheim
ADM:	Elaine B. Schunter
RSO:	Seymour C. Dewitt
PAO:	Marilyn E. Hulbert
IMO:	Russell M. Ikegami
ISO:	Brad Summers
AID:	George Jones
AID/REDSO:	Fred C. Fischer
AGR:	Henry Schmick
APHIS:	James P. Cavanaugh
FAA:	Ronald L. Montgomery (resident in Dakar)
LAB:	Lois A. Aroian
UNEP:	Richard Hoover
INS:	Donald J. Monica
MLO:	Col. David Swartzlander, USA
IRS:	David Robison (resident in Riyadh)
RETO:	Timothy H. Robinson (resident in Dakar)

Korea

Seoul (E)
82 Sejong-Ro
Chongro-ku
• Unit 15550
APO AP 96205-0001
Tel: [82] (2) 397-4114
Fax: 738-8845
USATO Address: Room 303
Leema Building 146-1
Susong-dong, Chongro-U
Tel: 397-4188
Fax: 720-792

AMB:	James T. Laney
AMB SEC:	Carol J. Mills
DCM:	Charles Kartman
POL:	Mark C. Minton
ECO:	Barbara Griffiths
COM:	Robert S. Connan
CON:	Kathryn Dee Robinson
ADM:	M. Bart Flaherty
RSO:	Benjamin C. Runner, Jr.
PAO:	William H. Maurer, Jr.
IMO:	James C. Norton
ISM:	Paul A. Converti
SCI:	Frederick Kenneth Crosher
CUS:	Reginald I. Duncan
EST:	F. Kenneth Crosher
ODA:	Col. William R. McKinney, USA
MAAG:	Col. Keith Young, USA
AGR:	John W. Child
APHIS:	Ray I. Miyamoto
ATO:	Charles T. Alexander
DEA:	Dannie West
FAA:	Frederick Lee (resident in Beijing)
INS:	Robert L. Butler
IRS:	Dennis Tsujimoto (resident in Tokyo)

**US Export Development Office/
US Commercial Center**
c/o US Embassy
Tel: [82] (2) 397-4212
Fax: 739-1628

DIR:	Robert M. Murphy

Pusan (C)
24, 2-Ka, Daechung-Dong, Chung-ku
Tel: [82] (51) 246-7791
Fax: 246-8859

PO:	Holcombe H. Thomas
BPAO:	William E. Richey

Kuwait

Kuwait (E)
P.O. Box 77
SAFAT, 13001 SAFAT, Kuwait
• Unit 6900
APO AE 09880-9000
Tel: [965] 242-4151 through 9
Fax: 244-2855
GSO Fax: 245-2490
FCS Fax: 244-7692
USIS Fax: 243-9706
OMC-K Fax: 242-4192
workweek: Saturday through Wednesday

AMB:	Ryan C. Crocker
AMB SEC:	Betty L. McNaughton
DCM:	Georgia J. Debell
POL:	Margaret Scobey
POL/MIL:	Peter C. McDevitt
ECO:	Paul H. Tyson
COM:	Johnny E. Brown
CON:	Kevin L. Richardson
ADM:	Lyle A. Dittmer
RSO:	Louis M. Possanza
PAO:	Mildred C. McCoo
IRS:	David Robison (resident in Riyadh)
VOA:	Terrance Donovan
FAA:	Dennis Beres (resident in Riyadh)

Kyrgyzstan

Bishkek (E)
Erkindik Prospect #66, 720002
Tel: [7] (3312) 22-29-20, 22-27-77, 22-26-31, 22-24-73
Afterhours Tel: 22-32-89

GSO Fax: 22-35-51
CON Fax: 22-32-10
Telex: 245133 AMEMB SU
AMB: Eileen A. Malloy
DCM: Douglas Kent
POL/NARC:
 Gene Coyle
POL/ECO: Neciz Quast
CON: Shawn Dorman
ADM: Ann Wright
GSO: Mark Cameron
RSO: Bob Hanni
 (resident in Almaty)
PAO: Bruce McGowan
IPO: Aurelius J. Manupella
FAA: Dennis B. Cooper
 (resident in Moscow)
AGR: Larry Panasuk
 (resident in Ankara)
IRS: Joe D. Hook
 (resident in Bonn)
RMO: Nancy Manahan
 (resident in Almaty)
USAID: C. G. Rushin-Bell

Laos

Vientiane (E)
Rue Bartholonie, B.P. 114
• Box V
APO AP 96546
Tel: [856] (21) 212581, 212582, 212585
Fax: 212584
Afterhours Tel: 212581
AMB: Victor L. Tomseth
AMB SEC: Linda A. Hayes
DCM: Alan W. Barr
POL/ECO: John L. Junk
CON/COM: Charles J. Jess
ADM: Terrence J. Daru
GSO: Dan B. Christenson
PAO: Kathleen L. Boyle
RSO: Gerard Lopez
 (resident in Bangkok)
FAA: David L. Knudson
 (resident in Singapore)

IPO: Roger M. Grovdahl
DEA: Edward J. Schlachter
 (resident in Udorn)
NAS: Albert L. Bryant

Latvia

Riga (E)
Raina Blvd. 7
LV-1510, Riga, Latvia
• PSC 78, Box R
APO AE 09723
Tel: [371] (2) 210-005
IDD: 782-0046
Afterhours Tel: 220-367
Fax: 226-530
IDD Fax: 782-0047
USIS Tel: 216-571
Fax: 216-478
IDD Tel: 782-0277
Fax: 782-0077
USAID Tel: 321-941
IDD Tel: 783-0068
Fax: 783-0067
MLT Tel: 335-137
IDD Fax: 783-0222
PC Tel: 212-187
IDD Fax: 782-0128
AMB: Larry C. Napper
AMB SEC: Marcia W. Vajay
POL: Douglas B. Wake
ECO/COM: Constance A. Phlipot
CON: Ellen M. Conway
IPO: Kenneth Knudsen
ADM: Susan Lee Pazina
GSO: Gyorgy Vajay
AID: Baudouin DeMarcken
PAO: Phillip R. Ives
RSO: Jeremy Zeikel
 (resident in Helsinki)
AGR: Thomas A. Hamby
 (resident in Stockholm)
FAA: J. Stuart Jamison
 (resident in Brussels)
ODA: Col. Scott B.
 Sonnenberg, USAF
 (resident in Stockholm)

An Entrepreneur's Directory to Foreign Service Officers

PC: Edward Block
EST: Stephanie Smith Kinney (resident in Copenhagen)
FAA: J. Stuart Jamison (resident in Brussels)
MLT: Col. Wayne Koppa
IRS: Joe D. Hook (resident in Bonn)

Lebanon

Beirut (E)
Antelias
• P.O. Box 70-840 or PSC 815, Box 2
FPO AE 09836-0002
Tel: [961] (1) 402-200, 403-300, 406-650, 406-651, 426-183, 417-774
Fax: 407-112
ADM Fax: 403-313
ODA Fax: 416-215

AMB: (Vacant)
AMB SEC: (Vacant)
CHG: Ronald L. Schlicher
POL/ECO: Melvin T. Ang
CON/COM: George W. Brazier III
ADM: James J. Kessinger, Jr.
RSO: David Haas
PAO: (Vacant) (contact CHG)
IPO: Hector F. Torres
AID: (Vacant) (contact CHG)
ODA/OMC: Ltc. Timothy B. Grimmett, USA
AGR: Forrest K. Geerken, Jr. (resident in Cairo)
LEGATT: Stephen P. Walker (resident in Athens)
FAA: Dennis Beres (resident in Riyadh)
IRS: David Robison (resident in Riyadh)

Lesotho

Maseru (E)
P.O. Box 333
Maseru 100 Lesotho
Tel: [266] 312-666
Fax: 310-116
USAID Tel: 313-954
USAID Telex: 4506 LO
USIA Tel: 312-335
Fax: 310-441

AMB: Bismarck Myrick
AMB SEC: Beverly J. Krause
DCM: Jeffrey Miotke
ADM/CON: Cassie Ghee
RSO: Thomas J. Colin (resident in Gaborone)
PAO: Denise N. Burgess
CPO: Ray Shankweiler
ODA: Col. Kim J. Henningsen, USA (resident in Pretoria)
SAO: Ltc. James Smaugh, USA
PC: Harvey Ramseur
AID: Gary Lewis
FAA: Ronald L. Montgomery (resident in Dakar)
AGR: James M. Benson (resident in Pretoria)
LAB: Thomas A. Shannon, Jr. (resident in Johannesburg)
IRS: Stanley Beesley (resident in London)

Liberia

Monrovia (E)
111 United Nations Dr.
• P.O. Box 10-0098
Mamba Point
Tel: [231] 226-370
Fax: 226-148

CHG: John W. Fuhrer
AMB SEC: (Vacant)
DCM: (Vacant)

POL/ECO/COM:
　　　　　　Curtis M. Stewart
CON:　　　Roger Daley
ADM:　　　Edward L. Howell
RSO:　　　John H. Frese
PAO:　　　J. Riley Sever
AID:　　　Lowell E. Lynch
POL/MIL/LAB:
　　　　　　Kathleen L. List
IMO:　　　Michael A. Bricker
CPO:　　　Joseph L. Deroche
ODA:　　　Ltc. Paul S. Cariker, USMC
　　　　　　(resident in Dakar)
FAA:　　　Ronald L. Montgomery
　　　　　　(resident in Dakar)
AGR:　　　Jonathan Gressel
　　　　　　(resident in Abidjan)
LAB:　　　Frederick B. Cook
　　　　　　(resident in Washington, DC)
IRS:　　　Frederick D. Pablo
　　　　　　(resident in Paris)

Lithuania

Vilnius (E)
Akmenu 6, 2600
• PSC 78, Box V
APO AE 09723
Tel: 370-2-223-031, 227-224
Fax: 670-6084
Afterhours Tel: 227-240

AMB:　　　James W. Swihart, Jr.
AMB SEC:　Doris McCourt
DPO/POL/ECO:
　　　　　　John C. Stepanchuk
POL:　　　Algis Avizienis
CON:　　　Steven Wangsness
COM:　　　Joan Edwards
　　　　　　(resident in Warsaw)
ADM:　　　Matthew Johnson
IPO:　　　Marcellus D. Davis
AID:　　　John Cloutier
PAO:　　　Viktor Sidabras
RSO:　　　Jeremy Zeikel
　　　　　　(resident in Helsinki)

AGR:　　　Roger A. Wentzel
　　　　　　(resident in Warsaw)
ODA:　　　Bg (s) Tiiu Kera, USAF
FAA:　　　J. Stuart Jamison
　　　　　　(resident in Brussels)
IRS:　　　Joe D. Hook
　　　　　　(resident in Bonn)

Luxembourg

Luxembourg (E)
22 Blvd. Emmanuel-Servais
2535 Luxembourg
• PSC 11
APO AE 09132-5380
Tel: [352] 460123
Fax: 46 14 01
Official mail, name/office
American Embassy Luxembourg
Unit 1410
Personal mail, name
American Embassy Luxembourg
PSC 9, Box 9500
APO AE 09123

AMB:　　　Clay Constantinou
AMB SEC:　Suzanne Chapman
DCM:　　　Michael Parmly
POL:　　　Duane Kramer
POL/ECO/COM:
　　　　　　Robert Faucher
CON:　　　Ruth W. Godfrey
ADM:　　　Tim Harley
RSO:　　　Frederick Mecke
　　　　　　(resident in Brussels)
IPO:　　　John W. Green
ODA:　　　Col. John Fairlamb, USA
　　　　　　(resident in Brussels)
ODC:　　　Ltc. Patrick Faure, USA
　　　　　　(resident in Brussels)
AGR:　　　Steven Yoder
　　　　　　(resident in The Hague)
FAA:　　　Carl Burleson
　　　　　　(resident in London)
CUS:　　　Paul Beaulieu
　　　　　　(resident in Paris)
IRS:　　　Joe D. Hook
　　　　　　(resident in Bonn)

Macedonia (the former Yugoslav Republic of)

Skopje (USLO)
ul. 27 Mart No. 5
9100 Skopje
• Pouch address: USLO Skopje
Department of State
Washington, DC 20521-7120
Tel: [389] (91) 116-180
Fax: 117-103
USAID: Velijko Vlahovich
26/11 Skopje 9100
Tel: 117-211/117-032
Fax: 118-105

COM:	Victor D. Comras
COM SEC:	JoAnn M. Rowe
POL:	Robert L. Sorenson
POL/ECO:	Mark Post
CON/ADM:	Adolfo A. Ramirez III
GSO:	Daria Darnell
IPO:	Dennis F. Hirst
USDLO:	James Bright
USIS:	Sonja Sweek
FAA:	Steven B. Wallace (resident in Rome)
AID:	Linda Gregory
IRS:	Larry J. Legrand (resident in Rome)

Madagascar

Antananarivo (E)
14-16 Rue Rainitovo
Antsahavola, B.P. 620
Tel: [261] (2) 212-57, 200-89 or 207-18
Telex USA EMB MG: 22202
101 Antananarivo
Fax: 234-539

AMB:	Dennis P. Barrett
AMB SEC:	Sophie G. Jorgensen
DCM:	Howard T. Perlow
POL:	James A. Knight
ECO:	Paul E. Rohrlich
COM:	K. Malaika Williams
CON:	Robert Kragie
ADM:	Garace A. Reynard

RSO:	Bruce F. Warren
PAO:	Mary Ann Ignatius
IPO:	Clifton L. Miller
AID:	Donald Mackenzie
FAA:	Ronald L. Montgomery (resident in Dakar)
PCD:	Robert Friedman
IRS:	David Robison (resident in Riyadh)

Malawi

Lilongwe (E)
P.O. Box 30016
Lilongwe 3, Malawi
Tel: [265] 783-166
Telex: 44627
Fax: 780-471
AID Tel: 782-455
USIS Tel: 782-992

AMB:	Peter R. Chaveas
AMB SEC:	Kerry L. Brougham
DCM:	Gregory W. Engle
ECO/COM:	Karen T. Levine
CON/POL:	Jill C. Lundy
ADM:	Anne W. Patchell
RSO:	Steven Chalupsky (resident in Harare)
PAO:	Robert L. Dance
IPO:	Donna Chick-Bowers
AID:	Cynthia F. Rozell
ODA:	Ltc. Gregory M. Saunders (resident in Maputo)
FAA:	Ronald L. Montgomery (resident in Dakar)
LAB:	Lois A. Aroian (resident in Nairobi)
IRS:	Stanley Beesley (resident in London)

Malaysia

Kuala Lumpur (E)
376 Jalan Tun Razak
50400 Kuala Lumpur
• P.O. Box No. 10035

50700 Kuala Lumpur
APO AP 96535-8152
Tel: [60] (3) 248-9011
Fax: 242-2207
COM/AGR *Fax:* 242-1866

AMB:	(Vacant)
AMB SEC:	Lois L. Bozilov
CHG:	Wendy Chamberlin
POL:	G. Nicholas Mauger III
ECO:	Deborah L. Linde
COM:	Paul Walters
CON:	Philip C. French
ADM:	Steven J. White
GSO:	Paul A. Wedderien
RSO:	John L. Tello
PAO:	Nicholas Mele
IPO:	Alexander Kleinsmith
ISM:	James L. Sundstrom
ODA:	Ltc. Donald R. Moran, USA
SAO:	Ltc. Russel Thurber II, USA
DEA:	Stephen H. Cassada
AGR:	Kent D. Sisson
FAA:	David L. Knudson (resident in Singapore)
CUS:	Donald K. Shruhan, Jr. (resident in Singapore)
IRS:	Charles W. Landry (resident in Singapore)

Mali

Bamako (E)
Rue Rochester NY and Rue Mohamed V
B.P. 34
Tel: [223] 225470
Telex: 2448 AMEMB MJ
Fax: 223712

AMB:	(Vacant)
AMB SEC:	Robin J. Welker
CHG:	Carolee Heileman
POL:	David A. Alarid
ECO/COM:	Douglas B. Dearborn
CON:	Franklin L. Milhous
ADM:	Mark M. Boulware
RSO:	Robert G. Reed
PAO:	Michael P. Pelletier
CPO:	Sebastian R. Failla
ISM:	Janet A. Cote (resident in Dakar)
AID:	Joel E. Schlesinger
ODA:	Ltc. Paul S. Cariker, USMC (resident in Dakar)
LAB:	Frederick B. Cook (resident in Washington, DC)
FAA:	Ronald L. Montgomery (resident in Dakar)
RETO:	Timothy H. Robinson (resident in Dakar)
IRS:	Frederick D. Pablo (resident in Paris)
RCON:	Thomas E. Cairns (resident in Dakar)

Malta

Valletta (E)
2nd Fl., Development House
St. Anne St.
Floriana, Malta
• P.O. Box 535
Valletta
Tel: [356] 23-59-60
Fax: 22-32-22

AMB:	Joseph R. Paolino, Jr.
DCM:	Charles N. Patterson, Jr.
SA:	Daniel F. Sheehan
ECO/COM/CON:	Paul J. Andersen
POL:	David Larsen
ADM:	John J. Finneuan, Jr.
RSO:	Stephen H. Jacobs (resident in Rome)
PAO:	Linda Cheatham
IPO:	Michael M. Pingree
AGR:	Frank A. Padovano (resident in Rome)

An Entrepreneur's Directory to Foreign Service Officers   **309**

FAA:	Steven B. Wallace (resident in Rome)	AMB:	Dorothy Myers Sampas
IRS:	Larry J. Legrand (resident in Rome)	AMB SEC:	Sharon S. Rault
		DCM:	Joseph D. Stafford
		POL:	Raymond D. Richart, Jr.

ECO/COM/CON: Steven Craig Walker

Marshall Islands

Majuro (E)
Oceanside, Long Island
Majuro, Republic of the Marshall Islands
Tel: (692) 247-4011
Fax: 247-4012
COM *Fax:* 247-7533
• Pouch: Majuro, 20521-4380
Via US Mail
P.O. Box 1379
Majuro, MH 96960-1379
No APO/FPO is available.

AMB:	David C. Fields
AMB SEC:	Kathleen A. Snider
DPO:	Thomas M. Murphy
ADM:	John W. Dinkelman
RSO:	Walter H. Sargent (resident in Manila)
USIA:	Ken Yates (resident in Honolulu)
FAA:	Barry Brayer (resident in Hawthorne, CA)
CUS:	Donald K. Shruhan, Jr. (resident in Singapore)
MLO:	Thomas Keene
IRS:	Dennis Tsujimoto (resident in Tokyo)

Mauritania

Nouakchott (E)
B.P. 222
Tel: [222] (2) 526-60 or 526-63
Telex: AMEMB 5558 MTN
Fax: 515-92
workweek: Sunday through Thursday

CON:	Thomas E. Cairns (resident in Dakar)
ADM:	Robert L. Lane
RSO:	Robert G. Reed (resident in Bamako)
ODA:	Ltc. Paul S. Cariker, USMC (resident in Dakar)
FAA:	Ronald L. Montgomery (resident in Dakar)
LAB:	Frederick B. Cook (resident in Washington, DC)
IMO:	Terrence Williamson (resident in Dakar)
IRS:	Frederick D. Pablo (resident in Paris)

Mauritius

Port Louis (E)
Rogers House (4th Fl.)
John Kennedy St.
Tel: [230] 208-9763 through 7
Fax: 208-9534

AMB:	Leslie M. Alexander
AMB SEC:	Judy Snyder
DCM:	Margaret C. Jones
POL:	Clyde Berryman
ECO/COM:	Jeanne L. Foster
CON:	Pamela Tremont
ADM:	Bonita S. Bissonette
RSO:	Bruce F. Warren (resident in Antananarivo)
PAO:	Susan Crystal
IPO:	Donna J. Law
FAA:	Ronald L. Montgomery (resident in Dakar)
LAB:	Lois A. Aroian (resident in Nairobi)

IRS: David Robison
(resident in Riyadh)
Port Louis is now responsible for Comoros.

Mexico
Mexico (E)
Paseo de la Reforma 305
06500 Mexico, D.F.
• P.O. Box 3087
Laredo, TX 78044-3087
Tel: [52] (5) 211-0042
Fax: 511-9980 and 208-3373
ATO: Parque Virreyes Building
Monte Pelvoux 220 (esq. Prado Sur)
PH-2
Lomas de Chapultepeo
1100 Mexico, D.F.

AMB:	James R. Jones
AMB SEC:	Gloria Gutierrez
DCM:	Charles Brayshaw
POL:	Barbro A. Owen
ECO:	Daniel L. Dolan
COM:	Kevin C. Brennan
CON:	Bruce A. Beardsley
CG:	Kathleen J. Mullen
ADM:	Russell F. King
RSO:	Jeffrey N. Pursell
SCI:	S. Armed Meer
RAMC:	Frederic C. Hassani
PAO:	William J. Dieterich
ISM:	Charles D. Wisecarver, Jr.
AID:	Arthur H. Danart
EPA:	Enrique Manzanilla
EST:	S. Ahmed Meer
AGR:	Daniel Conablo
APHIS (Reg. 6):	
	Dr. Peter J. Fernandez
ATO:	Marvin L. Lehrer
FAA:	Victor Tamariz (resident in Miami)
FAA/CASLO:	
	Don Rendon
LAB:	Richard T. Booth
INS:	Luis Garcia
NAS:	Kevin Brown
CUS:	Enrique Castro
ATF:	Luis E. Trejo
LEGATT:	Stanley A. Pimentel
DEA:	Horacio M. Ayala
ODA:	Col. Daniel O. Mason, USAMLO
	Col. Richard J. Teliska, USAF
IRS:	Daniel R. Dietz
FIN:	Jack V. Sweeney

USDA/AGR Trade Office (ATO)
Edificio Parque Virreyes
Monte Pelvoux No. 220
Esquina. Prado Sur
11000 Mexico D.F.
• P.O. Box 3087
Laredo, TX 78044-3087
Tel: [52] (5) 202-0434, 202-0168, and 202-0212
Fax: 202-0528
DIR: Marvin L. Lehrer

US Export Development Office
Liverpool 31
06600 Mexico, D.F.
Tel: [52] (5) 591-0155
Fax: 566-1115
DIR: Robert W. Miller

US Travel and Tourism Office
Plaza Comermex
M. Avila Camacho 1-402
11560 Mexico, D.F.
Tel: [52] (5) 520-2101
Fax: 202-9231
DIR: Peter F. Bohen

Ciudad Juarez (CG)
Chihuahua
Avenue Lopez Mateos 924 Norte
32000 Ciudad Juarez, Chihuahua
• P.O. Box 10545
El Paso, TX 79995-0545
Tel: (Visa Info Only) [52] (16) 134048
Tel: (all other calls) 113000
Fax: 169056

CG: Larry Colbert
CON: John P. Caulfield, Jr.
ADM: Brian W. Wilson
INS: Ramona Flores
IPO: James H. Porter

Guadalajara (CG)
JAL, Progreso 175
44100 Guadalajara
Jalisco, Mexico
• Box 3088
Laredo, TX 78044-3088
Tel: [52] (3) 825-29-98, 825-27-00
Fax: 826-6549

CG: Danny B. Root
COM: William B. Smith, Jr.
CON: Ronald J. Kramer
ADM: Julio T. Perez
BPAO: Marjorie Coffin
IPO: Jimmy Barrett
APHIS: Kenneth Bedat
FBU: Bernadino A. Gonzalez
LEGATT: Gilbert A. Alvarez
DEA: Samuel Herrera

Monterrey (CG)
N. L. Ave.
Constitucion 411 Poniente 64000
Monterrey, N.L.
Box 3098
Laredo, TX 78044-3098
Tel: [52] (8) 345-2120
Fax: 342-0177

CG: Eileen M. Heaphy
CG SEC: Frances M. Kendrick
POL: Norman Antokol
ECO: Mary Lee K. Garrison
COM: Robert O. Jones
CON: H. Richard Sindelar III
ADM: Judith I. Marvin
RSO: Wolfgang G. Fuchs
BPAO: Robert L. Hugins
IPO: Simon Guerrero
INS: Hipolito Acosta
CUS: Frederico Villalobos
DEA: (Vacant)
LEGATT: Alfredo Ortiz

Tijuana (CG)
B.C.N., Tapachula 96
22420 Tijuana
Baja California Norte
• P.O. Box 439039
San Diego, CA 92143-9039
Tel: [52] (66) 81-7400
Fax: 81-8016

CG: Norman A. Singer
CG SEC: Elizabeth A. Bobick
CON: George L. Summers
NIV: Peter E. Cozzens
ADM: Perry L. Holloway
BPAO: Nancy LeRoy
IPO: Arnold Olivio, Jr.
INS: Raul Ozuna

Hermosillo (C)
Son., Monterrey 141 Pre.
83260 Hermosillo, Sonora
• Box 3598
Laredo, TX 78044-3598
Tel: [52] (62) 17-2375
Fax: 17-2578

PO: William P. Francisco III
PO SEC: Jean C. Wax
CON: Frederick L. Kupke
ADM/GSO: Caroline B. Mangelsdorf
ECO: William D. Douglas
IPO/ISO: Rudy R. Garcia
CUS: Javier G. Vasquez
AGR/APHIS:
            Dennis Hannapel
DEA: Jeffrey Yllander

Matamoros (C)
Tamps., Ave. Primera 2002
87330 Matamoros, Tamaulipas
• Box 633
Brownsville, TX 78522-0633
Tel: [52] (88) 12-44-02
Fax: 12-21-71

PO: Atim E. Ogunba
CON/COM: Ricardo F. Zuniga
ADM: Douglas Koneff

Merida (C)
Yuc., Paseo M. Ontejo 453
97000 Merida, Yucatan

- Box 3087
  Laredo, TX 78044-3087
  Tel: [52] (99) 25-5011
  Fax: 25-6219
  PO: David R. van Valkenburg
  CON: John M. Desmond
  CUS: Robert Garcia

Nuevo Laredo (C)
Ramps., Calle Allende 3330
Col. Jardin
88260 Nuevo Laredo, Tamps.
- Drawer 3089
  Laredo, TX 78044-3089
  Tel: [52] (87) 14-0512
  Fax: 14-7984, ext. 128
  PO: Isiah L. Parnell

Micronesia

Kolonia (E)
P.O. Box 1286
Pohnpei
Federated States of Micronesia
96941
Tel: [691] 320-2187
Fax: 320-2186
AMB: March Fong Eu
AMB SEC: Susan L. Bigelow
DCM/POL/ECO:
 Stuart V. Brown
ADM: John W. Dinkelman
 (resident in Majuro)
RSO: Walter H. Sargent
 (resident in Manila)
PAO: Ken Yates
 (resident in Honolulu)
FAA: Barry Brayer
 (resident in Hawthorne, CA)
CUS: Donald K. Shruhan, Jr.
 (resident in Singapore)
IRS: Dennis Tsujimoto
 (resident in Tokyo)

Moldova

Chisinau (E)
Strada Alexei Mateeviei, #103
Tel: 373 (2) 23-37-72
Telex: 163261 EMB SU
Fax: 23 30 44
Afterhours: 23 7345
ADM: 22 24 66
AMB: Mary C. Pendleton
AMB SEC: Selina Berriman
POL/ECO: Louis Licht
ADM: Steven Slatin
GSO: Mark Moody
CON: Sarah Penhune
CPO: James Vanderpool
RSO: Harold Countryman
 (resident in Bucharest)
PAO: Jennifer Galenkamp
ODA: Ltc. Paul H. Nelson, USA
 (resident in Moscow)
AGR: William P. Huth
 (resident in Sofia)
FAA: Dennis B. Cooper
 (resident in Moscow)
IRS: Joe D. Hook
 (resident in Bonn)

Mongolia

Ulaanbaatar (E)
c/o American Embassy Beijing
Micro Region 11
Big Ring Rd.
- PSC 461, Box 300
  FPO AP 96521-0002
  Tel: [976] (1) 329-095 or 329-606
  Fax: 320-776
AMB: Donald C. Johnson
DCM/ADM:
 Llewellyn Hedgbeth
POL: Cheryl A. Martin
ECO/CON: C. Michael Konner
IPO: Marlin Tracy
AID: Chuck Howell

An Entrepreneur's Directory to Foreign Service Officers   **313**

PC: Jean E. Mead
PAO: Ann E. Welden
RSO: Donald Schurman
               (resident in Beijing)
ODA: Col. Rocky Roland,
               USAF
               (resident in Beijing)
FAA: Fred Laird
               (resident in Tokyo)
IRS: Dennis Tsujimoto
               (resident in Tokyo)

Morocco
Rabat (E)
2 Ave. de Marrakech
• PSC 74, Box 003
APO AE 09718
Tel: [212] (7) 76-22-65
Fax: 76-56-61
Afterhours Tel: 76-96-39
Telex: 31005M
USAID Fax: 70-79-30
USIS Fax: 75-08-63

AMB: Marc C. Ginsberg
AMB SEC: Lynda Dunn
DCM: Gary S. Usrey
POL: Joseph Mussomeli
ECO: James Yellin
POL/LAB: Elizabeth Martinez
               (resident in Casablanca)
CON: Elaine A. Zenoble
ADM: Richard E. Kramer
RSO: Lawrence H. Liptak
PAO: Robert B. Petersen
IMO: James Tuten
ISM: Lucille Smithson
AGR: Quintin Gray
AID: Michael Farbman
ODA: Col. Alan J. Tinder,
               USAF
ODC: Col. Grant Lorenz, USA
IRS: Frederick D. Pablo
               (resident in Paris)
FAA: J. Stuart Jamison
               (resident in Brussels)

Casablanca (CG)
8 Blvd. Moulay Youssef
• APO AE 09718 (CAS)
Tel: [212] (2) 26-45-50
Fax: 20-41-27
COM Fax: 22-02-59
Duty officer's cellular Tel. no: 13-4065

CG: Marcia Bernicat
POL/LAB: Elizabeth Martinez
ECO: Daniel K. Balzer
COM: Frederic J. Gaynor
CON: Shelley S. Midura
ADM: Sylvia Nasri
IPO: Raymond Harger
BPAO: Philip A. Frayne

Mozambique
Maputo (E)
Avenida Kenneth Kaunda 193
• P.O. Box 783
Tel: [258] (1) 49-27-97
Telex: 6-143 AMEMB MO
Fax: 49-01-14
USAID Tel: 49-07-26
Fax: 49-20-98
USIS Tel: 49-19-16
Fax: 49-19-18

AMB: Dennis Coleman Jett
AMB SEC: Lena R. Steinhoff
DCM: P. Michael McKinley
POL: Jon Danilowicz
ECO/COM: Joseph Ripley
CON: Philippa Deramus
ADM: John E. Olson
RSO: Stephen W. Sekellick
AID: Roger D. Carlson
ODA: Ltc. Paul D. Keller
PAO: Adrienne O'Neal
IRS: Stanley Beesley
               (resident in London)
LAB: Thomas A. Shannon, Jr.
               (resident in
               Johannesburg)
FAA: Ronald L. Montgomery
               (resident in Dakar)

Namibia

Windhoek (E)
Ausplan Building
14 Lossen St.
Private Bag 12029 Ausspannplatz
Windhoek, Namibia
Tel: [264] (61) 221-601
Fax: 229-792

AMB:	Marshall F. McCallie
AMB SEC:	Rosemary M. Patterson
DCM:	Katherine H. Peterson
POL:	Carl F. Troy
ECO/COM:	Philip R. Drouin
CON:	Robert Bruton
ADM:	Gordon R. Olson
RSO:	Larry D. Salmon
PAO:	Helen B. Picard
IPO:	Amanda Gilke
AID:	Edward Spriggs
ODA:	Ltc. Gary E. Walker, USA
FAA:	Ronald L. Montgomery (resident in Dakar)
AGR:	James Benson (resident in Pretoria)
LAB:	Thomas A. Shannon, Jr. (resident in Johannesburg)
IRS:	Stanley Beesley (resident in London)

Nepal

Kathmandu (E)
Pani Pokhari
Tel: [977] (1) 411179
Telex: 2381 AEKTM NP
Fax: 419963 Chancery 272357
USAID Tel: 270-144
Fax: 272357

AMB:	Sandy L. Vogelgesang
AMB SEC:	S. Anne Leverette
DCM:	Peter W. Bodde
POL/ECO:	Peter S. Gadzinski
POL/MIL:	Gary Bernsten
COM:	Craig Arness
CON:	Rekha Arness
ADM:	William Campbell
RSO:	Eric Levine
CPO:	Gary Cook
PAO:	David A. Queen
IPO:	Gary Cook
AID:	Frederick Machmer
ODA:	Ltc. James Dunn, USA (resident in Dhaka)
IRS:	Charles W. Landry (resident in Singapore)
FAA:	David L. Knudson (resident in Singapore)

Netherlands

The Hague (E)
Lange Voorhout 102
2514 EJ The Hauge
• PSC 71, Box 1000
APO AE 09715
Tel: [31] (70) 310-9209
Fax: 361-4688
COM Fax: 363-2985

AMB:	K. Terry Dornbush
AMB SEC:	Evelyn Nasro
DCM:	Michael Klosson
POL:	Bronson Percival
ECO:	Jack Croddy
COM:	Rafael Fermoselle
ADM:	Wajat Iqbal
RSO:	George Gaines
PAO:	Karl Olsson
IMO:	Peter Jenson
ODA:	Capt. Donald Roulstone, USN
ODC:	Col. Ronnie Lewis
AGR:	Steven Yoder
FAA:	Carl Burleson (resident in London)
IRS:	Joe D. Hook (resident in Bonn)
LAB:	Eleanore Raven-Hamilton

An Entrepreneur's Directory to Foreign Service Officers

Amsterdam (CG)
Museumplein 19
1071 DJ Amsterdam
• PSC 71, Box 1000
APO AE 09715
Tel: [31] (20) 5755 309
CG Fax: 5755 310
COM Fax: 5755 350

CG:	John W. Shearburn
CON:	Joseph B. Nowell
COM:	(Vacant)
USTTA:	Maximilian J. Ollendorff (resident in Paris)

Netherlands Antilles

Curacao (CG)
St. Anna Blvd. 19
• P.O. Box 158
Willemstad, Curacao
Tel: [599] (9) 613066
Fax: 616489
Duty Tel: 606870

CG:	Bernard J. Woerz
RSO:	Edward R. Napliello (resident in Caracas)
PAO:	Peter Peshazo (resident in Caracas)
AGR:	Larry Senger (resident in Caracas)
LEGATT:	Ralph Torres (resident in Caracas)
FAA:	Celio Young (resident in Miami)
IRS:	Charles Shea (resident in Caracas)

New Zealand

Wellington (E)
29 Fitzherbert Terr.
Thorndon, Wellington
• P.O. Box 1190
Wellington, PSC 467, Box 1
FPO AP 96531-1001
Tel: [64] (4) 472-2068
ADM Fax: 471-2380
EXEC Fax: 472-3537

AMB:	Josiah Horton Beeman
AMB SEC:	Shannon Lee Tracy
DCM:	Morton R. Dworken, Jr.
POL/ECO:	Evans J. R. Revere
ECO:	Elaine Garland
CON:	James E. Flynn
ADM:	Steven G. Leach
GSO:	Michael G. Bakalar
RSO:	John Henry Kaufmann (resident in Canberra)
PAO:	Timothy M. Randall
IPO:	David W. Smith
ODA:	Capt. Richard L. Norwood, USN
AGR:	Theodore Horoschak
FAA:	Fred Laird (resident in Tokyo)
CUS:	Donald K. Shruhan, Jr. (resident in Singapore)
LAB:	Karen E. Krueger
IRS:	Vivian Simon (resident in Sydney)

Auckland (CG)
4th Fl., Yorkshire General Building
Corner of Shortland and O'Connell Sts.
Auckland, Private Bag, 92022
Auckland
• PCS 467, Box 99
FPO AP 96531-1099
Tel: [64] (9) 303-2724
Fax: 366-0870
COM Fax: 302-3156

| CON: | Alcy R. Frelick |
| COM: | M. Philip Gates |

Nicaragua

Managua (E)
Km. 4½ Carretera Sur.
• APO AA 34021
Tel: [505] (2) 666010, 666013, 666015-18, 666026-27, 666032-34

Fax: 666046
USIS Fax: 663861
AMB: John F. Maisto
AMB SEC: Linda O. Swafford
DCM: Heather M. Hodges
POL: Frederick A. Becker
ECO/COM: Paul A. Trivelli
CON: Kathleen M. Daly
ADM: Russell L. Keeton
RSO: Lanny R. Bernier
PAO: Joseph N. McBride
IMO: Paul W. Eickman
AID: George W. Carner
ODA: Col. Lynn E. Lanzoni
AGR: Scott Bleggi
 (resident in San Jose)
APHIS: Dr. Alan Terrell
FAA: Ray Salazar
 (resident in Miami)
LAB: John Cushing
 (resident in Guatemala City)
IRS: Daniel R. Dietz
 (resident in Mexico City)

Niger
Niamey (E)
Rue Des Ambassades
B.P. 11201
Tel: [227] 72-26-61 through 4
Fax: 73-31-67
Telex: EMB NIA 5444 NI
AMB: John S. Davison
DCM: Ravic R. Huso
POL: Nan Mattingly
ECO/COM: James A. Stewart
CON: (Vacant)
ADM: Wilbert Stitt, Jr.
RSO: Raymond Lee Yates
PAO: Shirley O. Stanton
IPO: James A. Harrison, Jr.
ODA: Col. Kenneth Hibl
 (resident in Abidjan)

ODC: Maj. Stefan Arredondo, USA
FAA: Ronald L. Montgomery
 (resident in Dakar)
SAO: Maj. Douglas E. Lathrop, USA
ISM: Janet A. Cote
 (resident in Dakar)
RETO: Timothy H. Robinson
 (resident in Dakar)
IRS: Frederick D. Pablo
 (resident in Paris)

Nigeria
Lagos (E)
Eleke Crescent
• P.O. Box 554
Tel: [234] (1) 261-0097
Telex: 23616 AMEMLA NG
Fax: 261-0257
CON Fax: 261-2218
COM Fax: 261-9856
DEA Fax: 261-7874
USIS Fax: 263-5397
AID Fax: 261-4698
Family Health Serv. Fax: 261-2815
AMB: Walter C. Carrington
AMB SEC: Sandra K. Slaughter
DCM: Tibor P. Nagy, Jr.
POL: Robert E. Downey
ECO: Herbert Yarvin
COM: Walter Hage
CON: Philip Covington
ADM: William Gaines
IMO: Dennis Thatcher
RSO: David P. Manley
RMO: Dr. Gretchen McCoy
PAO: Thomas N. Hull
AID: Stephen Spielman
ODA: Maj. Lacy Ingram, USA
FAA: Ronald L. Montgomery
 (resident in Dakar)
SAO: (Vacant)
AGR: Maurice W. House
DEA: Edgar L. Moses

LAB: Jon Peter Dorschner
IRS: Federick D. Pablo
(resident in Paris)

Kaduna (USIS)
11 Maska Rd.
- P.M.B. 2060
Tel: [234] (62) 235990, 235992
Fax: 213312, 217491
BPAO: Bruce A. Lohof

Note: Kaduna State office closed September 30, 1994. The BPAO is the only officer remaining at post. All correspondence, mail, and inquiries should be directed to USLO, Abuja, Department of State, Washington, DC 20521-8300.

Ibadan (USIS)
OGC Enconsult House
- P.M.B. 5089
Tel: [234] (02) 810-0775, 810-2802
Fax: 810-1019
BPAO: Claud R. Young

Abuja (USLO)
9 Mambilla St. (off Aso Dr.)
Maitama District
- P.O. Box 5760
Garki Abuja
Tel: [234] (9) 523-0960
Fax: 523-0353

Liaison Office does not offer commercial services. Commercial Services are available at Embassy Lagos.

Officer in Charge:
   Timothy D. Andrews
ADM: Richard Ingram
POL: Russel Hanks
ECO/CON: Landon R. Taylor
BPAO: Claudia Anyaso
PC: George Spellman

Norway

Oslo (E)
Drammensveien 18
0244 Oslo
- PSC 69, Box 1000
APO AE 09707
Tel: [47] 22-44-85-50
Fax: 22-44-33-63
ADMIN Fax: 22-43-07-77
COM Fax: 22-55-88-03
POL/ECO Fax: 22-55-43-13
USIS Fax: 22-44-04-36

AMB: Thomas A. Loftus
AMB SEC: Sue Meyer
DCM: (Vacant)
POL/ECO: Harold E. Meinheit
COM: E. Scott Bozek
CON: Eli N. Lauderdale, Jr.
ADM: Stephen B. Williams
RSO: Joseph F. Noon
PAO: Michael T. Scanlin
IMO: Mark S. Buske
ODA: Capt. Robert H. Paleck, USN
ODC: Col. Daniel G. Penny, USAF
AGR: Margaret Dowling
(resident in Copenhagen)
LAB: David R. Galindo
FAA: Carl Burleson
(resident in London)
IRS: Stanley Beesley
(resident in London)
FBI: John E. Guido
(resident in London)

US Information Office closed in February 1994.

Oman

Muscat (E)
P.O. Box 202
Code No. 115
Medinat Qaboos switchboard: (968) 698-989
Afterhours: (968) 699-049
Fax: ODA 699-779
ECA: 699-669
POL/ECO/COM: 604-316

USAID: 797-778
GSO: 699-778
OMC: 604-327
USIS: 699-771
Health Unit: 699-088
workweek: Saturday through Wednesday

AMB:	David J. Dunford
AMB SEC:	Suzanne Chapman
DCM:	Elizabeth McKune
POL/ECO:	Roberta L. Chew
POL/MIL:	Robert G. Richer
ECO/COM:	Richard M. Eason
CON:	Manish K. Mishra
ADM:	Ernest J. Parkin, Jr.
RSO:	William M. Savich
IPO:	Chandra L. Smith
PAO:	Matthew R. Lussenhop
FBO:	Gregory K. Larson
ODA:	Ltc. Walter J. Cooner, Jr.
OMC:	Col. Tod J. Wilson
ECA:	Ltc. Jerry E. Bjornstad
ATO:	Edwin Porter (resident in Dubai)
FAA:	Dennis R. Beres (resident in Riyadh)
IRS:	David Robison (resident in Riyadh)

US Delegation to the Oman/American Joint Commission for Economic and Technical Cooperation
P.O. Box 3001
Code No. 112
Ruwi, Oman
Tel: (968) 703-000
Fax: 797-778

US CO-CHAIRMAN AMB: David J. Dunford
AID REP: Mark S. Matthews

Pakistan

Islamabad (E)
Diplomatic Enclave, Ramna 5
• P.O. Box 1048
Unit 62200
APO AE 09812-2200
Tel: [92] (51) 826161 through 79
Telex: 82-5864 AEISL PK
Fax: 214222
workweek: Sunday through Thursday

AMB:	John C. Monjo
AMB SEC:	Pamela H. Moore
DCM:	John C. Holzman
POL:	Eric A. Kunsman
ECO:	Rafael L. Marin
ADM:	Jeremy Nice
CON:	June H. Kunsman
RSO:	Ronald M. Mazen
PAO:	Ray Peppers
IMO:	Jane S. Longenecker
AGR:	Frank A. Coolidge
AID:	John S. Blackton
NAS:	John A. Parker
REF:	Caryl M. Courtney
DEA:	Michael Long
ODA:	Col. John B. Longenecker
ODRP:	Col. Frederick R. Wilhelm
IRS:	David Robison (resident in Riyadh)
FAA:	David L. Knudson (resident in Singapore)
MAAG:	BG John D. Howard, USA

Karachi (CG)
8 Abdullah Haroon Rd.
• Unit 64200
APO AE 09814-2400
Tel: [92] (21) 5685170 through 79
Telex: 82-21001 ACGK PK
Fax: 5680496
GSO Fax: 5683089
FCS Fax: 5681381
workweek: Sunday through Thursday

CG:	Mary Virginia Kennedy
CG SEC:	Susan C. G. Winner
POL/ECO:	Michael Owen

COM: Daniel Devito
CON: Kay L. Anske
ADM: Stephen B. Hogard
RSO: Keith Swinehart
BPAO: Peter Claussen
IPO: Carrie A. Ullman
ISM: Robert S. Blankenship
DEA: John Atlee
LOC: (Vacant)

Lahore (CG)
50 Shahrah-E-Bin Badees
(50 Empress Rd.)
Near Simla Hills
• Unit 62216
APO AE 09812-2216
Tel: [92] (42) 6365530 through 6365539
Fax: 6365177
workweek: Sunday through Thursday

CG: Eric D. Tunis
CG SEC: Judith A. Franco
POL: James F. Cole
ECO: (Vacant)
CON: Clyde L. Jones
ADM: Bruce F. Knotts
BPAO: Haynes R. Mahoney
IPO: Kenneth Spaulding
DEA: Robert A. Dinius

Peshawar (C)
11 Hospital Rd.
Peshawar Cantt, AC Peshawar
• Unit 62217
APO AE 09812-2217
Tel: [92] (521) 279801 through 279803
Telex: 52364 AMCON PK
Fax: 276712
workweek: Sunday through Thursday

PO: Richard H. Smyth
PO SEC: Jane B. McCarthy
ADM/POL: Kelly C. Degnan
POL/CON: Lynne M. Tracy
BPAO: David Mees
IPO: George F. Kaminski
DEA: James Hughes

Republic of Palau

Koror (E)
P.O. Box 6028
Republic of Palau 96940
Tel: (680) 488-2920
Fax: 488-2911

CHG: Richard G. Watkins
FAA: Barry Brayer
(resident in Hawthorne, CA)

Panama

Panama City (E)
Apartado 6959
Panama 5
Rep. de Panama, Unit 0945
APO AA 34002
Tel: [507] 227-1377
Fax: 227-1964
FBO Fax: 227-2128
GSO Fax: 225-2720

CHG: Oliver P. Garza
AMB SEC: Barbara Matchey
POL: John E. Bennett
ECO: Elizabeth Bollmann
COM: Americo Tadeu
CON: L. Bradley Hittle
ADM: Bernado Sigura-Giron
RSO: Paul P. Gaffney
PAO: Joe B. Johnson
AID: David E. Mutchler
DOD REP: Col. Benjamin Vega
AGR: Scott Bleggi
(resident in San Jose)
AGR/APHIS:
Dr. Eloisa Jones
AGR/ARS: Dr. John B. Welch
LAB: John Mohanco
CUS: William T. Long
IMO: Joseph E. Zeman
ICITAP: Robert Doguim
NAS: Paul T. Belmont
LEGATT: Luis Fernandez
FAA: Celio Young

PC: (resident in Miami)
Joseph W. Hindman
IRS: Charles Shea
(resident in Caracas)

Papua New Guinea
Port Moresby (E)
Douglas St.
• P.O. Box 1492
Unit 11026
APO AE 96553-4240
Tel: (675) 321-1455
Fax: 321-3423

AMB: Richard W. Teare
AMB SEC: Donna D. Linchangco
DCM: Edward J. Michal
POL: Royal M. Whartman
ECO/COM: Beatrice P. Soila
CON: Patrick W. Walsh
ADM: Mason S. Green
RSO: Bruce W. Tully
(resident in Jakarta)
PAO: Karl E. Stoltz
IPO: Alfred Begin
AID: Paul H. Greenough
ATO: Robert D. Fondahn
(resident in Singapore)
ODA: Col. Shelby T. Stevens, USA
(resident in Canberra)
FAA: Fred Laird
(resident in Tokyo)
CUS: Donald K. Shruhan, Jr.
(resident in Singapore)
IRS: Vivian L. Simon
(resident in Sydney)

Paraguay
Asuncion (E)
1776 Mariscal Lopez Ave.
Casilla Postal 402
• Unit 4711
APO AA 34036-0001
Tel: [595] (21) 213-715
Fax: 213-728

AMB: Robert E. Service
AMB SEC: Alice M. Weaver
DCM: Gerald C. McCulloch
POL: Alexander H. Margulies
ECO/COM: Francisco J. Fernandez
CON: Eigil V. Hansen
ADM: Franklin D. English
AGR: Max Bowser
(resident in Buenos Aires)
RSO: David C. Zebley
PAO: Mark T. Jacobs
IMO: Jorge Viscal
AID: Richard B. Nelson
ODA: Ltc. Alfonso Gomez, USA
ODC: Col. Raymond H. Becerril, USA
FAA: Santiago Garcia
(resident in Rio de Janeiro)
PC: Kristine B. Vega
IRS: Charles Shea
(resident in Caracas)

Peru
Lima (E)
Avenida Encalada
Cuadra 17
Monterrico, Lima
• P.O. Box 1995
Lima 1, or American Embassy (Lima)
APO AA 34031
Tel: [51] (12) 21-1202
Fax: 21-3543
Afterhours Tel: 33-2242
ADM: Larrabure y Unanue 110
Lima 1
Tel: (14) 33-0555
GSO Fax: 33-4588
CON: Grimaldo del Solar 346
Miraflores, Lima 18

Tel: (14) 44-3621
Fax: 47-1877
COM: Larrabure Y Unanue 110
Lima 1
Tel: 33-0555
Fax: 33-4687
USAID: Larrabure Y Unanue 110
Lima 1
Tel: 33-3200
Fax: 33-7034
AGR/FAS: Larrabure Y Unanue 110
Lima 1
Tel: 33-0555
Fax: 33-4623
USIS: Larrabure Y Unanue 110
Lima 1
Tel: 33-0555
Fax: 33-4635

AMB:	Alvin P. Adams, Jr.
AMB SEC:	Silvester Satcher
DCM:	James F. Mack
POL:	Stephen G. McFarland
ECO:	John R. Riddle
COM:	Ann Bacher
CON:	Thomas L. Holladay
ADM:	Alphonse Lopez
RSO:	Anthony Walters
IMO:	Frederick R. Sadler
PAO:	Pamela Corey-Archer
AID:	George Wachtenheim
ODA:	Capt. Manuel Y. Durazo, USN
MAAG:	Col. David Plumer
DMA:	John O. Gates
AGR/FAS:	Daryl Brehm (resident in Quito)
FAA:	Victor Tamariz (resident in Miami)
LEGATT:	William D. Godoy (resident in Montevideo)
NAS:	Sherman N. Hinson
IRS:	Charles Shea (resident in Caracas)

Philippines
Manila (E)
1201 Roxas Blvd.
APO AP 96440
Tel: [63] (2) 521-7116
Telex: 722-27366
AME PH, Fax: 522-4361
COM OFF 395 Senator Gil J. Puyat Ave.
Makati
Tel: 818-6674
Telex: 22708 COSEC PH

AMB:	John D. Negroponte
AMB SEC:	Katherine M. Astala
DCM:	Raymond F. Burghardt
POL:	E. Mason Hendrickson, Jr.
ECO:	Donald F. McConville
COM:	August Maffry, Jr.
COM rep to the ADB:	Janet Thomas
CON:	Richard R. Peterson
ADM:	Raymond J. Pepper
GSO:	Paul M. Hooper
RSO:	Walter H. Sargent
PAO:	Philip C. Harley
ISM:	R. Peter Rice
IMO:	Richard C. Kwaitkowski
AID:	Kenneth G. Schofield
ODA:	Col. Morrill E. Marston, USAF
JUSMAG:	Col. Wayne M. Barth, USA
AGR:	Lawrence E. Hall
FAA:	Fred Laird (resident in Tokyo)
LAB:	James J. Ehrman
INS:	Carlos Salazat (Acting)
IRS:	Dennis Tsujimoto (resident in Tokyo)

Asian Development Bank (Manila)
#6 ADB Ave.
Mandaluyong, Metro Manila
• P.O. Box 789
APO AP 96440
Tel: (632) 632-6050

Telex: 63587 ADB PN, 42205
ADBPM, and 29066 ADB PH
Fax: 632-4003, 632-6044
COM ADB OFF 395 Buenida Ave.,
Ext.
Makati, Metro Manila
Tel: 813-3248
Fax: 632-4003, 632-6044
US EXEC DIR: Linda TSAO Yang
US ALT EXEC DIR:
 N. Cinnamon Dornsife
COM/ADB: Janet G. Thomas

Cebu (C)
3rd Fl., PCI Bank Building
Gorordo Ave.
Lahug Cebu City 6000
• APO AP 96440
Tel: [63] (32) 311-261
Fax: 310-174

PO:	Lisa A. Piascik
CON/POL:	John R. Carlino
BPAO:	(Vacant)

Poland

Warsaw (E)
Aleje Ujazdowskie 29/31
• Unit 1340
APO AE 09213-1340
Tel: [48] (2) 628-3041
Telex: 817771 EMUSA PL
Fax: 628-8298

AMB:	Nicholas Andrew Rey
AMB SEC:	Rosalind Poynter
DCM:	James R. Hooper
POL:	Stephen D. Mull
ECO:	J. Aubrey Hooks
COM:	Maria Andrews
CON:	Laura Clerici
ADM:	W. Douglas Frank
RSO:	James T. Cronin
PAO:	Richard Virden
IMO:	John H. Gibbs
ISM:	Onnie Ogot
EST:	James W. Chamberlin

AID:	Suzanne Olds
ODA:	Col. Branko B. Marinovich, USA
AGR:	Roger A. Wentzel
FAA:	Steven B. Wallace (resident in Rome)
LAB:	Mathew Boyse
IRS:	Larry J. Legrand (resident in Bonn)

US Trade Center (Warsaw)
Aleje Jerozolimskie 56C
IKEA Building, 2nd Fl.
00-803 Warsaw
• Unit 1340
APO AE 09213-1340
Tel: [48] (2) 621-4515, 621,4216
625-4300
Fax: 621-6327

DIR:	Maria Andrews

Krakow (CG)
Ulica Stolarska 9
31043 Krakow
• Unit 1340
APO AE 09213-1340
Tel: [48] (12) 229764, 221400, 226040,
227793
Telex: 325350 KRUSA PL
Fax: 218292

CG:	Mary B. Marshall
POL/ECO:	Paulal Thied
CON:	Michael McCamman
ADM:	Leslie Degraffenried
BPAO:	John A. Matel

Poznan (CG)
Ulica Chopina 4
61708 Poznan
• Unit 1340
APO AE 09213-1340
Tel: [48] (61) 551088, 529587, 529874
Telex: 413474 USA PL
Fax: 530053

PO:	Janet M. Weber
CON:	David T. Morris
ADM:	Charles Ashley
BPAO:	Douglas Ebner

Portugal
Lisbon (E)
Avenida das Forcas Armadas
1600 Lisbon
• PSC 83
APO AE 09726
Tel: [351] (1) 726-6600, 726-6659, 726-8670, 726-8880
Fax: 726-9109
FCS Fax: 726-8914
USIS Fax: 726-8814

AMB:	Elizabeth Frawley Bagley
AMB SEC:	Beverly O. Harrison
DCM:	Sharon P. Wilkinson
POL:	David M. Adamson
ECO:	James M. McGlinchey
COM:	Miguel Pardo de Zela
CON:	David P. Bocskor
ADM:	Raymond A. Boneski
RSO:	Robert Q. Blackburn
PAO:	Kathleen A. Brion
AGR:	Franklin D. Lee (resident in Madrid)
FAA:	J. Stuart Jamison (resident in Brussels)
LAB:	James G. Davis
IMO:	Glenn A. Cockerill
ISO/ISM:	Elizabeth B. McGaffey
ODA:	Col. Steven G. Joseph, USAF
MAAG:	Capt. Grant W. Sassen, USN
IRS:	Frederick D. Pablo (resident in Paris)
ODC:	Col. Jesse M. Perez, USA

Ponta Delgada, Sao Miguel, Azores (C)
Avenida Infante D'Henrique
• PSC 76, Box 3000
APO AE 09720
Tel: [351] (96) 22216/7/8/9
Fax: 27216

PO:	Luis Espada-Platet
VC:	Mark H. Lunardi

American Business Center (Oporto)
Praca Conde de Samodaes
65, 4000 Porto
• APO AE 09726
Tel: [351] (2) 606-30-94 or 606-30-95
Fax: 600-27-37

DIR:	Miguel Pardo de Zela (resident in Lisbon)

Qatar
Doha (E)
149 Ali Bin Ahmed St.
Farig Bin Omran (opp. TV station)
• P.O. Box 2399
Tel: (0974) 864701/2/3
USLO Tel: 875140
COM Tel: 867460
Fax: 861669
USIS Tel: 351279, 351207
Fax: 321907

AMB:	Kenton W. Keith
AMB SEC:	Virginia Phillips
POL/ECO:	Marguerita D. Ragsdale
CON:	Michael Adler
ADM:	Scott R. Heckman
RSO:	Gary L. Caldwell (resident in Riyadh)
PAO:	Elizabeth Thornhill
CPO:	Bruce E. Peters
ATO:	Edwin Porter (resident in Dubai)
FAA:	Dennis Beres (resident in Riyadh)
IRS:	David Robison (resident in Riyadh)
USLO:	Ltc. Bruce W. Deane, USAF

Romania
Bucharest (E)
Strada Tudor Arghezi 7-9
• Unit 1315
APO AE 09213-1315
Tel: [40] (1) 210-4042, 210-0149

Telex: 11416
Fax: 210-0395
Afterhours Tel: 210-6384
CON Tel: 210-4042
Fax: 211-3360
AID Tel: 312-5565
Fax: 312-0508
AGR Tel: 210-4042
Fax: 210-0395
GSO Tel: 211-5658, 5731
Fax: 210-5567
Peace Corps Tel: 312-1289
Fax: 312-3004
USIS Tel: 210-4042
Fax: 210-0396
USIS Cultural Ctr. Tel: 312-1688, 1761, 1821
Fax: 211-5659

AMB:	Alfred H. Moses
DCM:	M. Michael Einik
AMB SEC:	Sheila Romine
POL:	Robert Whitehead
ECO:	Richard A. Rorvig
COM:	William H. Crawford
PO/CLUJ:	Nathan Bluhm
CON:	Susan Jacobs
ADM:	Charles Kinn
RSO:	Harold S. Countryman, Jr.
IPO:	Jerry Albright
ISM:	Lola A. Timmins
AID:	Richard J. Hough
ODA:	Col. Gary Chamberlan, USAF
PAO:	Christian Filostrat
PC:	Arthur J. Flanagan
AGR:	William P. Huth (resident in Sofia)
FAA:	Steven B. Wallace (resident in Rome)
IRS:	Larry J. Legrand (resident in Rome)

Clug-Napoca (BO)
International address US Branch Office
Universitatii 7-9
Etage 1
Cluj-Napoca, Romania 3400
• Unit 1315
APO AE 09213-1315
Tel: [40] (64) 19-38-15
Fax: 19-38-68
PO: Nathan Bluhm

Russia
Moscow (E)
Novinskiy Bul'var 19/23
• APO/AE 09721
Tel: [7] (095) 252-2451 through 59
Telex: 413160 USGSO SU
Fax: 956-4261
Afterhours Tel: 230-2001/2610
USAID Tel: 956-4281
Fax: 205-2813
USIS Tel: 956-4126/4246
Fax: 255-9766

AMB:	Thomas R. Pickering
AMB EXEC ASST:	Valorie N. Williams
DCM:	Richard M. Miles
POL:	William J. Burns
ECO:	Michael C. Mozur
COM:	John Peters
CON:	Michael W. Marine
ADM:	Peter S. Flynn
RSO:	Robert J. Franks
PAO:	Paul R. Smith
IMO:	John P. Boulanger
ISM:	Kent W. Huff
EST:	John C. Zimmerman
AID:	James A. Norris
ODA:	Brig. Gen. John C. Reppert
PC:	Douglas W. Frago
AGR:	Mary Revelt
FAA:	Dennis B. Cooper
LAB:	Jason H. Horowitz
FIN:	William C. Murden
IRS:	Joe D. Hook (resident in Bonn)

An Entrepreneur's Directory to Foreign Service Officers **325**

FBIS:	Mareen E. Cote
INS:	Irena Kip-Daigle
VOA:	Peter X. Collins
NASA:	Kenneth L. Mitchell
DOE:	Robin J. Copeland
LEGATT:	J. Michael Di Pretoro

US Commercial Office (Moscow)
Novinskiy Bul'var 15
Tel: [7] (095) 956-4255, 255-4848/4660 or (502) 224-1105
Fax: 230-2101, 224-1106

DIR:	John Peters

St. Petersburg (CG)
Furshtadtskaya Ulitsa 15
191028 St. Petersburg
• PSC 78, Box L
APO AE 09723
Tel: [7] (812) 275-1701, 274-8568, 274-8253, 274-8689
Fax: 110-7022 or 850-1473
Afterhours Tel: 274-8692
Emergency Tel: 271-6455

US Foreign Commercial Service
American Consulate General
Bolshaya Morskaya Ulitsa 57
190000 St. Petersburg
Tel: [7] (812) 110-6656, 110-6727, or 850-1902
Fax: 110-6479 or 850-1903
• Mail from the US: Commercial Section
American Consulate General
PSC 78, Box L
APO AE 09723

USIS
US Cultural and Information Center
Millionnaya Ulitsa 5
191065 St. Petersburg
Tel: [7] (812) 311-8905 or 119-8050
Fax: 119-8052

CG:	John Evans
CG SEC:	Frances Hester
DPO:	Jeffrey Garrison
POL/ECO:	Janet Speck
COM:	David Schneider
CON:	Adam Shub (Acting)
ADM:	Susan Garrison
RSO:	Gustavo Mejia
BPAO:	Mary Kruger
CPO:	Joe Hester

Vladivostok (CG)
Ulitsa Mordovtseva 12
• Pouch address: AmConGen Vladivostok
Department of State
Washington, DC 20521-5880
Tel: [7] (4232) 268-458/554 or 266-820
INMARSAT Tel/Fax: 011-7-50985-11011
Telex: 213206 CGVLAD SU
Fax: 268-445
CON Tel: 266-734

CG:	Desiree A. Millikau
POL/ECO:	Eric A. Jones
ADM:	Michael Scanlon
CON:	Donna Michaels
COM:	Timothy Smith
USIS:	Gregory Elftmann

Yekaterinburg (CG)
Ulitsa Gogolya 15A
• P.O. Box 400
620151 Yekaterinburg AmConGen
Yekaterinburg
Department of State
Washington, DC 20521-5890
Telex: 612-696 CONS SU
Tel: [7] (3432) 564619, 564191
Fax: 564515, 601-181
COM: 564736
CON: 564744
USIS: 564760

CG:	Dr. Howard J. T. Steers
POL/ECO/COM:	Jonathan Turak
ADM:	Warren D. Hadley
CON:	Brook Hefright

Rwanda
Kigali (E)
Blvd. de la Revolution
B.P. 28
Tel: [250] 75601/2/3
Fax: 72128, 7:30 am–5 pm
Amb.'s Off: 5 pm–6 pm 72127
CPU72126
USAID Tel: 74719
USAID Fax: 74735
USIS after 5 pm: 76339
Peace Corps: 76339

AMB:	David P. Rawson
AMB SEC:	Sandy McInturff
DCM:	(Vacant)
ECO/COM/CON:	(Vacant)
ADM:	Jerris Riordan
RSO:	Doug Allison (resident in Kampala)
PAO:	(Vacant)
IPO:	Richard McInturff
GSO:	Gary Herbst
AID:	Jack Hjelt
ODA:	Ltc. Thomas Odom
FAA:	Ronald L. Montgomery (resident in Dakar)
RETO:	Timothy H. Robinson (resident in Dakar)
IRS:	David Robison (resident in Riyadh)

Saudi Arabia
Riyadh (E)
Collector Rd. M
Riyadh Diplomatic Quarter
• Unit 61307
APO AE 09803-1307
International Mail: P.O. Box 94309
Riyadh 11693
Tel: [966] (1) 488-3800
USIS: P.O. Box 94310
Riyadh 11693
Fax: 488-3989
FCS Fax: 488-3237
POL/ECO Fax: 488-3278
Fax (General): 488-7360
ISC Fax: 488-7867
FMC Fax: 482-2765
GSO Fax: 488-7939
IRS Fax: 488-7351
ATO Tel: 488-3800, ext. 1560
Fax: 482-4364
workweek: Saturday-Wednesday (all posts)

AMB:	Raymond E. Mabus, Jr.
AMB SEC:	Deborah M. Paolini-Huff
DCM:	Theodore H. Kattouf
POL:	Albert A. Thibault, Jr.
POL/MIL:	Thomas W. Callow
ECO:	Frank S. Parker
COM:	John H. Steuber, Jr.
CON:	Richard C. Hermann
ADM:	Robert E. Davis, Jr.
RSO:	Gary L. Caldwell
PAO:	Samir Kouttab
IMO:	Randall R. Dudley
ODA:	Col. Gary W. Nelson
ATO:	John H. Wilson
USMTM:	Maj. Gen. William Boice
FAA:	Dennis Beres
FIN:	John R. Johnson
IRS:	David Robison
OMPSANG:	Brig. Gen. William L. Nash

Dhahran (CG)
Between Aramco Hdqtrs. and Dhahran Int'l. Airport
P.O. Box 81
Dhahran Airport 31931
• Unit 66803
APO AE 09858-6803
Tel: [966] (3) 891-3200
ADM Fax: 891-7416
COM Fax: 891-8332
CON Fax: 891-6816
EXEC Fax: 891-0464
GSO Fax: 891-3296
Afterhours: 891-2203

CG: David M. Winn
CG SEC: Susan I. McDowell
POL/MIL: Mark L. Andersen
ECO: John R. Sheil
COM: Thomas E. Moore
CON: Helen Bridget Burkart
ADM: Samuel A. Rubino
ITO: Robert A. Klawansky

Jeddah (CG)
Palestine Rd.
Ruwais
• P.O. Box 149
Jeddah 21411 or Unit 62112
APO AE 09811
Tel: [966] (2) 667-0080
ADM Fax: 669-3074
CON Fax: 669-3078
COM Tel: 667-0040
Fax: 665-8106
ATO Tel: 661-2408
Fax: 667-6196
USIS Tel: 660-6355
Fax: 660-6367
workweek: Saturday through Wednesday

CG: Charles L. Daris
CG SEC: Deborah Cherry
POL/ECO: Robert N. Bentley
COM: (Vacant)
CON: Jeanine E. Jackson
ADM: Mark H. Jackson
BPAO: John Moran
CPO: Elizabeth Whitt-Murphy
ATO: David Culver
 (resident in Riyadh)
FAA/CAAG: John Waltz
USGS: Kenneth A. Sargent
USMTM: Ltc. Herbert Holden, USMC

US Rep. to the Saudi Arabian US Joint Commission on Economic Cooperation (USREP/JECOR)
P.O. Box 5927
Riyadh
Tel: [966] (1) 464-0433
Telex: 201012

DIR: William Griever
DEP: Larry Bacon

Senegal
Dakar (E)
B.P. 49
Avenue Jean XXIII
Tel: [221] 23-42-96 or 23-34-24
USIS Tel: 23-59-28, 23-11-85
Telex: 21793 AMEMB SG
Fax: 22-29-91

AMB: Mark Johnson
AMB SEC: Cynthia F. Larre
DCM: Robert J. Kott
POL: Frankie Calhoun
ECO: Carol R. Kalin
RCON: Thomas E. Cairns
ADM: Robert J. McAnneny
RSO: Gary M. Gibson
PAO: James C. Pollock
IMO: Terrence K. Williamson
SAO: Maj. Clark Smith, USA
AID: Anne M. Williams
ODA: Ltc. Paul S. Cariker
SAO: Maj. Clark L. Smith
AGR: Jonathan Gressel
 (resident in Abidjan)
FAA: Ronald L. Montgomery
LAB: Frederick B. Cook
 (resident in Washington, DC)
RETO: Timothy H. Robinson
IRS: Frederick D. Pablo
 (resident in Paris)

Serbia-Montenegro
Belgrade (E)
American Embassy Belgrade
• Unit 1310
APO AE 09213-1310
Tel: [381] (11) 645-655
Telex: 11529 AMEMBA YU
Fax: 645-221

COM Fax: 645-096
CON Fax: 644-053

CM:	Rudolf V. Perina
EXEC SEC:	Phyliss D. Williams
DCM:	Lawrence E. Butler
POL:	Steven L. Blake
ECO:	Harvey S. Lee
COM:	(Vacant)
CON:	Robert E. Sorenson
ADM:	Robert M. Marshall
RSO:	Michael J. Darmiento
PAO:	John Brown
IPO:	George E. Williams
ODA:	Ltc. Robert W. Kershaw, USAF
AGR:	William P. Huth (resident in Sofia)
FAA:	Steven B. Wallace (resident in Rome)
IRS:	Larry J. Legrand (resident in Rome)

Seychelles

Victoria (E)
Box 148
• Unit 62501
APO AE 09815-2501 or Victoria House
Box 251
Victoria, Mahe, Seychelles
Tel: [248] 225256
Fax: 225189

AMB:	Carl Burton Stokes
AMB SEC:	Elka H. Hortoland
CHG/ADM:	(Vacant)
RSO:	Seymour C. Dewitt (resident in Nairobi)
CPO:	Dwight D. Bohnet
AID/REDSO:	Fred C. Fischer (resident in Nairobi)
LAB:	Lois A. Aroian (resident in Nairobi)
FAA:	Ronald L. Montgomery (resident in Dakar)

IRS:	David Robison (resident in Riyadh)

Sierra Leone

Freetown (E)
Corner of Walpole and Siaka Stevens Sts.
Tel: [232] (22) 226-481 through 226-485
AMB Tel: 226-155
DCM Tel: 227-192
Fax: 225-471

AMB:	(Vacant)
EXEC SEC:	Monika Dietrich Jennings
CHG:	Charles A. Ray
POL:	Donald C. Harwick
CON:	Thomas G. Rogan
RCON:	Thomas Cairns (resident in Dakar)
ADM:	Susan M. Selbin
RSO:	James D. Pelphrey
PAO:	Patricia L. Sharpe
IPO:	Paul C. Cox
LAB:	Frederick B. Cook (resident in Washington, DC)
ODA:	Ltc. Paul S. Cariker, USMC (resident in Dakar)
IRS:	Stanley Beesley (resident in London)
FAA:	Ronald L. Montgomery (resident in Dakar)

Singapore

Singapore (E)
30 Hill St.
Singapore 0617
• FPO AP 96534
Tel: (65) 338-0251
Fax: (65) 338-4550

AMB:	Timothy A. Chorba

An Entrepreneur's Directory to Foreign Service Officers **329**

AMB SEC: Virginia Ann Crawford
DCM: Emil M. Skodon
ECO/POL: Charles B. Jacobini
COM: Stephen Craven
CON: Frank C. Turley
ADM: Joseph Hilliard, Jr.
GSO: Martin P. Hohe
RSO: Dale McElhattan, Jr.
PAO: Dennis D. Donahue
IPO: Harry W. Lumley
ISM: John H. Varner, Jr.
ODA: Capt. William P. Cooper, USN
AID/RIG/AUDITOR:
 Richard C. Thabet
AID/IG/I/SFO:
 Philip Rodokanakis
ATO: Robert B. Fondahn
INS: David K. Johnston
SAO: Ltc. Dennis B. Fowler, USAF
CUS: Donald K. Shruhan, Jr.
RSPO: James E. Tyckoski
DEA: Larry M. Hahn
FAA: David L. Knudson
FAA/ILO: Craig Beard
IRS: Charles W. Landry

USIS/American Center MPH Building
Level 4
71-77 Stamford Rd.
Singapore 0617
Tel: [65] 334-0910
Fax: 334-2780
Commercial Services and Library
1 Colombo Ct.
Unit #05-16 Colombo Ct., Building
N. Bridge Rd.
Singapore 0617
Tel: 338-9722
Fax: 338-5010
Telex: RS25079 (SINGTC)
Fax: 338-5010

AGR/ATO OFF
541 Orchard Rd.
Unit 08-04
Liat Towers Building
Singapore 0923

Tel: [65] 737-1233
Fax: 732-8307

USAID/RIG/A
111 N. Bridge Rd.
No. 17-03 Peninsula Plaza
Singapore 0617
Tel: [65] 334-2766
Fax: 334-2541

FAA
Changi Airport Terminal 2
S. Finger, 4th Fl., Security
• Unit 048-002
International Area Office Director
and Field Office
Unit 048-006
Singapore 1781
Tel: [65] 543-1466, 545-5822
Fax: 543-1952 or 545-9722

Slovak Republic

Bratislava (E)
(Int'l) Hviezdoslavovo Namestie 4
81102 Bratislava
Tel: [42] (7) 330861 or 333338
EXEC Fax: 335439
ADM/POL/ECO Fax: 330096
AID Tel: 330667 or 331588
Fax: 334711
Peace Corps Tel: 5222358 or 5220209
Fax: 5222628
USIS Fax: 335-934

AMB: Theodore E. Russell
DCM/POL/ECO:
 Eleanor B. Sutter
POL: Stephen Pipkin
ECO/COM: Eugene S. Young
COM: Peter Repka
ADM: Marjorie Phillips
CON: Sharon V. Hurley
PAO: Helen McKee
AID: Patricia J. Lerner
IPO: Charles Reitz
RSO: Edward F. Gaffney (resident in Vienna)
ODA: Ltc. James Spears

AGR: Francis J. Tarrant (resident in Vienna)
CUS: Ivan E. Taborsky (resident in Vienna)
PC: Robert Blenker
FAA: Steven B. Wallace (resident in Rome)
IRS: Joe D. Hook (resident in Bonn)

Slovenia

Ljubljana (E)
Box 254, Prazakova 4
61000 Ljubljana or AmEmbassy Ljubljana
Department of State
Washington, DC 20521-7140
Tel: [386] (61) 301-427/472/485
Fax: 301-401
AID Tel: 131-5114
Fax: [386] (61) 301-401
USIS Cankarjeva 11 61000 Ljubljana
Tel: 125-8226 or 126-1169
Fax: 126-4284

AMB: Allan Wendt
AMB SEC: Doris Cabral-Jensen
POL/ECO: Mahlon Henderson
ADM/CON: David W. Ball
PAO: Domenick Dipasquale
IPO: (Vacant)
RSO: Edward Gaffney (resident in Vienna)
ODA: Col. John R. Miller, USAF (resident in Vienna)
AGR: Frank J. Tarrant (resident in Vienna)
LAB: John W. Zerolis (resident in Zagreb)
AID: (Vacant)
FAA: Steven B. Wallace (resident in Rome)
IRS: David Robison (resident in Riyadh)

Somalia

Mogadishu (USLO)
This separate Mission was moved in September 1994 to the premises of the US Embassy in Nairobi and renamed the Somalia Liaison Office. The International address is:
Samalia Liaison Office
US Embassy Nairobi
MOI/Haile Selassie Ave.
P.O. Box 30137
Nairobi, Kenya
APO Address: Somalia Liaison Office
US Embassy Nairobi
Unit 64100
APO AE 09831-4100
Pouch Address: Somalia Liaison Office
US Embassy Nairobi
Department of State
Washington, DC 20521-8900
Tel: 254-2-334141, ext. 409
Fax: 214543

Special Envoy: Daniel H. Simpson
DPO: Michael A. Ranneberger
POL: James C. Swan
MLO: Col. Stephen Ward
AID: Ronald E. Ullrich
FAA: Dennis Beres (resident in Riyadh)

South Africa

Pretoria (E)
877 Pretorius St.
• P.O. Box 9536
Tel: [27] (12) 342-1048
Fax: 342-2244
USIS Tel: 342-3006
Fax: 342-2090
AID Tel: 323-8869
Fax: 323-6443

AMB: Princeton N. Lyman
AMB SEC: Barbara Beckwith
DCM: Priscilla Clapp

POL: John Campbell
ECO: J. Michael Cleverley
COM: Millard W. Arnold, Jr. (resident in Johannesburg)
CON: Thomas Auld
ADM: John A. Collins
RSO: Alan M. Nathanson
IMO: Floyd H. Hagopian
PAO: John T. Burns
EST: Michael W. Holshey
AID: Leslie A. (Cap) Dean
FAA: Ronald L. Montgomery (resident in Dakar)
ODA: Col. Kim J. Henningsen, USA
AGR: James M. Benson
IRS: Stanley Beesley

Cape Town (CG)
Broadway Industries Centre
Heerengracht, Foreshore
Tel: [27] (21) 21-4280
Fax: 25-4151
USIS Tel: 461-0503
Fax: 461-303

CG: Charles B. Gurney
CG SEC: Anita Stockdale
ECO/COM: Matthew A. Meyer
CON: Mark T. Hill
IPO: Earle S. Greene
ADM: Stephanie L. Brown
ARSO: Daniel M. Wutrich
BPAO: Janet E. Garvey

Durban (CG)
Durban Bay House, 29th Fl.
333 Smith St.
Tel: [27] (31) 304-4737
Fax: 301-8206
USIS Tel: 305-5068
Fax: 304-2847

CG: Pamela Bridgewater
CG SEC: Karl Johnson
CON: J. Baxter Hunt III
BPAO: Paul Denig

Johannesburg (CG)
Kline Centre, 11th Fl.
Commissioner and Kruis Sts.
• P.O. Box 2155
Tel: [27] (11) 331-1681
Fax: 331-1327
USIS Tel: 838-2231
Fax: 838-3920
COM Tel: 331-3937
Fax: 331-6178

CG: Alan R. McKee
CG SEC: Dorothy J. Rushing
ECO: Alexander P. Bolling
COM: George Kachmar
CON: Richele Keller
ADM: Robert P. Kepner
IPO: James E. Barclay
IMS: Edward C. Saunders
BPAO: William J. Weinhold
MNL: Ruth Miles Henderson
LAB: Thomas A. Shannon, Jr.

Spain

Madrid (E)
Serrano 75
28006 Madrid or APO AE 09642
Tel: [34] (1) 577-4000
Fax: 577-5735
FCS Fax: 575-8655

AMB: Richard N. Gardner
AMB SEC: Jill Sykes
DCM: David N. Greenlee
POL: Richard M. Ogden
ECO: Emil Castro
COM: Emilio Iodice
POL/MIL: Enrique F. Perez
CON: Harry Jones
ADM: William J. Burke, Jr.
RSO: Kenneth E. Sykes
IMO: Bradford W. Ham
PAO: Brian Carlson
AGR: Franklin Lee
LAB: Arlen R. Wilson
SCI: Helen B. Lane

ODA:	Capt. James Tinsley, USN		
ODC:	Col. Judy W. George, USAF		
FAA:	J. Stuart Jamison (resident in Brussels)		
FAA/CAAG:	Rudolph J. Escobedo		
DEA:	George J. Faz		
LEGATT:	H. Enrique Ghimenti		
IRS:	Frederick Pablo (resident in Paris)		

Barcelona (CG)
Reilna Ellisenda 23
08034 Barcelona
• PSC 61, Box 0005
APO AE 09642
Tel: [34] (3) 280-2227
Fax: 205-5206
ADMIN Fax: 205-7764
USIS Fax: 205-5857
COM Fax: 205-7705

CG:	Carolee Heileman
CG SEC:	Marlene Curtain
COM:	Dorothy L. Lutter
CON:	Clyde I. Howard, Jr.
ADM:	Andrew D. Siegel
BPAO:	Angier M. Peavy

Bilbao (C)
Lehendakari Agirre 11-3
48014 Bilbao
• PSC 61, Box 0006
APO AE 09642
Tel: [34] (4) 475-8300
Telex: 32589 ACBIL E
Fax: 476-1240

PO:	Hilarion A. Martinez
CON:	Daniel Ross

SRI Lanka

Colombo (E)
210 Galle Rd.
Colombo 3
• P.O. Box 106

Tel: [94] (1) 448007
Telex: 21305 AMEMB CE
Fax: 437345
USAID 356 Galle Rd.
Colombo 3
Tel: 574333
Fax: 574264
USIS 44 Galle Rd.
Colombo 3
Tel: 421271
Fax: 449070
VOA: 228/1 Galle Rd., Colombo 4
Tel: *589245*
Fax: *502675*
Peace Corps 75 1/1 Kynsey Rd.
Colombo 8
Tel: *687617*

AMB:	Teresita C. Schaffer
AMB SEC:	Donna L. Millet
DCM:	John S. Boardman
POL:	Scott H. Delisi
ECO:	Nicholas H. Riegg
COM:	R. Bruce Neuling
CON:	Anne Winnifred Simon
ADM:	Judith A. Chammas
RSO:	John S. DiCarlo
PAO:	Duncan H. MacInnes
ODA:	Ltc. Carl A. Cockrum
AID:	David A. Cohen
IPO:	James E. Morgan
FAA:	David L. Knudson (resident in Singapore)
AGR:	Thomas Pomeroy (resident in New Delhi)
LAB:	Theodore S. Pierce
IRS:	Charles W. Landry (resident in Singapore)
VOA:	David M. Sites

Sudan

Khartoum (E)
Sharia Ali Abdul Latif
• P.O. Box 699
APO AE 09829
Tel: 74700, 74611

Telex: 22619 AMEM SD
AMB: Timothy M. Carney
AMB SEC: Shirley J. Dickman
DCM: Lawrence N. Benedict
POL/ECO: Lucien Vandenbroucke
CON: Sylvia Johnson
ADM: Gloria Benedict
RSO: James J. Burke
PAO: Jane Gaffney
IPO: Aziz Ahmed
USAID: Robert Russell
ODA: Ltc. Michale J. Berry, USA
REF: Eric P. Whitaker
FAA: Dennis Beres
(resident in Riyadh)
LAB: Lois A. Aroian
(resident in Nairobi)
IRS: David Robison
(resident in Riyadh)

Suriname
Paramaribo (E)
Dr. Sophie Redmondstraat 129
• P.O. Box 1821
AmEmbassy Paramaribo
Department of State
Washington, DC 20521-3390
Tel: [597] 472900, 477881, 476459
USIS: 475051
IPC: 476793
USIS Fax: 410025
GSO Fax: 479289
AMB Fax: 420800
ADM Fax: 410972

AMB: Roger R. Gamble
AMB SEC: Maria Del Rosario Heck
DCM: Ruth H. Van Heuven
POL/ECO: Daniel F. Christiansen
PRA: Robert V. Matthews
CON: David W. Renz
ADM: Eugene Aaron
RSO: Michael Richer
(resident in Georgetown)

PAO: Daniel McGaffie
(resident in Port-of-Spain)
ODA: Ltc. Leocadio Muniz
IPO: John E. Combs
AGR: Larry Senger
(resident in Caracas)
FAA: Celio Young
(resident in Miami)
LAB: Peggy Zabriskie
(resident in Bridgetown)
LEGATT: Rinaldo A. Campana
(resident in Caracas)
DEA: Richard Joyce
(resident in Curacao)

Swaziland
Mbabane (E)
Central Bank Building
Warner St.
• P.O. Box 199
Tel: [268] 46441/5
Fax: 45959
USAID Telex: 2016 WD
USAID Fax: 44770

AMB: John T. Sprott
AMB SEC: Barbara B. Jacquin
DCM: Michael E. Malinowski
POL/ECO/COM:
Richard Mark Kaminski
ADM: Stephen B. Hogard
RSO: Daniel Becker
(resident in Maputo)
PAO: Brooks A. Robinson
AID: Valerie Dickson-Horton
CPO: Joseph M. Suddath
FAA: Ronald L. Montgomery
(resident in Dakar)
AGR: James Benson
(resident in Pretoria)
LAB: Thomas A. Shannon, Jr.
(resident in Johannesburg)
IRS: Stanley Beesley
(resident in London)

Sweden

Stockholm (E)
Strandvagen 101
S-115 89 Stockholm, Sweden
Tel: [46] (8) 783-5300
Fax: 661-1964
CON Fax: 660-5879
FCS Fax: 660-9181
FAS Fax: 662-8495
USIS Fax: 665-3303
ODA Fax: 662-8046

AMB:	Thomas L. Siebert
AMB SEC:	Elizabeth A. Franke
DCM:	Gregory L. Johnson
POL:	Terrell R. Otis
ECO:	Lloyd R. George
COM:	Barbara Slawecki
CON:	Marianne U. Gustafson
ADM:	William J. Haugh
RSO:	Edward E. Fortney
PAO:	Barbara H. Nielson
IMO:	Forrest R. Partovi
ODA:	Col. Scott B. Sonnenberg, USAF
AGR:	Thomas A. Hamby
FAA:	Carl Burleson (resident in London)
LAB:	Hugh M. Neighbour
IRS:	Stanley Beesley (resident in London)

Switzerland

Bern (E)
Jubilaeumstrasse 93
3005 Bern
Tel: [41] (31) 357-7011
Telex: (845) 912603
Fax: 357-7344
CPU: 357-7201
USIS Fax: 357-7379
COM Fax: 357-7336
FAS Fax: 357-7363
ODA Fax: 357-7381

AMB:	M. Larry Lawrence
DCM:	Michael C. Polt
POL/ECO:	L. Allen Nelsen
COM:	Kay R. Kuhlman
CON:	Brian M. Flora
ADM:	Clyde L. Jardine, Jr.
AGR:	Craig A. Thorn (resident in Geneva/USTR)
RSO:	Peter D. Ford
PAO:	Samuels S. Westgate III
IPO:	Jimmie L. McCray
ODA:	Col. William H. Mitchell, USA
IRS:	Frederick D. Pablo (resident in Paris)
FAA:	J. Stuart Jamison (resident in Brussels)

Geneva (BO)
A Consular Agency is now open.
CON AGENT: John J. Kermisch

US Mission to the European Office of the UN and Other International Organizations (Geneva)
Mission Permanente des Etats-Unis
Route de Pregny 11
1292 Chambesy-Geneva, Switzerland
Tel: [41] (22) 749-4111
Telex: 412865 USGV
Fax: 749-4880

CM:	Daniel L. Spiegel
CM SEC:	Sharon Wells
DCM:	Leslie Gerson
IEA (ECO):	Stephen A. Schlaikjer
COM:	Paul Salmon
PSA (POL):	Peter Eicher
REFUGEE/MIG AFF:	John E. Lance
LEGAL AFF:	John R. Crook
ADM:	Ronald B. Rabens
PAO:	Larry R. Taylor
RSO:	Thomas McKeever
LAB:	Nicholas A. Stigliani
CPO:	Richard J. Aber
ISM:	Evelyn U. Putnam

An Entrepreneur's Directory to Foreign Service Officers 335

US Trade Representative (USTR)
Botanic Building
1-3 Avenue de la Paix
1202 Geneva, Switzerland
Tel: [41] (22) 749-4111
Fax: [41] (22) 749-5308

CM:	Booth Gardner
DCM:	Andrew L. Stoler
COM:	Paul Salmon
AGR:	Craig Thorn

US Delegation to the Conference on Disarmament (CD)
Botanic Building
1-3 Avenue De La Paix
1202 Geneva
Tel: [41] (22) 749-5355
Fax: 749-5326

US REP:	Stephen J. Ledogar
DEP REP:	James H. Madden
EXEC SEC:	John H. King
ACDA REP:	Katherine Crittenberger
DOE REP:	Dortohy Donnelly
JCS REP:	Capt. Greg Meyer, USN
OSD REPS:	Brian Knapp
	Ltc. Richard Baker
STATE REP:	Edward Ifft

Zurich (CG)
Switzerland, Zurich
American Consulate General
Zollikerstrasse 141
8008 Zurich
Tel: [41] (1) 422-27-33
EXEC Tel: 422-09-76
ADM Tel: 422-26-50
Fax: 383-98-14
COM Tel: 422-23-72
Fax: 382-26-55

CG:	Sheldon I. Krebs
CON:	Richard H. Wallen
COM:	Anthony J. Belfiglio

Syria

Damascus (E)
Abou Roumaneh
Al-Mansur St., No. 2
• P.O. Box 29
Damascus, Syria
Tel: [963] (11) 333-2814, 333-0788
USIS Tel: 333-1878, 333-8413
Telex: 411919 USDAMA
Fax: 2247938

AMB:	Christopher W. S. Ross
AMB SEC:	Phyllis G. Gain
DCM:	(Vacant)
POL:	Douglas C. Greene
ECO/COM:	David Rundell
CON:	Great C. Holtz
ADM:	Ronald L. Gain
RSO:	Justine Sincavage
PAO:	Alberto M. Fernandez
IMO:	Robert Arriaga
ODA:	Col. William Baker
AGR:	Forrest Geerken, Jr.
	(resident in Cairo)
FAA:	Dennis Beres
	(resident in Riyadh)
IRS:	David Robison
	(resident in Riyadh)

Tajikistan

Dushanbe (E)
Octyabrskaya Hotel
105A Prospect Rudaki
Dushanbe, Tajikistan 734001
Tel: [7] (3772) 21-03-56
Telex: (787) 20016

AMB:	R. Grant Smith
POL/ECO:	Brad Hanson
POL:	Martha Patterson
CON/GSO:	Elizabeth Sharrier
ADM:	Kenny R. Miller
RSO:	Robert F. Valente
	(resident in Tashkent)
AGR:	Larry Panasuk
	(resident in Ankara)
FAA:	Dennis B. Cooper
	(resident in Moscow)
IRS:	Joe D. Hook
	(resident in Bonn)

Tanzania
Dar Es Salaam (E)
36 Laibon Rd. (off Bagamoyo Rd.)
- P.O. Box 9123

Tel: [255] (51) 66010/1/2/3/4/5
Telex: 41250 USA TZ
Fax: 66701

AMB:	J. Brady Anderson
AMB SEC:	Katherine Radcliffe
DCM:	Steven A. Browning
POL:	Siria R. Lopez
ECO:	Michael W. O'Hare
COM:	Alexander C. Tabb
CON:	George H. Hogeman
ADM:	Moosa A. Valli
RAO:	Michael A. D'Andrea
RSO:	Charlene R. Lamb
PAO:	Kili S. Munshi
CPO:	Diane B. Peterson
ODA:	Ltc. Grant C. Hayes (resident in Harare)
AID:	Mark G. Wentling
AGR:	Henry Schmick (resident in Nairobi)
FAA:	Ronald L. Montgomery (resident in Dakar)
LAB:	Lois A. Aroian (resident in Nairobi)
IRS:	David Robison (resident in Riyadh)

Thailand
Bangkok (E)
95 Wireless Rd.
- APO AP 96546

Tel: [66] (2) 252-5040
Fax: 254-2990
COM 3rd Fl.
Diethelm Towers Building, Tower A
93/1 Wireless Rd., 10330
Tel: 255-4365 through 7
Fax: 255-2915

AMB:	David F. Lambertson
AMB SEC:	Loretta Dickson
DCM:	(Vacant)
POL:	Margaret K. McMillion
ECO:	John Medeiros
COM:	Carol Kim
CON:	Thomas P. Furey
ADM:	Jose J. Cao-Garcia
GSO:	Kathleen V. Hodai
RSO:	Gerard J. Lopez
PAO:	John Reid
CPO:	William O. Weatherford
ISM:	Wayne A. Buehrer
ODA:	Col. Edward J. Corcoran, USA
JUSMAG:	Col. Joshua Kiser, Jr. USA
CDC:	(Vacant)
NAS:	Allen E. Nugent
REF:	Edward H. Wilkinson
CUS:	Francisco P. Dominguez
INS:	Daniel Solis
AGR:	Peter Kurz
FAA:	David L. Knudson (resident in Singapore)
FAA/CASLO:	Wendell L. Sims
LAB:	Robert D. Griffiths
IRS:	Charles W. Landry (resident in Singapore)

Chiang Mai (CG)
Vidhayanond Rd.
- Box C
APO AP 96546

Tel: [66] (53) 252-629
Fax: 252-633

PO:	Judith A. Strotz
POL/CON:	Cecile Shea
ADM:	Karl Philip Albrecht
BPAO:	Stephen J. Thibeault

Udorn (C)
35/6 Supakitjanya Rd.
- Box UD
APO AP 96546

Tel: [66] (42) 244-270
Fax: 244-273

PO:	Brevard Stewart
POL:	Paul O. Mayer

An Entrepreneur's Directory to Foreign Service Officers

Togo
Lome (E)
Rue Pelletier Caventou and Rue Vauban
B.P. 852
Tel: [228] 21-77-17 and 21-29-91 through 94
Fax: 21-79-52

AMB:	Johnny Young
AMB SEC:	Patricia A. Collins
DCM:	Jeffrey C. Gallup
ECO/COM/CON:	Whitney Young Baird
ADM:	Marcia L. Norman
RSO:	Charles Hartley
PAO:	Theodore A. Boyd
IPO:	Richard A. Carpenter
FAA:	Ronald L. Montgomery (resident in Dakar)
ODA:	Col. Kenneth A. Hibl, USA (resident in Abidjan)
LAB:	Jon Peter Dorschner (resident in Lagos)
IRS:	Frederick D. Pablo (resident in Paris)

Trinidad and Tobago
Port-of-Spain (E)
15 Queen's Park W.
• P.O. Box 752
Tel: (809) 622-6372/6, 6176
Fax: 628-5462

AMB:	Brian J. Donnelly
DCM:	Joyce Simmons
POL:	Lloyd Moss
POL/MIL:	Timothy Inemer
ECO:	Donald Cleveland
CON:	Sandra J. Campbell
ADM:	George A. Forsyth
RSO:	Thomas A. Barnard
GSO:	Grenville Day
PAO:	Daniel McGaffie
CPO:	Ronnie J. Fontenot
AGR:	Larry Senger (resident in Caracas)
FAA:	Celio Young (resident in Miami)
LAB:	Peggy Zabriskie (resident in Bridgetown)
MLO:	Maj. Daniel Jacobson, USN
ODA:	Ltc. Clark Lynn II, USA (resident in Bridgetown)
NAV:	Capt. Aaron D. Lonquist, USA (resident in Caracas)
LEGATT:	Paul F. Nolan (resident in Bridgetown)
IRS:	Charles Shea (resident in Caracas)

Tunisia
Tunis (E)
144 Ave. de la Liberte
1002 Tunis-Belvedere
Tel: [216] (1) 782-566
Telex: 18379 AMTUN TN
Fax: 789-719
Telex: 14307 USATO
Fax: 785-345

AMB:	Mary Ann Casey
AMB SEC:	Harriett Page
ADM:	Allan V. Ellsbury
DCM:	Warren E. Littrel, Jr.
POL:	Robert O. Blake, Jr.
ECO:	David J. Peashock
COM:	Paul C. O'Friel
CON:	June E. Cochran
RSO:	Doyle E. Cooper
PAO:	James L. Bullock
IPO:	Norman McKone
ISO:	Gregory M. Rice
FSI:	Nazeh Y. Daher
AID:	David Painter
ATO:	Evans "Duffy" Browne
AGR:	Evans "Duffy" Browne
ODC:	Col. Edward Tice
LAB:	Anthony Benesch

ODA: Col. Eugene M. Mensch II, USA
USLOT: Col. James J. Poland, USAF
IRS: Frederick D. Pablo (resident in Paris)
FAA: J. Stuart Jamison (resident in Brussels)

Turkey

Ankara (E)
110 Ataturk Blvd.
• PSC 93, Box 5000
APO AE 09823
Tel: [90] (312) 468-6110 through 6128
Fax: 467-0019
USIS Tel: 468-6102 through 6106
Fax: 467-3624 (EXEC OFF) and 468-6145
GSO Fax: 467-0057
FAS Fax: 467-0056
COM Fax: 467-1366
CON Fax: [90] (312) 468-6131

AMB: Marc Grossman
AMB SEC: Hulya Kilgore
DCM: James H. Holmes
POL: Richard K. McKee
POL/MIL: James K. Connell
ECO: C. Eugene Dorris
COM: James M. Wilson
CON: Lucy P. Uncu
ADM: William Eaton
EST: John L. Brady
RSO: Douglas J. Rosenstein
PAO: David Arnett
IMO: Franklin B. Pressley, Jr.
AGR: Larry L. Panasuk
FAA: Steven B. Wallace (resident in Rome)
LAB: Philip Dale Dean, Jr.
ODA: Col. Ron A. Anthony, USAF
ODC: Maj. Gen. John Welde
IRS: David Robison (resident in Riyadh)

Istanbul (CG)
104-108 Mesrutiyet Caddesi, Tepebasi
• PSC 97, Box 0002
APO AE 09827-0002
Tel: [90] (212) 251 36 02
Telex: 24077 ATOT-TR
GSO Fax: 251-2554
ADM Fax: 251-3632
EXEC Fax: 251-3218
COM Fax: 252-2417
CON Fax: 252-7851

CG: Jerrold Mark Dion
CG SEC: Barbara A. Hering
POL: James B. Bond
ECO: Oscar W. Clyatt
COM: John G. H. Muehlke, Jr.
CON: Roger J. Daley
ADM: Christopher Stillman
RSO: William R. Harmon
BPAO: Donald Terpstra
IPO: Robert L. Hensley

Adana (C)
Ataturk Caddesi
• PSC 94
APO AE 09824
Tel: [90] (322) 453-9106, 545-2145, 454-3774
Fax: 457-6591

PO: Elizabeth Shelton
POL/ECO: Olaf North Otto III
ADM/CON: Steven A. Goodwin

Turkmenistan

Ashgabat (E)
6 Teheran St.
Yubilenaya Hotel
Tel: [7] (3632) 51-13-06, 24-49-25
Fax: 51-13-05
After Duty Hours: 52-03-09
Telex: 064-228-124 USAS RU

AMB: Joseph S. Hulings III
POL/ECO: Douglas Archard

ADM: Lewis Elbinger
IPO: T. Michael Jackson
CON: Benjamin Webber
AGR: Larry Panasuk
(resident in Ankara)
RSO: Robert F. Valente
(resident in Tashkent)
FAA: Dennis B. Cooper
(resident in Moscow)
IRS: Joe D. Hook
(resident in Bonn)
GSO: Michael Dixon

Uganda
Kampala (E)
Parliament Ave.
• P.O. Box 7007
Tel: [256] (41) 259792/3/5
Fax: 259794
ADM Tel: 259792
Fax: 241863

AMB: E. Michael Southwick
AMB SEC: Grace Maxine Wade
DCM: Wayne J. Bush
POL: Janet E. Beik
ECO/COM: Stanley Morris
CON: Beverly J. Berg
CON/POL: Robert Dewitt
ADM: Frank W. Skinner, Jr.
GSO: John Moos
RSO: Doug Allison
PAO: Judith M. Butterman
CPO: Robert E. Claus
FAA: Ronald L. Montgomery
(resident in Dakar)
AID: Donald B. Clark
LAB: Lois A. Aroian
(resident in Nairobi)
IRS: David Robison
(resident in Riyadh)

Ukraine
Kiev (E)
10 Yuria Kotsyubinskovo
252053 Kiev 53
Tel: [7] (044) 244-7349
24 hr. Tel: 244-3745
Telex: 131142 CGKIV SU
Fax: 244-7350
COM Fax: 417-1419

AMB: William Green Miller
AMB SEC: Jacqueline Voorhees
DCM: James F. Schumaker
POL: Bruce Connuck
ECO: Natalie Jaresko
COM: Stephen Wasylko
CON: Walter Davenport
ADM: Harry E. Young, Jr.
RSO: Scott Bultrowizc
IPO: Mark J. Chalkley
PAO: Robert Heath
AGR: Mary Revelt
(resident in Moscow)
ODA: Ltc. John Sherkus
FAA: Dennis B. Cooper
(resident in Moscow)
AID: Gregory Huger
IRS: Joe D. Hook
(resident in Bonn)

United Arab Emirates
Abu Dhabi (E)
Al-Sudan St.
• P.O. Box 4009
Pouch: AmEmbassy Abu Dhabi
Department of State
Washington, DC 20521-6010
Tel: [971] (2) 436-691 or 436-692
Afterhours Tel: 434-457
Fax: 434-771
ADM Fax: 435-441
CON Fax: 435-786
USIS Fax: 434-802
USLO Fax: 434-604
COM: Blue Tower Building, 8th Fl.
Shaikh Khalifa Bin Zayed St.
Tel: (2) 345-545
Fax: (2) 331-374
workweek: Saturday–Wednesday

AMB: William A. Rugh
AMB SEC: Carmen S. Ryan
DCM: Bruce D. Strathern
POL: Stephen L. Kontos
ECO: Paul R. Siekert
COM: Charles Kestenbaum
CON: Michelle M. Bernier-Toth
ADM: Jay N. Anania
RSO: Jeffrey W. Culver
PAO: Magda S. Siekert
IPC: Jefrey S. Myers
ODA: Col. Samuel D. McCormick
USLO: Col. Paul F. Barb
IRS: David Robison (resident in Riyadh)
FAA: Dennis Beres (resident in Riyadh)
FIN: Marvin L. Wolfe (resident in Riyadh)

Dubai (CG)
Dubai International Trade Center 21st Fl.
• P.O. Box 9343
Pouch AMCONGEN Dubai
Department of State
Washington, DC 20521-6020
Tel: [971] (4) 313-115
Fax: 314-043
COM Tel: 313-584
Fax: 313-121
USIS Tel: 314-882
ATO Tel: 313-612/314-063
Fax: 314-998
NRCC Tel: 311-888
Fax: 315-764
workweek: Saturday–Wednesday

CG: David D. Pearce
POL/ECO: David J. Whiddon
POL/MIL: Geoffrey H. Barnes
COM: Terry Sorgi
CON: James J. Turner
RSO/ADM: F. Scott Gallo
ATO: Edwin Porter
ODA: LCdr. Timothy A. Zimmerman, USN
NRCC: LCdr. Raymond Rodriguez
AGR: Edwin Porter

Note: Neither post has access to APO/FPO.

United Kingdom

London, England (E)
24/31 Grosvenor Sq., W. 1A 1AE
• PSC 801, Box 40
FPO AE 09498-4040
Tel: [44] (171) 499-9000
Fax: 409-1637
COM-FCS Fax: 408-8020
CON Fax: 495-5012
The ATO office is closed.

AMB: William J. Crowe, Jr.
AMB SEC: Brooke S. Jaffe
DCM: Timothy E. Deal
POL: Michael J. Habib
ECO: Thomas H. Gewecke
COM: Charles A. Ford
COM rep to the EBRD:
 Thomas Kelsey
CON: Max N. Robinson
ADM: Nicholas S. Baskey
RSO: Clifton W. Flowers
PAO: Michael O'Brien
IMO: Joseph T. Yanci
SCI: Ray Arnaudo
INS: Richard H. Gottlieb
ODA: Capt. Joseph E. Hart
ODC: Col. Russell T. Bolt
AGR: Richard L. Barnes
LAB: Dan E. Turnquist
CUS: Thomas A. McDermott
POLAD: Michael L. Durkee, USNAVEUR
DEA: John W. Featherly
FAA: Carl Burleson
FAA/CASLO:
 Jeffrey Coghill
FIN: William McFadden
SAO: (Vacant)
USTTA: Margaret "B." Corkery

USSS: Barry Smith
IRS: Stanley Beesley
FBI: John Guido

Belfast Northern Ireland (CG)
Queen's House
14 Queen St., BT1 6EQ
• PSC 801, Box 40
APO AE 09498-4040
Tel: [44] (1232) 328-239
Fax: 224-8482

CG: Kathy Stephens
CON: Thomas M. Ramsey
RSO: Clifton W. Flowers
(resident in London)
AGR: Richard Barnes
(resident in London)

Edinburgh, Scotland (CG)
3 Regent Ter. EH7 5BW
• PSC 801, Box 40
FPO AE 09498-4040
Tel: [44] (131) 556-8315
Fax: 557-6023

CG: Bobette Orr
RSO: Clifton W. Flowers
(resident in London)

European Bank for Reconstruction and Development
1 Exchange Square
London EC2A 2EH
Tel: [44] (171) 338-6502
Fax: 338-6487

EXEC DIR: James H. Scheuer
ALT DIR: Lee F. Jackson
COM: (Vacant)

United States

US Mission to the United Nations (USUN)
799 United Nations Plaza
New York, NY 10017-3505
Tel: (212) 415-4050
Afterhours Tel: 415-4444
Fax: 415-4443

US REP: Amb. Madeleine K. Albright
US REP SEC:
  Suzanne McPartland
DEP US REP:
  Amb. Edward W. Gnehm, Jr.
ALT US REP FOR SPECIAL POL AFF: Amb. Karl F. Inderfurth
US REP TO ECOSOC:
  Amb. Victor Marrero
DEP US REP TO ECOSOC:
  John W. Blaney
DEP US REP FOR MANAGEMENT AND UN REFORM:
  Amb. David E. Birenbaum
EXEC ASST: Stuart E. Jones
EXEC ASST WASH OFC:
  Elaine K. Shocas
SPECIAL ADV AND COUNSEL:
  David J. Scheffer
POL: Cameron R. Hume
INT LEGAL:
  Robert B. Rosenstock
PRESS: James P. Rubin
HOST COUNTRY:
  Robert C. Moller
UN RES MGT:
  Linda S. Shenwick
ADM: Wayne K. Logsdon
MSC: Col. William R. Clontz, USA
RSO: Michael Viggiano

US Mission to the Organization of American States (USOAS)
Department of State
Washington, DC 20520
Tel: (202) 647-9376
Fax: 647-0911

US REP: Amb. Harriet C. Babbitt
DEP US REP:
  Sarah R. Horsey-Barr
POL: William W. Milan
ECO: Lee M. Peters

BUD INT ORG:
    Joan E. Segerson
EDUC AND CULT:
    Margarita Riva-
    Geoghegan
ADM: Jay A. Rini

Uruguay
Montevideo (E)
Lauro Muller 1776
• APO AA 34035
Tel: [598] (2) 23-60-61 or 48-77-77
Fax: 48-86-11
AMB: Thomas J. Dodd
AMB SEC: Aili Kiuru
DCM: Gerald J. Whitman
POL: John A. Ritchie
ECO/COM: Robert A. Gehring
ADM: Robert D. Goldberg
CON: Daniel D. Darrach
RSO: James J. Walsh
            (resident in Buenos
Aires)
PAO: Cynthia F. Johnson
IPO: Christopher Bonsteel
AID: Robert J. Asselin, Jr.
ODC/MAAG:
            Col. William A. Jordan,
            USAF
AGR: Max F. Bowser
            (resident in Buenos
            Aires)
CUS: Roberto J. Fernandez
DEA: Leonard H. Williams
LAB: Glenda Gaye Maris
IRS: Charles Shea
            (resident in Caracas)
FAA: Santiago Garcia
            (resident in Rio de
            Janeiro)
PC: Jose Ralls
LEGATT: David W. Shrimp

Uzbekistan
Tashkent (E)
82 Chilanzarskaya
Tel: [7] (3712) 77-14-07, 77-10-81
Fax: 77-69-53
Telex: (64) 116569 USA SU
USIS *Fax:* 89-12-24
AMB: Henry L. Clarke
AMB SEC: Kelly G. Taylor
DCM: Sharon White
POL/ECO: Dorothy Delahanty
ADM: John Gieske
COM: John Breidenstine
PAO: Anthony W. Sariti
RSO: Robert F. Valente
IPO: Robert Popchak
AGR: Larry Panasuk
            (resident in Ankara)
CON/GSO: Joan Polaschik
FAA: Dennis B. Cooper
            (resident in Moscow)
IRS: Joe D. Hook
            (resident in Bonn)

Venezuela
Caracas (E)
Avenida Francisco de Miranda and
Avenida Principal de la Floresta
• P.O. Box 62291
Caracas 1060-A or APO AA 34037
Tel: [58] (2) 285-222 or 285-3111
Telex: 25501 AMEMB VE
Fax: 285-0366
ATO is closed.
AMB: Jeffrey Davidow
AMB SEC: Celestina Renteria
DCM: Robert B. Morley
POL: Thomas M. Tonkin
ECO: Charles Ahlgren
COM: Edgar Fulton
CON: James R. Blanford
ADM: Arnold N. Munoz
RSO: Edward R. Napoliello
PAO: Peter C. Deshazo

IPO:	Richard McCloughan	AMB:	Josiah Horton Beeman
ISM:	Paul D. Lane		(resident in Wellington)
CUS:	Robert Benavente	CHG:	Robert T. Yamate
DEA:	Leo Arreguin	RSO:	John Henry Kaufmann
ODA:	Col. Michael Kenna, USAF		(resident in Canberra)
		FAA:	Fred Laird
MILGP:	Col. Hugh Scruggs, USA		(resident in Tokyo)
		IRS:	Vivian Simon
FBO:	Knox Burchett		(resident in Sydney)
AGR:	Larry Senger		
FAA:	Victor Tamariz (resident in Miami)		
IRS:	Charles Shea		
NAS:	Joel Cassman		
LEGATT:	Ralph Torres		

Republic of Yemen

Sanaa (E)
Dhahr Himyar Zone
Sheraton Hotel District
- P.O. Box 22347

Sanaa, Republic of Yemen
Tel: [967] (1) 238-843/52
Fax: 251-563
USIS Tel: 216-973
Fax: 203-364
USAID Tel: 231-529
Fax: 231-578
workweek: Saturday–Wednesday

Vietnam

Hanoi (USLO)
7 Lang Ha
Ba Dinh District
- PSC 461, Box 400

FPO AP San Francisco 96521-0002
Tel: [84] (4) 431500
Fax: 350484

Chief USLO:	James H. Hall
Deputy Chief:	Christopher W. Runckel
PO SEC:	Patricia R. Limeri
ECO/POL:	Scot A. Marciel
CON:	Charles Neary
GSO:	Richard K. Pruett
IPO:	Carl J. Giampietro
RSO:	Philip E. Jornlin
FAA:	David L. Knudson (resident in Singapore)

AMB:	David G. Newton
AMB SEC:	Loren Mealey
DCM:	Allen J. Kepchar
POL:	Richard Jarvis
POL/MIL:	Peter Enzminger
ECO/COM:	Gregory Hicks
CON:	David Stone
ADM:	Joseph F. Cuadrado
RSO:	Robert Reca
PAO:	John Kincannon
RMO:	Scott Kennedy
ODA:	Ltc. Ted Seel, USA
IPO:	Kenneth Hill
AID:	William McKinney
ATO:	John H. Wilson (resident in Riyadh)
FAA:	Dennis Beres (resident in Riyadh)
IRS:	David Robison (resident in Riyadh)

Western Samoa

Apia (E)
5th Fl., Beach Rd.
- P.O. Box 3420

Apia
Tel: (685) 21-631
Fax: 22-030

Zaire

Kinshasa (E)
310 Avenue des Aviateurs
• Unit 31550
APO 09828
Tel: [243] (12) 21533, 34, or 35
Telecel: (88) 43608
Fax: (88) 43805, ext. 2308 or 43467

AMB:	(Vacant)
CHG:	John M. Yates
DCM:	Gerald W. Scott
POL:	Alfred F. Fonteau
ECO/COM:	Edward L. Williams
CON:	Dale L. Rumbarger
ADM:	Walter Greenfield
RSO:	Kenneth W. Kayatin
PAO:	Mary C. Yates
IPO:	James T. Tuten
AGR:	Jonathan Gesel (resident in Abidjan)
FAA:	Ronald L. Montgomery (resident in Dakar)
AID:	Wayne J. King
IRS:	Frederick D. Pablo (resident in Paris)
ODA:	Mary A. Becka
OFDA:	Lynette Simon

Zambia

Lusaka (E)
Corner of Independence and United Nations Aves.
• P.O. Box 31617
Tel: [260] (1) 250-955 or 252-230
Front Office Tel: 254-301
Afterhours Tel: 252-234
Telex: AMEMB ZA 41970
Fax: 252-225
AID Tel: 254-303 through 6, ext. 212
Fax: 254-532
USIS Tel: 227-993 through 4, ext. 211
Fax: 226-523

AMB:	Roland K. Kuchel
AMB SEC:	Beverly McLaurin
DCM:	Michael Arietti
POL:	Donald Gatto
ECO/COM:	Necia L. Quast
CON:	Donald Heflin
ADM:	Sharon A. Lavorel-Rutherford
RSO:	Jo Ann Moore
PAO:	Stedman Howard
CPO:	Dale Johnson
FAA:	Ronald L. Montgomery (resident in Dakar)
AGR:	James M. Benson (resident in Pretoria)
LAB:	Lois A. Aroian (resident in Nairobi)
AID:	Fred E. Winch
IRS:	Stanley Beesley (resident in London)

Zimbabwe

Harare (E)
172 Herbert Chitepo Ave.
• P.O. Box 3340
Tel: [263] (4) 794-521
COM 1st Fl.
Century House West
36 Baker Ave.
Tel: 728-957
Telex: 24591 USUSFCS ZW
Fax: 796488

AMB:	Johnny Carson
AMB SEC:	Antonette De Melo
DCM:	George M. Staples
POL:	Virginia E. Palmer
ECO/COM:	J. Anthony Holmes
CON:	David W. Abell
ADM:	Stephen J. Nolan
RSO:	Steven J. Chalupsky
PAO:	Lucy Hall
IMO:	Danny D. Lockwood
AGR:	James Benson (resident in Pretoria)
LAB/ECO:	Gregg Morrow
AID:	Peter Benedict
ODA:	Ltc. Grant Hayes

FAA: Ronald L. Montgomery
       (resident in Dakar)
IRS: Stanley Beesley
       (resident in London)

Taiwan

Unofficial commercial and other relations with the people of Taiwan are conducted through an unofficial instrumentality, the American Institute in Taiwan, which has offices in Taipei and Kaohsiung. AIT Taipei operates an American Trade Center, located at the Taipei World Trade Center. The addresses of these offices are:

American Institute in Taiwan
#7 Lane 134
Hsin Yi Rd. Section 3
Taipei, Taiwan
Tel: [886] (2) 709-2000
Afterhours Tel: 709-2013
Fax: 702-7675

American Trade Center
Room 3207
International Trade Building
Taipei World Trade Center
333 Keelung Rd. Section 1
Taipei 10548, Taiwan
Tel: [886] (2) 720-1550
COM Fax: 757-7162

American Institute in Taiwan
5th Fl.
#2 Chung Cheng 3rd Rd.
Kaohsiung, Taiwan
Tel: [886] (7) 224-0154/7
Fax: 223-8237

For further information, contact:
Washington, DC
Office of the American Institute in Taiwan
1700 N. Moore St., Suite 1700
Arlington, VA 22209-1996
Tel: (703) 525-8474
Fax: 841-1385

Abbreviations and Symbols

ACM	Assistant Chief of Mission
ADM	Administrative Section
ADV	Adviser
AGR	Agricultural Section (USDA/FAS)
AID	Agency for International Development
ALT	Alternate
AMB	Ambassador
AMB SEC	Ambassador's Secretary
APHIS	Animal and Plant Health Inspection Service Officer
APO	Army Post Office
ARSO	Assistant Regional Security Officer
ATO	Agricultural Trade Office (USDA/FAS)
BCAO	Branch Cultural Affairs Officer (USIS)
Bg	Brigadier General
BIB	Board for International Broadcasting
BO	Branch Office (of Embassy)
BOB/EUR	Board of Broadcasting, European Office
BPAO	Branch Public Affairs Officer (USIS)
B.P.	Boite Postale
BUD	Budget
C	Consulate
CA	Consular Agency/Agent
CAO	Cultural Affairs Officer (USIS)
Capt	Captain (USN)
CDC	Centers for Disease Control

Cdr	Commander	DSA	Defense Supply Adviser
CEO	Cultural Exchange Officer (USIS)	E	Embassy
CG	Consul General, Consulate General	ECO	Economic Section
		ECO/COM	Economic/Commercial Section
CG SEC	Consul General's Secretary	EDO	Export Development Officer
CHG	Charge d'Affaires		
CINCAFSOUTH	Commander-in-Chief Allied Forces Southern Europe	ERDA	Energy Research and Development Administration
CINCEUR	Commander-in-Chief U.S. European Command	EST	Environment, Science, and Technology
		EX-IM	Export-Import
CINCUSAFE	Commander-in-Chief U.S. Air Forces Europe	FAA	Federal Aviation Administration
CINCUSAREUR	Commander-in-Chief U.S. Army Europe	FAA/CASLO	Federal Aviation Administration Civil Aviation Security Liaison Officer
Col	Colonel		
CM	Chief of Mission	FAA/FSIDO	Federal Aviation Administration Flight Standards International District Office
COM	Commercial Section (FCS)		
CON	Consul, Consular Section		
COUNS	Counselor	FIC/JSC	Finance Committee and Joint Support Committee
C.P.	Caixa Postal		
CPO	Communications Program Officer	FIN	Financial Attache (Treasury)
CUS	Customs Service (Treasury)	FODAG	Food and Agriculture Organizations
DAC	Development Assistance Committee	FPO	Fleet Post Office
DCM	Deputy Chief of Mission	IAEA	International Atomic Energy Agency
DEA	Drug Enforcement Agency	IAGS	Inter-American Geodetic Survey
DEP	Deputy	ICAO	International Civil Aviation Organization
DEP DIR	Deputy Director		
DIR	Director	IMO	Information Management Officer
DOE	Department of Energy		
DPAO	Deputy Public Affairs Officer (USIS)	IO	Information Officer (USIS)
DPO	Deputy Principal Officer	IPO	Information Program Officer

IRM	International Resources Management	PO SEC	Principal Officer's Secretary
IRS	Internal Revenue Service	POL	Political Section
		POL/LAB	Political and Labor Section
ISM	Information Systems Manager	POLAD	Political Adviser
		POL/ECO	Political/Economic Section
JUS/CIV	Department of Justice, Civil Division	Radm	Rear Admiral
JUSMAG	Joint US Military Advisory Group	RCON	Regional Consular Affairs Officer
LAB	Labor Officer	REDSO	Regional Economic Development Services Office
LO	Liaison Officer		
Ltc	Lieutenant Colonel		
LEGATT	Legal Attache	REF	Refugee Coordinator
M	Mission	REP	Representative
Mg	Major General	RES	Resources
MAAG	Military Assistance Advisory Group	RHUDO	Regional Housing and Urban Development Office
MILGP	Military Group		
MSG	Marine Security Guard	ROCAP	Regional Officer for Central American Programs
MSC	Military Staff Committee	RPSO	Regional Procurement and Support Office
MIN	Minister		
MLO	Military Liaison Office	RSO	Regional Security Officer
MNL	Minerals Officer		
NARC	Narcotics	SAO	Security Assistance Office
NATO	North Atlantic Treaty Organization		
		SCI	Scientific Attache
NAS	Narcotics Affairs Section	SEC DEL	Secretary of Delegation
NCIS	Naval Criminal, U.S.	SHAPE	Supreme Headquarters Allied Powers Europe
OAS	Organization of American States		
ODA	Office of the Defense Attache	SLG	State and Local Government
ODC	Office of Defense Cooperation	SR	Senior
		STC	Security Trade Control
OIC	Officer in Charge	UNEP	United Nations Environment Program
OMC	Office of Military Cooperation	UNESCO	United Nations Educational, Scientific, and Cultural Organizations
PAO	Public Affairs Officer (USIS)		
PO	Principal Officer		

UNIDO	United Nations Industrial Development Organization
USA	United States Army
USAF	United States Air Force
USDA/APHIS	Animal and Plant Health Inspection Service
USEU	US Mission to the European Union
USGS	US Geological Survey
USINT	United States Interests Section
USIS	United States Information Service
USLO	United States Liaison Office
USMC	United States Marine Corps
USMTM	US Military Training Mission
USN	United States Navy
USNATO	US Mission to the North Atlantic Treaty Organization
USOAS	US Mission to the Organization of American States
USOECD	US Mission to the Organization for Economic Cooperation and Development
USTTA	US Travel and Tourism Agent
USUN	US Mission to the United Nations
VC	Vice Consul
VOA	Voice of America

State Zip Codes

In conjunction with the U.S. Postal Service's new system of 9-digit ZIP Codes, the Department of State has assigned a unique 4-digit number to each Foreign Service post. All mail sent through the Department's pouch system (for posts without APO/FPO addresses) should add the 4-digit number to the current ZIP Code 20521. For example, the new ZIP Code for Abidjan would be 20521-2010; for Abu Dhabi, 20521-6010. Refer the following list for each Foreign Service post's unique number.

Abidjan	2010
Abu Dhabi	6010
Accra	2020
Adana	5020
Addis Ababa	2030
Algiers	6030
Almaty	7030
Amman	6050
Amsterdam	5780
Ankara	7000
Antananarivo	2040
Apia	4400
Ashgabat	7070
Asmara	7170
Asuncion	3020
Athens	7100
Auckland	4370
Baghdad	6060
Baku	7050
Bamako	2050
Bandar Seri Begawan	4020
Bangkok	7200
Bangui	2060
Banjul	2070
Barcelona	5400
Barranquilla	3040

An Entrepreneur's Directory to Foreign Service Officers   **349**

Beijing	7300	Dar Es Salaam	2140
Beirut	6070	Dhahran	6310
Belfast	5360	Dhaka	6120
Belgrade	5070	Djibouti	2150
Belize	3050	Doha	6130
Berlin	5090	Dubai	6020
Bern	5110	Dublin	5290
Bilbao	5410	Durban	2490
Bishkek	7040	Dushanbe	7090
Bissau	2080	Dusseldorf	5160
Bogota	3030	Edinburgh	5370
Bombay	6240	Florence	5670
Bonn	7400	Frankfurt	7900
Bordeaux	5580	Freetown	2160
Brasilia	7500	Fukuoka	4310
Bratislava	5840	Gaborone	2170
Brazzaville	2090	Geneva (M)	5120
Bridgetown	3120	Georgetown	3170
Brisbane	4130	Guadalajara	3280
Brussels (USNATO - M)	5230	Guangzhou	4090
Brussels (E)	7600	Guatemala City	3190
Bucharest	5260	Guayaquil	3430
Budapest	5270	The Hague	5770
Buenos Aires	3130	Halifax	5500
Bujumbura	2100	Hamburg	5180
Bukavu	2240	Hamilton	5300
Cairo	7700	Hanoi	4550
Calcutta	6250	Harare	2180
Calgary	5490	Havana	3200
Canberra	7800	Helsinki	5310
Cape Town	2480	Hermosillo	3290
Caracas	3140	Ho Chi Minh City	7160
Casablanca	6280	Hong Kong	8000
Cebu	4230	Islamabad	8100
Chengdu	4080	Istanbul	5030
Chiang Mai	4040	Jakarta	8200
Chisinau	7080	Jeddah	6320
Ciudad Juarez	3270	Jerusalem	6350
Cluj-Napoca	1315	Johannesburg	2500
Colombo	6100	Kaduna	2260
Conakry	2110	Kampala	2190
Copenhagen	5280	Karachi	6150
Cotonou	2120	Kathmandu	6190
Curacao	3160	Khabarovsk	5870
Dakar	2130	Khartoum	2200
Damascus	6110	Kiev	5850

Kigali	2210	Moscow	5430
Kingston	3210	Munich	5190
Kinshasa	2220	Muscat	6220
Kolonia	4120	Naha	4320
Koror	4260	Nairobi	8900
Krakow	5140	Naples	5700
Kuala Lumpur	4210	Nassau	3370
Kuwait	6200	N'Djamena	2410
La Paz	3220	New Delhi	9000
Lagos	8300	Niamey	2420
Lahore	6160	Nice	5610
Leipzig	5860	Nicosia	5450
Libreville	2270	Nouakchott	2430
Lilongwe	2280	Nuevo Laredo	3340
Lima	3230	Oporto	5330
Lisbon	5320	Oran	6040
Ljubljana	7140	Osaka-Kobe	4330
Lome	2300	Oslo	5460
London	8400	Ottawa	5480
Luanda	2550	Ouagadougou	2440
Lusaka	2310	Panama City	9100
Luxembourg	5380	Paramaribo	3390
Lyon	5590	Paris	9200
Madras	6260	Perth	4160
Madrid	8500	Peshawar	6170
Majuro	4380	Phnom Penh	4540
Malabo	2320	Ponta Delgada	5340
Managua	3240	Port-au-Prince	3400
Manama	6210	Port Louis	2450
Manila	8600	Port Moresby	4240
Maputo	2330	Porto Alegre	3070
Marseille	5600	Port-of-Spain	3410
Martinique	3250	Poznan	5050
Maseru	2340	Prague	5630
Matamoros	3300	Praia	2460
Mbabane	2350	Pretoria	9300
Medan	4190	Pusan	4270
Melbourne	4140	Quebec	5520
Merida	3320	Quito	3420
Mexico City	8700	Rabat	9400
Milan	5690	Rangoon	4250
Minsk	7010	Recife	3080
Monrovia	8800	Reykjavik	5640
Monterrey	3330	Riga	4520
Montevideo	3360	Rio de Janeiro	3090
Montreal	5510	Riyadh	6300

Rome	9500	Tegucigalpa	3480		
St. George's	3180	Tel Aviv	9700		
St. Petersburg	5440	Thessaloniki	5060		
San Jose	3440	Tijuana	3350		
San Salvador	3450	Tirana	9510		
Sanaa	6330	Tokyo	9800		
Santiago	3460	Toronto	5530		
Santo Domingo	3470	Trieste	5720		
Sao Paulo	3110	Tunis	6360		
Sapporo	4340	Udorn	4060		
Sarajevo	7130	Ulaanbaatar	4410		
Seoul	9600	Valletta	5800		
Seville	5490	Vancouver	5540		
Shanghai	4100	Vatican City	5660		
Shenyang	4110	Victoria	2510		
Singapore	4280	Vienna	9900		
Skopje	7120	Vientiane	4350		
Sofia	5740	Vilnius	4510		
Stockholm	5750	Vladivostok	5880		
Strasbourg	5620	Warsaw	5010		
Stuttgart	5200	Wellington	4360		
Surabaya	4200	Windhoek	2540		
Suva	4290	Yaounde	2520		
Sydney	4150	Yekaterinburg	5890		
Taipei, Ait	4170	Yerevan	7020		
Tallinn	4530	Zagreb	5080		
Tashkent	7110	Zurich	5130		
Tbilisi	7060				

Appendix I
Personality Profile Evaluation for Career Choices

Sample Personality Test*

One of the most influential tools for interpersonal success in business is a psychological theory of Carl Jung's. In 1921, Jung proposed the "type" theory—that is, that each of us is predisposed to certain personality tendencies, which Jung arranged in four dimensions. Some individuals, Jung says, are by nature more extroverted, some more introverted. Some spend their energy handling details while others try to grasp the big picture. Some are predominantly logical, some emotional. Some are data gatherers, while others draw conclusions.

Within this range of personality attributes lie the seeds for most interpersonal conflict in business. It's easy to understand how an individual set upon making decisions can be frustrated by the efforts of a coworker to ferret out more and more details. A manager who operates through logic and objectivity can be driven up the wall by a fellow manager who wants to proceed using seat-of-the pants intuition or heart-of-hearts emotion.

Jung's insights were extended and formalized by Katherine Briggs and Isabel Briggs Myers, developers of the Myers-Briggs Type Indicator; by David Keirsey and Marilyn Bates, in the Keirsey Temperament sorter; and by others.

We offer our own easy-to-score instrument, based on the insights of Jung. We call it the Bell/Smith Personality Assessment.

*Source: Arthur H. Bell and Dayle M. Smith, *Winning with Difficult People* (Baron's Educational Series, 1991) pp. 12–24. Reprinted by permission.

353

Here's how this evaluation works. You enter your "a" or "b" choices on the scorecard after the questions. You can then use your results to understand more deeply your own personality predispositions and tendencies.

Why get to know yourself? Because only then can you understand why certain other personality types are difficult for you. Once you've scored the questions to determine your top four personality tendencies, you can use the following descriptions to understand in detail how these tendencies influence your business life.

By the way, if you're shy about taking personality tests, you're not alone. Many people don't like tests of any kind, especially when the results will be compared with others' results. But take heart: the Bell/Smith Personality Assessment is simply a quick, general guide to some of your most basic habits of mind. You can't fail the test and you can't ace it—and neither can any of your coworkers.

The Bell/Smith Personality Assessment will help you recognize *four* aspects of your personality and behavior from these possibilities:

1. *The Member (M).* This personality trait predisposes you to enjoy the company of others. The Member joins groups willingly, seeks ways to include others in activities, and may tend to avoid tasks that must be accomplished alone. The Member relies on the consensus of the group for important decisions and may hesitate to form or express personal opinions without having them validated first by the group. The Member derives emotional strength and support from belonging, popularity, and the respect of others.

2. *The Self (S).* This personality trait predisposes you to individual initiation and solitary work habits. The Self joins groups only for a compelling reason, and even then only for the period of the task at hand. The Self looks with suspicion upon widely held opinions and group think. When faced by tasks too extensive or difficult for a single person to accomplish, the Self opts to divide work tasks into portions that can each be managed by individuals. The Self derives emotional strength from measuring up to personal standards, not the judgment of others.

3. *The Juggler (J).* This personality trait predisposes you to minute-by-minute, seemingly practical adjustments to changing conditions. The Juggler manages to keep many tasks in progress at once, all in a partial state of completion. The panic of impending deadlines and the unpredictability of interruptions and emergencies are all energizing and challenging for the Juggler. It is a matter of pride to the Juggler that he or she can "handle" situations, "cope," and eventually see projects through to fulfillment. The Juggler derives emotional strength from a

Personality Profile Evaluation for Career Choices

sense of sustained busy-ness as well as a conviction of his or her own specialness and value to the group.

4. *The Planner (P).* This personality trait predisposes you to place details, individual facts, and other data into patterns. The Planner then clings to these patterns tenaciously, for they serve to organize an otherwise bewildering array of discrete items. The Planner is resistant to receiving disorganized data before a plan has been developed; but after the planning state, he or she welcomes information, particularly insofar as it supports the designated plan. The Planner derives emotional strength from a conviction of his or her usefulness, as a shaping influence, on disorderly projects and groups. To a degree, the Planner also derives emotional strength simply from the nature of the plan developed—its symmetry, scope, and interrelation of parts.

5. *The Thinker (T).* This personality trait predisposes you toward finding, or attempting to find, logical links between thoughts, ideas, concepts, facts, details, and examples. The Thinker insists on postponing action until he or she "figures out" the underlying causes, effects, and relative accuracy or truth of mental propositions and assertions. When in a data-gathering mode, the Thinker is intent on "knowing more"; but when in assimilation and ratiocinating modes, the Thinker may reject or postpone new input of any kind. The Thinker derives emotional strength from the satisfaction of reaching logically defensible solutions to problems. Whether anyone acts on the basis of those solutions is less important to the Thinker than the success of the mental processes involved in arriving at them.

6. *The Empathizer (E).* This personality trait predisposes you to focus on the emotional content of situations, as experienced personally or by others. The Empathizer appraises new information or a new situation first according to its emotional potential: How do I feel about this? How do others feel? Who will be hurt? Who will be happy? The answers to these questions play a prominent role in shaping the Empathizer's eventual point of view and action regarding the new information or situation. The Empathizer derives emotional strength from his or her self-image as a sensitive, caring individual and, often, from the gratitude and friendship of those targeted for his or her empathy.

7. *The Closer (C).* This personality trait predisposes you to make conclusions, judgments, and decisive acts (sometimes contrary to established procedures). The Closer is generally impatient with delays urged by others for additional thought, research, or planning. The Closer often grants that the whole truth is not known, but argues that enough of the truth is available for decision making. This personality type can be deaf

to input that does not contribute directly to finalizing projects and processes. The Closer derives emotional strength from his or her reputation in the group as an action-oriented, no-nonsense decision maker and from the satisfaction of having used power and daring to manage difficult problems and personalities.

8. *The Researcher (R).* This personality trait predisposes you to postpone judgment and action so long as it is possible to acquire new information. The Researcher craves certainty and suspects conclusions reached without consideration of all the evidence. The Researcher frequently ignores both time and resource constraints in pressing on with the search for additional data. In communicating that data to others, the Researcher may not be able to successfully organize and summarize the data gathered, since these activities both involve the drawing of tentative conclusions. The Researcher derives emotional strength from the "treasure hunt" excitement of investigation, from the strong influence his or her findings have upon eventual planning, and from the admiration of the group when such findings are announced.

Before determining where you may fit in these personality categories, try a brief experiment with one or more friends or coworkers. Photocopy the following list of questions and have each participant use it as an "answer sheet." Allow each participant to have access to the eight personality type descriptions above. Begin the experiment by having each participant choose a letter from the list of personality type descriptions for each of the following:

As the sole owner of a company, I would choose type _____ for CEO.
As a vice president of the company, I would prefer to work for type _____ as CEO.
As a manager in the company, I would prefer type _____ as my fellow managers.
As a line employee in the company, I would prefer to work for type _____ as my manager.
As a secretary in the company, I would prefer to work for type _____ as a manger.
As a manager, I would prefer to have type _____ as my secretary.
I would prefer to have type _____ as my spouse or significant other
I would prefer to have type _____ as my only child.

Now compare results. Where differences in responses occur, discuss reasons for your choices.

Finally, decide what these results can teach us about dealing successfully with difficult people. Do you understand how easily differing personality types can fall into conflict? The same person you've identified as an S.O.P. (source of pain) may have simultaneously branded *you* an S.O.P. Interpersonal difficulty, in other words, lies in the eye of the beholder.

Determining Your Personality Profile

The following instrument is intended to serve the reader as an approximate guide to his or her personality type. It should be used in conjunction with the Jungian types identified earlier in this chapter.

Directions: Read each question and allow your initial response to guide your answer. (In some cases, you may not have a strong preference for either answer. Choose the answer that you agree with most.)

1. At a social gathering, do you usually
   a. make conversation with many people?
   b. make conversation with only a few people?
2. In learning about a new subject, do you prefer
   a. to follow a step-by-step approach?
   b. to grasp the big picture first?
3. Do your friends value you most for
   a. what you think?
   b. what you feel?
4. Most important achievements have been due to
   a. a lot of hard work and a little luck.
   b. a lot of luck and a lot of hard work.
5. During school years did you consider yourself
   a. popular with many people?
   b. popular with a few people?
6. In learning about a company, would you prefer to hear about
   a. what employees are doing?
   b. what employees may be able to do?
7. In meeting new people, do you form impressions based on
   a. their appearance and actions?
   b. personal chemistry?

8. When shopping, do you select items
   a. carefully?
   b. impulsively?
9. At work do you prefer jobs that
   a. bring you in contact with many people?
   b. bring you in contact with only a few people?
10. In your opinion, is speculation about unidentified flying objects
    a. foolish?
    b. interesting?
11. Picturing yourself as a manager of others, would it be most important for you to be
    a. firm?
    b. friendly?
12. In arranging a deal between parties, would you
    a. make sure all details were spelled out in writing?
    b. allow trivial details to be left to good faith between the parties?
13. Do you consider yourself to have
    a. many close friends?
    b. a few close friends?
14. Do you think national leaders should be
    a. informative?
    b. imaginative?
15. When someone confides in you about a personal problem, do you first
    a. try to think of a solution?
    b. feel sympathy?
16. In romantic relationships, should bonds and understandings between the parties by
    a. stated clearly?
    b. left partially unstated?
17. When meeting strangers, do you
    a. take the initiative in showing friendliness?
    b. wait for sign of friendliness on their part?

18. Should children be raised to
    a. learn practical skills and behaviors as soon as they are ready?
    b. enjoy childhood fantasies as long as possible?
19. In general human affairs, is it most dangerous to show
    a. too little emotion?
    b. too much emotion?
20. In taking a test, would you prefer to deal with
    a. questions with definite answers?
    b. questions that are open-ended?
21. Do you find unexpected encounters with previous acquaintances
    a. enjoyable?
    b. somewhat uncomfortable?
22. Do you prefer a poem that
    a. has a single clear meaning?
    b. has many possible meanings?
23. In voting for a congressional representative, do you favor
    a. an intelligent, cool-headed candidate?
    b. a passionate and well-intentioned candidate?
24. Do you prefer dates that are
    a. carefully planned in advance?
    b. spontaneous?
25. In going out to lunch with friends, would you prefer to eat with
    a. many friends?
    b. one or two friends?
26. Presidents of companies should be thoroughly
    a. practical.
    b. aware.
27. Would you prefer that acquaintances passing through your city
    a. make specific arrangements to see you in advance of their trip?
    b. call on the spur of the moment when they arrive?
28. When given a time for arrival at a social gathering, are you
    a. usually right on time?
    b. usually somewhat late?

29. When on the phone, do you usually
    a. make most of the conversation?
    b. respond in brief comments to what the other person is saying?
30. In general, would you prefer to read
    a. a letter to the editor in a newspaper?
    b. a modern poem?
31. Do you prefer to see movies that
    a. reveal social conditions?
    b. produce tears or laughter?
32. In preparing for a job interview, do you think you should prepare to talk more about
    a. your achievements?
    b. your future plans and goals?
33. If forced to accept dormitory accommodations during a conference, would you prefer to stay in a room
    a. with a few other compatible conference participants?
    b. alone?
34. In general, do you act on the basis of
    a. the situation at hand?
    b. your mood?
35. If you were hiring employees to work for you, should they be primarily
    a. intelligent and creative?
    b. loyal and dedicated?
36. In choosing a name for a child, the parents should
    a. decide upon possible names well before the child is born.
    b. wait until the child is born to settle upon the right name.
37. In making a consumer complaint, would you prefer to
    a. call the company?
    b. write the company?
38. When performing an ordinary work task, do you prefer to
    a. do it in a traditional way?
    b. try your own way of doing it?

39. In court, judges should
    a. follow the letter of the law.
    b. show leniency when they think it is appropriate.
40. If you are given a project to complete, would you prefer to turn it in
    a. by a set deadline?
    b. when you feel it is ready to turn in?
41. When introducing two of your friends who do not know each other, do you
    a. tell them each a bit of information about the other?
    b. let them make their own conversation?
42. Which is worse for an adult?
    a. To be too idealistic.
    b. To be too much in a routine.
43. When you listen to a speech, do you prefer a speaker who
    a. proves his or her points?
    b. feels deeply about what he or she is saying?
44. At the end of the day, do you spend more time thinking about
    a. what you did during the day?
    b. what you will do tomorrow?
45. In planning your ideal vacation, would you choose a place where
    a. you can meet family and friends?
    b. you can be alone or with only one or two friends?
46. Which mental activity appeals more to you?
    a. analysis.
    b. prediction.
47. Which would be more important to you if you were president of a company?
    a. that all employees understood their job responsibilities thoroughly.
    b. that all employees felt part of the company family.
48. If you were a member of a project team, would you prefer to be most active during the
    a. completion stage of the project?
    b. initial conceptualization of the project?

49. In learning a new skill, would you prefer to be taught
    a. as part of a small class?
    b. one-on-one by a tutor?
50. In choosing leisure reading, would you be more likely to choose
    a. a historical novel?
    b. a science fiction novel?
51. In planning your career, should you
    a. plan all career moves well in advance?
    b. go with the flow of opportunity?
52. In writing an epitaph for an admired industry leader, should the inscription pay tribute to the person's
    a. accomplishments?
    b. aspirations?
53. Do you think the primary purpose of meetings in business is
    a. to get to know one another and build team spirit?
    b. to get work done as efficiently as possible?
54. Do you consider yourself as having a good head for
    a. facts?
    b. speculation?
55. The most important quality that employees can have is
    a. individual initiative.
    b. team spirit.
56. As a rule, do you consider yourself
    a. a hard worker?
    b. easygoing?
57. If your employer wanted to honor you at a luncheon, would you prefer that the luncheon be attended
    a. by many company employees?
    b. by your employer and only one or two others?
58. In general, which quality has been more valuable to human progress?
    a. common sense.
    b. inspired insight.

Personality Profile Evaluation for Career Choices

59. What is the best thing that can be said about a retiring employee?
    a. He or she was excellent at his or her job.
    b. He or she cared about fellow workers.
60. At the time they become engaged to be married, a couple should
    a. set a definite date for the wedding.
    b. leave the wedding date open for a while.

Scoring

Transfer your answers as checks in the appropriate spaces below:

1a ___	b ___	2a ___	b ___	3a ___	b ___	4a ___	b ___
5a ___	b ___	6a ___	b ___	7a ___	b ___	8a ___	b ___
9a ___	b ___	10a ___	b ___	11a ___	b ___	12a ___	b ___
13a ___	b ___	14a ___	b ___	15a ___	b ___	16a ___	b ___
17a ___	b ___	18a ___	b ___	19a ___	b ___	20a ___	b ___
21a ___	b ___	22a ___	b ___	23a ___	b ___	24a ___	b ___
25a ___	b ___	26a ___	b ___	27a ___	b ___	28a ___	b ___
29a ___	b ___	30a ___	b ___	31a ___	b ___	32a ___	b ___
33a ___	b ___	34a ___	b ___	35a ___	b ___	36a ___	b ___
37a ___	b ___	38a ___	b ___	39a ___	b ___	40a ___	b ___
41a ___	b ___	42a ___	b ___	43a ___	b ___	44a ___	b ___
45a ___	b ___	46a ___	b ___	47a ___	b ___	48a ___	b ___
49a ___	b ___	50a ___	b ___	51a ___	b ___	52a ___	b ___
53a ___	b ___	54a ___	b ___	55a ___	b ___	56a ___	b ___
57a ___	b ___	58a ___	b ___	59a ___	b ___	60a ___	b ___
___	___	___	___	___	___	___	___ TOTAL
M	S	J	P	T	E	C	R

In each pair, circle the letter that corresponds to your highest core. These suggest dominant aspects of your personality. The letters, of course, refer to the eight personality descriptions presented earlier in the chapter.

How to Interpret Your Scores

Your totals on the scorecard will suggest relative tendencies toward four of the eight possible personality-trait predispositions. The higher the score, the more intense that trait in your total personality.

Why four dominant traits? None of us consistently acts in accordance with one personality pattern. Instead, various traits (such as those you've identified through the Trait Indicator) interact—often in unpredictable ways—to produce the whole personality known as "you."

Let's say, for example, that you have identified yourself as Member, a Juggler, an Empathizer, and a Closer. Read through the descriptions of those personality traits and reflect upon how those traits interact in your personality. Perhaps in times of stress, one or more traits come to the fore. Perhaps some traits are evident at home while others are dominant at work.

What do you gain from such reflection? You come to know your own predispositions more accurately—and, in so doing, prepare yourself to choose companies, colleagues, and a career path that best suit your personality preferences and strengths.

Appendix J
Helpful Reference Guides for the International Job Search

American Firms: Subsidiaries and Affiliates in Brazil (Brazilian Government Trade Bureau).
American Register of Exporters and Importers (American Register of Exporters and Importers, Inc.).
American Subsidiaries of German Firms (German-American Chamber of Commerce).
Asian Markets: A Guide to Company and Industry Information (Washington Researchers Publishing).
Banks of the World (Fritz Knopp Verlag).
Bureau of International Commerce, Trade Lists (U.S. Department of Commerce).
Career Guide, The: Dun's Employment Opportunities Directory (Dun & Bradstreet).
Careers in International Affairs (G. Sheehan, Georgetown University School of Foreign Service).
Current European Directories (G. P. Henderson, CBD Research, Ltd.).
Directory of American Firms Operating in Foreign Countries (Uniworld Business Publications).
Directory of American Firms Operating in Foreign Countries (World Trade Academy Press).
Directory of European Industrial and Trade Associations (Gale Research Co.).
Directory of Executive Recruiters (Kennedy and Kennedy, Inc.).
Directory of Foreign Firms Operating in the United States (Uniworld Business Publications).
Directory of Foreign Manufacturers in the United States (Georgia State University College of Business Administration).

Directory of Japanese Firms and Offices in the U.S. (Japan Trade Center).
Directory of Jobs and Careers Abroad (Vacation Work Publications).
Directory of National Trade and Professional Associations of the United States (Columbia Books).
Directory of Opportunities in International Law (W. A. Stanback, University of Virginia School of Law).
Directory of Organizations Concerned with Environmental Research (State University College at Fredonia).
Directory of Overseas Summer Jobs (D. Woolworth, Writers Digest).
Directory of Resources for Cultural and Educational Exchanges and International Communication (U.S. International Communication Directory).
Directory of U.S. Firms Operating in Latin America (Pan American Union).
Directory of U.S.-Based Agencies Involved in International Health Assistance (National Council for International Health, Washington, DC).
Directory of United States Subsidiaries of British Companies (British-American Chamber of Commerce).
Directory of Work Study in Developing Countries (D. Leppard, Vacation Work Publications).
Dun & Bradstreet Exporter's Encyclopedia (Dun & Bradstreet International).
Dun's Latin America's Top 25,000 (Dun & Bradstreet).
Encyclopedia of Associations (Gale Research Co.).
Europe's 15,000 Largest Companies (ELC Publishing, Ltd.).
Global Marketplace, The (M. Moskowitz, Macmillan).
International Bankers Directory (Rand-McNally).
International Business Travel and Relocation Directory (Gale Research Co.).
International Business Woman, The (M. L. Rossman, Greenwood Press).
International Consultant, The (P. Guttman, Cantrell Corporation).
International Directory for Youth Internships (Council for Intercultural Studies and Programs).
International Directory of Corporate Affiliations (National Register Publications Company).
International Jobs Bulletin (University Placement Center, Southern Illinois University, Carbondale, IL).
Jane's Major Companies of Europe (Jane's Yearbooks).
Major Companies of Europe (Graham & Trotman).
Major Companies of Europe (R. M. Whiteside, ed. Graham & Trotman).
National Job Bank, The (Bob Adams, Inc.).
Newspaper International (National Register Publishing Company).
O'Dwyer's Directory of Public Relations (J. R. O'Dwyer Co., Inc.).
Overseas Business Reports [monthly] (U.S. Department of Commerce, Washington, DC).
Peterson's Guide to Business and Management Jobs (Peterson's Guides).
Peterson's Guide to Engineering, Science, and Computer Jobs (Peterson's Guides).
Principal International Business (Dun & Bradstreet).
Principal International Businesses (Dun's Marketing Services, Inc.).
Study and Teaching Opportunities Abroad (P. McIntyre, U.S. Government Printing Office).

Teach Overseas: The Educator's World-Wide Handbook and Directory to International Teaching Overseas (Maple Tree Publishing Co.).
Technical Assistance Programs of U.S. Non-Profit Organizations (American Council of Voluntary Agencies for Foreign Service).
U.S. Non-Profit Organizations in Development Assistance Abroad (Technical Assistance Information Clearing House).
U.S. Voluntary Organizations and World Affairs (Center for War/Peace Studies).
Ulrich's International Periodicals Directory (Bowker Press).
Who Owns Whom (Dun & Bradstreet, Ltd.).
World Directory of Environmental Research Centers (Orix Press).
World Directory of Multinational Enterprises, The (J. Stopford, ed. Gale Research, Inc.).
Worldwide Chamber of Commerce Directory (Johnson Publishing Co., Inc.).

Index

A2Z, 72
AB Volvo, 150
Accounting positions, 82
AccuFind, 72
Acquisitions editors, 103
Actors, 92
Administrative assistance, financial services/banking, 93
Administrative officers, 257
Advertising, 137-138
   positions, 82-83
      advertising sales, 82
      copy writer, 82
      design layout specialist, 82-83
Advertising sales, 82
Aerospace and armaments industry, 136
AFL-CIO, 237
Agency for International Development, 237
Agents:
   customs, 95
   loan, 94
   real estate, 105
   sales, 100
   talent, 92
   travel, 107
Agricultural Development Council, 237
Agricultural officers, 256
Agriculture, 152-153
AID mission directors, 257
AIESEC-US Association, 237
Airborne Express, 133-134
Airbus Industrie, 136
Airlines Industry, 136-137
Alabama:
   employers with foreign offices, 157-158
   Federal Job Information Center, 241
   U.S. Department of Commerce printed information, 245
Alaska:
   employers with foreign offices, 158-159
   Federal Job Information Center, 241
   U.S. Department of Commerce printed information, 245
Albania, foreign service officers, 260
Alcatel Alsthom, 140
Algeria, foreign service officers, 260
Allen-Bradley Company:
   Inc., 110
      Systems Division, 198
Alliancz AG Holding, 144
Allied Chemical/Menickens, 180
Allied Corporation/Birmingham, 157-158
Allied Domecq PLC, 143
Allied Signal Corporation, 160

Alta Vista, 72
Aluminum Company of America, 202
Amax, 166-167
Amerace Corporation (Elastimold), 123
American Canadian Caribbean Line, 156
American companies/organizations, 2-3
American Council on Education, 238
American Cyanamid Company, 191
American Express Company—Travel Related Services, 116
American Field Service, 238
American Graduate School of International Management, 238
American Greeting Corporation, 124
American Home Products Corporation 195
American Pipe Division/Southwest, 159
American President Companies, Ltd., 132
American Standard, Inc., 111
Ameron Pipe Division/Southwest, 159-160
Amoco Foam Products Company, 204
Amoco Oil Company, 198
AMP, Inc., 115
Amphenol Corporation, 167
AMSCO, 207
Angola, foreign service officers, 260-261
Anheuser-Busch Companies, Inc., 186
Animal and plant health inspection service officers, 256
Announcers/hosts, radio/television, 102
Ansel International, 110
Application package:
   application forms, 30
   and desktop publishing, 34
   personal background statement at end of, 34, 235
   responses to, 31-32
   using a personal contact in, 27-31
Applied sciences position, 83
Appraisers, 94
Architect drafting, 86
Architects, 72
Argentina:
   foreign service officers, 261
   major companies in, 110
Arizona:
   employers with foreign offices, 159-160
   Federal Job Information Center, 241
   U.S. Department of Commerce printed information, 246
Arkansas:
   employers with foreign offices, 169-161
   Federal Job Information Center, 241
   U.S. Department of Commerce printed information, 246
Armenia, foreign service officers, 261-262
Armstrong World Industries, Inc., 116

Index

369

Arthur D. Little, Inc., 183
Art liaison, 83
Art Opportunities, 83-84
Ashland, Inc., 178-179
Asia, Internet job listings, 73
Asian Development Bank, 238
Associated Press, 125-126
Association for International Practical Training, 238
Associations, finding international jobs with, 237-240
Association of Teachers of English as a Second Language (TESOL), 238
AT&T International, 120
A. T. Cross Company, 203
Atlantic Richfield Company/Alaska Region, 159
Atlantis Youth Exchange, 153
Au Pair Company, The, 151
Australia:
  foreign service officers, 262-263
  Internet job listings, 73
  major companies in, 110
  work permit and visa, 62
  World Trade Center, 219
Austria:
  foreign service officers, 263
  major companies in, 111
  work permit and visa, 62
Automotive services position, 84
Auto rental, 84
Auto repair, 84
AVX Corporation, 120
Azerbaijan, foreign service officers, 263-264

Bahamas, foreign service officers, 264
Bahrain:
  foreign service officers, 264-265
  World Trade Center, 219
Baker Hughes, Inc., 130
Bandag, Inc., 133
Bangladesh, foreign service officers, 265
Banking, 93-94, 137
Bank of New York Company, Inc., The, 115
Bank tellers, 94
Barbados, foreign service officers, 265
Barclays PLC, 137
Bartenders, 98
BASF, 215
BASF Group, 138
Bausch & Lomb, Inc., 122
Baxter Healthcare Corporation, 121
Bayer, 215
Bayerische Motoren Werke AG, 149
BCE, Inc., 148
Beatrice/Hunt-Wesson, Inc., 198-199
Bechtel Group, Inc., 113
Belarus, foreign service officers, 265-266
Belgium:
  foreign service officers, 266-267
  major companies in, 111
  World Trade Center, 219-220
Belize, foreign service officers, 267
Bell & Howell Company, 161-162
Bell Helicopter/Textron, 129, 205
Benin, foreign service officers, 267-268
Berlitz Language Centers, 15
Bermuda, foreign service officers, 268
Bertelsmann AG, 147
B. F. Goodrich Company, 199
Bio-Rad Laboratories, 132
Black & Decker Corporation, 110, 180-181
Blind ad, 20-22
Block Drug Company, Inc., 117
Blount/Oregon Cutting Systems Division, 201
Boeing Company, 129

Boise Cascade Corporation, 172
  Specialty Paperboard Division/Pressboard Products, 208
Bolivia, foreign service officers, 268
Bookkeeping positions, 82
Borden, Inc., 112
Borg-Warner Corporation/New Bedford Gear, 182-183
Borland International, Inc., 131
Bose Corporation, 117
Bosnia-Herzegovina, foreign service officers, 268-269
Botswana, foreign service officers, 269
Brazil:
  foreign service officers, 269-271
  major companies in, 112
  World Trade Center, 220
Bridgestone, 215
Briggs & Stratton Corporation, 211-212
Bristol-Meyers Squibb, 112
Bristol-Meyers U.S. Pharmaceutical and Nutrition, 175
British Aerospace, 136
British Airways PLC, 136
British Petroleum Co., PLC., 146
British Telecommunications PLC, 148
Brown & Williamson Tobacco Corporation, 179
Brunei, foreign service officers, 271
Brunswick Corporation, 172-173
  Defense Division, 101-102, 162
BTR Sealing Systems, 177
Bulgaria:
  foreign service officers, 271
  World Trade Center, 220
Bureau of International Aviation, 238
Bureau of International Labor Affairs, 238
Burkina Faso, foreign service officers, 271-272
Burma, foreign service officers, 272
Burnham & Morrill Division/IC Industries, 180
Burns International Security Services, 134
Burr-Brown Corporation, 160
Burundi, foreign service officers, 272
Business brokers, 92-93
Business Council for International Understanding, 238
Business services and advertising, 137-138
Business skills trainers, 91
Buyer, retail/wholesale, 106

Cabinet makers, 86
Cabot Corporation, 123
Cadbury Schweppes PLC, 141
Calgon Corporation, 111
California:
  employers with foreign offices, 161-166
  Federal Job Information Center, 241
  U.S. Department of Commerce printed information, 246
California Pellet Mill Company, 120
Cambodia, foreign service officers, 272-273
Cameroon, foreign service officers, 273
Campbell Soup Company, 188
Canada:
  foreign service officers, 273-274
  Internet job listings, 73
  major companies in, 112
  work permit and visa, 63
  World Trade Center, 220-221
Canon, Inc., 145
Cape Verde, foreign service officers, 274-275
Cargill Incorporated, 117
Carlton Hotel, 169
Carnation Company, 162-163
Carnegie Endowment for International Peace, 238
Carpenters, 87
Carrefour, 142
Casio, 215
Casterbridge Tours, Ltd., 155
Caterers, 98
Caterpillar, Inc., 173

Central African Republic, foreign service officers, 275
Central Intelligence Agency, 238
Cessna Aircraft Company, 177-178
Chad, foreign service officers, 275
Chamber of Commerce of the United States, 238
Charitable/religious organization positions, 84-85
    field worker, 84-85
    fundraiser, 85
    grant manager, 85
Charles Schwab, Inc., 73
Chauffeurs, 89-90
Chemical industry, 138-139
Chemists, 83
Chevron USA (Hawaii Division), 171
Chief of Mission, 256
Childcare Agency, 151
Child/eldercare, 90, 151-152
Chile:
    foreign service officers, 275-276
    major companies in, 113
China:
    foreign service officers, 276-277
    major companies in, 113
Chrysler Corporation, 168
Cifra, S.A., 142
Cigna Corporation, 125
Citicorp, 126-127
Claims processor, 99
Clipper Cruise Lines, 114
Clorox Company, 118
Club Mediterranee, 156, 216
Club Mediterranee SA, 143
Coach drivers, 107
Coaches, 106-107
Coca-Cola Company, 110, 171
Cold calls, 22-27
Coleman Company, 207
Colgate-Palmolive Company, 122
Colombia:
    foreign service officers, 277-278
    major companies in, 114
    World Trade Center, 221
Colorado:
    employers with foreign offices, 166
    Federal Job Information Center, 241
    U.S. Department of Commerce printed information, 246
Colt Industries/Holley Carburetor Division, 186
Columbian Rope Company, 127
Comedian, 92
Commercial Intertech Corporation, 123
Commercial officers, 256
Committee for Economic Development, 238
Communications programs officers, 257
Compagnie de Saint-Gobain SA, 138
Compagnie des Machines Bull, 139
Compaq Computers Corporation, 129
Computer Associates International, Inc., 116
Computer equipment industry, 139
Computer Sciences Corporation, 163
Computing positions, 85-86
    assembly, 85-86
    programmers, 85
    sales, 86
    service, 86
    systems analyst, 86
    trainer, 86
Conagra, 128, 188
Congo:
    foreign service officers, 278
    World Trade Center, 221
Congressional Budget Office, 238
Congressional Research Service, 238
Connecticut:
    employers with foreign offices, 166-168
    Federal Job Information Center, 242

U.S. Department of Commerce printed information, 246
Conoco, Inc., 120, 187-188
Construction:
    materials and furniture, 138
    positions, 86-88
        architect drafting, 86
        cabinet makers, 86
        carpenters, 87
        contractors/contractor's representatives, 87
        electricians, 87
        floor-covering specialists, 87
        glass specialists, 87
        painters, 87-88
        plumbers, 88
        project foremen, 88
        roofers, 88
        structural engineers, 88
Consular officers, 257
Consultant, 88-89
    cultural coach, 88-89
    industrial troubleshooting, 89
    international liasion, 89
    management processors, 89
    market analysts, 89
Consumer appliances industry, 139-140
Container Corporation of America, 171
Contractors/contractor's representatives, 87
Cooks/chefs, 90
Cooper Air Tools/Division of Cooper Industries, 203-204
Copyreaders, 104
Copywriters, advertising positions, 82
Core Laboratories, 114
Corning International, 113
Costa Rica:
    foreign service officers, 278
    major companies in, 114
Cote D'Ivoire, foreign service officers, 278-279
Council on International Educational Exchange, 238
Councils, finding international jobs with, 237-240
Counselors, 96
Credit Lyonnais, 137
Croatia, foreign service officers, 279
Cuba:
    foreign service officers, 279
    World Trade Center, 221
CUC International, Inc., 112
Cultural coach, 88-89
Cuna Mutual Insurance Group, 121-122
Curtiss-Wright Corporation, 191-192
Customs agents, 95
Cyprus:
    foreign service officers, 279-280
    World Trade Center, 221
Czech Republic, foreign service officers, 280

Daiei, Inc., 142
Dai-Ichi Kangyo Bank, Ltd., 137
Daimler-Benz, 216
    Aktiengesellschaft, 149
Dana Corporation/Engine Products Division, 166
Dayco Products, Inc., 134
DDB Needham Worldwide, Inc., 111
DejaNews, 72
Delaware:
    employers with foreign offices, 168
    Federal Job Information Center, 242
    U.S. Department of Commerce printed information, 246
Dell Computer Corporation, 131
Del Monte Corporation, 124
Denmark:
    foreign service officers, 280-281
    major companies in, 115
    work permit and visa, 63
    World Trade Center, 221
Dentsu, Inc., 137

Index

Deputy Chief of Mission, 256
Design layout specialist, advertising positions, 82-83
Desktop publishing, and application package, 35
Deutsche Bank AG, 137
Developmental editors, 104
Dexter Corporation, The, 132
DH Technology, Inc., 119
Digital Equipment Corporation, 126, 194
Dillingham Construction Pacific, 171-172
Dispatchers, 107
District of Columbia:
   employers with foreign offices, 168-169
   Federal Job Information Center, 242
   U.S. Department of Commerce printed information, 246
Djibouti, foreign service officers, 281
Document processors, 94, 95
   real estate, 105-106
Domestic services, 89-91
   chauffeurs, 89-90
   child-/eldercare, 90
   cooks/chefs, 90
   personal secretaries, 90
   residence managers, 90
   security services, 90
   tutors, 91
Domestic work, 151-152
Dominican Republic, foreign service officers, 281
Domino's Pizza, Inc., 129
Dow Chemical Company, 119
Dow Jones & Company, Inc., 128
Dresser Industries, Inc., 122-123
   Wayne Division, 181
Drew Industrials, 178

Eastman Kodak Company, 113
Ebasco Overseas Corporation, 126
Ecology and Environment, Inc., 115
Economic officers, 256
Ecuador, foreign service officers, 281-282
Educational/training sales, 91
Education/training, 91-92
   business skills trainers, 91
   educational/training sales, 91
   language coaches, 91
   teachers, 91-92
   testing specialists, 92
EG & G, Inc., 132
Egypt:
   major companies in, 115-116
   World Trade Center, 221
Egypt (Arab Republic of), foreign service officers, 282-283
E.I. Du Pont de Nemours, 168
Electricians, 87
Electric Library, 72
Electronic equipment industry, 140-141
Elf Aquitaine, 146
Eli Lilly and Company, 110, 175
Elizabeth Arden Company, 122
El Salvador, foreign service officers, 283
Embassies obtaining information and applications from, 229-235
Embassy attaches, 96
Emerson Electric Co., 186-187
Emery Worldwide, 124
Emhart Corporation/Warren Division, 184
Employment, *See* International employment
Encyclopedia Britanica, Inc., 121
Engineers, 83
English, teaching, 153
English Language School International, 154
Entertainment, 92
   talent agents, 92
Entrepreneurial ventures, 92-93
   business broker, 92-93
   franchiser, 93
   small business owner, 93

   venture capitalist, 93
Environment, science and technology (EST) officers, 256
Equatorial Guinea, foreign service officers, 283-284
Ernst & Young, 118
ESCO Corporation, 200-201
Estonia, foreign service officers, 284
Ethiopia, foreign service officers, 284
Eurocamp Summer Jobs, 156
Euro Disney, 155-156
Euro-Pair Agency, 151
Europe, Internet job listings, 74
Evergreen Group, 142
Excite, 72
Exxon Chemical Company, 114

Fabricator, 94-95
Falk Corporation, Inc., 112
Fax machine, 32
Federal Republic of Germany, foreign service officers, 288-290
F. Hoffmann-La Roche, 216
Fiat, 216
Fiat SPA, 149
Figgie International, Inc., 121
Fiji, foreign service officers, 285
Financial attachés, 256
Financial services/banking, 93-94
   administrative assistance, 93
   appraisers, 94
   bank tellers, 94
   document processors, 94
   investment/portfolio managers, 94
   loan agents, 94
Finland:
   foreign service officers, 285
   major companies in, 116
   work permit and visa, 63
Firestone Tire and Rubber Company, 163
Fitness instructors, 107
Fletcher Challenge Ltd., 138
Floor-covering specialists, 87
Florida:
   employers with foreign offices, 169-170
   Federal Job Information Center, 242
   U.S. Department of Commerce printed information, 247
Fluor Corporation, 163-164
FMC Corporation Spring Hill Plant, 210
Food and beverage products, 141-142
Food preparation, 98
Ford foundation, 238
Foreign Agriculture Service, 238
Foreign-based companies with U.S. offices, 215-218
Foreign Commercial Service, 238
Foreign service officers, 255-353
Formosa Plastics Corporation, 138
Foster Parents Plan International, 238
France:
   foreign service officers, 285-287
   major companies in, 116-117
   work permit and visa, 63
   World Trade Center, 221-222
Franchiser, 93
Freeport-McMoran, Inc., 119
Freight and shipping, 142
Fried, Krupp AG Hoesch-Krupp, 145
Fritz Companies, 117
Fruehauf Corporation, 202
Fuji Photo Film Co., Ltd., 147
Fujitsu, Ltd., 139
"Full disclosure" advertising, 22
Fuller Company, 131
Fundraiser, 85

Gabon, foreign service officers, 287
GAF Corporation, 184
Gallery sales management, 84

Gambia, foreign service officers, 287
Gannett Company, Inc., 132
Garment industry, 94-95
  fabricator, 94-95
  modeling, 95
  promotions, 95
  sales representative, 95
Garrett Aireseach, 164
General Accounting Office (GAO), 238
General Dynamics Corporation, 133
General Electric Company (GE), 115
General Foods Corporation, 201
General Instrument Corporation, 123
General merchandise, 142-143
General Motors Corporation (GM), 115
General Services Administration (GSA), 238
General Tire, Inc., 128
Genesco, Inc., 186
Georgia:
  employers with foreign offices, 170-171
  Federal Job Information Center, 242
  foreign service officers, 287-288
  U.S. Department of Commerce printed information, 247
Georgia-Pacific Corporation, 207-208
Gerber Products Company, 114
Gerber Scientific, 167
Germany:
  major companies in, 117
  work permit and visa, 63
Getz Brothers Company, Inc., 164
Ghana, foreign service officers, 290
Glass specialists, 87
Global resources, Internet job listings, 74
Goldman Sachs & Company, 113
Goodyear Tire & Rubber Company, 114
Government, 95-96
  customs agents, 95
  document processors, 95
  embassy attaches, 96
  public services, 96
Government agencies, finding international jobs with, 237-240
Grace Offshore, 180
Grant managers, 85
Graphics specialists, 104
Greece:
  foreign service officers, 290-291
  major companies in, 117-118
  work permit and visa, 64
Grenada, foreign service officers, 291
Greyhound Corporation, 164
Grooming/care, pets, 103
Groupe Danone, 141
Group sales, 98
Guardian Industries Corporation, 119
Guatemala, foreign service officers, 291
Guide, tours, 107
Guinea, foreign service officers, 292
Guinea-Bissau, foreign service officers, 292
Guinness PLC, 141
Guyana, foreign service officers, 292-293

Haiti, foreign service officers, 293
Harley-Davidson, Inc., 212
Havas S.A., 147
Hawaii:
  employers with foreign offices, 171-172
  U.S. Department of Commerce printed information, 247
Healthcare, 96-97
  counselors, 96
  health plan sales/administration, 96
  hospital maintenance workers, 96
  laboratory/diagnostic technicians, 96-97
  massages, 97
  nurses, 97
  office administrators/assistants, 97
  personal health assistants, 97
  physicians, 97
Health plan sales/administration, 96
Heineken, 216
Helene Curtis Industries, Inc., 125
Hertz Corporation, 131, 186
Hess Language School, 154
Hewlett-Packard Company, 164-165
Hitachi, 140, 216
H.J. Heinz Company, 125
Hobart Corporation, 205-206
Hoechst AG, 138
Holiday Inns Worldwide, 112, 205
Holy See, The, foreign service officers, 293
Honda Motor Co., Ltd., 149
Honduras, foreign service officers, 293-294
Hong Kong:
  foreign service officers, 294
  major companies in, 118
  World Trade Center, 222
Hong Kong Telecommunications, Ltd., 148
Hospitality industry, 98
  bartenders, 98
  caterers, 98
  food preparation, 98
  hotel/restaurant management, 98
  promotions/group sales, 98
  waiters, 98
Hospital maintenance workers, 96
HotBot, 72
Hotel/restaurant management, 98
Hotel Sofitel, 156
Hotels/restaurants, 143
Household products, 143
House writers, 104
Hungary:
  foreign service officers, 294-295
  major companies in, 118-119
  World Trade Center, 222
Hunt Consolidated, Inc., 206
Hyatt International Corporation, 156
Hyundai, 216

IBM Infomarket, 72
Iceland, foreign service officers, 295
ICF Kaiser Engineers, 128
Idaho:
  employers with foreign offices, 172
  U.S. Department of Commerce printed information, 247
Illinois:
  employers with foreign offices, 172-174
  Federal Job Information Center, 242
  U.S. Department of Commerce printed information, 247
Immigration and Naturalization Service officers, 257
IMO Industries, 131
Import/export, 99
  merchandisers, 99
  sales representatives, 99
  shipping specialists, 99
Inco Ltd., 145
India:
  foreign service officers, 295-296
  major companies in, 119
  work permit and visa, 64
  World Trade Center, 222
Indiana:
  employers with foreign offices, 174-175
  Federal Job Information Center, 242
  U.S. Department of Commerce printed information, 248
Indonesia:
  foreign service officers, 296-297
  major companies in, 119-120

Index

World Trade Center, 222
Industrial troubleshooting, 89
Information services, 147-148
Information systems managers, 257
InfoSeek, 72
Ingersoll-Rand Company, 111
Inlingua Schools of Language, 15
Inland Motor/Kollmorgen Corporation, 208-209
Institute of International Education, 238
Insurance, 99-100
  claims processors, 99
  office managers/administrative assistants, 99
  sales agents, 100
Insurance industry, 144
Intel Corporation, 127
Inter-American Development Bank, 238
Inter-Exchange, 152
Interior design/decorating, 100
Interlingua Centre, 151
International Association for the Exchange of Students for Technical Experience, 239
International Atomic Energy Agency, 239
International Center for Language Studies, 15
International Data Group, Inc., 133
International Development Corporation Agency, 239
International employers, making direct contact with, 3
International employment:
  advise about seeking, 39-44
  application packages, 19-38
  benefits of choosing, 3-5
  and blind ads, 20-22
  career field, choosing, 13-14
  and cold calls, 22-27
  contents of, 19
  and "full disclosure" advertising, 22
  languages, 14-16
  myths about, 6-8
  work experience, 16-17
International Fund for Agricultural Development, 239
International Institute for Studies and Training, 239
International job interviews:
  accepting/postponing/refusing an international job offer, 54-56
  after the interview, 53-56
  appearance, 46
  eye contact, 48
  first impressions, 47
  impressions of the office staff, 46
  interruptions, dealing with, 48
  interview answers, 47, 48-49
  preparing for, 45-56
  questions
    about attitudes and intelligence, 50-53
    about education, 49
    about skills and work experience, 49-50
International League for Human Rights, 239
International liasion, 89
International Monetary Fund, 239
International Paper Pine Bluff Mill, 161
International representative, art, 84
International resumes, 33-38
  samples of, 35-38
International Schools Association, 239
International School Services, 154
International Trade Administration, 239
Internet:
  finding jobs abroad through, 71-80
  job sites on, 72-74, 75-80
  Monster Board, 74-75
  searching for company job listings on, 72
Investment/portfolio managers, 94
Iowa:
  employers with foreign offices, 175-177
  Federal Job Information Center, 242

U.S. Department of Commerce printed information, 248
Iraq, foreign service officers, 297
Ireland:
  foreign service officers, 297
  major companies in, 120
  work permit and visa, 64
Israel:
  foreign service officers, 297-298
  major companies in, 120-121
  work permit and visa, 64
  World Trade Center, 222
Italy:
  foreign service officers, 298-299
  major companies in, 121
  work permit and visa, 64
  World Trade Center, 222-223
Ito-Yokado Co., Ltd., 142
ITT Corporation, 116
Ivory Coast, World Trade Center, 223

Jamaica:
  foreign service officers, 299-300
  major companies in, 121-122
James River Corporation, 133
Japan:
  foreign service officers, 300-301
  major companies in, 122
  work permit and visa, 64-65
  World Trade Center, 223
J. C. Penney Company, Inc., 133, 169
Job interview, *See* International job interview
Johnson & Johnson, 118
Johnson Control, Inc. Automotive Systems Group, 184
John Wiley & Sons, Inc., 197
Jordan, foreign service officers, 301-302
Journalists, 104

Kansas:
  employers with foreign offices, 177-178
  Federal Job Information Center, 242
  U.S. Department of Commerce printed information, 248
Kazakstan, foreign service officers, 302
Kendall International, 133
Kentucky:
  employers with foreign offices, 178-179
  Federal Job Information Center, 242
  U.S. Department of Commerce printed information, 248
Kenya, foreign service officers, 302
Key Officers Guide, 256
KFC Corporation, 123
Kikkoman, 216
Kimberly-Clark Corporation, 120
Kirin Brewery Co., Ltd., 141
KLM Royal Dutch Airlines, 136
Knoll International, 134
Korea, foreign service officers, 303
Kraft General Foods International, 118
Kuwait:
  foreign service officers, 303
  major companies in, 122-123
Kyrgyzstan, foreign service officers, 303-304

Laboratory/diagnostic technicians, 96-97
Laboratory technician positions, 83
Labor officers, 257
L. A. Gear, Inc., 130
Language coaches, 91
Languages, 14-16
Language schools, 15-16
Laos, foreign service officers, 304
Latvia, foreign service officers, 304-305
Layout/design specialists, 104-105
Lebanon, foreign service officers, 305
Legal attachés, 257

Legal/paralegal services, 100
Lesotho, foreign service officers, 305
Levi Strauss Associates, Inc., 127
Liberia, foreign service officers, 305-306
Line workers, 100
Linguex, 15
Lintas: Worldwide, 119
Liquid Carbonic Corporation, 127
Lithuania, foreign service officers, 306
Litton Industries, Inc., 130
Lloyd's of London, 144
Loan agents, 94
Lockheed Corporation, 165
London Au Pair & Nanny Agency, 151
L'Oreal SA, 143
Lotus Development Corporation, 120
Louisiana:
  employers with foreign offices, 179-180
  Federal Job Information Center, 242
  U.S. Department of Commerce printed information, 248
LTV Steel Co., 121
Lubrizol Corporation, 113
Luxembourg:
  foreign service officers, 306
  major companies in, 123
  work permit and visa, 65
Lycos, 72

McCann-Erickson Worldwide, 113
Macedonia, foreign service officers, 307
McKinley Group, Inc., 72
McKinsey & Company, Inc., 116
MacMillan Bloedel Ltd., 147
Macro Systems, Inc., 119
Madagascar, foreign service officers, 307
Magellan, 72
Maiawi, foreign service officers, 307
Maico Hearing Instruments, Inc., 185
Mail merge, 26
Maine:
  employers with foreign offices, 180
  Federal Job Information Center, 242
  U.S. Department of Commerce printed information, 248
Malaysia:
  foreign service officers, 307-308
  major companies in, 123-124
  World Trade Center, 223
Mali, foreign service officers, 308
Malta, foreign service officers, 308-309
Management processes, 89
Manufacturer's representatives, 100-101
Manufacturing, 100-101
  line workers, 100
  manufacturer's representatives, 100-101
  mechanical specialists, 101
  personnel specialists, 101
  process engineers, 101
  quality inspectors, 101
  training specialists, 101
Manville Sales, 210-211
Marathon Oil, 213
Marine biologists, 83
Maritime Administration, 239
Markem Corporation, 189
Market analysts, 89
Marriott Corporation, 156
Marshall Islands, foreign service officers, 309
Maryland:
  employers with foreign offices, 180-181
  Federal Job Information Center, 242
  U.S. Department of Commerce printed information, 248
Masonite Corporation, 130

Massachusetts:
  employers with foreign offices, 181-183
  Federal Job Information Center, 242
  U.S. Department of Commerce printed information, 248
Massages, 97
Matco, 176
Matsushita Electric, 139, 216
Mattel, Inc., 132
Mauritania, foreign service officers, 309
Mauritius, foreign service officers, 309
McGraw-Hill Companies, Inc., The, 196
Mead Container, 173-174
Mechanic, 108
Mechanical specialists, 101
Media (radio/television), 102
Medical products (pharmaceuticals), 144
Medtronic, Inc., 125
Memorex/Telex Computer Products, Inc., 200
Merchandisers, 99
Merck & Company, Inc., 117
MetaCrawler, 72
Metals and mining, 145
Mexico:
  foreign service officers, 310-312
  major companies in, 124
  work permit and visa, 65
Michelin, 216
Michigan:
  employers with foreign offices, 183-184
  Federal Job Information Center, 242
  U.S. Department of Commerce printed information, 248
Micronesia, foreign service officers, 312
Military installations, temporary employment at, 155
Minnesota:
  employers with foreign offices, 184-185
  Federal Job Information Center, 242
  U.S. Department of Commerce printed information, 249
Minolta Co., Ltd., 147
Mississippi:
  employers with foreign offices, 185-186
  Federal Job Information Center, 242
  U.S. Department of Commerce printed information, 249
Missouri, 186-187
  employers with foreign offices, 186-187
  Federal Job Information Center, 242
  U.S. Department of Commerce printed information, 249
Modeling, 95
Modern Language Association, 239
Modine Manufacturing Company, 111
Moldova, foreign service officers, 312
Mongolia, foreign service officers, 312-313
Monsanto Company, 126
Monster board, 74-75
Montana:
  employers with foreign offices, 187
  Federal Job Information Center, 242
  U.S. Department of Commerce printed information, 249
Moore Corporation Ltd., 145
Morocco:
  foreign service officers, 313
  work permit and visa, 65
Motorola, Inc., 112, 194-195
Motorola Radio Products Group, 169-170
Mozambique, foreign service officers, 313
MPB Corporation, 190
Musicians, 92
Mutual/United of Omaha Insurance Co., 188-189
M. W. Kellogg Company, 206

Nalco Chemical Company, 114
Namibia, foreign service officers, 314
National Association for Foreign Student Affairs, 239
National Association of Foreign Trade Zones, 239
National Can Corporation, 181-182

Index

National Foreign Trade Council, 239
National Geographic Society, 239
National Science Foundation, 239
National Semiconductor Corporation, 133
Nature et Progres, 153
Nebraska:
  employers with foreign offices, 187-188
  Federal Job Information Center, 242
  U.S. Department of Commerce printed information, 249
NEC Corporation, 140, 217
Nepal, foreign service officers, 314
Nestle, Ltd., 141, 217
Netherlands:
  foreign service officers, 314-315
  major companies in, 124-125
  work permit and visa, 65
  World Trade Center, 223
Netherlands Antilles, foreign service officers, 315
Nevada:
  employers with foreign offices, 188
  Federal Job Information Center, 242
  U.S. Department of Commerce printed information, 249
New Hampshire:
  employers with foreign offices, 189-190
  Federal Job Information Center, 243
  U.S. Department of Commerce printed information, 249
New Jersey:
  employers with foreign offices, 190-193
  U.S. Department of Commerce printed information, 249
New Mexico:
  employers with foreign offices, 193-194
  Federal Job Information Center, 243
  U.S. Department of Commerce printed information, 249
Newsweek International, 127
New York:
  employers with foreign offices, 194-198
  Federal Job Information Center, 243
  U.S. Department of Commerce printed information, 250
New Zealand:
  foreign service officers, 315
  major companies in, 125
  work permit and visa, 65-66
Nicaragua, foreign service officers, 315-316
Niger, foreign service officers, 316
Nigeria:
  foreign service officers, 316-317
  World Trade Center, 223
Nintendo Co., Ltd., 139
Nippon Steel Corporation, 145
Nippon Telegraph and Telephone Corp., 148
Non-U.S. nationals, working legally in the U.S., 67-69
Norplex Division/Allied Signal, 176
North Carolina:
  Federal Job Information Center, 243
  U.S. Department of Commerce printed information, 250
North Dakota:
  employers with foreign offices, 198
  Federal Job Information Center, 243
  U.S. Department of Commerce printed information, 250
Northern Telecom, Inc., 185
Northrop Grumman Corporation, 195-196
Northwest Airlines, Inc., 122
Norway:
  foreign service officers, 317
  major companies in, 125-126
  work permit and visa, 66
Novo Nordisk A/S, 144
Nurses, 97

Occidental Chemical PVC Divisions, 202-203
Office administrators/assistants, 97
Office equipment, 145-146
Office of International Health, 239
Office managers/administrative assistants, 99

Ogilvy & Mather, 124
Ohio:
  employers with foreign offices, 198-200
  Federal Job Information Center, 243
  U.S. Department of Commerce printed information, 250
Oil and gas industry, 146
Oki Electric Industry Co., Ltd., 140
Okista, 151
Oklahoma:
  employers with foreign offices, 200-201
  Federal Job Information Center, 243
  U.S. Department of Commerce printed information, 250
Olin Defense Systems Group, 209
Olivetti Group, 139
Oman, foreign service officers, 317-318
Open Text, 72
Operation Crossroads Africa, 239
Oregon:
  employers with foreign offices, 201-202
  Federal Job Information Center, 243
  U.S. Department of Commerce printed information, 250
Organization of American States, 239
Oscar Mayer Foods Corporation, 212
Osram Sylvania, Inc., 189-190
Otis Elevator Company: World Headquarters, 118
Overseas Education Association, 239
Owens-Illinois, Inc., 192-193
  Machine Division, 174
Ozite Corporation, 174

Pacific Architects & Engineers, Inc., 128
Packard-Hughes Interconnect, 160-161
Paine Webber, 166
Painters, 87-88
Pakistan:
  foreign service officers, 318-319
  major companies in, 126
Palau, foreign service officers, 319
Panama, foreign service officers, 319-320
Paper and lumber products, 147
Papua New Guinea, foreign service officers, 320
Paraguay, foreign service officers, 320
Parke Davis-Rochester, 184
Parker Drilling Company, 123
Passports, 57-59
  obtaining, 58-59
  regional passport agencies, 59
Peace Corps, 239
Pearson, 217
Pennsylvania:
  employers with foreign offices, 202-203
  Federal Job Information Center, 243
  U.S. Department of Commerce printed information, 250-251
Penrod Drilling Corporation, 118
People's Republic of China, World Trade Center, 223-224
Pepsico Foods International, 134
Perkin-Elmer Corporation, 131
Perrier, 215
Personal health assistants, 97
Personality profile evaluation, 353-364
Personal secretary, 90
Personnel specialists, 101
Peru:
  foreign service officers, 320-321
  major companies in, 126-127
Petrofina SA, 146
Petroleos de Venezuela, 146
Pet services, 103
Pfizer, Inc., 117
Philip Morris Companies, Inc., 196
Philippines:
  foreign service officers, 321-322

major companies in, 127
Philips, 217
Philips Electronics N.V., 140
Philips Petroleum Company, 126
Phillips-Van Heusen Corporation, 112
Photographers, 105
Photographic equipment, 147
Physicians, 97
Pillsbury Company, 185-186
Pinkerton's, Inc., 187
Pirelli SPA, 150
Pitney Bowes, Inc., 132, 209
Pittway Corporation, 110
Playskool, Inc., 203
Playtex Apparel, Inc., 124
Plumbers, 88
Point, 72
Poland:
   foreign service officers, 322
   major companies in, 127-128
Political officers, 257
Portugal:
   foreign service officers, 323
   major companies in, 128
   work permit and visa, 66
   World Trade Center, 224
PPG Industries, 211
Premark International, Inc., 110
Primerica Corporation, 121
Printers, 105
Process engineers, 101
Pro Filia, 152
Programmers, 85
Program specialists, radio/television, 102
Project foremen, 88
Promotions, 95, 98
Property management, 106
PSA Peugeot Citrogen, 149
Public afairs officers, 257
Public services, 96
Publishing, 103
   acquisitions editor, 103
   copyreaders, 104
   developmental editors, 104
   graphics specialists, 104
   house writers, 104
   and information services, 147-148
   journalists, 104
   layout/design specialists, 104-105
   photographers, 105
   printers, 105
   sales/marketing representatives, 105
Puerto Rico, U.S. Department of Commerce printed information, 251

Qatar, foreign service officers, 323
Quaker Chemical Corporation, 130
Quality inspectors, 101
Quantas Airways United, 136
Quantegy, Inc., 158
Quebecor, Inc., 137

Ralston Purina Company, 113, 166
Rank Organization PLC, 143
Rayovac Corporation, 212-213
Raytheon Company, 123, 183
Real estate, 105-106
   agents, 105
   document procesors, 105-106
   property management, 106
Reckitt & Colman, PLC, 143
Redken Laboratories, Inc., 125
Reed Tool Company, 129
Regional passport agencies, 59

Regional security officers, 257
Relaciones Culturales Internacionales, 152
Relations Internaationales, 152
Reliance Electric Company, 131
Residence managers, 90
Resistoflex Company/Division of Crane Company, 197-198
Resort work, 156
Resource officers, 256
Retail sales, automobiles, 84
Retail/wholesale, 106
Reuters Holdings PLC, 147
Revlon, Inc., 161
Reynolds Metals Company, 122
Rhode Island:
   employers with foreign offices, 203-204
   Federal Job Information Center, 243
   U.S. Department of Commerce printed information, 251
Rhone-Poulenc S.A., 139
Ricoh Company, Ltd., 145
Riegel Textile Corporation, 204
Roche Group, 144
Rockefeller Foundation, 239
Rockwell International Corporation, 130
   Avionics Group, 176-177
Rohm & Haas Company, 124
Rolls-Royce PLC, 136
Romania, foreign service officers, 323-324
Roofers, 88
Rosemount, Inc., 115
Rowan Companies, Inc., 120
Royal Dutch/Shell Group, 146
Rubbermaid, Inc., 119
Russell Corporation, 111
Russia:
   foreign service officers, 324-325
   major companies in, 128
   work permit and visa, 66
Rust International, Inc., 129
Rwanda, foreign service officers, 326
Ryder Systems, Inc., 170

Saab-Scania Holdings Group, 150
Saatchi & Saatchi Company PLC, 138
Safeway Stores, 213
Sales:
   computers, 86
   pets, 103
   radio/television, 102
Sales agents, 100
Sales/marketing representatives, 105
Sales representatives, 95, 99
Sales/stocking clerks, retail wholesale, 106
Salomon, Inc., 196-197
Sample personality test, 353-364
Sandoz Ltd., 144
Sanyo Electric Co., Ltd., 140
Sara Lee, 125, 174-175
Sargent & Greenleaf, Inc., 179-180
Saudi Arabia:
   foreign service officers, 326-327
   major companies in, 129
   World Trade Center, 224
Save the Children, 240
S.C.A. Soldive, 153
Schering Laboratories, 170
Schering-Plough Corporation, 193-194
Schlegel Corporation, 118
SCI Systems, Inc., 158
Seagate Technology, Inc., 128
Searle Company, 126
Sears, Roebuck & Company, 172
Security assistance officers, 257
Security services, 90
Senegal, foreign service officers, 327

Index

Sensormatic Electronics Corporation, 111, 170-171
Serbia-Montenego, foreign service officers, 327-328
Service, computers, 86
Seychelles, foreign service officers, 328
Shanghai Petrochemical Co., Ltd., 139
Sharp Corporation, 146
Shipping specialists, 99
Shiseido Company, Ltd., 143
Shullep International, Inc., 178
Siemens, 217
Siemens AG, 141
Sierra Leone, foreign service officers, 328
Siliconix, 132
Simplicity Pattern Company, Inc., 130
Sinclair International, 158
Singapore:
    foreign service officers, 328-329
    major companies in, 129
    World Trade Center, 224
Singapore Airlines Limited, 136
Sister Cities International, 240
Skidmore, Owings & Merrill, 126
Skil-Bosch Corporation, 175
Slovak Republic, foreign service officers, 329-330
Slovenia, foreign service officers, 330
Small business owner, 93
Smith-Kline Beecham PLC, 144
Society for International Development, 240
Somalia, foreign service officers, 330
Sonat Offshore, 116
Sony Corporation, 140, 217
Sotheby's Holdings, Inc., 130
South Africa:
    foreign service officers, 330-331
    major companies in, 130
    World Trade Center, 224
South Carolina:
    employers with foreign offices, 204-205
    Federal Job Information Center, 243
    U.S. Department of Commerce printed information, 251
South Dakota:
    employers with foreign offices, 205
    Federal Job Information Center, 243
    U.S. Department of Commerce printed information, 251
South Korea:
    major companies in, 130
    World Trade Center, 224
Southland Corporation, 122
Spain:
    foreign service officers, 331-332
    major companies in, 131
    work permit and visa, 66
    World Trade Center, 224
Sports, 106-107
    coaches, 106-107
    fitness instructors, 107
SPS Technologies, 203
    Inc., 115
SRI International, 129, 165-166
Sri Lanka, foreign service officers, 332
Standard Commercial Corporation, 110, 133
Stanley Works, The, 167-168
Steelcase, Inc., 185
Stewart-Warner Corp/South Wind Division, 175-186
Stone & Webster Engineering, 183-184
Stone & Webster, Incorporated, 197
Store management, retail/wholesale, 106
Structural engineers, 88
Sudan, foreign service officers, 332-333
Sundstrand Data Control, Inc., 209-210
Sun Electric Corporation, 124
Sundstrand Data Control, Inc., 209-210
Suriname, foreign service officers, 333

Swaziland, foreign service officers, 333
Sweden:
    foreign service officers, 334
    major companies in, 131
    work permit and visa, 66-67
    World Trade Center, 224-225
Switzerland:
    foreign service officers, 334-335
    major companies in, 132
    work permit and visa, 67
    World Trade Center, 225
Syria, foreign service officers, 335
Systems analyst, 86

Taiwan:
    major companies in, 132
    World Trade Center, 225
Tajikistan, foreign service officers, 336
Talent agents, 92
Tambrands, Inc., 128
Tanzania, foreign service officers, 336
Tate & Lyle, PLC, 142
Tax preparation positions, 82
TDK, Inc., 199-200
Teacher of English to Speakers of Other Languages (TESOL), 240
Teachers, 91-92
Teaching Abroad, 153
Technicians, radio/television, 102
Telecommunications, 148-149
Teledyne, Inc., 128
Telefonica de Espana, S.A., 148
Telefonos de Mexico, s.A., 148
Teleglobe, Inc., 149
Tellabs Operations, Inc., 116
Temporary international employment, 151-156
Tenneco, Inc., 206
Tennessee:
    employers with foreign offices, 205
    Federal Job Information Center, 243
    U.S. Department of Commerce printed information, 251
TESOL Job Placement Service, 153
Testing specialist, 92
Texas:
    employers with foreign offices, 205-207
    Federal Job Information Center, 243
    U.S. Department of Commerce printed information, 251-252
Texas Instruments, Inc., 124
Textron, Inc., 125
Thailand:
    foreign service officers, 336
    major companies in, 133
    World Trade Center, 225
Thomas & Betts, 131
Thomson Corporation, 147-148
3M Company, 113
Thyssen, 217
Ticket clerk, 108
Togo, foreign service officers, 337
Tokio Marine and Fire, 144
Tokyo Language Institute, 154
Toshiba Corporation, 141, 217
TOTAL, 146
Tourist industry, 107
Toys "R" Us, Inc., 117
Trade information centers, 259
Trainer, computers, 86
Training specialists, 101
Transportation (air/rail/bus), 107-108
    coach drivers, 107
    dispatchers, 107
    mechanics, 108
    ticket clerks, 108

Travel agents, 107
Trinidad and Tobago, foreign service officers, 337
Trinova Corporation, 121
Triton Energy Corporation, 114
Tunisia, foreign service officers, 337-338
Turkey:
   foreign service officers, 338
   major companies in, 133
   work permit and visa, 67
   World Trade Center, 225
Turkmenistan, foreign service officers, 338-339
Tutoring, 91, 153-154
Tyson Foods, Inc., 118

Uganda, foreign service officers, 339
Ukraine, foreign service officers, 339
Unilever, 217-218
Union Bank of Switzerland, 137
Union Camp Corporation, 122
Union Carbide Corporation, 120
Union Pacific Corporation, 189
United Arab Emirates, foreign service officers, 339-340
United Board for Christian Higher Education in Asia, 240
United Kingdom:
   foreign service officers, 340-341
   major companies in, 133-134
   World Trade Center, 225
United Nations, 240
United Nations Children's Fund, 240
United States:
   foreign service officers, 341-342
   World Trade Center, 225-227
United States Information Agency, 240
Universal Care, 152
Universal Foods Corporation, 112
Universal Language Institute, 154
Uruguay, foreign service officers, 342
U.S. Civil Service Commission, 240
U.S. Committee for UNICEF, 240
U.S. Customs Service, 240
U.S. Department of Agriculture, 240
U.S. Department of Commerce, 240
   country desk officers, 258
   obtaining country and business information from, 245-253
U.S. Department of Defense, 240
U.S. Department of State, 240
   coordinator for business affairs, 258
   country desk officers, 258
U.S. Department of Transportation, 240
U.S. Immigration and Naturalization Service, 240
U.S. International Trade Commission, 240
U.S. Student Travel Service, 240
US West, Inc., 126
Utah:
   employers with foreign offices, 207-208
   Federal Job Information Center, 243
   U.S. Department of Commerce printed information, 252
Utilities, 149
Uzbekistan, foreign service officers, 342

Varian Eimac, 208
Vehicle and parts manufacturing, 149-150
Vendex International, N.V., 142
Venezuela, foreign service officers, 342-343
Venture capitalist, 93
Vermont:
   employers with foreign offices, 208
   Federal Job Information Center, 243
   U.S. Department of Commerce printed information, 252

Veterinarians, 103
VF Corporation, 114
Vietnam, foreign service officers, 343
Virginia:
   employers with foreign offices, 208-209
   Federal Job Information Center, 243
   U.S. Department of Commerce printed information, 252
Visas, 57-58
   obtaining, 60
   requirements for, 62-67
Vishay Intertechnology, 121
Voice of America, 240
VTN Corporation, 129

Wackenhut Services, Inc., 189
Waiters, 98
Wales, World Trade Center, 227
Walt Disney World, 169
Wang Laboratories, Inc., 111, 201-202
Washington:
   employers with foreign offices, 209-210
   Federal Job Information Center, 243
   U.S. Department of Commerce printed information, 252
Washington, D.C., *See* District of Columbia
Waterford Wedgwood PLC, 143
WebCrawler, 72
Western Samoa, foreign service officers, 343
West Germany, World Trade Center, 227
West Virginia:
   employers with foreign offices, 210-211
   U.S. Department of Commerce printed information, 252
Weyerhaeuser Company, 182, 210
Whirlpool Corporation, 119, 161
White Consolidated Industries, 199
Williams Companies, Inc., 200
William Wrigley Jr. Company, 127
Willing Workers on Organic Farms (WWOOF), 152
Wisconsin:
   employers with foreign offices, 211-213
   Federal Job Information Center, 243
   U.S. Department of Commerce printed information, 252
Work permits, 57-58
   obtaining, 60-61
   requirements for, 62-67
World Health Organization, 240
World Tourism Organization, 240
World Trade Centers, using in the job search, 219
World Trade Centers Association, 240
Writers, radio/television, 102
Wyoming:
   employers with foreign offices, 213
   Federal Job Information Center, 243
   U.S. Department of Commerce printed information, 252

Xerox Corporation, 159

Yachts/cruise lines/fishing boats/commercial shipping, 155
Yahoo!, 72
Yamaha, 218
Yemen, foreign service officers, 343
Yugoslavia, World Trade Center, 227

Zaire, foreign service officers, 344
Zale Corporation, 206-207
Zambia, foreign service officers, 344
Zambia Consolidated Copper Mines, 145
Zimbabwe, foreign service officers, 344-345